A History and Anthology of
Award-winning Materials in
Journalism, Letters, and Arts

Series Editor:
Heinz-Dietrich Fischer
Ruhr University, Bochum
Federal Republic of Germany

ART & NONFICTION LITERATURE

Volume 7

K. G. Saur
München · New York · Providence · London ·
Paris 1994

THE PULITZER PRIZE ARCHIVE

A History and Anthology of
Award-winning Materials in
Journalism, Letters, and Arts

Series Editor:
Heinz-Dietrich Fischer
Ruhr University, Bochum
Federal Republic of Germany

PART C: NONFICTION LITERATURE
Volume 7

K · G · Saur
München · New Providence · London
Paris 1994

American History Awards 1917 - 1991

From Colonial Settlements to the Civil Rights Movement

Edited with general and special
introductions by
Heinz-Dietrich Fischer
in cooperation with
Erika J. Fischer

K · G · Saur
München · New Providence · London
Paris 1994

Gefördert durch Prof. Dr. Dietrich Oppenberg
aus Mitteln der Stiftung Pressehaus NRZ
Essen

Die Deutsche Bibliothek – CIP-Einheitsaufnahme

The Pulitzer prize archive : a history and anthology of award-
winning matrials in journalism, letters, and arts / ser. ed.:
Heinz-Dietrich Fischer. – München ; New Providence ; London ;
Paris : Saur.
ISBN 3-598-30170-7
NE: Fischer, Heinz-Dietrich [Hrsg.]
Vol. 7 : Pt. C, Nonfiction literature. American history awards 1917 – 1991 :
from colonial settlements to the civil rights movement / ed.
with general and special introd. by Heinz-Dietrich Fischer in
cooperation with Erika J. Fischer. – 1994.
ISBN 3-598-30177-4

PREFACE

Among the awards that carry the name of Joseph Pulitzer (1847-1911) and which were established in Pulitzer's will of 1903 there are not only prizes to honour works in different categories of journalism but also in the arts. One of these prizes for literary products was defined as awarding authors "for the best book of the year upon the history of the United States." This Pulitzer Prize for American History, John Hohenberg stresses, "remains in substantially the same form today, 'the best' having been replaced by 'a distinguished.' It was discovered very early in the risky business of prize-giving," Hohenberg explains, "that an award for 'the best' of anything invariably created an unnecessary amount of argument and the Pulitzer authorities dropped the term."

The present volume of the *Pulitzer Prize Archive* deals with this special literary award, established in 1917, and its development until now. At the same time the book marks the beginning of a three-volume series handling the Pulitzer Prizes for non-fictional book publications. As the history award's definition was wide-ranged from its beginning on, books on rather all historical eras, topics and aspects were allowed to take part in the competition. Consequently strongly different publications were awarded with a Pulitzer Prize in the course of time. Among the Prize-winning works count historical overall views as well as more detailed examinations and problem-orientated case studies with topics from outside the political history.

As the awarded books in the history category sometimes were published more than once and sometimes as pocket books or otherwise licensed, the problem of copyright for reprinting short sequences was not easy to solve. Furthermore, it was difficult to choose particularly those text portions which were to a certain extend representative for the work as a whole and which could be understood without knowing the book's entire content. Different authors as well as the publishers to whom we addressed generously agreed to this practice, so that - next to the detailed presentation and analysis of the prize's history based upon the jury reports - short text examples could be presented to the reader.

The following Pulitzer Prize winners or their descendants kindly agreed to reprint text passages: Professor Bernard Bailyn (Harvard University, Cambridge, Mass.), Mr. Daniel J. Boorstin (Washington, D.C.), Professor James MacGregor Burns (Williams College, Williamstown, Mass.), Mrs. Charlotte R. Cremin (New York, N.Y.), Mr. Anthony Dangerfield (Santa Barbara, Cal.), Professor Michael G. Kammen (Cornell University, Ithaca, N.Y.), Mr. Stanley Karnow (Potomac, Md.), Professor Leonard W. Levy (Ashland, Or.), Professor Leon F. Litwack (University of California, Berkeley, Cal.), Professor Thomas K. McCraw (Harvard University, Cambridge, Mass.), Mrs. Helga Sandburg (Cleveland, Oh.), Professor Laurel Thatcher Ulrich (University of New Hampshire, Durham, N.H.).

Thanks shall also be delivered to the following employees of the copyright-departments of different publishing companies who showed much understanding and sympathy and by this contributed to the publication of the present book: Mr. John Bauco (Oxford University Press, New York), Mrs. Teresa Buswell (Houghton Mifflin Company, New York), Mrs. Carol Christiansen (Bantam Doubleday Dell Publishing Group, Inc., New York), Mr. Robert A. Clark (The Arthur H. Clark Company, Spokane, Wash.), Mr. Frederick T. Courtright (Macmillan Publishing Company, New York), Mrs. Florence B. Eichin (Penguin Books USA, Inc., New York), Mrs. Patricia Flynn (Random House, Inc., and Alfred A. Knopf, Inc., New York), Mrs. Edith Golub (Macmillan Publishing Company, New York), Ms. Becky Hemperly (Little, Brown and Company, Publishers, Boston, Mass.), Mrs. Judi Kincaid (Harcourt Brace & Company, Orlando, Fla.), Mrs. Beth Kiley Kinder (Harvard University Press, Cambridge, Mass.), Mrs. Patricia Kratz (University Press of New England, Hanover, N.H.), Mrs. Helen McKenna (Yale University Press, London), Mrs. Patricia Newforth (Indiana University Press, Bloomington, Ind.), Mrs. Mimi Ross (Henry Holt and Company, Inc., New York), Mrs. Mary E. Ryan (W. W. Norton & Company, Inc., New York), Mrs. Erika Seidman (Farrar, Straus and Giroux, Inc., New York), Mrs. Kathy Shaer (The University of North Carolina Press, Chapel Hill, N.C.), Mr. Kevin J. Sullivan (Simon & Schuster, Inc., New York), Mrs. Kathy Train (Irvington Publishers, New York), N.N. (Harper Collins Publishers, New York), N.N. (Princeton University Press, Princeton, N.J.).

In a very special manner Prof. Dr. Dietrich Oppenberg (publisher of the NRZ Neue Ruhr/Rhein Zeitung, Essen, and head of the ECON book publishing company, Düsseldorf) took part in the genesis of the book. Mr. Edward M. Kliment (Pulitzer Prize Office at Columbia University, New York) again helped by contributing important material and by giving varied kind of information meanwhile Mr. Carroll Brown (President of the American Council on Germany, New York) arranged important contacts. Further help to the authors was given by Mrs. Ursula Bauer (New York), Mr. Klaus T. Hille (Düsseldorf), Prof. Dr. Heinz Peters (Ratingen). Prof. Dr. Günther Pflug (Frankfurt a.M.), Mr. Jörg Strackbein (Düsseldorf) and Mr. Hendrik B. van Opstal (Frankfurt a.M.).

For different helpful services in preparing the book our thanks are given to: Mrs. Rachel Baxter (K. G. Saur Publishing Co., Munich), Mrs. Sheila Carney (Journalism Library at Columbia University, New York), Mr. Frank J. Carroll (The Library of Congress, Washington, D.C.), Mrs. Karen Furey (The American Council on Germany, New York), Mr. Larry Heinzerling (The Associated Press, New York), Mrs. Brigitte James (Library of the USIA at the United States Embassy, Bonn), Mr. Philipp Schmitz (The American Council on Germany, New York), and Mrs. Monika Schröder (Library of the John F. Kennedy Institute for North America Studies at the Free University, Berlin).

At the Department of Journalism and Communication of the Ruhr-Universität Bochum it was first of all Mrs. Ingrid Dickhut who contributed to this volume being published in good time. She not only computerized main parts of the text but also prepared the layout and developed the index. Miss Friederike Erlinghagen helped in creating the biographical sketches of the Pulitzer Prize winners occuring in the book and finally Mr. Olaf Jubin, Mr. Jürgen Niemann, M.A., and Mr. Oskar Stodiek, M.A., coped with the proof-reading and researched on different special topics. We wish to thank all who helped to realize this volume, as it was finally a product of well-organized and trusting team work!

Bochum, FRG
August, 1993

E.J.F./H.-D.F.

THIS VOLUME IS DEDICATED TO

DEAN G. ACHESON (1893 - 1971)

- PULITZER PRIZE WINNER 1970 -

ON HIS 100TH BIRTHDAY

CONTENTS

XVIII

INTRODUCTION

HISTORY AND DEVELOPMENT OF THE PULITZER PRIZE FOR AMERICAN HISTORY

by Heinz-Dietrich Fischer

In his will Joseph Pulitzer not only established the institutionalized awards for outstanding performances in the press[1] but also for exceptional literary works of fiction and non-fiction. Since the introduction of the Pulitzer Prizes in 1917, a special category was dedicated to one aspect of non-fiction literature: "For the best book of the year upon the history of the United States."[2] "In a moment of pedagogical grandeur," writes John Hohenberg, "Henry Adams once informed his publisher that history is 'the most aristocratic of all literary pursuits.' ... Adams accurately reflected the nature of the conservative historical scholarship of his time, which so critically influenced the beginnings of the Pulitzer Prizes in both history and biography. The older generation of American historians, the distinguished amateurs, had been accustomed to write about their country in the romantic, uplifting tradition of George Bancroft and Francis Parkman; and, although dazzled by the style and scholarship of John Lothrop Motley and William Hickling Prescott, few others had tried to write significantly about lands other than their own."[3] The style of such historians, outlined here by Hohenberg, definitely influenced the jury's decision at Columbia University in the first few years of the Pulitzer Prizes, as to which historical description or analysis should win the prize for the best historical or biographical work of non-fiction.

The majority of contemporary historians, states Hohenberg, "had been content with the heroic American imagery of their elders. Indeed, for those like Bancroft who were determined on deeper research, they found the expense to be a considerable burden. Thus the historian, in Adams' words, had to be 'rich as well as educated' if he intended to amount to much. Not many had been formally trained to write history, but some had entered

---

1 Cf. Heinz-Dietrich Fischer/Erika J. Fischer (Eds.), The Pulitzer Prize Archive, Vols. 1-3: Reportage Journalism; Vols. 4-6: Opinion Journalism, Munich - London - New York - Paris 1987 - 1992.
2 Quoted from Don C. Seitz, Joseph Pulitzer - His Life and Letters, New York 1924, p. 462.
3 John Hohenberg, The Pulitzer Prizes. A History of the Awards in Books, Drama, Music, and Journalism, New York - London 1974, p. 61.

academe and helped to create the professional historians of later years who often broke with tradition ... The professional historian ... had established himself as a force in academe by the time the first Pulitzer History Prize was awarded, but control of the honor at first rested mainly with those who espoused the genteel tradition. There were two reasons for this. First (Columbia University President) Nicholas Murray Butler was scarcely the type of educator who would have accepted at once the progressive, revisionist historians. ... Equally as important as Butler's conservatism was the discouraging reality, of which (Columbia University's Secretary) Frank D. Fackenthal complained, that few American historians were members of the American Academy of Arts and Letters, from which the early jurors were drawn. Even when members of the affiliated National Institute of Arts and Letters were included, the pool still was too small to make much difference. It fell, therefore, to Professor Barrett Wendell of Harvard to set the pattern for the first awards in history as the jury chairman from 1917 through 1920 ... Wendell's associates on the History Juries in the early years were men who were very much to his liking."[4]

Hohenberg stresses that "the cult of the gentleman amateur dominated the Pulitzer Prize selections of this group, beginning with Ambassador Jusserand's *With Americans of Past and Present Days* in 1917. They blandly overlooked the underlying theme of Pulitzer's will that Americans should be honored, since it was not specifically stated in the terms of the history award."[5] The first jury report (John H. Finley, Worthington C. Ford and Barrett Wendell) gives only a partial explanation as to why the book on American history by the long-serving French ambassador in Washington - who reportedly enjoyed a close and confidential relationship with all American presidents since 1902[6] - was the first to win the award: "The jury is of (the) opinion that, for various reasons, none of the four books submitted for the prize 'for the best book of the year upon the history of the United States' deserves much distinction." Nevertheless the jury unanimously recommended, "that the prize of $ 2,000, for the best book of the year upon the history of the United States be awarded to His Excellency, J. J. Jusserand, Ambassador of France to the United States, for his book entitled *With Americans of Past and Present Days*, published by Charles

---

4   *Ibid.*, pp. 61 f.
5   *Ibid.*, p. 63.
6   Cf. Harry J. Carman, History Awards, in: *Columbia Library Columns* (New York), Vol. 6/No. 3, May 1957, p. 37.

Scribners Sons, of New York, in 1916."[7] The Advisory Board accepted the jury's proposal and gave the Pulitzer Prize for history to the Frenchman, Monsieur Jusserand.[8]

In the following year, the same jury as in 1917 was to decide on the award of a Pulitzer Prize in the history category. At the end of April 1918, the jury unanimously proposed that James Ford Rhodes' *A History of the Civil War, 1861-1865*[9] should be awarded the prize. As this book, which John Hohenberg calls "a truly distinguished work,"[10] was also valued by the Advisory Board, the Pulitzer Prize was awarded to Rhodes.[11] A slightly different jury from its predecessor (Worthington C. Ford, Henry Dwight Sedgwick and Barrett Wendell) was to judge over the books entered for the history category in March 1919. In their report to the Advisory Board the members of the jury stated that they, even after careful consideration, "find themselves unable to say that any of the books is at once so important and so well written as unquestionably to deserve ... a prize. They therefore ... recommend that the prize be not awarded for the year 1918."[12] The Advisory Board accepted this proposal and voted for "no award" in the history category.[13] One year later, in March 1920, the same jury voted clearly and definitely for one candidate in this category. The history jury was "unanimous in awarding the prize to Justin Harvey Smith for his book entitled *The War with Mexico*."[14] Again, the Advisory Board did not contradict the jury's proposal, and awarded Smith the prize for his work.[15]

During the first years of Pulitzer Prize history, Barrett Wendell was not only a permanent member of the different juries but also their chairman. In 1921, the task of making a suitable proposal for the history category was handed over to a new jury (Worthington C. Ford, John B. McMaster and William R. Thayer), which took over from the "Wendell team." The jury's chairman, William R. Thayer, told the Advisory Board after finishing the first selection, "that the committee to award the Pulitzer Prize for American

7   John H. Finley/Worthington C. Ford/Barrett Wendell, Report of the Pulitzer Prize History Jury, Boston, May 8, 1917, pp. 1 f.
8   Columbia University (Ed.), The Pulitzer Prizes 1917-1991, New York 1991, p. 57.
9   John H. Finley/Worthington C. Ford/Barrett Wendell, Report of the Pulitzer Prize History Jury, Boston, April 24, 1918, p. 1.
10 John Hohenberg, The Pulitzer Prizes, *op. cit.*, p. 63.
11 Columbia University (Ed.), The Pulitzer Prizes, *op. cit.*, p. 57.
12 Worthington C. Ford/Henry Dwight Sedgwick/Barrett Wendell, Report of the Pulitzer Prize History Jury, Boston, March 18, 1919, pp. 1 f.
13 Columbia University (Ed.), The Pulitzer Prizes, *op. cit.*, p. 57.
14 Worthington C. Ford/Henry Dwight Sedgwick/Barrett Wendell, Report of the Pulitzer Prize History Jury, Boston, March 19, 1920, p. 1.
15 Columbia University (Ed.), The Pulitzer Prizes, *op. cit.*, p. 57.

History names *The Victory at Sea*, by Admiral Wm. S. Sims, as best deserving the prize among the books submitted."[16] Again, the Advisory Board agreed and bestowed the award on William Sowden Sims and his collaborator, Burton J. Hendrick.[17] In 1922 the process of selecting a Pulitzer Prize winner was comparatively easy. The jury (Worthington C. Ford, Charles Downer Hazen and John B. McMaster) unanimously found *The Founding of New England*, by James Truslow Adams, "in every respect deserving,"[18] as it says in the report. The Advisory Board agreed to this proposal and named Adams the Pulitzer Prize winner in the history category.[19] In spring 1923, the jury consisted of the same members as in the years before, thus constituting a team with some considerable experience. Although this particular jury report is recorded as missing, there are several hints that the jury unanimously proposed that Charles Warren be awarded a Pulitzer Prize for his book *The Supreme Court in United States History*.[20] As there were no contradictions from the Advisory Board, the well-known lawyer became the Pulitzer Prize winner in 1923.[21]

"No one on the Advisory Board," Hohenberg summarizes the first period in the history of awarding Pulitzer Prizes, "raised a question about any of these works, for they were considered eminently satisfactory selections at the time. Some, in fact, still have the respect of professional historians of various persuasions and at least one, the Rhodes work, is still recommended reading for students of American history. It is remarkable that Rhodes, Smith, Adams, Warren, and Hendrick, Admiral Sim's collaborator, all were self-made historians who came into the profession from a variety of other endeavors ... While the day of the gentleman amateur was by no means over, the professional historians came into their own during the changing era of the late 1920s and the early 1930s. In a time of unequaled economic stress, when the faith of tens of millions of Americans in self-government was being tried as never before, new voices demanded attention in academe and new views of the American past had to be taken into account by those who were trying to shape the nation's future."[22] The experienced jury of the previous two years (Worthington C. Ford, Charles Downer Hazen and John

---

16 Worthington C. Ford/John B. McMaster/William R. Thayer, Report of the Pulitzer Prize History Jury, Boston, May 8, 1921, p. 1.
17 Columbia University (Ed.), The Pulitzer Prizes, *op. cit.*, p. 57.
18 Worthington C. Ford/Charles Downer Hazen/John B. McMaster, Report of the Pulitzer Prize History Jury, Boston, March 22, 1922, p. 1.
19 Columbia University (Ed.), The Pulitzer Prizes, *op. cit.*, p. 57.
20 Cf. John Hohenberg, The Pulitzer Prizes, *op. cit.*, p. 63.
21 Columbia University (Ed.), The Pulitzer Prizes, *op. cit.*, p. 57.
22 John Hohenberg, The Pulitzer Prizes, *op. cit.*, pp. 63, 107.

B. McMaster) was also given the task of deciding on the award winner in 1924. The members unanimously decided to propose that Charles Howard McIlwain be awarded the prize for his book *The American Revolution - A Constitutional Interpretation*, published by the Macmillan Company.[23] As the proposal was accepted by the Advisory Board, McIlwain - whom Hohenberg reports as being the "less controversial professional"[24] among the applicants of 1924 - received the Pulitzer Prize for the history category.[25]

As early as 1925, the dominant trend among the juries in the first few years of the Pulitzer Prizes of making a unanimous proposal to the Advisory Board was to come to an end. The jury (James Truslow Adams, Worthington C. Ford and Charles Downer Hazen) had to judge between twenty-three books in the history category and came to a more differentiated evaluation of the material than in the years before. The jury members considered three books to be worthy for the final choice, namely: *The Colonial Background of the American Revolution*, by Charles M. Andrews; *The American States during and after the Revolution, 1775-1789*, by Allan Nevins; *A History of the American Frontier*, by Frederic L. Paxson. "The final decision rests upon the scope, manner of treatment, and evidence of research shown in Professor Paxson's volume," it says in the jury report.[26] The Advisory Board followed the jury's suggestion and awarded Paxson with the Pulitzer Prize in the history category.[27] This was not to be the case in 1926, when the same jury members as in the year before had to select among the entries (the number of which is not recorded) for a first proposal to the Advisory Board. The first selection narrowed the field down to the following titles and authors: *Great Britain and the American Civil War*, by Ephraim D. Adams; *Jefferson and Hamilton*, by Claude Bowers; *A History of the United States, Vol. VI*, by Edward Channing; *L'Esprit Révolutionnaire en France et aux Etats-Unis*, by Bernard Faÿ.[28]

This list of finalists was the only common basis the three jury members could reach in their evaluation of the entries, because their opinions on the books and authors differed to a high extent. Jury member James T. Adams,

---

23   Worthington C. Ford/Charles Downer Hazen/John B. McMaster, Report of the Pulitzer Prize History Jury, Boston, March 24, 1924, p. 1.
24   John Hohenberg, The Pulitzer Prizes, *op. cit.*, p. 108.
25   Columbia University (Ed.), The Pulitzer Prizes, *op. cit.*, p. 57.
26   James Truslow Adams/Worthington C. Ford/Charles Downer Hazen, Report of the Pulitzer Prize History Jury, Boston, March 9, 1925, p. 1.
27   Columbia University (Ed.), The Pulitzer Prizes, *op. cit.*, p. 57.
28   Cf. James Truslow Adams/Worthington C. Ford/Charles Downer Hazen, Reports of the Members of the Pulitzer Prize History Jury, Boston - London - New York, February/March 1926.

for example, put his case for his two favorite authors as follows: "1. Faÿ and, if no foreigner can be chosen, 2. Bowers."[29] As Adams' colleague Worthington C. Ford was more or less of the same opinion, he wrote to the Advisory Board that "the decision of a majority of the jury ... is in favor of Bernard Faÿ ... As the terms of award do not expressly call for an American product - an exception belonging to it alone - we assume that the work of a foreigner is eligible ... Should it appear that our interpretation of the rules is wrong and only an American work is eligible, the decision is in favor of Claude Bowers ..."[30] The third jury member, Columbia University Political Science Professor Charles D. Hazen, took a stand against this proposal with the following words: "In regard to Bernard Faÿ's *L'Esprit Révolutionnaire en France et aux Etats-Unis*, I think that the fact that it is in a foreign language ought to be decisive against its receiving the prize. Any book in any other language than English would have a very small audience in this country. Mr. Pulitzer had in mind, I imagine, the encouragement and the reward of American creative effort in the various lines in which he established prizes ... Claude Bowers' *Jefferson and Hamilton* I consider to be nearly everything a history ought not to be ... Professor Ephraim D. Adams' *Great Britain and the American Civil War* on the other hand is, in my judgment the best historical work in the American field that has appeared in several years ... My second choice would be Channing's *History of the United States* ..."[31] Faced by these dissonances in the jury's proposal, the Advisory Board took its traditional right to make an independent decision, and awarded the prize to Edward Channing.[32]

In 1927, the task of assessing entries for the history category was given to the same jury as in the year before. Evidently alluding to the dissonances of the preceding jury report, it states in the 1927 report - signed by the jury's chairman - to the Advisory Board: "I am happy to say that the members of the Jury ... unite on *Pinckney's Treaty - A Study of America's Advantage from Europe's Distress, 1783-1800*, by Samuel Flagg Bemis ... That work is selected because of its thorough and wide research, its use of the material, and its intelligent interpretation of a diplomatic incident of wide result. The only work which came into competition was one by Mr. Adams, whose

---

29 Letter from Worthington C. Ford, London, to Professor Charles Downer Hazen, New York, February 11, 1926, p. 1.
30 Letter from Worthington C. Ford, London, to Frank D. Fackenthal, New York, February 11, 1926, pp. 1 f.
31 Letter from Charles Downer Hazen, New York, to Frank D. Fackenthal, New York, March 11, 1926, pp. 1-5.
32 Columbia University (Ed.), The Pulitzer Prizes, *op. cit.*, p. 57.

presence on the Jury naturally precluded its consideration."[33] The Advisory Board saw no reason to reject this proposal and as a consequence awarded the Pulitzer Prize for history to Samuel F. Bemis.[34] In 1928, when eighteen entries were in competition with one another for the Pulitzer Prize for history, the jury again consisted of the same members. The jurors were "unanimous in recommending for the award ... Vernon Louis Parrington's two volumes issued under the general title of *Main Currents in American Thought* ... The decision rests upon the following considerations: that the work is original in conception and in performance; it shows research and scholarship; and it throws fresh light upon many aspects of our history. It is penetrating and acute."[35] The Advisory Board members were entirely persuaded by this praise and awarded Vernon L. Parrington with the Pulitzer Prize for history.[36]

In 1929 - with exactly the same jury in office as in the previous year - nineteen entries were assessed for the award. "The members of the jury," it says in their report, "are unanimous in selecting Fred Albert Shannon's *The Organization and Administration of the Union Army, 1861-1865*. That work is selected because of its wide investigation, its close and generally correct handling of facts, and the main purpose of the book which has been supported in such a way as not to confuse by a multiplicity of facts hastily thrown together after the manner of an academic essay. We believe it to be fully entitled to the award."[37] The Advisory Board agreed to this proposal, thus awarding the prize to Fred A. Shannon.[38] After looking through the incoming material, the jury of 1930 (James Truslow Adams, Charles Downer Hazen and Burton J. Hendrick) was not able to vote unanimously for one entry. "I regret to report," the jury chairman wrote to the Advisory Board, "that the members of the Jury ... have been unable to agree unanimously on any work ... The published work in history during the year has generally been considered as singularly disappointing, and, indeed, the jury would prefer not to award the prize at all this year unless the terms require it. I believe they do, and therefore the jury attempted to reach a decision. The two books that received most consideration were Van Tyne's

33 Letter from Worthington C. Ford to Frank D. Fackenthal (in the name of the Pulitzer Prize History Jury), Boston, March 16, 1927, p. 1.
34 Columbia University (Ed.), The Pulitzer Prizes, *op. cit.*, p. 57.
35 James Truslow Adams/Worthington C. Ford/Charles Downer Hazen, Report of the Pulitzer Prize History Jury, Boston, March 10, 1928, p. 1.
36 Columbia University (Ed.), The Pulitzer Prizes, *op. cit.*, p. 57.
37 James Truslow Adams/Worthington C. Ford/Charles Downer Hazen, Report of the Pulitzer Prize History Jury, Boston, March 13, 1929, p. 1.
38 Columbia University (Ed.), The Pulitzer Prizes, *op. cit.*, p. 57.

VERNON L. PARRINGTON

Main Currents in American Thought   I

THE COLONIAL MIND (1620-1800)

Of Parrington's Pulitzer Prize study of men and ideas in America, Henry Seidel Canby wrote: "This is a work of the first importance, lucid, comprehensive, accurate as sound scholarship should be, and also challenging, original in its thinking, shrewd, and sometimes brilliant. . . . It is a genuine history of ideas, clearly seen, tirelessly followed, admirably analyzed. Indeed it is the book which historians and critics of American literature have been waiting and hoping for."

In this volume Parrington treats of such makers of the American mind as Thomas Hooker, Roger Williams, Samuel Sewall, Increase and Cotton Mather, Jonathan Edwards, Alexander Hamilton, John Adams, Tom Paine, and Thomas Jefferson.

Volumes I and II of *Main Currents in American Thought* are now being reprinted without the third, fragmentary, posthumously published volume.

A Harvest/HBJ Book
Harcourt Brace Jovanovich, Inc.

Cover drawings by Milton Glaser
of Cotton Mather, Joel Barlow, and Benjamin Franklin

War of Independence and Bowers' *Tragic Era*. The former received one vote, and the latter two, for the prize. The minority member who voted for Van Tyne's book considers it a scholarly work, displaying sane and balanced judgments, embodying the latest knowledge on its subject, written in a clear and attractive style."[39] Contradictory to the opinion of the jury majority, the Advisory Board decided to award Claude H. Van Tyne with the Pulitzer Prize in the history category.[40]

The members of the history jury in 1931 (Charles Downer Hazen, Burton J. Hendrick and M. A. DeWolfe Howe), declared in their report that they were "unanimously and strongly of the opinion that *The Coming of the War*, by Professor Schmitt, should receive the award ... The work is not only far above any other published by an American historian during the year 1930 but is an outstanding event in American scholarship. It is the result of ten years' laborious research, pursued with meticulous regard for the truth only. The presentation of the material is admirable. It is as impartial as it is possible for human judgment to be. The style is lucid, and the book will interest the general reader as well as the scholar ... The only point that might possibly constitute an objection to the award in the opinion of some is the subject, which they might consider to be in the realm of European rather than American history. It is, however, the unanimous opinion of the Committee that this is not a valid objection in this case. The World War, although it started in Europe, was participated in by the United States ... Unless you disagree with us on the eligibility of the subject matter," the jury put to the members of the Advisory Board, "we strongly urge that the prize be conferred on Professor Schmitt. In case of such disagreement, which we trust will not arise, we unanimously suggest as an alternative Professor Morison's *Founders of the Bay Colony* ... In importance it is not comparable to Professor Schmitt's, but it is interesting, and scholarly. It is a good book but not an outstanding one."[41] After having evaluated the pro and contra arguments, the Advisory Board followed the jury's favoured proposal and awarded the Pulitzer Prize for history to Bernadotte E. Schmitt.[42]

In 1932 the Pulitzer Prize History jury was identical to the preceding one. In their address to the Advisory Board the jury members were of "the opinion that General Pershing's *My Experiences in the World War* is the

---

39 James Truslow Adams/Charles Downer Hazen/Burton J. Hendrick, Report of the Pulitzer Prize History Jury, Boston, March 25, 1930, p. 1.
40 Columbia University (Ed.), The Pulitzer Prizes, *op. cit.*, p. 57.
41 Charles Downer Hazen/Burton J. Hendrick/M. A. DeWolfe Howe, Report of the Pulitzer Prize History Jury, Boston, March 25, 1931, p. 1 f.
42 Columbia University (Ed.), The Pulitzer Prizes, *op. cit.*, p. 57.

best work of the year and the one which should receive the award. We have seriously considered three or four others, namely *King Cotton Diplomacy*, by Frank Lawrence Owsley; *The Epic of America*, by James Truslow Adams, and *The Martial Spirit*, by Walter Millis, but we are of the opinion that Pershing has not only written the most authoritative, the most penetrating and the most decisive account of our own part in the war but that he has presented a finer spirit in narration than any of the others, more objectivity, more fullness, and more balance."[43] As one of the jury members put it, Pershing's book is epic "in the sense that it is a great national story, displaying the American character in its finest aspects. It has drama, too, for we constantly feel two motives working in antagonism - the determination of European Powers that America should play no decisive part in the war, and the determination of Pershing that it should. The complete demonstration that the war would have ended very differently had it not been for Pershing's strong character and his insistence on maintaining the dignity of the American effort also makes it a great chapter in American history, - and the whole story is told with the utmost modesty."[44] Although a book concerning World War I had already been awarded a Pulitzer Prize in the previous year, the Advisory Board did not hesitate to once again give preference to this subject, and awarded the prize to John J. Pershing.[45]

In 1933, the jury's composition remained the same as in the two preceding years. Nevertheless the team was confronted with an unexpected problem which it had never before encountered. "We have not been able," the jury chairman wrote to the Advisory Board, "to reach a unanimous agreement, but two of us ... are of the opinion that the prize should be given to the book of Professor Frederick J. Turner, entitled *The Significance of Sections in American History* ... This is a selection of studies made by Professor Turner during the years of his teaching, on many subjects in American history ... These studies have been selected by certain of his friends from Professor Turner's work. They treat important aspects of the evolution of American civilization in a thorough and fresh way, are based upon a wide reading of sources, and are clear and careful in their point of view ... They represent slow and thorough research and are destined to exercise a distinct influence upon the thought of attentive and reflecting Americans ... They are briefly, carefully, justly, and judicially presented by

---

43 Charles Downer Hazen/Burton J. Hendrick/M. A. DeWolfe Howe, Report of the Pulitzer Prize History Jury, Boston, March 22, 1932, p. 1.
44 *Ibid.*
45 Columbia University (Ed.), The Pulitzer Prizes, *op. cit.*, p. 57.

" the best book of the year upon history of the United States. "

THE SIGNIFICANCE
OF SECTIONS IN

AMERICAN
HISTORY

By
FREDERICK JACKSON TURNER

With an Introduction by MAX FARRAND

PULITZER PRIZE
FOR HISTORY: 1932

HENRY HOLT AND COMPANY
One Park Avenue New York

There are American ideals. We are members of
one body, though it is a varied body. It is
inconceivable that we should follow the evil
path of Europe and place our reliance upon
triumphant force. We shall not become cynical and convinced that sections, like European
nations, must dominate their neighbors and
strike first and hardest. However profound
the economic changes, we shall not give up our
American ideals and our hopes for man, which
had their origin in our own pioneering experience, in favor of any mechanical solution
offered by doctrinaires educated in Old World
grievances. Rather, we shall find strength to
build from our past a nobler structure, in
which each section will find its place as a
fit room in a worthy house. We shall cour-
ageously maintain the American system expressed by nation-wide parties, acting under sectional and class compromises. We shall continue to
present to our sister continent of Europe the
underlying ideas of America as a better way of
solving difficulties. We shall point to the
Pax Americana, and seek the path of peace on
earth to men of good will.

XXX

the author and merit high consideration. Two of the Committee, therefore, recommend that this book ... be given the Pulitzer Prize ... The other member of the Committee ... does not agree with our decision and wishes to recommend, in its stead, the book of Mr. Mark Sullivan on *Our Times, 1909-1914* ... These two books are the only ones suggested by the jury for the award. We therefore refrain from discussing other volumes which we have considered but which we do not recommend."[46] As the Advisory Board accepted the jury's majority proposal, the Pulitzer Prize was given to Frederick J. Turner.[47]

Although in 1934 the Pulitzer Prize history jury consisted of the same persons as in the years before, it was difficult for them to reach a unanimous agreement on one of the thirty-one entries. Of the following books, the jury gave serious consideration to: *Our Earliest Colonial Settlements, their Diversities of Origin and Later Characteristics*, by Charles M. Andrews; *Divided Loyalties*, by Lewis Einstein; *History of Our Times, Vol. V: Over Here, 1914-1918*, by Mark Sullivan. Sullivan's book, the chairman of the jury wrote to the Advisory Board, "in the opinion of a majority of our Committee" is "a careful and vivid account of our participation in the World War, of the events in which America took part, of the personalities that participated in those events, of what they said and did, of the measures adopted by our government and people during this crisis ... Two members of the Committee ... recommend that Mark Sullivan's book be given the Pulitzer Prize ..., as it seems to us a mistake not to award it unless for very grave reasons, - for example, if all the works presented were too poor to merit consideration. I am enclosing herewith," the chairman's report finished, "the dissenting opinion of the other member of the Committee ... who does not believe in bestowing the prize upon any book submitted this year."[48] "In the interest of the prestige of the Prize," the third juror expressed his doubts, "I feel that its omission in a year which has produced no book of commanding fitness for the award would do more good than harm."[49] Not following any of the jury's proposals, the Advisory Board made an independent decision to award the prize to Herbert Agar's *The People's Choice*,[50] a book that is not mentioned in the jury report at all.

46 Charles Downer Hazen/Burton J. Hendrick/M. A. DeWolfe Howe, Report of the Pulitzer Prize History Jury, Boston, March 17, 1933, pp. 1 f.
47 Columbia University (Ed.), The Pulitzer Prizes, *op. cit.*, p. 57.
48 Charles Downer Hazen/Burton J. Hendrick, Majority Report of the Pulitzer Prize History Jury, New York, March 15, 1934, pp. 1 f.
49 M. A. DeWolfe Howe, Minority Report of the Pulitzer Prize History Jury, Boston, March 13, 1934, p. 1.
50 Columbia University (Ed.), The Pulitzer Prizes, *op. cit.*, p. 57.

After the Advisory Board recommended Agar's book for the Pulitzer Prize in history, "there wasn't a peep from the jurors," writes John Hohenberg, and continues: "When the prize was announced, however, the roof fell in. Lewis Gannett in the *New York Herald-Tribune* blasted Agar's essays on the presidency as an appeal 'for American Fascism.' His paper wondered darkly if there was 'some unnamed power behind the Pulitzer throne.' And the *New York Evening Post* called for the discontinuance of the prizes. There had never been such an outburst over the history prize. Actually, whatever the demerits of the book, Agar himself was no Fascist. He was the *Louisville Courier-Journal*'s London correspondent, later became its editor ... The controversy had one major effect. It discouraged the Board from further intervention in the field of history, very largely leaving the judgments to the professionals who were the dominant factor in the juries. Actually, even to their critical contemporaries, the work that had been done by the jurors from 1917 through 1935 appeared to have been good. Malcolm Cowley of the *New Republic*, who seldom had anything pleasant to say about any of the Pulitzer awards, conceded in 1935 that the Pulitzer history prizes 'have been consistently better than the others, even though there have been occasional lapses like the choice of General Pershing in 1932 and of Herbert Agar in 1934.' With the exception of ... 1940 and ... 1942, professional historians dominated the history award from 1935"[51] onwards, so that after the controversy over Herbert Agar's award, the Pulitzer Prizes in the history category were awarded without the occurrence of similar disputes.

This was to become evident as early as 1935, when the jury members (Guy Stanton Ford, Charles Downer Hazen and Burton J. Hendrick) put forward a common proposal from a selection of thirty-eight entries. "We unanimously recommend," it says in the jury report, "that the Prize be given to Charles McLean Andrews ... for his book on *The Colonial Period of American History*, the result of more prolonged study and mature scholarship than any other volume submitted this year, or, for that matter, in most previous years ... Another fine production submitted this year is that of Allen French, *The First Year of the American Revolution*."[52] The Advisory Board accepted the jury's first choice and named Charles McLean Andrews the Pulitzer Prize winner in the history category.[53] An identical jury in 1936

---

51   John Hohenberg, The Pulitzer Prizes, *op. cit.*, p. 157.
52   Guy Stanton Ford/Charles Downer Hazen/Burton J. Hendrick, Report of the Pulitzer Prize History Jury, New York, March 19, 1935, p. 1.
53   Columbia University (Ed.), The Pulitzer Prizes, *op. cit.*, p. 57.

had the task of assessing the work of more than thirty candidates for the award. "Many of these books are of inferior quality or are on local or limited subjects," reads the jury report, "and ought not to be considered worthy of recommendation. But we are unanimously of the opinion that there is one clearly outstanding and superior work that possesses the qualities that are desired for this prize and for which it should be awarded. This is the volume submitted by Professor Andrew Cunningham McLaughlin ... and entitled *The Constitutional History of the United States* ... In view of the conspicuous and outstanding merits of this book, we as a jury have no other recommendation to make. The book is far superior in every particular to any other work submitted to us this year. We heartily commend it to the consideration of the Advisory Board."[54] Here, the convincing arguments for Andrew C. McLaughlin were accepted, and he was awarded the Pulitzer Prize.[55]

In 1937, an identical jury was once again able to reach a unanimous vote. From a selection of more than forty entries, the Advisory Board was told that "we are unanimously in favor of making the award to Van Wyck Brooks for his *Flowering of New England*, by far the best of the series. This book is, both from the point of view of the material examined and analyzed and from the point of view of the literary skill and charm of the author, by far the leading work that has come to our attention and we heartily recommend that it be given the Pulitzer Prize in view of its conspicuous and outstanding merits."[56] There were no objections raised on the part of the Advisory Board, so Van Wyck Brooks was awarded the prize.[57]

Finding a Prize winner in 1938 was more problematic. A nearly new jury (James P. Baxter III, Guy Stanton Ford and Arthur M. Schlesinger Sr.) was totally divided in their judgment on the entries. As a consequence it took much time and effort to choose one favourite from five finalists. While two jury members proposed to award the prize to Paul Buck's *Road to Reunion*, the third juror was strictly opposed to this suggestion. This member was of the opinion that *A History of Chicago* by Bessie Pierce, a book given third rank by the other two jurors, deserved the Pulitzer Prize. Another book, *The Monroe Doctrine, 1867-1907*, by Dexter Perkins, was alternatively

54 Guy Stanton Ford/Charles Downer Hazen/Burton J. Hendrick, Report of the Pulitzer Prize History Jury, New York, March 10, 1936, p. 1.
55 Columbia University (Ed.), The Pulitzer Prizes, *op. cit.*, p. 57.
56 Guy Stanton Ford/Charles Downer Hazen/Burton J. Hendrick, Report of the Pulitzer Prize History Jury, New York, March 19, 1937, p. 1.
57 Columbia University (Ed.), The Pulitzer Prizes, *op. cit.*, p. 57.

favoured by two jury members, the third juror, however, placed it fifth.[58] The Advisory Board finally followed the proposal of the jury's majority and awarded Paul Herman Buck with the Pulitzer Prize in the history category.[59]

In spring 1939, when the same persons again made up the Pulitzer Prize jury for history, there was no disagreement on the preferred candidate for the award. "The committee is unanimous in choosing for first place, Mr. Frank L. Mott's *A History of American Magazines*. In the opinion of the committee this work stands far in front of any of the others named in the panel of their possible choices," the jury report put its case for the book, and went on to state that, "Mr. Mott's work blazes a trail in a new and unworked field. It is itself a monumental study, of exact scholarship, and extraordinarily skillful in its arrangement of a mass of complex and hitherto unstudied material."[60] Although there were some other titles mentioned in the jury report, the vote for Frank Luther Mott was that clear and evident that the Advisory Board agreed to confer the award on the historian who specialized in the history of magazines.[61] In 1940, when the same jury evaluated the entries, a common proposal was achieved during the discussions. "Quite independently," it says in the jury report, "all three came to agreement on five possible titles out of the forty-four that were submitted ...: 1. Carl Sandburg, *Abraham Lincoln - The War Years*; 2. R. G. Albion, *The Rise of New York Port, 1815-1860*; 3. L. B. Shippee, *Canadian-American Relations, 1849-1874*; 4. Perry Miller, *The New England Mind - The Seventeenth Century*; 5. C. A. and Mary Beard, *America in Midpassage* ... The first choice, Sandburg's *Lincoln*," as it says in the report later on, was an extraordinary effort, "both in substance and form, an achievement worthy of the reward to which we recommend it."[62] Although it was not entirely clear if the book about Lincoln should not rather have been placed in the biography category, the Advisory Board awarded the Pulitzer Prize for history to Carl Sandburg.[63]

Once again, in 1941, all jury members stayed in office. After drawn-out committee discussions, the jurors formulated their position as follows: "The recommendation for No. 1 rank goes to the late Marcus Lee Hansen, of the

---

58 James P. Baxter III/Guy Stanton Ford/Arthur M. Schlesinger Sr., Report of the Pulitzer Prize History Jury, Minneapolis, March 14, 1938, pp. 1-4.
59 Columbia University (Ed.), The Pulitzer Prizes, *op. cit.*, p. 57.
60 James P. Baxter III/Guy Stanton Ford/Arthur M. Schlesinger Sr., Report of the Pulitzer Prize History Jury, Minneapolis, March 14, 1939, p. 1 ff.
61 Columbia University (Ed.), The Pulitzer Prizes, *op. cit.*, p. 57.
62 James P. Baxter III/Guy Stanton Ford/Arthur M. Schlesinger Sr., Report of the Pulitzer Prize History Jury, Minneapolis, March 12, 1940, pp. 1 ff.
63 Columbia University (Ed.), The Pulitzer Prizes, *op. cit.*, p. 57.

University of Illinois, primarily for his volume on *The Atlantic Migration* ... which ... is a sweeping and beautifully organized presentation of the background of the whole immigration movement to America in the 19th century ... The presentation is unencumbered by too much detail but moves securely upon the rock bottom of patiently accumulated data. The style is smooth and gives a sense of an amazing maturity of mind ... The volume by Dean Theodore C. Blegen on the *Norwegian Migration to America - The American Transition* is in the same general field as Professor Hansen's but of an entirely different character. Professor Blegen has taken the story of one people as his theme ... The third ranking goes to the volume by Professor Ralph H. Gabriel, of Yale, on *The Course of American Democratic Thought - An Intellectual History Since 1815* ... It is well written, some would say very well written, and a considerable number better written possibly than the first two ... Miss Debo's volume with a rather blind title, *And Still the Waters Run*, is devoted to five civilized tribes of the Indian territory, and their treatment by the many uncivilized white men with whom they had to deal in that area ... Fifth place ... goes to the volume by Professor Edward S. Corwin of Princeton, entitled *The President - Office and Powers*. Like everything that Professor Corwin does, there is in this volume the manifestation of great scholarship, a keen and penetrating mind with original and independent views."[64] The Advisory Board considered the first-ranked book to be worthy of an award and gave the Pulitzer Prize to Marcus Lee Hansen.[65]

In 1942, the jury remained the same, and its members decided to draw up a list of five finalists from a total of almost fifty entries. In their report the jury members first of all wanted "to indicate that when books written by newcomers, authors unknown to us, meet ... (the award) qualifications we are as ready to crown them as though they had been written by scholars long known to us by outstanding achievements. So far as any of us know Miss Leech, to whose volume *Reveille in Washington* is given the first award, had not done nor had she distinguished herself in historical work. We were agreed, however, that in this volume she has given a complete and satisfying picture, well based on sound historical work, of the capital of the nation during four most critical years ... We ranked Professor Dexter Perkins' *Hand Off - A History of the Monroe Doctrine* second because it represents the summation of a life work on an important topic ... Third,

---

64　James P. Baxter III/Guy Stanton Ford/Arthur M. Schlesinger Sr., Report of the Pulitzer Prize History Jury, Minneapolis, March 19, 1941, pp. 1-6.
65　Columbia University (Ed.), The Pulitzer Prizes, *op. cit.*, p. 57.

Wecter's *The Hero in America* is next to Miss Leech's book the most interestingly written from the standpoint of style and organization ... Fourth, Dr. Burnett's volume *(The Continental Congress)* is, like Perkins' volume, the summation of a lifetime of work ... Fifth, Van Doren's *Secret History of the American Revolution* ... reads well ... It represents a considerable amount of library and archival labor."[66] The Advisory Board decided to award the first-ranked author and named Margaret Leech the Pulitzer Prize winner in the history category.[67]

Consisting of the same members, the jury of 1943 decided on a list of three outstanding works, of "the following ranking: 1. Esther Forbes, *Paul Revere* ...; 2. Wood Gray, *Hidden Civil War* ...; 3. Douglas S. Freeman, *Lee's Lieutenants* ... Beyond this grouping of the first three," the jury report continued, "it would be difficult to find from our interchange any unity of opinion and, if there were, any strong conviction that books below the first three should be seriously considered for the Pulitzer Prize ... The first problem in connection with Forbes was to make sure that it represented history and not essentially biography. It bears the name of a very interesting colonial character who, from the standpoint of history, had the misfortune to get into poetry first. Miss Forbes has disengaged him from that, suppressed and subordinated him to the history of Boston and the pre-Revolutionary community ... Wood Gray is a young man in the field of American history ... This is his first major effort: *The Hidden Civil War* ... is really a very exceptional first product of a young scholar ... Mr. Freeman had the idea first of writing the history of the Army of Northern Virginia. By request he turned aside to write a volume on Lee first, which received the Pulitzer biographical Prize some years ago.[68] The three volumes on Lee are now to be followed by three volumes on his lieutenants ... The first volume of the lieutenants is an interesting account of the building up of the corps of officers, one after another tried out to the demonstration of failure or success or mediocrity. It is skillfully done ..."[69] The Advisory Board accepted the explanation why the book on *Paul Revere* should not be placed in the Biography category and awarded Esther Forbes the Pulitzer Prize for history.[70]

---

66 James P. Baxter III/Guy Stanton Ford/Arthur M. Schlesinger Sr., Report of the Pulitzer Prize History Jury, Washington, D.C., March 11, 1942, pp. 1-4.
67 Columbia University (Ed.), The Pulitzer Prizes, *op. cit.*, p. 58.
68 Cf. *ibid.*, p. 60.
69 James P. Baxter III/Guy Stanton Ford/Arthur M. Schlesinger Sr., Report of the Pulitzer Prize History Jury, Washington, D.C., March 16, 1943, pp. 1-3.
70 Columbia University (Ed.), The Pulitzer Prizes, *op. cit.*, p. 58.

The former jurors were in office again in 1944. The jurors were this time "unanimous in recommending for first place the volume by Merle Curti, *The Growth of American Thought*," and justified their choice as follows: "In general the volumes submitted this year, at least the half dozen or so that merited serious consideration, gave us a better basis for selection of a significant contribution to American history than last year ... The volume by Mr. Curti is one of the most creditable achievements of recent American historical scholarship. It is in a sense a pathbreaking work. It stands out in a field that has been treated only fragmentarily. It ranges over all that has been done, adds great masses of original data, and organizes this material in an exceptionally skillful manner. It is an unusual synthesis of a great body of material ranging in time from our earliest to our latest history. By reason of its breadth and suggestiveness it is likely to stimulate a series of further needed studies ... As to the other volumes," the report went on, the jury was "less certain or convinced about the rating or the order in which they should be placed. By combining the comments and expressed or implied ratings, it would appear that Bernard DeVoto's volume, *The Year of Decision*, was runner-up ... Close behind it, and by one judge ranked ahead of it, was Bemis' *The Latin American Policy of the United States* ... We were unanimous in rating the second volume of Freeman's *Lee's Lieutenants* as fourth."[71] As the vote for the first-placed book was the most convincing, the Advisory Board named Merle Curti the Pulitzer Prize winner for history.[72]

In 1945, when the same persons again formed the history jury, their report to the Advisory Board briefly named the following finalists: "Number 1 is Douglas Freeman's third volume of *Lee's Lieutenants*; Number 2 is Dixon Wecter's *When Johnny Comes Marching Home*; Number 3 is Krout and Fox's *The Completion of Independence* ... Following these but not requiring special comment are Mrs. Alice Felt Tyler's *Freedom's Ferment*, and then Bailey's *Woodrow Wilson and the Lost Peace*, and Perkins' *America and Two Wars*.[73] This list, which was followed by additional information some days later,[74] was entirely rejected by the Advisory Board. Instead of following the jury's proposals the Advisory Board awarded Stephen Bonsal the prize for his book *Unfinished Business*.[75] For the first

---

71 James P. Baxter III/Guy Stanton Ford/Arthur M. Schlesinger Sr., Report of the Pulitzer Prize History Jury, Washington, D.C., March 16, 1944, pp. 1 f.
72 Columbia University (Ed.), The Pulitzer Prizes, *op. cit.*, p. 58.
73 James P. Baxter III/Guy Stanton Ford/Arthur M. Schlesinger Sr., Brief note of the Pulitzer Prize History Jury, Washington, D.C., March 10, 1945, p. 1.
74 Cf. James P. Baxter III/Guy Stanton Ford/Arthur M. Schlesinger Sr., Report of the Pulitzer Prize History Jury, Washington, D.C., March 12, 1945, pp. 1-4.
75 Columbia University (Ed.), The Pulitzer Prizes, *op. cit.*, p. 58.

time since the controversy on Herbert Agar's award - which was more than a decade before - the Advisory Board took its proper right to award someone who was not on the jury's list at all. The Pulitzer Prize was awarded for a book, Hohenberg remarks on this latest dispute, that was "a diary of the Peace Conference of World War I, written by a former war correspondent. It wasn't a popular decision. The Board's prejudice in favor of one of its own, a widely known newspaperman, did not sit well with many historians, even though the jury itself made no public protest."[76] As a consequence, one of the jurors temporarily resigned from the committee and was replaced by a new member of the jury, whilst the other two members remained in office.[77]

In 1946, this partially newly-formed jury (James P. Baxter III, Guy Stanton Ford and Thomas J. Wertenbaker) "unanimously voted for Schlesinger's work ... Their report concluded that *The Age of Jackson* will survive 'and date a new approach by future scholars' to the Jacksonian era."[78] The Advisory Board accepted the jury's suggestion and awarded Arthur M. Schlesinger Jr.[79] - who was the son of Arthur M. Schlesinger Sr., a history jury member for many years - with the Pulitzer Prize. In 1947, James P. Baxter III left the jury again and Schlesinger Sr. rejoined it. Baxter, as it says in a letter, had "resigned ... in order to make it possible for his book *Scientists Against Time* to be considered for the competition."[80] In the history jury's report "the five outstanding publications" were, "in the order named: 1. James P. Baxter III, *Scientists Against Time* ...; 2. Lawrence H. Gipson, *The British Empire Before the Revolution* ...; 3. Burton J. Hendrick, *Lincoln's War Cabinet* ...; 4. Alfred H. Bill, *The Beleaguered City* ...; 5. Donald M. Nelson, *Arsenal of Democracy* ... Baxter's book," it says of their first choice, "describes the contributions of American scientists to the winning of World War II. An exceedingly difficult subject to handle, he tells the story in terms understandable to the lay reader and reveals many important facts for the first time. His manuscript was carefully checked by scientists before publication. The account reads well, with occasional flashes of humor. It seems certain to be a work of permanent value."[81]

---

76 John Hohenberg, The Pulitzer Prizes, *op. cit.*, p. 214.
77 N.N., The Pulitzer Prize Jurors 1946, from a type-written list in the Pulitzer Prize Office, undated.
78 John Hohenberg, The Pulitzer Prizes, *op. cit.*, p. 213.
79 Columbia University (Ed.), The Pulitzer Prizes, *op. cit.*, p. 58.
80 Letter from Arthur M. Schlesinger Sr., Harvard University, Cambridge, Mass., to Dean Carl W. Ackerman, Graduate School of Journalism, Columbia University, New York, May 22, 1947, p. 1.
81 Theodore C. Blegen/Arthur M. Schlesinger Sr., Report of the Pulitzer Prize History Jury, Cambridge, Mass., March 10, 1947, p. 1.

Obviously these arguments persuaded the Advisory Board to award James P. Baxter III the Pulitzer Prize for history.[82]

In 1948, when James P. Baxter III rejoined the jury to select the best of seventy-nine entries together with Theodore C. Blegen and Arthur M. Schlesinger Sr., the proposals to the Advisory Board were as follows: 1. Bernard DeVoto, *Across the Wide Missouri*; 2. Samuel Eliot Morison, *History of United States Naval Operations in World War II*; 3. Allan

---

82 Columbia University (Ed.), The Pulitzer Prizes, *op. cit.*, p. 58.

Nevins, *Ordeal of the Union*; 4. Lloyd Morris, *Postscript to Yesterday*; 5. T. J. Wertenbaker, *The Puritan Oligarchy*.[83] "These recommendations," it says in the jury report, "are unanimous. All five of these works have the merit of maintaining scholarly standards and at the same time being well enough written to interest the thoughtful general reader. DeVoto's book presents a masterly account of the mountain fur trade both as a business and a way of life. It is an original treatment based on personal acquaintance with the area concerned and on years of research in the original documents. One Juror commented, 'The effect on me was so powerful that I plan to spend part of next summer driving through the territory discussed.' The volume contains many colored and uncolored sketches, done at the time, which are skillfully woven into the body of the narrative. DeVoto's style is sinewy and informal as befits his theme ... Morison ... writes with dash and distinction as well as with authority ... Nevins ... does not write as well as Morison ... Morris'... (book) is thoughtful and mature and enlivened by much brilliant writing ... Wertenbaker attempts a fresh study of a pretty shopworn theme."[84] As the vote for the first-ranked book was the most convincing one, the Advisory Board awarded Bernard DeVoto with the Pulitzer Prize in the history category.[85]

A history jury slightly different from the preceding one (James P. Baxter III, Theodore C. Blegen and Merle Curti) stated in the 1949 jury report, that "three books ... stand out above all others in the competition ... One of them is the best work of American literary history, another the best study in American economic history, a third the best work in American political history, to appear for years. We had no difficulty in concluding these were the three books of the year, but because it is difficult to measure literary, political or economic history in terms of the other two, it has not been easy for us to pick a first choice ... After the interchange of correspondence and telephone calls we have finally reached a unanimous agreement to recommend Roy Franklin Nichols, *The Disruption of American Democracy*. The two other books that made the competition this year unusually keen, were the three-volume *Literary History of the United States*, edited by Spiller, Thorp, Canby and Johnson; and Edward C. Kirkland's *Men, Cities and Transportation - A Study in New England History, 1820-1900* ... We have finally agreed to recommend Nichols' book for first choice," the report

83 James P. Baxter III/Theodore C. Blegen/Arthur M. Schlesinger Sr., Report of the Pulitzer Prize History Jury, New York, March 18, 1948, p. 1.
84 *Ibid.*, pp. 1 f.
85 Columbia University (Ed.), The Pulitzer Prizes, *op. cit.*, p. 58.

adds, "because it represents the most penetrating study of American politics yet made for the period just preceding the Civil War, and because we believe that it will have a major influence on American historical writing. Working over an old field with fresh insight, and extraordinary skill in mobilizing his materials, Nichols has produced a book with important implications for the larger theme of American Democracy."[86] These arguments were accepted by the Advisory Board, which, as a consequence, awarded the Pulitzer Prize for history to Roy Franklin Nichols.[87]

In 1950, the jury was reshuffled again (Theodore C. Blegen, Merle Curti and Arthur M. Schlesinger Sr.). Five authors and books were considered for the Pulitzer Prize and ranked in the following order: "1. L. H. Gipson, *The Great War for the Empire*; 2. O. W. Larkin, *Art and Life in America*; 3. S. E. Morison, *History of United States Naval Operations in World War II*, vols. IV and V; 4. L. C. Hunter, *Steamboats on the Western Rivers*; 5. S. F. Bemis, *John Quincy Adams and the Foundations of American Foreign Policy* ... Gipson's undertaking ... is one of the great individual historical enterprises of our generation ... Larkin's book is a skillful and original attempt to correlate artistic achievements with social and other conditions in the history of the American people, and it is bountifully illustrated and attractively written. Its greatest merit perhaps lies in its point of view ... Morison's volumes, like his preceding ones, are distinguished for judgment, knowledge and graphic description ... Hunter's book is of narrower scope than those that have been mentioned, but it is marked by exhaustive research and by the skillful weaving of economic, technological and social factors into his account. It seems unlikely that this job will ever need to be done over again. Bemis's account treads more familiar territory, but it too is meaty and based on painstaking research ..."[88] After a number of years in which the Advisory Board had accepted the jury's first-ranked proposal, the decision was different this time. In awarding Oliver W. Larkin with the Pulitzer Prize for history, the Advisory Board demonstrated their preference for the second-placed candidate on the jury's list.[89]

Only two members (Merle Curti and Arthur M. Schlesinger Sr.) formed the jury in 1951, and had to select from sixty-eight entries. The following five books were finally placed on the jury's list: "1. *The Old Northwest -*

---

86 James P. Baxter III/Theodore C. Blegen/Merle Curti, Report of the Pulitzer Prize History Jury, Williamstown, Mass., March 7, 1949, pp. 1 f.

87 Columbia University (Ed.), The Pulitzer Prizes, *op. cit.*, p. 58.

88 Theodore C. Blegen/Merle Curti/Arthur M. Schlesinger Sr., Report of the Pulitzer Prize History Jury, Cambridge, Mass., March 10, 1950, pp. 1 f.

89 Columbia University (Ed.), The Pulitzer Prizes, *op. cit.*, p. 58.

Columbia University
in the City of New York

Ocker— 1/16
J. Jury 1/28

NOMINATION FOR A PULITZER PRIZE IN LETTERS

To be filed with the Secretary of the Advisory Board on or before February 1

NOMINATION OF   ACROSS THE WIDE MISSOURI by Bernard DeVoto

In accordance with the provisions of the will of the late Joseph Pulitzer, the Pulitzer Prizes in Journalism and in Letters, and the Pulitzer Traveling Scholarships, open alike to men and women, will be awarded in May, 1917, and each successive year thereafter.

Nominations of candidates for any one of the Pulitzer Prizes must be made in writing on or before February 1 of each year, addressed to the Secretary of the Advisory Board, Graduate School of Journalism, Columbia University, New York 27, on forms that may be obtained on application to Dean Carl W. Ackerman, the Secretary.

Each nomination for a prize must be accompanied by four copies of any book submitted by any competitor for a prize, or on his behalf, which must be delivered at the time of nomination to the Secretary of the Advisory Board. Competition for a prize will be limited to work published during the calendar year ending December 31 next preceding; in the case of the drama prize, consideration will be of works produced during the twelve months April 1 to March 31 inclusive. Nomination of a play should be made while it is being performed.

The following awards will be made annually as Prizes in Letters:

	Check Here

(1) For distinguished fiction published in book form during the year by an American author, preferably dealing with American life, Five hundred dollars ($500).   **1.**

(2) For the original American play, which shall represent in marked fashion the educational value and power of the stage, preferably dealing with American life, Five hundred dollars ($500).   **2.**

(3) For a distinguished book of the year upon the history of the United States, Five hundred dollars ($500).   **3.**   X

(4) For a distinguished American biography or autobiography teaching patriotic and unselfish services to the people, illustrated by an eminent example, Five hundred dollars ($500).   **4.**

(5) For a distinguished volume of verse published during the year by an American author, Five hundred dollars ($500).   **5.**

(*a*) Indicate by a cross (✕) in the margin of the description of the several prizes, the particular prize for which the nomination is made.

(*b*) Name of the proposer of the candidate, if other than the competitor.
Paul Brooks

(*c*) Proposer's present address.
Houghton Mifflin Company
2 Park Street
Boston 7, Massachusetts

Pioneer Period 1815-1840, by R. Carlyle Buley; 2. *The Papers of Thomas Jefferson*, edited by Julian P. Boyd; 3. *And the War Came*, by Kenneth M. Stampp; 4. *Church and State in the United States*, by Anson Phelps Stokes; 5. *Breaking the Bismarck Barrier*, by Samuel Eliot Morison ... Professor Buley has written a readable, well-formed history based upon contemporary sources, written and printed, and containing valuable illustrations and maps. This book should interest laymen as well as scholars. Boyd's edition of Jefferson's writings and papers is a monumental undertaking ... Many of the explanatory notes are historical and bibliographical essays of the highest importance ... Stampp ... is particularly interesting in discussing the economic considerations which caused Northern business at first to want to appease the South and then to insist on a 'Tough' policy ... Stokes's massive treatment of the relations of church and state in America commands admiration because of the thoroughness of his research and the intrinsic value of the material he presents ... Morison ... was an actual observer of much that he describes, but he also draws upon formal and informal sources of both the Allies and the enemy. He writes with unusual distinction of style."[90] The first-ranked book was once again accepted by the Advisory Board. The Pulitzer Prize in the history category was awarded to R. Carlyle Buley.[91]

As the 1952 jury report (by Merle Curti and Arthur M. Schlesinger Sr.) is considered to be lost, it is impossible to completely reconstruct the details of the selection process. Oscar Handlin was awarded with the Pulitzer Prize in the history category by the Advisory Board for his book *The Uprooted*.[92] John Hohenberg describes Handlin's work as a "classic study of European immigration to America," and he adds with respect to the titles awarded in the preceding years: "Nearly all of these works, in one way or another, served to broaden the field of the American historian and the best of them, particularly Handlin's book, set high standards for innovative scholarship. The balance of responsibility for historical literature had long since swung toward the academics whose work was very largely subsidized by their universities or by private foundations and away from the non-institutionalized writers of the type of Douglas Southall Freeman and Carl Sandburg. But now and then, one of the unaffiliated would turn up in the mass of academic literature with a work that simply demanded attention."[93]

90 Merle Curti/Arthur M. Schlesinger Sr., Report of the Pulitzer Prize History Jury, Cambridge, Mass., March 15, 1951, pp. 1 f.
91 Columbia University (Ed.), The Pulitzer Prizes, *op. cit.*, p. 58.
92 *Ibid.*
93 John Hohenberg, The Pulitzer Prizes, *op. cit.*, p. 215.

In the course of the history of the Pulitzer Prizes it would sometimes be the case that historians who were not part of the professional establishment would be presented with the award. After having received the Pulitzer Prize for history, however, these men became objects of public and professional interest - whether they were professional historians or not.

In 1953, the smaller, two-member jury was still in office, and had seventy books to evaluate. The following five titles were selected by the jurors: "1. George Dangerfield, *The Era of Good Feelings*; 2. William L. Langer and S. Everett Gleason, *The Challenge to Isolation, 1937-1940*; 3. Carl F. Wittke, *Refugees of Revolution - The German Forty-Eighters in America*; 4. Bell I. Wiley, *The Life of Billy Yank - The Common Soldier of the Union*; 5. T. Harry Williams, *Lincoln and His Generals* ... Dangerfield's book perhaps comes closest to being a work of literary art. His account is also founded on solid and careful research ... The book is replete with brilliant characterizations, stimulating reflections and fresh insights and should be of as much interest to the layman as to the professional historian ... The work by Langer and Gleason ... has a panoramic sweep, and the authors evidence an unusual mastery of global politics always tempered by precision of scholarship ... Wittke tells the story of the defeated German revolutionists who fled to the United States in 1848 ... Much of his material is drawn from German-language newspapers. It is the first time that the story has been told so completely or so well ... (Wiley's book) is an ant's-eye view of the (Civil) war containing much that is picturesque and interesting ... William's book ... is an extremely perspicuous work."[94] The Advisory Board saw no reason to reject the first-ranked proposal and named George Dangerfield the Pulitzer Prize winner in the history category.[95]

Although there is no jury report from 1954 either, the process of finding a Pulitzer Prize winner is nevertheless fairly easy to trace. John Hohenberg was quite successful in closing the information gaps, and referring to the small number of non-professional historians to win the Pulitzer Prize for American History, he writes of the winner of that year: "Bruce Catton, a former newspaperman and former public official, was such a historian and the book that brought him prominence was his study of the last year of the Civil War, *A Stillness at Appomattox*. The two-member jury in history for 1954, Professors Curti and Schlesinger Sr., were understandably conditioned to think of the fine work of their fellow professionals - the mas-

94 Merle Curti/Arthur M. Schlesinger Sr., Report of the Pulitzer Prize History Jury, Cambridge, Mass., March 5, 1953, pp. 1 f.
95 Columbia University (Ed.), The Pulitzer Prizes, *op. cit.*, p. 58.

sive and authoritative study by William L. Langer and S. Everett Gleason, *The Undeclared War*; Clinton Rossiter's *Seed-time of the Republic*; and Perry Miller's *The New England Mind from Colony to Province*. But they did include Catton's book with this comment: '*A Stillness at Appomattox* is ... a moving book, with good character portraits and vivid portrayal of the sights, sounds, and feelings of the battlefield. The scholar will find little new in it, but few scholarly accounts approach this one in re-creating the human side of the war.' ... Over the jury's choice *The Undeclared War*, ... the Board voted for Catton, without dissent, thus recognizing a new and unaffiliated historian and continuing the long line of nonprofessionals that had begun with Henry Adams to leave their mark on the Pulitzer Prizes."[96]

The jury in 1955, consisting of the same two members as in the years before, had to evaluate seventy-two books. Five titles were considered worthy of a Pulitzer Prize: "1. Paul Horgan, *Great River - The Rio Grande in North American History*; 2. Lewis Atherton, *Main Street on the Middle Border*; 3. Leonard D. White, *The Jacksonians*; 4. Clement Eaton, *A History of the Southern Confederacy*; 5. Thomas J. Pressly, *Americans Interpret Their Civil War* ... Horgan's *Great River* ... is an imaginative and charmingly written account of the Rio Grande and the peoples it affected from pre-Columbian times down to the present. The author enriches his canvas with a wealth of incident, topographical description and human drama without losing the reader in a maze of detail ... This attractive and informative work should make an appeal to both laymen and scholars ... Atherton's *Main Street on the Middle Border* ... deals with the small town in Middle Western life in the period 1865-1950 ... A new approach to the subject, it is amply buttressed with research and written in a vigorous and generally interesting style ... White's *The Jacksonians* ... is a pioneer work in its field ... Eaton's *History of the Southern Confederacy* ... reads easily and is the best we have of the Confederacy ... Pressly's *Americans Interpret Their Civil War* ... is a thoughtful, well-written and stimulating study of the shifting interpretations of the causes of the great sectional conflict from the war period itself to the present day ... The book has excited an unusual amount of controversy in historical circles."[97] Confronted with the merits of all books mentioned in the report the Advisory Board decided to accept the first-ranked proposal and awarded the Pulitzer Prize for history to Paul Horgan.[98]

---

96 John Hohenberg, The Pulitzer Prizes, *op. cit.*, pp. 215 f.
97 Merle Curti/Arthur M. Schlesinger Sr., Report of the Pulitzer Prize History Jury, Cambridge, Mass., March 8, 1955, pp. 1 f.
98 Columbia University (Ed.), The Pulitzer Prizes, *op. cit.*, p. 58.

An entirely new jury (Harry J. Carman and C. Vann Woodward) presented the Advisory Board with a list of five finalists in 1956 which consisted of the following titles and authors: 1. Hofstadter, *The Age of Reform*; 2. Hofstadter and Metzger, *A History of Academic Freedom in the United States*; 3. Bridenbaugh, *Cities in Revolt*; 4. Higham, *Strangers in the Land*; 5. Hidy and Hidy, *Pioneering in Big Business*.[99] Although there were no additional reasons given for the jury's choice and ranking the Advisory Board accepted this small list and awarded Richard Hofstadter with the Pulitzer Prize for his book *The Age of Reform*.[100] The same jurors formed the committee in 1957, and it was their unanimous decision to propose George F. Kennan's *Russia Leaves the War - Soviet-American Relations 1917-1920* for a Pulitzer Prize. The jury ranked four further candidates as follows: 2. Perry Miller, *Errand into the Wilderness*; 3. Kenneth M. Stampp, *The Peculiar Institution*; 4. Arthur Link, *Wilson - The New Freedom*; 5. H. K. Beale, *Theodore Roosevelt and the Rise of America to World Power*; 6. John Hope Franklin, *The Militant South*. "Possibly some might object," the jurors added, "that the Kennan volume does not deal primarily with the history of the United States ... (We) feel, however, that those who established the award did not have in mind that it should be narrowly interpreted ... Certainly, the changes which have occurred in the history of the world during the last half century have both broadened and deepened the content of American history greatly. The Kennan volume deals with one of these major changes which has affected and continues to affect the course of American civilization."[101] The Advisory Board was entirely persuaded that the jury's choice was correct and awarded George F. Kennan with the Pulitzer Prize in the history category.[102]

After forty years of awarding Pulitzer Prizes it was time to take stock of the Prize's development and its history as well as finding a winner in 1958. "As scholarship," one of the two history jurors remarked, "most of the history volumes, but not all, for which Pulitzer Awards have been received have stood the test of time. Even some of those which have been challenged on the basis of factual content or interpretation, or both, have been a source of stimulation to unnumbered thousands of readers and research students ... Undoubtedly, in some years another set of judges might have selected for

99 Harry J. Carman/C. Vann Woodward, Report of the Pulitzer Prize History Jury, New York, February 27, 1956, p. 1.

100 Columbia University (Ed.), The Pulitzer Prizes, *op. cit.*, p. 58.

101 Harry J. Carman/C. Vann Woodward, Report of the Pulitzer Prize History Jury, New York, February 19, 1957, p. 1 f.

102 Columbia University (Ed.), The Pulitzer Prizes, *op. cit.*, p. 58.

the award volumes other than those that were chosen. Were one to hazard a guess, however, as to the number of 'mistakes' made in this respect, it is this writer's belief that it would be very small."[103] The author of this comment, Harry J. Carman, formed the jury in the history category together with C. Vann Woodward, as in 1957. "Despite the thin crop of history books this year," it says in their report, "the five listed here are without question Pulitzer material ...: 1. Bray Hammond, *Banks and Politics in America from the Revolution to the Civil War*; 2. Victor S. Mamatey, *The United States and East Central Europe, 1914-1918*; 3. Arthur M. Schlesinger Jr., *Crisis of the Old Order*; 4. Herbert Feis, *Churchill, Roosevelt, Stalin*; 5. Frank L. Mott, *History of American Magazines* ... Mamatey is a sound scholar but his book is of limited scope. There is not the slightest doubt that Bray Hammond's volume is the best of the lot."[104] The Advisory Board thought the same, and named Bray Hammond the Pulitzer Prize winner in the history category.[105]

The newly elected jury of 1959 (John A. Krout and Roy F. Nichols) proposed, after evaluating the material, awarding the Pulitzer Prize to "the late Leonard D. White and to Jean Schneider for their work *The Republican Era, 1869-1901*. We are, in reality," the jury report continues, "recommending that the Prize be awarded to them for the whole series of books which they have published: *The Federalists*, *The Jeffersonians*, *The Jacksonians*. These together with the volume published in 1958 (*The Republican Era*) have contributed a new technique to historical scholarship. This series of volumes has broken new ground in the field of historiography. Before these works appeared, we knew little or nothing of administrative history. We now have a complete and perceptive history of the American phase of this subject written from sources never before used for such purpose and shaped by an original conceptualization which has made a pattern for future writing in the field. White and Schneider had no models; they had to construct their own and have done such a difficult task most effectively."[106] Further books considered were: Shelby Foote, *The Civil War - A Narrative*; Daniel J. Boorstin, *The Americans - The Colonial Experience*; George E. Mowry, *The Era of Theodore Roosevelt*. "All of these volumes," the jury explained with regards to the finalists from the

---

103 Harry J. Carman, History Awards, *op. cit.*, pp. 37 f.
104 Harry J. Carman/C. Vann Woodward, Report of the Pulitzer Prize History Jury, New York, March 31, 1958, p. 1.
105 Columbia University (Ed.), The Pulitzer Prizes, *op. cit.*, p. 58.
106 John A. Krout/Roy F. Nichols, Report of the Pulitzer Prize History Jury, New York, March 12, 1959, p. 1.

second rank onwards, "deal with subjects which have been repeatedly presented by historians of the American scene. None is either original in conception or rich in new interpretations."[107] Because of this clear difference in quality between the first-ranked title and the other finalists, it was evident to the Advisory Board that Leonard D. White and Jean Schneider should be awarded the Pulitzer Prize.[108]

The same jury took office again in 1960. In their report the jurors made a clear case for awarding the prize "to Professor Henry F. May for his book *The End of American Innocence*, a distinguished contribution to intellectual history ... This is in a real sense a pioneer work based upon an extraordinary amount of research. It sets a much needed pattern for intellectual history which has hitherto been rather amorphous. Our second choice is Hodding Carter's *The Angry Scar*. It is a judicious treatment of the history of Southern Reconstruction ... This is an able interpretation but it is not the original or path breaking analysis that we find our first choice to be. Our third choice is Margaret Leech's *In the Days of McKinley*. This is a well-written, intensive account of the years at the end of the last century. It has much to commend it, but it is absorbing rather than critical. The author finds little to question in this so-called golden age."[109] Meanwhile two members of the parallel-working Biography/Autobiography jury, where Margaret Leech's book was evaluated before being transferred to the history category, stated: "Here is a first class and fascinating performance ... Miss Leech's story, told with literary skill and scholarship of a high order, has a freshness that accounts in part for her achieving what many might regard as impossible: she makes William McKinley a flesh-and-blood man, ... an exciting experience."[110] Although her book on McKinley was only placed third in this category, the Advisory Board awarded Margaret Leech with the Pulitzer Prize for history.[111]

In 1961, the same two-member jury cast an unanimous vote for one candidate. "We recommend," it says in the jury-report, "that the prize be awarded to Herbert Feis for his study entitled *Between War and Peace - The Potsdam Conference* ... Two other volumes ranked high in our estimate but they are not close to Herbert Feis' work. They are John C. Miller, *The*

---

107 John A. Krout/Roy F. Nichols, Additional Report of the Pulitzer Prize History Jury, New York, April 3, 1959, p. 1.

108 Columbia University (Ed.), The Pulitzer Prizes, *op. cit.*, p. 58.

109 John A. Krout/Roy F. Nichols, Report of the Pulitzer Prize History Jury, New York, March 15, 1960, p. 1.

110 Quoted from John Hohenberg, The Pulitzer Prizes, *op. cit.*, p. 277.

111 Columbia University (Ed.), The Pulitzer Prizes, *op. cit.*, p. 58.

Federalist Era, 1789-1801 ... and Bernhard Knollenberg, *The Origin of the American Revolution, 1759-1766* ... We honor Herbert Feis for his wide-ranging examination of the sources, his originality in presenting his findings and the superior literary craftsmanship that distinguishes his book."[112] The Advisory Board accepted this praise and delivered the Pulitzer Prize for history to Herbert Feis.[113]

The 1962 jury report - written again by John A. Krout and Roy F. Nichols - named three finalists. First choice given in this report was Lawrence H. Gipson's book *The Triumphant Empire - Thunder Clouds Gather in the West, 1763-1766*: "It is a project of unusual significance in its comprehensive scope, its use of a tremendous amount of source material, its analytic competence, its lucid style, and its contribution to historical understanding ... Second choice: Thomas D. Clark's *The Emerging South* ... handles one of the most difficult problems in our historiography with rare capacity ... Third choice: Clement Eaton, *The Growth of Southern Civilization, 1790-1860* ... has neither the originality nor the significance of new interpretation which mark the other two."[114] The Advisory Board had no reason to dispute this opinion and, as a consequence, awarded Lawrence H. Gipson the Pulitzer Prize.[115]

The same jurors as in the previous years had to select the winner of the Pulitzer Prize from forty-seven entries in 1963. The following list was the result of their discussions: (1.) Constance McLaughlin Green, *Washington — Village and Capital, 1800-1878*; (2.) Richard S. Dunn, *Puritans and Yankees* ...; (3.) John Dos Passos, *Mr. Wilson's War*. "Among these three," the jury members stated in their report, "we have no strong preference. We have placed Constance Green's volume first because it presents new material on the development of our capital city in such a way as to make more meaningful the history of the nation during the first three-quarters of the nineteenth century."[116] The Advisory Board was persuaded by this argument and awarded the prize to Constance McLaughlin Green.[117] In 1964, when two new members (Lawrence H. Chamberlain and Elting E. Morison) formed the jury, the proposal to the Advisory Board consisted of

112　John A. Krout/Roy F. Nichols, Report of the Pulitzer Prize History Jury, New York, January 11, 1961, p. 1.
113　Columbia University (Ed.), The Pulitzer Prizes, *op. cit.*, p. 58.
114　John A. Krout/Roy F. Nichols, Report of the Pulitzer Prize History Jury, Philadelphia, Pa., January 9, 1962, pp. 1 f.
115　Columbia University (Ed.), The Pulitzer Prizes, *op. cit.*, p. 58.
116　John A. Krout/Roy F. Nichols, Report of the Pulitzer Prize History Jury, Tempe, Ar., January 10, 1963, p. 1.
117　Columbia University (Ed.), The Pulitzer Prizes, *op. cit.*, p. 58.

the following three titles: *The Civil War*, by Shelby Foote; *Here Lies Virginia*, by Ivor Noel Hume; and *Puritan Village*, by Sumner Chilton Powell. "Of the three books," the jury report states, "we cite as deserving special consideration for the Prize, we believe that the work of Mr. Powell is clearly superior to the other two and therefore we designate it as our choice for the prize ... Mr. Powell has worked a very small piece of ground with great resource and patience and considerable success."[118] In this case too, the Advisory Board accepted the jury's proposal and named Sumner Chilton Powell the Pulitzer Prize winner for history.[119]

The 1965 jury (Paul Horgan and Richard B. Morris) was faced with extraordinary problems in their selection of the finalists in the history category. Although they agreed on a list of three books, the jury admitted in their report to the Advisory Board, that "a final selection from among them is not easy to make, considering the variety of themes and the contrasts in literary manners which they represent ...: First choice: *When the Cheering Stopped*, by Gene Smith: For the new light it throws upon a critical episode in the history of the Presidency, for the absorbing readability of its telling, and for the contemporary significance of its subject. Second choice: *Diplomat among Warriors*, by Robert Murphy: For the importance of its contribution to the eye-witness history of vital phases of World War II and subsequent events, for the honesty of its view, and for the unstudied animation of its style. Third choice: *The Greenback Era*, by Irwin Unger: For its scholarly excellence, for its examination and demonstration of a new theory of historical forces at work in the post-Civil War period, and for its literary quality."[120] The jury report further comments on the third-ranked title: "It is bound to exercise a major influence on the revisionism of the historiography of this period for a long time to come. It is not too much to say that the book is superbly researched. In purely intellectual values, it is probably the most significant of the books in this final choice of three."[121] These last points in particular probably persuaded the Advisory Board to award Irwin Unger with the Pulitzer Prize[122] instead of following the jury's proposal.

The year 1966 brought a number of problems to the new jury - again consisting of three members (Henry F. Graff, Oscar Handlin and Margaret L.

---

118 Lawrence H. Chamberlain/Elting E. Morison, Report of the Pulitzer Prize History Jury, New York, January 21, 1964, pp. 1 f.
119 Columbia University (Ed.), The Pulitzer Prizes, *op. cit.*, p. 58.
120 Paul Horgan/Richard B. Morris, Report of the Pulitzer Prize History Jury, New York, undated (1965), p. 4.
121 *Ibid.*, p. 3.
122 Columbia University (Ed.), The Pulitzer Prizes, *op. cit.*, p. 58.

Pulitzer) - which put forward a two-ranked list: Richard B. Morris, *The Peacemakers*, and Perry Miller, *Life of the Mind in America*. "Mrs. Pulitzer and Mr. Graff," it states in the jury report, "vote for Richard B. Morris ... They feel strongly that it is head and shoulders above all other history books published in 1965. They consider it to be a splendid example of narrative history dealing with a grand theme (the Great Powers and American Independence) in a grand fashion ... Mr. Handlin's opinion is that Mr. Morris's book is certainly based upon sound and thorough research ... But, he states, he cannot find that it adds at all to the understanding of the subject ... Mr. Handlin votes for Perry Miller ... Mr. Handlin believes that imperfect and fragmentary as this posthumous book is, it is a distinguished work. It offers, he maintains, a fresh view of a whole subject, which will evoke continuing discussion and thought ... Mrs. Pulitzer and Mr. Graff gave to Mr. Handlin's choice the careful thought it deserves. Upon re-reading Miller, however, they concluded decisively that despite the merits of what Mr. Miller was able to accomplish before his death it seems to them inappropriate to recommend for a Pulitzer Prize an unfinished book containing less than a quarter of the material which the author had intended to include."[123] In spite of the contradictions of two jury members, the minority's vote was finally decisive. As a consequence the Advisory Board awarded the Pulitzer Prize to Perry Miller[124] who had already been a finalist in the Pulitzer Prize history category in the mid-fifties.[125]

The jurors of 1967 (Julian P. Boyd, Lyman H. Butterfield and Henry Steele Commager) were confronted with seventy-six entries. "The general level of both scholarship and literature was high," the jury report stressed, "half of the books submitted to us were worthy of serious consideration, and eight or ten were good enough to have justified an award ... There was, at an early stage, general agreement on the five or six best books of the year, and it is only fair to list these: Goetzmann, *Exploration and Empire* ...; Merk, *Monroe Doctrine and American Expansionism* ...; Morgan, *Congress and the Constitution* ...; De Conde, *The Quasi-War with France* ...; Blodgett, *The Gentle Reformers* ...; Young, *The Washington Community* ... After considerable discussion and several meetings the choice boiled down to the first two books on this list, and eventually the committee reached unanimous and harmonious agreement on a first choice: Goetzmann, *Exploration and Em-*

123 Henry F. Graff/Oscar Handlin/Margaret L. Pulitzer, Report of the Pulitzer Prize History Jury, New York, December 18, 1965, p. 1.
124 Columbia University (Ed.), The Pulitzer Prizes, *op. cit.*, p. 58.
125 Cf. John Hohenberg, The Pulitzer Prizes, *op. cit.*, p. 215.

Exploration & Empire

The Explorer and the Scientist in the Winning of the American West

William H. Goetzmann

Winner of the Pulitzer Prize in History, 1967

pire - The Explorer and the Scientist in the Winning of the American West. This book is not only a most remarkable achievement for a young man, but a tremendous book in its own right, tremendous in size, in imagination and in interpretation ... It is learned and scholarly, built on a massive documentary foundation. In conception, in research, in its findings, and in its interpretation, it is strikingly original ... This book is one of those seminal books which will, assuredly, inspire a dozen other books, for Goetzmann has opened up by-ways of history not only unexplored but even unsuspected ... Finally, *Exploration and Empire* is written with real literary distinction."[126] In view of this exceptional praise the Advisory Board followed the jury's proposal and awarded the Pulitzer Prize to William H. Goetzmann.[127]

In 1968, there were nearly no problems in finding a winner in the history category, because the jury (Julian P. Boyd, Louis Morton and Harold C. Syrett) "unanimously agreed to recommend to the Advisory Board that the award ... be given to Professor Bernard Bailyn's *The Ideological Origins of the American Revolution* ... This in their opinion," the report continues, "is a work of such originality, distinction, and enduring value for the understanding of the Revolution as to make it pre-eminent among all the nominations for the award. The jurors feel, however, that certain other works submitted are worthy of high commendation ...: George B. Tindall, *The Emergence of the New South*; Alfred E. Young, *The Democratic Republicans of New York*; John Blum, *The Morgenthau Diaries*; John A. Hawgood, *America's Western Frontiers*."[128] There was no doubt for the Advisory Board as to award Bernard Bailyn in 1968.[129] The Pulitzer Prize History jury of 1969 (Bruce Catton, Henry Steele Commager and Ernest Samuels) came to the unanimous proposal to award Leonard Levy's book *The Origins of the Fifth Amendment*. "This struck all of us as a most distinguished work," it says in the jury's evaluation, "thoroughly researched, and in its findings reflecting mature consideration and balanced judgment ... In addition, it is a landmark book which must be examined by anyone who seeks a real understanding of this important issue ... It was the first choice of all of us, and we are happy to commend it for the prize."[130] Although the report proposed two further finalists, namely Winthrop D. Jordan's *White Over Black* and John G.

---

126 Julian P. Boyd/Lyman H. Butterfield/Henry Steele Commager, Report of the Pulitzer Prize History Jury, Amherst, Mass., February 2, 1967, p. 1.
127 Columbia University (Ed.), The Pulitzer Prizes, *op. cit.*, p. 58.
128 Julian P. Boyd/Louis Morton/Harold C. Syrett, Report of the Pulitzer Prize History Jury, Princeton, N.J., December 30, 1967, p. 1.
129 Columbia University (Ed.), The Pulitzer Prizes, *op. cit.*, p. 59.
130 Bruce Catton/Henry Steele Commager/Ernest Samuels, Report of the Pulitzer Prize History Jury, New York, December 23, 1968, p. 1.

Sproat's *The Best Men*, the Advisory Board awarded Leonard W. Levy with the Pulitzer Prize.[131]

Four finalists were chosen at the end of the jury's discussion in 1970. Catherine Drinker Bowen, Lyman H. Butterfield and J. Russell Wiggins named the following authors and books: "First choice: Dean Acheson, *Present at the Creation*; second choice: Gordon S. Wood, *The Creation of the American Republic, 1776-1787*; third choice: Bruce Catton, *Grant Takes Command*; fourth choice: Robert K. Murray, *The Harding Era* ... Dean Acheson's ... pages are wonderfully informative and enlightening, giving an unusual, always authentic perspective on how the United States government conducts its foreign affairs in peace and in war ... Here is notable literary distinction, also an honesty that is not hidden by the irony, the sophistication, and truly elegant wit ... Wood demonstrates that in rebelling against British rule the Americans appealed to the assumptions of the best British political thought of the age - the classic Whig doctrines derived from Locke and the 'Commonwealthmen' ... This is a ... big, thick-textured and highly cerebral book. It would be foolish to pretend that it is for everybody ... Bruce Catton's ... account of the Army of the Potomac's approach to Richmond is a magnificent description of Grant's hit-and-slide tactics that ought to help demolish the legend of Grant as a frontal assault specialist. Catton's narrative depicts this sliding assault vividly and shows how Grant maneuvered around Lee's right flank after each engagement ... Murray's book ... is an important work, not only for its tendency to right the record itself, but for its revealing, indeed brilliant, demonstration of how the myths about the period arose in the journalism of the time."[132] The Advisory Board did not hesitate to award the prize to Dean Acheson, even though his book was distinctly biographical in character.[133]

The history jurors in 1971 (Julian P. Boyd, Leonard W. Levy and Louis Morton) were - despite their agreement on a number of questions - unable to reach a unanimous proposal in their report to the Advisory Board. The majority, i.e. Levy and Morton, proposed for first place *Roosevelt, the Soldier of Freedom, 1940-1945*, by James MacGregor Burns for a Pulitzer Prize. "It is difficult sometimes," one reads in their report, "to distinguish between biography and history and in this case it is particularly difficult to do so. Burns' book ... is a distinguished work of history whose focus is President

---

131 Columbia University (Ed.), The Pulitzer Prizes, *op. cit.*, p. 59.
132 Catherine Drinker Bowen/Lyman H. Butterfield/J. Russell Wiggins, Report of the Pulitzer Prize History Jury, New York, January 6, 1970, pp. 1-3.
133 Columbia University (Ed.), The Pulitzer Prizes, *op. cit.*, p. 59.

LEONARD W. LEVY

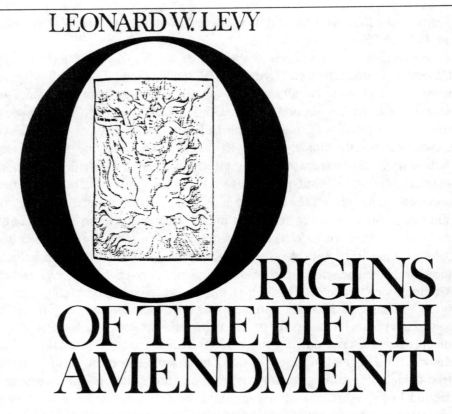

ORIGINS OF THE FIFTH AMENDMENT

The Right Against Self-Incrimination

(Winner of the Pulitzer Prize in History for 1969)

No part of the Constitution has aroused greater controversy in recent years than the Fifth Amendment's clause on the right against self-incrimination; yet no clause has been so neglected by historians. A landmark in the study of constitutional origins, Professor Levy's book probes the intentions of the framers of the Fifth Amendment, and reveals the ideas, events, and circumstances that lie behind this bulwark of a free society.

The story, which encompasses some of the basic legal problems of English society, starts even before Magna Carta, with the beginnings of the accusatorial system of justice in England. Concentrating upon the Tudor and early Stuart period, Professor Levy examines the English background of the struggle against arbitrary rule; and he shows how the issues that racked England in the sixteenth and seventeenth centuries reflected religious, political, and philosophical conflicts. He traces the echoes of those conflicts in the American colonies before the Revolution, and follows the details of the establishment of this right in one of the Amendments to the Constitution.

Roosevelt ... Not only does it place the President in a new perspective but it also offers new interpretations of the period and constitutes a major contribution to that period. Moreover it is written with clarity, vigor and grace ... For second place we recommend Lawrence A. Cremin, *American Education - the Colonial Experience, 1607-1783.*"[134] The third jury member, Julian P. Boyd, explained his minority opinion as follows: "I share some of my colleagues' regard for Burns' *Roosevelt* (book), but I think it is primarily a biography and should be judged in that category. I rejected Cremin's *American Education* partly because of my agreement with my colleagues that this is the first of a series of volumes and that it would be better to wait until other volumes have appeared before making a decision. But, aside from this, I do have serious reservations about the work ... My first choice is (Clifford K.) Shipton's *Harvard Graduates* ..., an aspect of the history of Harvard University as seen through the lives of its graduates."[135] Having evaluated the different arguments and positions the Advisory Board decided to award the Pulitzer Prize to MacGregor Burns.[136]

The jury members who had to decide on the award in 1972 (W. Frank Craven, Louis Morton and T. Harry Williams) were "unanimous in recommending the following: ... Carl Degler, *Neither Black Nor White*, ... is a brilliant book; short, well-written and breaks new ground ... Our second choice is Adam Ulam, *The Rivals*, ... an extremely intelligent and learned work on the relations between Russia and the United States in the period since 1945 ... Finally, the third place (though a very close third) is Morison's *European Discovery of America* ..., distinguished, beautifully crafted, exciting to read and a major contribution."[137] The Advisory Board awarded Carl Degler with the Pulitzer Prize.[138] In 1973 the task of finding a Pulitzer Prize winner was given to a new jury (Harold M. Hyman, Leonard W. Levy and Harold C. Syrett). The jurors "unanimously and enthusiastically," it says in their report to the Advisory Board, proposed for the Pulitzer Prize "Michael Kammen, *People of Paradox - An Inquiry Concerning the Origins of American Civilization* ... The jury considered this book to be in a class by itself. For second place the jury, again by unanimous vote, selected John W. Blassingame, *The Slave Community - Plantation Life in the Antebellum South* ...

---

134 Leonard W. Levy/Louis Morton, Majority Report of the Pulitzer Prize History Jury, Hanover, N.H., January 8, 1971, p. 1.
135 Julian P. Boyd, Minority Report of the Pulitzer Prize History Jury, Princeton, N.J., January 12, 1971, pp. 1 f.
136 Columbia University (Ed.), The Pulitzer Prizes, *op. cit.*, p. 59.
137 W. Frank Craven/Louis Morton/T. Harry Williams, Report of the Pulitzer Prize History Jury, Hanover, N.H., December 27, 1971, p. 1.
138 Columbia University (Ed.), The Pulitzer Prizes, *op. cit.*, p. 59.

The jurors were not able to agree on their third and fourth choices," which were: David McCullough, *The Great Bridge*; David S. Lovejoy, *The Glorious Revolution in America*; Sydney E. Ahlstrom, *A Religious History of the American People*; Pauline Maier, *From Resistance to Revolution*.[139] The Advisory Board took little account of the other titles and named Michael Kammen the winner in 1973.[140]

A lot of work had to be done by the jurors in 1974 (Louis Morton, Willie Lee Rose and Boyd Shafer) in their selection of a suitable winner. "The task of the History Jury," it is written in the report, "was particularly difficult this year, partly because of the large number of volumes submitted, well over 100, and partly because there were so many excellent works to be considered ... We were able finally to agree on the first two choices but not on the third choice. We are unanimous in recommending as our first choice ... Daniel J. Boorstin's *The Americans - The Democratic Experience* ... It is an important book, ranking with such multi-volume histories of the United States as those by Rhodes and McMaster. For second choice, we are unanimous in recommending Stephen Thernstrom's *The Other Bostonians* ... It is a clear, readable, statistical essay on social mobility in the United States. It is one of the best works in quantitative history we have encountered and the author is particularly frank in dealing with the shortcomings as well as the advantages of his method. For third choice Professor Shafer recommends Kevin Starr's *Americans and the California Dream* ... He found it ... beautifully written ... Professor Rose and Louis Morton selected for third place Warren L. Cook's *Flood Tide of Empire - Spain and the Pacific Northwest, 1543-1819* ... This volume is grand in scope ..., is based on original sources, is deeply researched and extremely attractive in format. It is a volume not likely to be superseded for a very long time."[141] There was no doubt for the Advisory Board to award Daniel J. Boorstin with the Pulitzer Prize.[142]

When the jury members of 1975 (David Herbert Donald, Walter LaFeber and James M. McPherson) met for the first time, sixty-one books were presented for evaluation. Following discussions lasting for some months the following decision was expressed in the report: "Our unanimous first choice ... is *Salem Possessed - The Social Origins of Witchcraft*, by Paul Boyer and Stephen Nissenbaum ... (It) is the very best example of the new social hi-

139 Harold M. Hyman/Leonard W. Levy/Harold C. Syrett, Report of the Pulitzer Prize History Jury, New York, December 21, 1972, p. 1.
140 Columbia University (Ed.), The Pulitzer Prizes, *op. cit.*, p. 59.
141 Louis Morton/Willie Lee Rose/Boyd Shafer, Report of the Pulitzer Prize History Jury, Hanover, N.H., January 3, 1974, pp. 1 f.
142 Columbia University (Ed.), The Pulitzer Prizes, *op. cit.*, p. 59.

story of which we are aware, for this study, which ostensibly deals with only one small New England town, raises very broad questions concerning the transformation of American life at the end of the seventeenth century, a transformation from a religion-oriented to a commerce-oriented society. A major work, elegantly conceived and superbly executed, *Salem Possessed* is in our judgment the most distinguished book in American History published during 1974. For second place the jury, again by unanimous vote, selects *All God's Dangers - The Life of Nate Shaw*, by Theodore Rosengarten ... For third place the jury unanimously recommends *Roll, Jordan, Roll - The World The Slaves Made*, by Eugene D. Genovese."[143] In a separate additional vote the jury proposed, "to award, in addition to the regular prizes in History and Biography, a Special Citation to *Jefferson and His Time*, by Dumas Malone ... We believe that Malone's work is one of the most important and distinguished studies now in progress in either American History or Biography."[144] Surprisingly, the Advisory Board awarded Dumas Malone not as one would expect with the Special Citation award proposed by the jury, but with the regular Pulitzer Prize for history.[145]

By proposing Paul Horgan's book *Lamy of Santa Fe* for the Pulitzer Prize, the history jury in 1976 (Bernard Bailyn, Linda Kerber and Arthur M. Schlesinger) decisively favoured one entry. "It is substantial and highly informative history," the jury report states, "covering a wide range of life in the old west from a remarkably fresh point of view ... This is both a moving literary achievement and an historical work of enduring importance. Other books received serious consideration from the jury and should be noted: Martin Sherwin, *A World Destroyed* ...; Francis Jennings, *The Invasion of America* ...; Ernest May, *The Making of the Monroe Doctrine* ...; W. Averell Harriman and Elie Abel, *Special Envoy to Churchill and Stalin* ...; Richard Kohn, *Eagle and Sword*."[146] The Advisory Board found no reason to dispute the decision to award the prize to Paul Horgan.[147] The jury members of 1977 (Michael Kammen, Leonard W. Levy and Kathryn Kish Sklar) were in the comfortable position of being able to present a clear favorite for the award. They unanimously voted that the Pulitzer Prize should "be awarded to *The Impending Crisis*, by David M. Potter. Although we disagreed on a

---

143 David Herbert Donald/Walter LaFeber/James M. McPherson, Report of the Pulitzer Prize History Jury, Cambridge, Mass., December 28, 1974, pp. 1 f.

144 David Herbert Donald/Walter LaFeber/James M. McPherson, Additional proposal of the Pulitzer Prize History Jury, Cambridge, Mass., December 28, 1974, p. 1.

145 Columbia University (Ed.), The Pulitzer Prizes, *op. cit.*, p. 59.

146 Bernard Bailyn/Linda Kerber/Arthur M. Schlesinger, Report of the Pulitzer Prize History Jury, New York, January 22, 1976, pp. 1 f.

147 Columbia University (Ed.), The Pulitzer Prizes, *op. cit.*, p. 59.

rank-ordering of runners-up," the jury report continues, "we agreed in ranking *The Impending Crisis* as number one. This is so superior a book that it would rank high in a competition among Pulitzer Prize winners over the years." Further books being in the closer choice were: Herbert Gutman's *The Black Family*, Lester Cappon's *Atlas of American History*, Irving Howe's *World of our Father's*, Richard Kluger's *Simple Justice*, Henry May's *The Enlightenment in America*, James McPherson's *Abolitionist Legacy* and Joseph Lash's *Roosevelt and Churchill*.[148] The Advisory Board, however, kept to the jury's first-ranked proposal and awarded the Pulitzer Prize posthumously to David M. Potter; Don E. Fehrenbacher had completed the manuscript.[149]

No less than one hundred and thirty-five titles were to be assessed by the jury (David Herbert Donald, David Hackett Fischer and Richard Kohn) in 1978. Despite the high number of entries there was only *one* book seriously discussed in the report. "The jury unanimously recommends," it says in the text, "that the ... Pulitzer Prize in History be awarded to *The Visible Hand - The Managerial Revolution in American Business*, by Alfred D. Chandler Jr. All three members agree that this is a distinguished book, a work of enormous scholarship, which is likely to have a broad and lasting impact ..., one of those very rare books that is at once a broad synthesis of an enormous literature ... and also a highly original interpretation ..."[150] The Advisory Board accepted this unanimous proposal and named Alfred D. Chandler Jr. the Pulitzer Prize winner in 1978.[151] The jurors in 1979 (John Higham, Martin Ridge and Harold C. Syrett) again presented a list of three titles, ranked as follows: "1. Anthony F. C. Wallace, *Rockdale*; 2. Don E. Fehrenbacher, *The Dred Scott Case*; 3. Philip Greven, *The Protestant Temperament* ... We placed *Rockdale* first ... because it is a remarkably original and successful example of an interdisciplinary approach to local history ... We considered *The Dred Scott Case* a truly superior and thorough monograph of major importance ... It will undoubtedly remain the definitive book on the subject ... We were all impressed by Greven, *The Protestant Temperament*, which seeks to revise many currently held views of intellectual history in colonial America."[152] The Pulitzer Prize Board, as the former Advi-

148 Michael Kammen/Leonard W. Levy/Kathryn Kish Sklar, Report of the Pulitzer Prize History Jury, La Verne, Cal., December 23, 1976, pp. 1-3.
149 Columbia University (Ed.), The Pulitzer Prizes, *op. cit.*, p. 59.
150 David Herbert Donald/David Hackett Fischer/Richard Kohn, Report of the Pulitzer Prize History Jury, Cambridge, Mass., December 30, 1977, pp. 1-3.
151 Columbia University (Ed.), The Pulitzer Prizes, *op. cit.*, p. 59.
152 John Higham/Martin Ridge/Harold C. Syrett, Report of the Pulitzer Prize History Jury, Craryville, N.Y., December 12, 1978, pp. 1 f.

sory Board was now called, did not accept the first book on the list, awarding the prize instead to Don E. Fehrenbacher,[153] who already had helped to bring a Pulitzer Prize to David M. Potter two years before.

The jury in 1980 (Don E. Fehrenbacher, William H. Goetzmann and Martin Ridge) agreed on a list consisting of three titles, which were presented "in alphabetical *not* rank order" as follows: Leon F. Litwack, *Been in the Storm So Long*; Gary B. Nash, *The Urban Crucible*; John D. Unruh, *The Plains Across*. "Each book," the jury report stresses, "is an outstanding contribution to the field of American history, and each will remain of lasting significance ... Leon F. Litwack's ... book is a pleasure to read and is perhaps all the more powerful in its effect ... Gary B. Nash's ... book is vigorously written as befits a reinterpretation. John D. Unruh's ... (book is) a work of magisterial comprehensiveness and penetrating insights ..."[154] The Board preferred Litwack's book and awarded him with the Pulitzer Prize.[155] The jurors in 1981 (Suzanne Garment, William H. Goetzmann and Karl Joachim Weintraub) again selected three titles and presented them in the following alphabetical order: Lawrence A. Cremin, *American Education - The National Experience, 1783-1876*; David Kennedy, *Over Here - The First World War and American Society*; Lyle Koehler, *A Search for Power - the 'weaker sex' in Seventeenth Century New England*. "Though we were requested to submit the nominations in alphabetical order," one can read in the jury report, "we feel obliged to say that the book by Lawrence A. Cremin, in our view, ranks substantially above the others."[156] This hint was accepted by the Pulitzer Prize Board, who awarded the prize for history to Lawrence A. Cremin.[157]

The following list of three titles was set up by the jurors (John M. Blum, Eric Foner and John W. Toland) in 1982 - again in alphabetical order of the names: George Frederickson, *White Supremacy*; Akira Iriye, *Power and Culture*; C. Vann Woodward, *Mary Chesnut's Civil War*. The report states with respect to the rank order of these three titles proposed by the jury: "1a. C. V. Woodward, *Mary Chesnut's Civil War*. One of the only two outstanding books among the entire group ... It is a special work. The jury believes the book fully merits a Pulitzer Prize. A question has arisen as to whether

153 Columbia University (Ed.), The Pulitzer Prizes, *op. cit.*, p. 59.
154 Don E. Fehrenbacher/William H. Goetzmann/Martin Ridge, Report of the Pulitzer Prize History Jury, San Marino, Cal., December 26, 1979, pp. 1 f.
155 Columbia University (Ed.), The Pulitzer Prizes, *op. cit.*, p. 59.
156 Suzanne Garment/William H. Goetzmann/Karl Joachim Weintraub, Report of the Pulitzer Prize History Jury, Stanford, Cal., December 11, 1980, p. 1.
157 Columbia University (Ed.), The Pulitzer Prizes, *op. cit.*, p. 59.

the prize in American history should be awarded for a work of historical editing. If (the Board concludes) that such a work does not conform to the criteria for that prize, then the jury strongly urges a special Pulitzer award for this book. 1b. George Frederickson, *White Supremacy*. The other of the only two outstanding books among the entire group. It is a work of impeccable scholarship and historical imagination. Provocative in its judgments, it provides a remarkable tour de force of comparative analysis and illuminates the histories of both American and South African societies. 3. Akira Iriye, *Power and Culture*. This book is well below the other two. At the same time, it is a work of impressive research and intellectual significance ... If (the Board) should decide to give the Woodward book an award in a special category, then a third book to list as a nominee in American history would properly be James Jones, *Bad Blood*."[158] Despite the formal criticism pronounced by the jury, the Pulitzer Prize Board awarded the history prize to C. Vann Woodward for his book *Mary Chesnut's Civil War*.[159]

No problems arose when awarding the Pulitzer History Prize in 1983. An entirely new jury (Aileen S. Kraditor, Leon F. Litwack and Robert V. Remini) put their proposal to the Board with the following alphabetical list of authors and titles: Rhys Isaac, *The Transformation of Virginia, 1740-1790*; Robert Middlekauff, *The Glorious Cause - The American Revolution, 1763-1789*; Bertram Wyatt-Brown, *Southern Honor - Ethics and Behavior in the Old South*. "We wish only to state," the jurors wrote to the Pulitzer Prize Board, "that in literary excellence, we find Rhys Isaac's *The Transformation of Virginia* and Robert Middlekauff's *The Glorious Cause* to be superior to Bertram Wyatt-Brown's *Southern Honor*. But the scholarly importance and imaginative qualities of *Southern Honor* we deemed sufficient to merit a nomination."[160] The Pulitzer Prize Board was in favour of Rhys L. Isaac and awarded him with the Prize for history.[161] In 1984, when a slightly different jury from the former one (Bernard Bailyn, George Frederickson and David M. Kennedy) was in office, the jury report begins: "It was clear at the start that 1983 was not a strong year for history and that there would be difficulty selecting a volume sufficiently distinguished to merit this national award," and continues: "One member of the Jury thought well of Dewey W. Grantham's *Southern Progressivism* ... Another book that was discussed in

158 John M. Blum/Eric Foner/John W. Toland, Report of the Pulitzer Prize History Jury, New Haven, Conn., December 7, 1981, pp. 1 f.
159 Columbia University (Ed.), The Pulitzer Prizes, *op. cit.*, p. 59.
160 Aileen S. Kraditor/Leon F. Litwack/Robert V. Remini, Report of the Pulitzer Prize History Jury, Berkeley, Cal., December 30, 1982, p. 1.
161 Columbia University (Ed.), The Pulitzer Prizes, *op. cit.*, p. 59.

some detail was John L. Thomas's *Alternative America* ... The third book discussed (was) John M. Cooper Jr.'s *The Warrior and the Priest* ... The Jury feels that none of the books are major works ... The Jury cannot, therefore, recommend to the Pulitzer Board any of the volumes received for the award in history."[162] The Board accepted this vote and decided for the first time since 1919 that "no award" should be given in the history category.[163]

Selecting from a total of eighty-three entries, the 1985 jury (Robert Dallek, David Herbert Donald and Joan Hoff-Wilson) considered three titles to be worthy of a Pulitzer Prize, namely: "(1) Thomas K. McCraw, *Prophets of Regulation - Charles Francis Adams, Louis D. Brandeis, James M. Landis, and Alfred E. Kahn* ... is an extraordinary book of outstanding merit ... (2) Francis Paul Prucha, *The Great Father - The United States Government and the American Indians* ... is a work of great erudition, based on exhaustive research ... (3) Joel Williamson, *The Crucible of Race - Black-White Relations in the American South Since Emancipation* ... deals with a fascinating topic of broad general interest and of great historical significance ... Though we have reservations about two of these books, we feel that any one of them is worthy of a Pulitzer Prize."[164] The Board favoured the first-ranked title and awarded Thomas K. McCraw with the Pulitzer Prize.[165] In 1986, the history jury (Catherine Clinton, C. Vann Woodward and Bertram Wyatt-Brown) named four finalists in the report which starts with the following reservation: "The two following books ... have been approved by all three members of the History Jury: Forrest McDonald, *Novus Ordo Seclorum - The Intellectual Origins of the Constitution* ...; Walter A. McDougall, ... *the Heavens and the Earth - A Political History of the Space Age* ... The following book ... (has) been approved by two members of the History Jury ...: Kerby A. Miller, *Emigrants and Exiles - Ireland and the Irish Exodus to North America.*" Dissenting from the two other jurors a minority report added the following book by Jacqueline Jones: *Labor of Love, Labor of Sorrow - Black Women.*[166] The Board voted for Walter A. McDougall who, as a consequence, received the Pulitzer Prize for history.[167]

---

162 Bernard Bailyn/George Frederickson/David M. Kennedy, Report of the Pulitzer Prize History Jury, Cambridge, Mass., January 10, 1984, pp. 1 f.
163 Columbia University (Ed.), The Pulitzer Prizes, *op. cit.*, p. 59.
164 Robert Dallek/David Herbert Donald/Joan Hoff-Wilson, Report of the Pulitzer Prize History Jury, Cambridge, Mass., December 30, 1984, pp. 1-3.
165 Columbia University (Ed.), The Pulitzer Prizes, *op. cit.*, p. 59.
166 Catherine Clinton/C. Vann Woodward/Bertram Wyatt-Brown, Report of the Pulitzer Prize History Jury, Hamden, Conn., undated (ca. December 1985), pp. 1-3.
167 Columbia University (Ed.), The Pulitzer Prizes, *op. cit.*, p. 59.

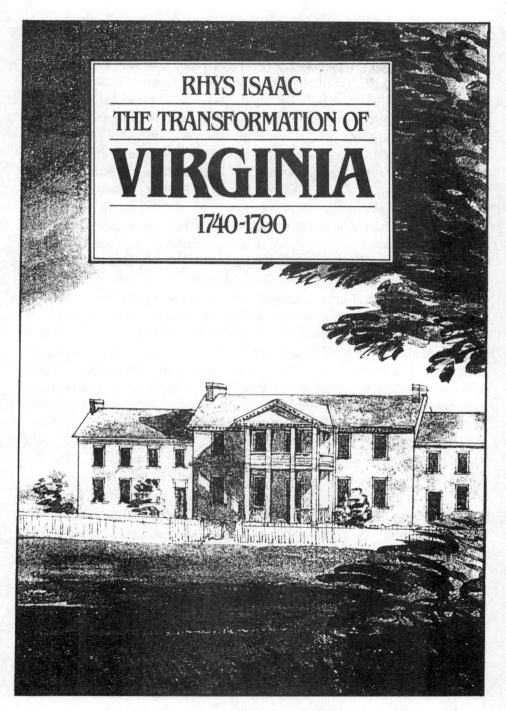

RHYS ISAAC
THE TRANSFORMATION OF
VIRGINIA
1740-1790

Although the jurors in the year 1987 (John Bodnar, Drew Gilpin Faust and Gordon S. Wood) agreed on a list consisting of three names, they ordered the titles according to their preferences rather than alphabetically: 1. *Bearing the Cross*, by David J. Garrow; 2. *Voyagers to the West*, by Bernard Bailyn; 3. *Eisenhower at War*, by David Eisenhower. Garrow's book that dealt with Martin Luther King Jr. was appreciated properly in the jury report as a "vivid portrait of the complex relationship between the man and the movement he came to symbolize ... *Voyagers to the West* is a masterful study of eighteenth-century British immigration to British North America ... The ultimate achievement of David Eisenhower is a meticulous reconstruction of the day to day operations that his grandfather faced."[168] The Board decided to award the second-ranked proposal, namely Bernard Bailyn, who had already won a Pulitzer Prize in the history category in 1968.[169] The 1988 jury (Alice Kessler-Harris, Gary B. Nash and Joel H. Silbey) again presented a list in alphabetical order in which they put forward: "Robert Bruce, *The Launching of Modern American Science*; David Montgomery, *The Fall of the House Labor*; Charles Rosenberg, *The Care of Strangers* ... Bruce is particularly skilled at presenting scientific thought clearly and elucidating the complex connections between science and society ... Montgomery's book ... is a thorough, detailed and painstaking empirical presentation of labor's situation ... Rosenberg presents an extremely valuable insight into the history of American society ..."[170] The members of the Pulitzer Prize Board were in favour of Robert V. Bruce and named him the Pulitzer Prize winner for history.[171]

In 1989, when the jurors (Jean Harvey Baker, David Herbert Donald and John Toland) had to evaluate nearly eighty entries, they selected the following four "strongest candidates for the prize ...: (1) Taylor Branch, *Parting the Waters - America in the King Years, 1954-63*, ... is the fullest and most revealing account ever written of the struggle for black equality ... (2) Eric Foner, *Reconstruction - America's Unfinished Revolution, 1863-1877*, ... is a beautifully crafted history of an important and neglected period ... (3) James M. McPherson, *Battle Cry of Freedom - The Civil War Era*, ... will without doubt be the standard work in its field for the coming generation ... (4) Neil Sheehan, *A Bright Shining Lie - John Paul Vann and America in*

---

168 John Bodnar/Drew Gilpin Faust/Gordon S. Wood, Report of the Pulitzer Prize History Jury, Providence, R.I., December 24, 1986, pp. 1-4.
169 Columbia University (Ed.), The Pulitzer Prizes, *op. cit.*, p. 59.
170 Alice Kessler-Harris/Gary B. Nash/Joel H. Silbey, Report of the Pulitzer Prize History Jury, Ithaca, N.Y., December 28, 1987, pp. 1 f.
171 Columbia University (Ed.), The Pulitzer Prizes, *op. cit.*, p. 59.

Vietnam, ... is the most brilliantly written (book) of the four volumes we have recommended."[172] The high quality of all four books was also appreciated by the Pulitzer Prize Board which - for the first time in the history of Pulitzer Prizes in this category - awarded two books at the same time, namely the works of Taylor Branch and James M. McPherson.[173]

In 1990 the jury (William H. Goetzmann, Christine Leigh Heyrman and Leon F. Litwack) again named three finalists in alphabetical order: "Hugh Honour, *The Image of the Black in Western Art,* Volume 4, Parts I and II: From the American Revolution to World War I ... This is a work of extraordinary sweep and originality, illuminating white attitudes toward blacks ... No study by any historian has recorded with such startling clarity the black image in the white mind — the ways in which white artists painted, drew, and carved representations of black men and women ... Thomas P. Hughes, *American Genesis - A Century of Invention and Technological Enthusiasm, 1870-1970* ... This is a thoughtful book that examines in depth the ways in which the United States rose to world technological dominance. Hughes' book is a well written and widely researched sophisticated survey not only of American technology but of the larger philosophical mind sets and social structures that caused its development ... Stanley Karnow, *In Our Image - America's Empire in the Philippines* ... Few historians in the West have written about the involvement of the United States in Southeast Asia with the skill, insight, and balance of Stanley Karnow. His most recent book ... represents the most distinguished effort in this field to date ... *In Our Image* offers a compelling story, a model of narrative history as it should be written ... That masterful rendering of the tragic and the absurd in American efforts at colonization and Filipino strivings toward independence merits the honor of the Pulitzer Prize in History."[174] Also from the Pulitzer Prize Board's point of view the latter-named book was the most brilliant, thus Stanley Karnow was awarded the much-coveted prize.[175]

The jurors in 1991 (Robert V. Bruce, Drew Gilpin Faust and Joel H. Silbey) agreed on a proposal that consisted of four finalists: Lizabeth Cohen, *Making a New Deal - Industrial Workers in Chicago, 1919-1939*; Hugh Davis Graham, *The Civil Rights Era - Origins and Development of National Policy*; Kenneth M. Stampp, *America in 1857 - A Nation on the*

---

172 Jean Harvey Baker/David Herbert Donald/John Toland, Report of the Pulitzer Prize History Jury, Cambridge, Mass., December 20, 1988, pp. 1-3.
173 Columbia University (Ed.), The Pulitzer Prizes, *op. cit.*, p. 59.
174 William H. Goetzmann/Christine Leigh Heyrman/Leon F. Litwack, Report of the Pulitzer Prize History Jury 1990, undated, pp. 1-3.
175 Columbia University (Ed.), The Pulitzer Prizes, *op. cit.*, p. 59.

COLUMBIA UNIVERSITY

KNOW ALL PERSONS BY THESE PRESENTS THAT

BERNARD BAILYN

HAS BEEN AWARDED

THE PULITZER PRIZE IN HISTORY

FOR

"VOYAGERS TO THE WEST"

IN WITNESS WHEREOF IT HAS CAUSED THIS CERTIFICATE TO BE
SIGNED BY THE PRESIDENT OF THE UNIVERSITY
AND ITS CORPORATE SEAL TO BE HERETO AFFIXED
ON THE SIXTEENTH DAY OF APRIL IN THE YEAR OF OUR LORD
ONE THOUSAND NINE HUNDRED AND EIGHTY-SEVEN

Michael I. Sovern

PRESIDENT

BERNARD BAILYN'S SECOND PULITZER PRIZE CERTIFICATE

Brink; Laurel Thatcher Ulrich, *A Midwife's Tale - The Life of Martha Ballard, Based on Her Diary, 1785-1812.*[176] The Pulitzer Prize Board's decision was to confer the award to the latter-named title, so that the Pulitzer Prize for history was given to Laurel Thatcher Ulrich.[177]

That is the end of the line so far, but Pulitzer History Prizes may be awarded as long as men reflect on their past. And as long as they do this by writing books, there may be a competent jury which decides on a book's quality either by presenting or not presenting it with an award. Passing judgment on quality, of course, will always to some extent be a matter of subjectivity. Subjectivity, however, can - or rather must - be accepted if the criteria which lead to a decision are open and clear. This does not necessarily mean that a "good" decision is an unanimous one. The path which leads to an award should be comprehensible, not necessarily straight. Evidently, criteria for quality change with the members of the jury as well as with the subjects of the books. But one can see from the jury reports that some characteristics are continually required of all history books, from 1917 up to the present: e.g. a "new" subject of public interest, scholarship, exceptional style, carefully arranged facts and a clear distinction between information and the author's standpoint.

The future of the Pulitzer history awards is now as open as history itself, and as the creativity of American authors who write about it. Writing about history is still a challenge, particularly if "an old order passes" and the "new world is more free but less stable."[178] Finally, authors who compete for a Pulitzer Prize are not only chroniclers but also actors. This fact is even more important if the history in which they act can be characterized as a crisis. "From our revolution to the Civil War," Bill Clinton says, addressing all Americans including American historians, "to the Great Depressions, to the civil rights movement, our people have always mustered the determination to construct from these crises the pillars of our history."[179]

May this general appeal reach American authors and the jurors in the Pulitzer Prize system who judge on their works. This judging of books always means extremely hard work to be done by the jury members. Among the 590 book titles entered in the 1990 Pulitzer Prize competition there were 79

---

176 Columbia University (Ed.), The 75th annual Pulitzer Prizes in Journalism, Letters, Drama and Music, New York, April 9, 1991, press release, pp. 5 f.
177 Columbia University (Ed.), The Pulitzer Prizes, *op. cit.*, p. 59.
178 William Jefferson Clinton, Inaugural Address, Washington, D.C., January 20, 1993.
179 *Ibid.*

MEMBERS OF THE PULITZER PRIZE BOARD IN APRIL, 1993

Front Row, left to right: Burl Osborne, James V. Risser, Joan Konner, Michael I. Sovern, Claude F. Sitton, Sissela Bok, Meg Greenfield, Edward Seaton. - *Back Row*, left to right: Peter R. Kann, Marilyn Yarbrough, Jack Fuller, Geneva Overholser, Helen Vendler, Walter Rugaber, Russell Baker, John S. Driscoll in the history category.[180] "Some of the book publishers," J. Douglas Bates states, "flood the competition in the same way some newspapers do. In its quest for (the) 1990 prizes, Alfred A. Knopf has entered fifty-eight books; that's almost ten per cent of the books submitted by all publishers combined ... Others are playing the numbers game, too ... For Knopf, its fifty-eight books add up to $ 1,160 in entry fees and far more than that in the value of complimentary copies for all the judges. But what's that compared to the extra royalties that might accrue if one of those fifty-eight should win the Pulitzer? Knopf editors obviously think the strategy works, and other houses are clearly following the same practice. The Pulitzer is the one award that publishers think consistently helps sell books",[181] - and that is true for the works sent in for the American History category, too.

---

180 J. Douglas Bates: The Pulitzer Prize. The Inside Story of America's Most Prestigious Award, New York 1991, p. 164.
181 *Ibid.*, pp. 164 f.

SELECTIONS FROM
AWARD-WINNING ENTRIES

REMARKS ABOUT THE SELECTIONS CRITERIA

While selecting portions from Pulitzer prize-winning books in the category *American History* and preparing them for republication by extract the editors were guided by the following ten principles:

* There is a short biography of every prize-winner at the beginning of each chapter, ranging up to the year when the award was bestowed.

* The biographical information about the prize-winners is based on the biographical notes attached to the award-winning entries as well as various biographical reference works.

* Although the awards were bestowed each time for a particular book of the respective author reasons of size made it unavoidable to present in each single case merely short passages as a sample of the text.

* The portions from the books to be reprinted were selected so as best to illustrate the focus mentioned in the reasons of the award respectively in the jury reports.

* All of the following reprinted passages were taken from the first print edition of the books in question, which also provided the basis for the awarding of the prize.

* As a consequence of the limitation of size in most cases not even one complete chapter or subchapter could be presented but only an "appetizer."

* The editors added headings to all of the reprinted book portions in order to describe each topic as succinctly as possible.

* Precise bibliographical data including indication of pages are given so that the excerpts can be found in the respective first print editions.

* Paragraphs and other typographic peculiarities in the original book portions were left unchanged, and also no editing or shortening of the original texts took place.

* Corrections were made in the reprinted passages only in cases of obvious typographical errors or garbled lines in the original texts.

1917 AWARD

ABOUT THE AMERICANS
IN VARIOUS HISTORICAL PHASES

BY

JEAN J. JUSSERAND

Jean Adrien Antoine Jules Jusserand (born on February 18, 1855, in Lyon, France) entered the diplomatic service of France at the end of the nineteenth century. From 1898 to 1902 he was the French minister to Denmark, afterwards he represented France as the ambassador to the United States. He stayed in this position for many years, and he made friends with several Presidents of the U.S. Jean Jusserand became member of the Grand Cross Legion of Honor, and he received honorary doctorates from quite a number of American institutions of higher education, among them the University of Chicago, Columbia University, Harvard University, New York University, Temple University, Princeton University, New York State University, Yale University, George Washington University, St. John University and Washington University of St. Louis, Mo. From his early years on, Jusserand has been the author of several book publications, e.g. *English Wayfaring Life; English Novel in the Time of Shakespeare; Piers Plowman; Les sports et jeux d'exercise dans l'ancienne France; A Literary History of the English People*. In 1916 Jean J. Jusserand published his book *With Americans of Past and Present Days* which earned him the Pulitzer Prize for history in the following year.

PIERRE L'ENFANT DESIGNS THE FEDERAL CITY

[Source: J(ean) J. Jusserand: With Americans of Past and Present Days, New York: Charles Scribner's Sons, 1916, pp. 162 - 166; reprinted by permission of the Macmillan Publishing Company, New York, N.Y.]

The same year in which the New York Federal Hall had seen the inauguration of the first President, the chance of his life came to L'Enfant. He deserved it, because he not only availed himself of it, but went forth to meet it, giving up his abode in New York, "where I stood at the time," he wrote later, "able of commanding whatever business I liked." This was the founding of the federal city.

The impression was a general one among the French that those insurgents whom they had helped to become a free nation were to be a great one, too. Leaving England, where he was a refugee during our Revolution, Talleyrand decided to come to the United States, "desirous of seeing," he says in his memoirs, "that great country whose history begins." General Moreau, also a refugee, a few years later spoke with the same confidence of the future of the country: "I had pictured to myself the advantages of living under a free government; but I had conceived only in part what such happiness is: here it is enjoyed to the full. ... It is impossible for men who have lived under such a government to allow themselves ever to be subjugated; they would be very great cowards if they did not perish to the last in order to defend it."

L'Enfant, with his tendency to see things "en grand," could not fail to act accordingly, and the moment he heard that the federal city would be neither New York nor Philadelphia, nor any other already in existence, but one to be built expressly, he wrote to Washington a letter remarkable by his clear understanding of the opportunity offered to the country, and by his determined purpose to work not for the three million inhabitants of his day, but for the one hundred of ours, and for all the unborn millions that will come after us.

The letter is dated from New York, 11th of September, 1789. "Sir," he said, "the late determination of Congress to lay the foundation of a city which is to become the capital of this vast empire offers so great an occasion of acquiring reputation to whoever may be appointed to conduct the execution of the business that your Excellency will not be surprised that my ambition and the desire I have of becoming a useful citizen should lead me to wish a share in the undertaking.

"No nation, perhaps, had ever before the opportunity offered them of deliberately deciding on the spot where their capital city should be fixed. ... And, although the means now within the power of the country are not such as to pursue the design to any great extent, it will be obvious that the plan should be drawn on such a scale as to leave room for that aggrandizement and embellishment which the increase of the wealth of the nation will permit it to pursue at any period, however remote. Viewing the matter in this light, I am fully sensible of the extent of the undertaking."

Washington knew that L'Enfant was afflicted, to be sure, with an "untoward" temper, being haughty, proud, intractable, but that he was honest withal, sincere, loyal, full of ideas, and remarkably gifted. He decided to intrust him with the great task, thus justifying, a little later, his selection: "Since my first knowledge of the gentleman's abilities in the line of his profession, I have received him not only as a scientific man, but one who has added considerable taste to professional knowledge; and that, for such employment as he is now engaged in, for prosecuting public works and carrying them into effect, he was better qualified than any one who had come within my knowledge in this country." The President informed L'Enfant that he was to set to work at once, and so bestir himself as to have at least a general plan to show a few months later, when he himself would return from a trip South. On March 2, 1791, Washington announced to Colonel Dickens, of Georgetown, the coming of the major: "An eminent French military engineer starts for Georgetown to examine and survey the site of the federal city." A few days later the arrival of "Major Longfont" was duly recorded by the *Georgetown Weekly Ledger*.

L'Enfant's enthusiasm and his desire to do well and quickly had been raised to a high pitch. He reached the place a few days later and found it wrapped in mist, soaked in rain, but he would not wait. "I see no other way," he wrote to Jefferson on the 11th, "if by Monday next the weather does not change, but of making a rough draft as accurate as may be obtained by viewing the ground in riding over it on horseback, as I have already done yesterday through the rain, to obtain a knowledge of the whole. ... As far as I was able to judge through a thick fog, I passed on many spots which appeared to me really beautiful, and which seem to dispute with each other [which] commands."

When he could see the place to better advantage, his admiration knew no bounds. In an unpublished letter to Hamilton he says: "Now, when you may probably have heard that I am finally charged with delineating a plan for the city, I feel a sort of embarrassment how to speak to you as advantageously as I really think of the situation determined upon; for, as there is no doubt, I must feel highly interested in the success of the undertaking, I become apprehensive of being charged with partiality when I assure you that no position in America can be more susceptible of grand improvement than that between the eastern branch of the Potomac and Georgetown."

A few weeks later L'Enfant was doing the honors of the spot to a brother artist, the painter Trumbull, just back from Yorktown, where he had been sketching in view of his big picture of the surrendering of Cornwallis, and who wrote in his autobiography: "Then to Georgetown, where I found Major L'Enfant drawing his plan of the city of Washington; rode with him over the ground on which the city has since been built. Where the Capitol now stands was then a thick wood." (May, 1791)

1918 AWARD

ABOUT THE STAGES
OF THE CIVIL WAR

BY

JAMES F. RHODES

James Ford Rhodes (born on May 1, 1848, in Cleveland, Oh.) attended as a special student New York University and the University of Chicago, but he was never graduated. After having spent more than a year in Europe from 1867 to 1868, he returned to the United States in order to follow in his father's footsteps and start a career in the coal and iron business. After a few years' service in another firm, in 1874 he became associated with Rhodes & Company and with his brother Robert. He never got the idea of writing until 1885, when he decided to retire from business. Eight years later, the first two volumes of the *History of the United States from the Compromise of 1850* were published. Five further volumes followed in the years until 1906. In 1898 James F. Rhodes was elected president of the American Historical Association. He also became member of the American Academy of Arts and Letters and of the American Academy of Arts and Sciences. Several prizes were awarded to him, among them the Loubat prize of the Berlin Academy of Science. Rhodes, who consorted with the political and literary leaders of his generation, also received several honorary doctorates, e.g. from Western Reserve University, Harvard University, Yale University, the University of Wisconsin, New York University and Princeton University. James F. Rhodes won the Pulitzer Prize for history in 1918 for *A History of the Civil War, 1861-1865*, which had been published the year before.

SOME BASIC LIFE CONDITIONS IN THE NORTH

[Source: James Ford Rhodes: A History of the Civil War, 1861-1865, New York: The MacMillan Company, 1917, pp. 341 - 345; reprinted by permission of the Macmillan Publishing Company, New York, N.Y.]

Life at the North during the war resembled that of most civilized communities which had full communication with the outside world. Business went on as usual, schools and colleges were full, churches were attended and men and women had their recreations. Progress was made in the mechanical sciences and arts. Men strove for wealth or learning; and the pursuit of fame was by no means confined to military and political circles. Nevertheless, that supreme business, the war, left its stamp on all private concerns and on every mode of thought. This was especially remarkable during the first eighteen months when the patriotic volunteers were individually encouraged by the sympathy and enthusiasm of those at home. "What of the war! Isn't it grand!" exclaimed Phillips Brooks in May, 1861. As late as the summer of 1862 the excellent character of the soldiers was noted. "Our army," wrote Asa Gray on July 2, "is largely composed of materials such as nothing but a high sense of duty could keep for a year in military life." "Our best young men," said Agassiz in a private letter of August 15, "are the first to enlist; if anything can be objected to these large numbers of soldiers, it is that it takes away the best material that the land possesses." "In all the country districts the strong young men were gone."

Times were hard at the commencement of the war and continued so until the autumn of 1862. "People are getting dreadfully poor here," wrote Phillips Brooks from Philadelphia. The New York *Tribune* referred to "our paralyzed industry, obstructed commerce, our overloaded finances and our mangled railroads." All sorts of economies were practised. Coffee and sugar rose enormously in price. Many families mixed roasted dandelion root with pure coffee while others made their morning beverage from parched corn or rye; some substituted brown for white sugar. One by one luxuries disappeared from the table and few were ashamed of their frugal repasts. The wearing of plain clothes became a fashion as well as a virtue. The North was for the most part a community of simple living. Opera was only occasional, theatres were few and the amusements took on a character adapted to the life. A popular lecture, a concert, a church sociable with a charade turning on some striking event of the war, a gathering of young men and women to scrape lint for the wounded, a visit perhaps to a neighboring camp to witness a dress parade of volunteers — these were the diversions from the overpowering anxiety weighing upon the people. Personal grief was added to the national anxiety. "In many of our dwellings," wrote Harriet Beecher Stowe, "the very light of our lives has gone out."

With great trials were mingled petty inconveniences arising from derangement of the country's finances. Gold began to sell at a premium in January, 1862, and disappeared from circulation; but this was no hardship to the mass of the people for gold had not been used largely as currency and there was a ready substitute for it in State bank-notes and the United States legal tenders. But the advance in gold was followed by a similar advance in silver. Silver change became an article of speculation and was bought at a premium by brokers; much of it was sent to Canada and by July 1, 1862, it seems to have practically disappeared from circulation. Its sudden disappearance brought forth diverse remedies. Individuals, prompter in action than municipalities or the general government, flooded the country with shinplasters — small notes in denominations of from 5 to 50 cents, promises to pay of hotels, restaurants, business houses and country dealers. For a short while copper and nickel cents commanded a premium and various metal tokens were issued by tradesmen to take their place as well as that of the small silver coins. Secretary Chase, in a letter of July 14, 1862, to the Chairman of the Committee of Ways and Means of the House of Representatives, said that "the most serious inconveniences and evils are apprehended" unless the issues of shinplasters and metal tokens "can be checked and the small coins of the government kept in circulation or a substitute provided." He proposed either to debase the silver coinage of the fractional parts of a dollar or to legalize in effect the use of postage and other stamps as currency. Congress, by Act of July 17, 1862, prohibited the issue of shinplasters by private corporations or individuals, provided for the issuance to the public of postage and other stamps and declared that, under certain limitations, these were receivable in payment of dues to the United States and were redeemable in greenbacks. People naturally preferred the stamps to the promises to pay of private individuals and hastened to the post offices to be supplied therewith, but what they here gained in soundness they lost in convenience. The gummy back, flimsy texture, small surface and light weight of the stamps rendered them the most imperfect circulating medium ever known in the United States. For one thing, the making of change in the course of small transactions proved a laborious business because of the intrusion of a common denomination of 3 cents (the stamp most frequently employed and the one of which there was the greatest supply) into the convenient decimal system. The counting out of 2, 3, 5 and 10 cent stamps became intolerable when large quantities of change were required, so that in places where various sorts of tickets were sold, the stamps were put up in small envelopes marked in large figures, 10, 25 and 50 cents, as the case might be. This mitigated the nuisance only in part as cautious persons would insist on opening the envelopes and counting the stamps in order to see whether the contents tallied with the figure outside. The stamps became dirty and mutilated; losing their adhesive power they were unfit for postage. They had proved a poor substitute for shinplasters. But relief from both evils was afforded almost simultaneously by the Treasury Department and by various municipalities.

From the language of Chase's recommendation for the use of postage and other stamps as currency and from the provisions of the statute, it would be impossible to divine the relief which was eventually forthcoming. The Secretary, in accordance with the Act of July 17, 1862, had made an arrangement with the Postmaster-General for a supply of postage stamps, but it being "soon discovered that stamps prepared for postage uses were not adapted to the purposes of currency," he proceeded to construe the law liberally and issue a postage currency. This was in the form of small notes of which the 25 and 50 cent denominations were about a quarter the size of a dollar bill, the 5 and 10 cent somewhat smaller. On the 5 cent note was a facsimile of the 5 cent postage stamp, the vignette being Jefferson's head; for the 25 cent note this vignette appeared five times. Of similar design were the 10 and 50 cent notes, the vignette on the 10 cent stamp being Washington's head.

1919 AWARD

ABOUT THE WITHHOLD
OF THE HISTORY PRIZE

BY

THE ADVISORY BOARD

Since the members of the 1919 Pulitzer Prize History Jury in their report declared themselves unable to single out any book published during the preceding year, the Advisory Board of the Columbia School of Journalism accepted the jury's proposal to give no award in this category.

NAMES OF THE BOARD MEMBERS VOTING FOR "NO AWARD"

Nicholas Murray Butler	Columbia University
Solomon B. Griffin	*Springfield* (Mass.) *Republican*
John L. Heaton	*The New York World*
George S. Johns	*St. Louis Post-Dispatch*
Victor F. Lawson	*Chicago Daily News*
St. Clair McKelway	*Brooklyn Daily Eagle*
Charles R. Miller	*The New York Times*
Edward P. Mitchell	*The New York Sun*
Ralph Pulitzer	*The New York World*
Melville E. Stone	*The Associated Press*
Charles H. Taylor	*Boston Globe*
Samuel C. Wells	*Philadelphia Press*

1920 AWARD

ABOUT THE CENTRAL
ASPECTS OF THE WAR WITH MEXICO

BY

JUSTIN H. SMITH

Justin Harvey Smith (born on January 13, 1857, in Boscawen, N.H.) attended the Union Theological Seminary from 1879 to 1881. But instead of proceeding to the ministry he went into the publishing business, in which he stayed until 1898. The following year he became professor of modern history at Dartmouth College. Here began his work as a productive scholar with the publication of *The Troubadours at Home in 1899*. All of his later works lay in the field of American history, e.g. *Arnold's March from Cambridge to Quebec; The Historie Booke; Our Struggle for the Fourteenth Colony: Canada and the American Revolution; The Annexation of Texas.* Smith wrote also many articles in historical journals. In 1908 he resigned his professorship to devote his time entirely to historical research. In 1917 he became chairman of the American Historical Association. Two years later, Justin H. Smith published his work in two volumes entitled *The War with Mexico*, for which, in 1920, the Pulitzer Prize for history was awarded to him.

THE SITUATION AROUND THE SANTA FE AREA

[Source: Justin H. Smith: The War with Mexico, Vol. 1, New York: The MacMillan Company, 1919, pp. 284 - 287; reprinted by permission of the Macmillan Publishing Company, New York, N.Y.]

NOT only Tamaulipas and Chihuahua but New Mexico lay within the scope of the government's war policy, and certain features of the situation made the outlook in that quarter peculiarly inviting.

The province was cut into an eastern and a western section by the Rio Grande, which ran approximately north and south; and usage divided the best settled part of it into the Río Arriba (Upstream) district near Santa Fe, the capital, which lay some twenty miles east of the great river, and the Río Abajo (Downstream) district, which had for its metropolis Albuquerque, a small town on the Rio Grande about seventy-five miles to the southwest. According to a recent census the population was 100,000, of which the greater part belonged in the lower district; and more than half the wealth also was attributed to that section. The caravan trade, which made its way from Independence, Missouri, to Santa Fe, Chihuahua, Lagos and even Mexico City, gilded the name of the province, for it had advanced rapidly from the humble beginnings of 1821, and now employed 1200 men, involved a capital of some two millions, and usually paid a net profit of thirty or forty per cent on the goods transported. The favorable climate believed to prevail in New Mexico was an additional source of interest.

The political situation appeared singularly promising. In March, 1845, the war department of Mexico admitted publicly that the northern sections of the country were "abandoned and more than abandoned" by the general government. Sensible Mexicans held that the connection of the province with their miserable system involved injury instead of benefit.

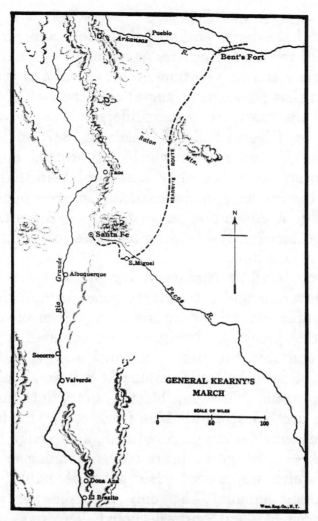

GENERAL KEARNY'S
MARCH

SCALE OF MILES

The people received no protection against the ravages of the
Indians. The national troops were a constant menace to the
citizens. If a man desired to give his note for $3000, he was
compelled to pay eight dollars for stamped paper. The duties
and extortions levied upon the caravan merchants increased
the price of their goods; and of late the central government
had been trying to deprive the provincial authorities of money
and the people of comforts by stopping that business entirely.

The citizens appeared weary of oppression. They would not
pay the taxes. It was found necessary in 1845 to excuse them

from one of the most profitable but most annoying imposts. Indifference toward the general government — a natural return for its neglect and its vexations — prevailed, and the continual changes in that government aggravated the lack of patriotism. Indeed, there was more than indifference. A move to follow the example of Texas had been made in 1837, and the idea of joining the United States, which had existed in that year, became so strong by the early months of 1846 that representatives of the province in the national Congress openly avowed it. Finally, a revolution against misgovernment, that had recently occurred in the neighboring state of Sonora, appeared to offer a strong hint.

All power, civil and military, lay in the hands of Manuel Armijo, governor and comandante general; and that of itself was an ample ground for insurrection. Born of disreputable parents, this precious adventurer had achieved a career still more disreputable. A man of unusual energy, though now a mountain of flesh, he could assume at will an air of ingenuous affability; could threaten, bluster, brag, intrigue or coax; and when dressed up in his blue frock coat, with blue striped pantaloons, shoulder straps, a red sash, and plenty of gold lace, could look — although at heart only a cunning and cowardly robber — quite impressive. His personal habits were said to be grossly immoral; his only principle was to succeed; and his type of mind, shrewd though low, was indicated by one of his favorite sayings, "It is better to be thought brave than to be so." Such force, cleverness and lack of scruple had naturally made him rich. His family now owned Albuquerque and the neighboring estates. His position and close relations with the priests gave him a firm hold on the ecclesiastical arm; it was believed that an understanding with the savages enabled him to use them against his enemies; and he engaged rather deeply in the American trade. Yet his ambition was not yet satisfied; and he entertained the idea, it would seem, of making the province an independent country.

1921 AWARD

ABOUT THE NAVAL
STRATEGY IN WORLD WAR I

BY

WILLIAM S. SIMS / BURTON J. HENDRICK

William Sowden Sims (born on October 15, 1858, in Port Hope, Canada) was appointed to the U.S. Naval Academy and was graduated in 1880. He was naval attaché at the American embassies in Paris and St. Petersburg from 1897 to 1900. In the following two years he served on board of several battleships belonging to the Asiatic Fleet, before he started working in the Bureau of Navigation at the Navy Department. From 1907 to 1909 he assumed the additional duty as a naval aide to the President. During World War I he commanded the American naval operations in European waters. In 1919 Sims, who had been promoted through grades to the rank of a rear admiral two years before, became member of the Grand Legion of Honor. - *Burton Jesse Hendrick* (born on December 8, 1870, in New Haven, Conn.) became editor of the *New Haven Morning Post* in 1896. Three years later he joined the staff of the *New York Evening Post*. From 1905 to 1913 he worked on the staff of the *McClure's Magazine*, then he became associated editor of *World's Work*. Moreover, Hendrick was member of the National Institute of Arts and Letters. He is also the author of several book publications, among them *The Story of Life Insurance; The Age of Big Business* and the biography *Life and Letters of Walter H. Page, American Ambassador to Great Britain, 1913-1918*. In 1921 William S. Sims and Burton J. Hendrick became the co-winners of the Pulitzer History award for *The Victory at Sea*, which had appeared the year before.

AMERICAN DESTROYERS IN FULL ACTION

[Source: William Sowden Sims/Burton J. Hendrick: The Victory at Sea, Garden City, N.Y. - Toronto: Doubleday, Page & Company, 1919/1920, pp. 130 - 133; reprint permission in public domain.]

The Admiralty in London was thus the central nervous system of a complicated but perfectly working organism which reached the remotest corners of the world. Wherever there was a port, whether in South America, Australia, or in the most inaccessible parts of India or China, from which merchantmen sailed to any of the other countries which were involved in the war, representatives of the British navy and the British Government were stationed, all working harmoniously with shipping men in the effort to get their cargoes safely through the danger zones. These danger zones occupied a comparatively small area surrounding the belligerent countries, but the safeguarding of the ships was an elaborate process which began far back in the countries from which the commerce started. Until about July, 1917, the world's shipping for the most part had been unregulated; now for the first time it was arranged in hard and fast routes and despatched in accordance with schedules as fixed as those of a great railroad. The whole management of convoys, indeed, bore many resemblances to the method of handling freight cars on the American system of trans-continental lines. In the United States there are several great headquarters of freight, sometimes known as "gateways," places, that is, at which freight cars are assembled from a thousand places, and from which the great accumulations are routed to their destinations. Such places are Pittsburg, Buffalo, St. Louis, Chicago, Minneapolis, Denver, San Francisco — to mention only a few. Shipping destined for the belligerent nations was similarly assembled, in the years 1917 and 1918, at six or eight great ocean "gateways," and there formed into convoys for "through routing" to the British Isles, France, and the Mediterranean. Only a few of the ships that were exceptionally fast — speed in itself being a particularly efficacious protection against submarines — were permitted to ignore this routing system, and dash unprotected through the infested area. This was a somewhat dangerous procedure even for such ships, however, and they were escorted whenever destroyers were available. All other vessels, from whatever parts of the world they might come, were required to sail first for one of these great assembling points, or "gateways"; and at these places they were added to one of the constantly forming convoys. Thus all shipping which normally sailed to Europe around the Cape of Good Hope proceeded up the west coast of Africa until it reached the port of Dakar or Sierra Leone, where it joined the convoy. Shipping from the east coast of South America — ports like Rio de Janeiro, Bahia, Buenos Aires, and Montevideo — instead of sailing directly to Europe, joined the convoy at this same African town. Vessels which came to Britain and France by way of Suez and Mediterranean ports found their great stopping place at Gibraltar — a headquarters of traffic which, in the huge amount of freight which it "created," became almost the Pittsburg of this mammoth transportation system. The four "gateways" for North

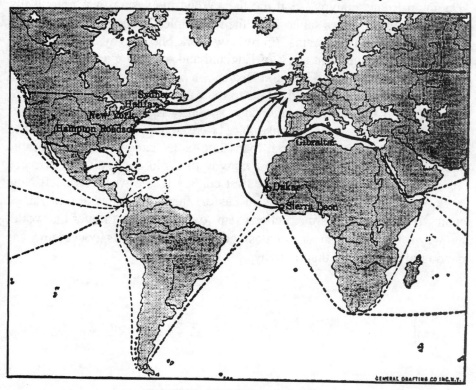

ROUTES OF THE CONVOYS

This diagram shows the courses of world commerce under the convoy system. The great ports of Sydney, Halifax, New York, and Hampton Roads in North America; of Gibraltar in Europe; and Dakar and Sierra Leone in Africa, were the places where shipping destined for Entente nations was formed into convoys. Thus, all ships from the west coast of South America, the Gulf of Mexico, and southern ports of the United States had to sail first to Hampton Roads where they were formed into a convoy and sent across the ocean to the war zone. When the system got into perfect working order, these convoys sailed on a rigid time-table like railroad trains.

America and the west coast of South America were Sydney (Cape Breton), Halifax, New York, and Hampton Roads. The grain-laden merchantmen from the St. Lawrence valley rendezvoused at Sydney and Halifax. Vessels from Portland, Boston, New York, Philadelphia, and other Atlantic points found their assembling headquarters at New York, while ships from Baltimore, Norfolk, the Gulf of Mexico, and the west coast of South America proceeded to the great convoy centre which had been established at Hampton Roads.

In the convoy room of the Admiralty these aggregations of ships were always referred to as the "Dakar convoy," the "Halifax convoy," the "Hampton Roads convoy," and the like. When the system was completely established the convoys sailed from their appointed headquarters on regular schedules, like railroad trains. From New York one convoy departed every sixteen days for the west coast of England and one left every sixteen days for the east coast. From Hampton Roads one sailed every eight days to the west coast and one every eight days to the east coast, and convoys from all the other convoy points maintained a similarly rigid schedule. The dates upon which these sailings took place were fixed, like the arrivals and departures of trains upon a railroad time-table, except when it became necessary to delay the sailing of a convoy to avoid congestion of arrivals. According to this programme, the first convoy to the west coast left New York on August 14, 1917, and its successors thereafter sailed at intervals of about sixteen days. The instructions sent to shipmasters all over the world, by way of the British consulates, gave explicit details concerning the method of assembling their convoys.

1922 AWARD

ABOUT THE FOUNDING
OF NEW ENGLAND STATES

BY

JAMES T. ADAMS

James Truslow Adams (born on October 18, 1878, in Brooklyn, N.Y.) was graduated from the Polytechnical Institute of Brooklyn in 1898. Two years later, he earned the Master's degree at Yale University. After his examinations he entered a New York Stock Exchange firm, where he worked for the following twelve years. From early in the First World War on, he prepared data with the Colonel House Commission for the Peace conference in Paris in 1919. There, he assumed detailed special duty. Before, Adams had become captain of the Military Intelligence Division. James T. Adams was member of quite a number of highstanding academic institutions, e.g. the American Academy of Arts and Letters, the National Institute of Arts and Letters and the American Historical Association. Adams was also a very productive writer; among his works are *Memorials of Old Bridgehampton* and *History of Town of Southampton*. In 1921 *The Founding of New England* by James T. Adams was published. One year later, the Advisory Board of the Columbia School of Journalism declared it the winner in the Pulitzer Prize History category.

THE GREAT MIGRATION IN THAT REGION

[Source: James Truslow Adams: The Founding of New England, Boston: The Atlantic Monthly Press, 1921, pp. 118 - 121; reprinted by permission of Little, Brown and Company, Publishers, Boston, Mass.]

DURING the years that the Pilgrims had thus been struggling to found a tiny commonwealth on an inhospitable bit of the long American coast-line, events had been moving rapidly on the more crowded stage of the Old World. In France, the power of the Huguenots had been hopelessly crushed by the fall of Rochelle in 1628; while in England, affairs were evidently approaching a crisis, due to the incompetence of the government of Charles, with its disgraceful military failures abroad, and its illegal financial exactions at home. No one was safe from the ruin of his fortune or the loss of his freedom. The nobility and gentry, subject to the imposition of forced loans, faced imprisonment if they refused to pay; and those below the rank of gentleman were the unwilling hosts of a horde of ruffians, the unpaid and frequently criminal soldiery returned from unsuccessful foreign ventures, and billeted upon them by the government. The laws against Catholics were largely suspended to please the Queen, who was of that faith, and the prospects were daily growing darker for the Puritan and patriot elements, both within and without the Church. Religious toleration as an avowed governmental policy was not, as yet, seriously considered by any considerable body of men outside of Holland, the notable example of which country had failed to influence England, where the control of the church was evidently passing into the hands of Laud and his party. The time had thus come when the King must face a united opposition of the soundest men in the country — of those who feared alike for their property, their liberty, and their religion.

The formation of the Puritan party, drawing into its fold men animated by any or all of these motives, in varying proportions, coincided with the beginning of the great increase in emigration to Massachusetts, which was to carry twenty thousand persons to the shores of New England between 1630 and 1640. But if attention is concentrated too exclusively upon the history of the continental colonies in North America, and, more particularly, of those in New England, the impression is apt to be gained that this swarming out of the English to plant in new lands was largely confined to Massachusetts and its neighbors, and to the decade named. The conclusion drawn from these false premises has naturally been that Puritanism, in the New England sense, was the only successful colonizing force. We do not wish to minimize the value of any deeply felt religious emotion in firmly planting a group of people in a new home. Such value was justly recognized by one of the wisest practical colonizers of the last century, who was not himself of a religious temperament, but who, to secure the firm establishment of his colony, would "have transplanted the Grand Lama of Tibet with all his prayer wheels, and did actually nibble at the Chief Rabbi." The Puritan colonies, nevertheless, not only were far from being the only permanent ones, but themselves were not always equally successful; and it is well to point out that many elements, besides peculiarity of religious belief, entered into the success of the New England colonies, as contrasted with the conspicuous failure of the Puritan efforts in the Caribbean.

At the beginning of the increased emigration to Massachusetts, colonizing, indeed, had ceased to be a new and untried business. To say nothing of the numerous large and small French, Dutch, and Spanish settlements firmly established in the New World, and the English already planted on the mainland, the latter nation had successfully colonized the islands of Bermuda in 1612, St. Kitts in 1623, Barbadoes and St. Croix in 1625, and Nevis and Barbuda three years later. By the time John Winthrop led his band to the shores of Massachusetts Bay, besides the five hundred Dutch in New Amsterdam, ten thousand Englishmen were present, for six

months of each year, in Newfoundland, engaged in the fisheries
there; nine hundred had settled permanently in Maine and
New Hampshire; three hundred within the present limits of
Massachusetts; three thousand in Virginia; between two and
three thousand in Bermuda; and sixteen hundred in Barbadoes; while the numbers in the other colonies are unknown.
The figures are striking also for the year 1640, or slightly later,
at which date the tide is too often considered as having flowed
almost wholly toward the Puritan colonies of New England
for the preceding ten years. The number in Massachusetts at
that time had risen to fourteen thousand, in Connecticut to
two thousand, and in Rhode Island to three hundred. Maine
and New Hampshire however, contained about fifteen hundred,
Maryland the same number, Virginia nearly eight thousand,
Nevis about four thousand, St. Kitts twelve to thirteen thousand, and Barbadoes eighteen thousand six hundred. There are
no contemporary figures for Barbuda, St. Croix, Antigua, Mont-
serrat, and other settlements. At the end, therefore, of what
has often been considered a period of distinctly Puritan emigration, we find that approximately only sixteen thousand
Englishmen had taken their way to the Puritan colonies, as
against forty-six thousand to the others; which latter figure,
moreover, is undoubtedly too low, owing to the lack of statistics just noted. Nor does the above statement take into
account the thousands of Englishmen who emigrated to Ireland
during the same period, and whose motives were probably
similar to those animating the emigrants to the New World,
however different their destinations may have been. There
had, indeed, been a "great migration," resulting in an English
population in America and the West Indies, by 1640 or there-
about, of over sixty-five thousand persons; but it is somewhat
misleading to apply the term solely to the stream of emigrants
bound for the Puritan colonies, who were outnumbered three
to one by those who went to settlements where religion did
not partake of the "New England way." Although young

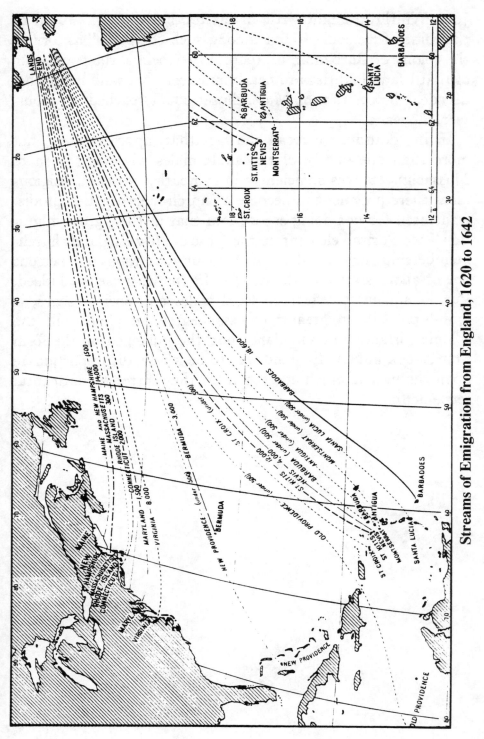

Streams of Emigration from England, 1620 to 1642

John Winthrop might write of his brother that it "would be the ruine of his soule to live among such company" as formed the colony of Barbadoes in 1629, nevertheless, the population of that island had risen to nearly nineteen thousand in another decade, whereas that of Massachusetts had reached only fourteen thousand.

If, in addition, we recall the fact that, approximately, not more than one in five of the adult males who went even to Massachusetts was sufficiently in sympathy with the religious ideas there prevalent to become a church member, though disfranchised for not doing so, we find that in the "great migration" the Puritan element, in the sense of New England church-membership, amounted to only about four thousand persons out of about sixty-five thousand. In the wider sense, indeed, Puritanism, in its effect on legal codes and social usages, is found present, in greater or less degree, in almost all the colonies, island and mainland, but the influence of the form that it took in New England was to be wholly disproportionate upon the nation which evolved from the scattered continental settlements.

1923 AWARD

ABOUT THE SUPREME COURT IN U.S. HISTORY

BY

CHARLES WARREN

Charles Warren (born on March 9, 1868, in Boston, Mass.) received a Master's degree at Harvard University in 1889. During the following three years he attended Harvard Law School. He was admitted to bar in 1892, and practiced at Boston in changing association with different colleagues until 1914. For the following four years he occupied the office of the assistant attorney general of the United States in Washington. Moreover, he was honorary vice president of the American Society of International Law, trustee of the New England Conservatory of Music and member of the Massachussets Historical Society. Warren is also the author of a large number of book publications, e.g. *The Girl and the Governor; History of the Harvard Law School and Early Legal Conditions in America* and *History of the American Bar, Colonial and Federal, to 1860*. With *The Supreme Court in United States History*, a publication in three volumes, Charles Warren won the Pulitzer Prize of 1923 for the best book on American history published in the preceding year.

THE TIMES OF SLAVERY AND STATE DEFIANCE

[Source: Charles Warren: The Supreme Court in United States History, Vol. 2, Boston: Little, Brown and Company, 1922, pp. 479 - 483; reprinted by permission of Little, Brown and Company, Publishers, Boston, Mass.]

In the years 1848-49, the Court may be said to have reached its height in the confidence of the people of the country. While there were extremists and radicals in both parties, in the North as in the South, who inveighed against it and its decisions, yet the general mass of the public and the Bar had faith in its impartiality and its ability. The old partisan bitterness towards Chief Justice Taney had largely passed away, and even an ardent anti-slavery Senator, like William H. Seward, wrote to Taney of "the high regard which, in common with the whole American people, I entertain for you as the head of the Judicial Department." Congressional attacks upon the Court had almost entirely ceased, and the serious attempts to destroy its most vital jurisdiction, which had been made during the last twenty years of Marshall's Chief Justiceship, seemed now to be forgotten and abandoned.

Only one subject — slavery — seemed likely to involve the Court once more in partisan controversy. Thus far, no serious complications had arisen in connection with this subject; and Martin Van Buren, writing his autobiography about this time, said, with keen perception, that since the Bank of the United States had "happily ceased to exist, we have not only been exempted from any such overwhelming convulsions as those caused by it, but the Supreme Court has occupied itself with its legitimate duties — the administration of justice between man and man — without being, as formerly, constantly assailed by applications for latitudinarian construction of the Constitution, in support of enormous corporate pretensions. We might, perhaps, have expected that in such a calm, even Mr. Jefferson's alarm, if he had lived to see, would, at least in some degree, have subsided; but this state of things can only be expected to last until a similar or equally strong interest is brought under discussion, of a character to excite the whole country and to enlist the sympathies of a majority of the Court, and requiring the intervention of that high tribunal to sustain its unconstitutional assumptions, by unauthorized and unrestrained construction. Whether the institution of domestic slavery is destined to be such an interest, remains to be seen."

The question thus presented by Van Buren was soon answered. For in the summer of 1848, the Court was thrown into the midst of the seething

THE SENATE CHAMBER IN 1850

political issue, when a Whig Senator, John M. Clayton of Delaware, conceived the idea that the question of the power of Congress over slavery in the Territories and in the States annexed from Mexico might properly be settled by the Court. By the introduction of a bill for this purpose, he set in motion a train of circumstances which led directly to the crash of the Court's reputation, nine years later, in the Dred Scott decision. For many years after the Missouri Compromise in 1820, the question of Congressional authority over slavery in the Territories had lapsed as a serious issue in politics, or as a cause of serious division among statesmen. With the close of the Mexican War, however, the status of slavery in the newly acquired territory became a flaming question; and on February 19, 1848, Calhoun introduced in the Senate a resolution announcing the dogma that Congress had no power to prohibit slavery in the Territories. The next year, when the bill to admit Oregon as a State was debated, he advanced the further contention that the Constitution itself, upon its extension to the Territories, carried with it the institution of slavery — "the doctrine of the self-extension of slavery into all the Territories by the self-expansion of the Constitution over them."

But while this issue was not acute in relation to Oregon, which lay north of the Missouri Compromise line, it had become exceedingly grave in connection with the bills which were proposed for the admission of

California as a State and of New Mexico as a Territory (New Mexico then embracing the present States of Arizona, Utah, Nevada and parts of Colorado, Wyoming and the present New Mexico). Hot debate ensued over the question of the respective rights of Congress and of the Territorial and State Legislatures to establish or prohibit slavery. In the summer of 1848, Senator Clayton brought forward his unfortunate proposal for a compromise, in a bill providing: first, for the admission of Oregon with its existing laws against slavery so far as not incompatible with the Constitution; second, for the admission of California and New Mexico, with a prohibition against the passage of laws by their Territorial Legislatures either establishing or prohibiting slavery; third, for the right of an appeal to the Supreme Court of the United States from the Territorial Courts.

By this plan, Clayton argued, the whole question as to the power of Congress over slavery in the Territories would be referred to the Supreme Court for its decision. "The bill leaves the entire question in dispute to the Judiciary," he said. "Any man who desires discord will oppose the bill. But he who does not desire to distract the country by a question merely political, will be able, by voting for this bill, to refer the whole matter to the Judiciary. In any case, in which it may be deemed important, any lawyer can carry the question to the Supreme Court. ... The people being law-abiding, will submit to the decision of that Court which occupies the highest place in their confidence. ... In this dark and gloomy hour, that is the dial-plate which glitters through and which will, I trust, guide us to a safe and harmonious result." Opinions varied greatly in the Senate, however, as to the wisdom of implicating the Court in so delicate and so explosive a question.

1924 AWARD

ABOUT THE BACKGROUND
OF THE AMERICAN REVOLUTION

BY

CHARLES H. MCILWAIN

Charles Howard McIlwain (born on March 15, 1871, in Saltsburg, Pa.) earned the Bachelor's degree at Princeton University in 1894. Three years later, he was admitted to bar of Allegheny County, Pa. From 1898 to 1901 he taught Latin and history at the Kiskiminetas School, before he earned the Master's degree at Harvard University in 1903. The same year he became professor of history at Miami University, before he assumed the position of preceptor at Princeton University in 1905. Six years later, he changed to Harvard University and became there assistant professor of history. In 1916 he received a professorship of history and government. In his function as editor, McIlwain published *Wraxall's Abridgement of the New York Indian Records (1678-1751)* and *The Political Works of James I.* Moreover, he wrote himself *The High Court of Parliament and Its Supremacy.* Charles H. McIlwain won the Pulitzer Prize for history of 1924 for *The American Revolution - A Constitutional Interpretation*, which had been published the year before.

TRIALS OF A CONSTITUTIONAL INTERPRETATION

[Source: Charles Howard McIlwain: The American Revolution: A Constitutional Interpretation, New York: The MacMillan Company, 1923, pp. 1 - 6; reprinted by permission of the Macmillan Publishing Company, New York, N.Y.]

The American Revolution began and ended with the political act or acts by which British sovereignty over the thirteen English colonies in North America was definitely repudiated. All else was nothing but cause or effect of this act. Of the causes, some were economic, some social, others constitutional. But the Revolution itself was none of these; not social, nor economic, nor even constitutional; it was a political act, and such an act cannot be both constitutional and revolutionary; the terms are mutually exclusive. So long as American opposition to alleged grievances was constitutional it was in no sense revolutionary. The moment it became revolutionary it ceased to be constitutional. When was that moment reached? The Americans stoutly insisted during the whole of their contest with Parliament to the summer of 1776 that their resistance was a constitutional resistance to unconstitutional acts. If their claim was justified the American Revolution can hardly be said to have occurred much before May, 1776. For it was the basis of the contemporary American contention that Parliament could constitutionally pass no act affecting the internal polity of the colonies, and hence no colonial opposition to such acts could be revolutionary. Only when the opposition was turned against an authority that was constitutional could this opposition be truly revolutionary; and for the Americans there was but one such authority, not the Parliament but the Crown. For them, therefore, the struggle continued to be merely a constitutional struggle for the recovery of legal rights and the redress of illegal wrongs up to the point where the power of the Crown was touched. The basis of their contention was a clear-cut distinction between the King in Parliament and the King out of Parliament, and so late as October 26, 1774, they solemnly assured George III that they wished "not a diminution of the prerogative."

On the other hand it can scarcely be expected that English statesmen who had declared in the solemn form of a statute that the English Parliament "had, hath, and of right ought to have" sufficient power and authority to bind the American colonies, subjects of the Crown of Great Britain in all cases whatsoever, would regard American opposition to Parliament's practical application of this power in such statutes as the Massachusetts Government Act as a merely "constitutional" opposition, or their resistance to its enforcement as anything less than revolutionary. For these English statesmen, the Revolution of 1688-9 had ended the older sharp distinction between the King in Parliament and the King out of Parliament. Prerogative had become for them only such part of the ancient discretionary right of the Crown as Parliament saw fit to leave untouched. All rights of the Crown in the dominions, as well as in the Realm, were now completely under the control of Parliament, since William and Mary had sworn in their coronation oath to govern the Kingdom "and the dominions thereunto belonging according to the statutes in Parliament agreed on."

On this interpretation it is obvious that the acts of the Americans had ceased to be constitutional and became revolutionary in character long before they ceased to protest their loyalty to the "best of Kings." They must be considered so from the first time the power of Parliament constitutionally to bind the colonies was definitely denied. This occurred long before 1776.

The bare statement of these two inconsistent and conflicting views at once suggests the first constitutional problem. When did the first revolutionary act occur? What is the date of the American Revolution? Is it coincident with the first definite breach of the royal prerogative, or should it be found in the earlier repudiation of Parliament's authority? No answer can possibly be made to this important question one way or the other till the conflicting constitutional views of the Americans and the English Parliament are carefully compared and some conclusion reached on their respective merits; and this conclusion itself must be based upon the constitutional precedents to be found in the whole historical development of the English constitution up to the time of the American struggle.

When did the train of constitutional development begin which led in continuous sequence to the first act that may be called revolutionary? Who were the real adversaries in this constitutional struggle, and which of them was constitutionally "right"? These are a few of the questions that occur to one who attempts to make a general survey of this period. The answers they have received are singularly contradictory and frequently unconvincing, and this after all the painstaking research of recent years. The purpose of this brief study is to try if possible to narrow these constitutional questions until they become susceptible of clear and definite treatment, if not of conclusive answers. We shall not be concerned with the intricate network of "causes," economic, social, or political, tremendous as is the importance of them all. They must be at the background of our minds, not the foreground.

Thus stripped of its constitutional non-essentials the American Revolution seems to have been the outcome of a collision of two mutually incompatible interpretations of the British constitution, one held by the subjects of the British King in America, the other by a majority in the British Parliament. This result was a breach of the constitution not based upon and not warranted by the earlier precedents in the constitution's growth...

The struggle popularly called the American Revolution, up to its latest constitutional phase, was a contest solely between the Americans and Parliament. The Crown was not involved. No question of prerogative was at issue. If the King was at all implicated, it was the King in Parliament only and as a constituent part thereof, not the King in Council. The struggle did not touch the prerogative till after George III's Proclamation of Rebellion of August 23, 1775, and in fact can hardly be safely dated earlier than the formal declaration of the Virginia Convention on June 29, 1776, that "the government of this country, as formerly exercised under the crown of Great Britain, is *totally dissolved*" or Congress's resolution of May 15, 1776, recommending to the various colonies the adoption of popular constitutions, with its famous preamble which declares that "it appears absolutely irreconcileable to reason and good Conscience, for the people of these colonies now to take the oaths and affirmations necessary for the support of any government under the crown of Great Britain, and it is necessary that the exercise of every kind of authority under the said crown should be totally suppressed, and all the powers of government exerted, under the authority of the people of the colonies."

1925 AWARD

ABOUT THE FRONTIER DEVELOPMENT OF THE U.S.

BY

FREDERIC L. PAXSON

Frederic Logan Paxson (born on February 23, 1877, in Philadelphia, Pa.) earned the Bachelor's degree of science at the University of Pennsylvania in 1898. During the following five years he held a Harrison scholarship. At that time, he also worked as instructor in history in several secondary schools. In 1902 he was graduated from Harvard University. The year after, he assumed the position of assistant professor of history at the University of Colorado, and in 1904 Paxson became professor of history within the same institute. Another two years later, he changed to the University of Michigan and from 1910 on, he held a professorship of American history at the University of Wisconsin. In the summer of the same year, he did research in the British archives as an associate member of the Carnegie Institution. At the end of the First World War, he served as a major in the United States Army and was there in charge of the economic mobilization section of the historical branch within the war plans division of the General Staff. In 1924 he became member of the Committee on Management of the Dictionary of American Biography. Furthermore, Frederic L. Paxson published as author quite a number of books, among them *The Independence of the South American Republics; The Last American Frontier; The Civil War; The New Nation; Recent History of the United States.* In 1924 Frederic L. Paxson wrote *History of the American Frontier*, which earned him the Pulitzer Prize for history one year later.

THE BOUNDARY LINE IN EARLY 19TH CENTURY

[Source: Frederic L. Paxson: History of the American Frontier, 1763-1893, Boston - New York: Houghton Mifflin Company/The Riverside Press, 1924, pp. 111 - 115; reprinted by permission of Houghton Mifflin Company, New York, N.Y.]

THIRTY-SEVEN years after the British Government placed a limit to western expansion at the watershed of the Appalachians, the people of the colonies had grown in number from perhaps 1,600,000 to 5,300,000, and in the region then closed to their entry nearly a million settlers had taken up their homes and built a new civilization. In 1800 this border area produced the party of Jefferson that took possession of the Federal Government. Even Americans were not prepared in their minds for the sudden shift of political power. The English bewilderment and dismay at the loss of the American colonies was fully paralleled by eastern discouragement at the victory of the Republicans. All along the seaboard, persons of position were irritated at the control by a new democracy. The resentment was keenest east of the Hudson, and here the unwillingness to endure it was most nearly uniform. There were Democratic-Republicans everywhere, for everywhere there were young voters, men without property, and farmers struggling under the burden of their debt. But the sectional distribution of interests and the uniformity of the West behind the leadership of Jefferson are so manifest that the year 1800 becomes the dividing point between two chapters of political history. The background of popular movements for the next two decades is to be found along the frontier revealed by the census of 1800. Not only its political theory and party practice, but its numerical strength, social and religious habits, and changing relation to the eternal problem of its land, are needed to show it as it was.

In the ten years after the first census of 1790, the population of the United States increased about thirty-five per cent, from 3,900,000 to 5,300,000. The increase would have been great enough to disarrange relationships under any condition; it was the more notable because it came almost exclusively from excess of births over deaths. There was so little immigration that it may be ignored. The Americans of 1800 were American born of American

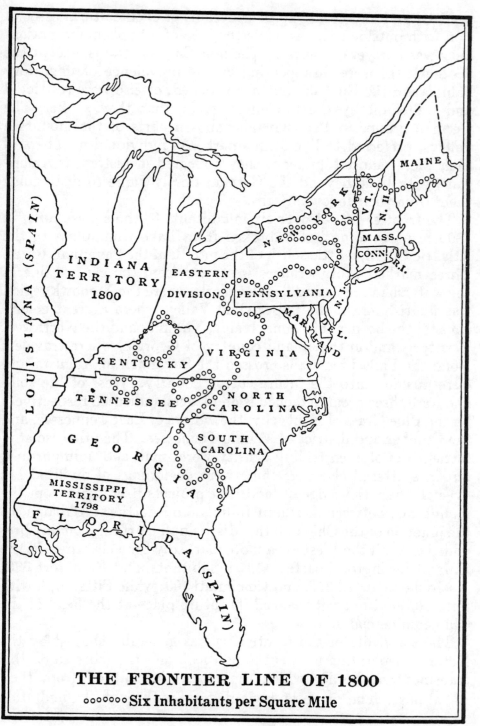

THE FRONTIER LINE OF 1800
∘∘∘∘∘∘∘ Six Inhabitants per Square Mile

parents, and had ceased to be conscious of even cultural association with outside sources, while the idea of a hyphenated nation-
ality was not yet conceived. The non-English strains, except the
Scotch-Irish, were disappearing as the prevalence of migratory
habits, and the English language widened; or else were restricted
and walled-off by the foreign language that they spoke. The
German groups in Pennsylvania, and in parts of the mountain
valleys, preferred to live a life apart. As individual members of
their race acquired influence they appeared in history as Americans, with little beyond the German family name to distinguish
them from their fellow citizens.

The frontier line of over six inhabitants to the square mile, in
1800, runs winding but unbroken from Lake Champlain to the
Atlantic Ocean, a little south of the mouth of the Savannah River.
Three marked protuberances westward from the general line of
the watershed are in middle New York, where the Mohawk region
was flourishing, in the upper Ohio Valley where a great colony
covered the borders of Pennsylvania, Virginia, and the Northwest
Territory, and in the upland country of Georgia, where travelers
along the Falls Line trails crossed the Savannah at Augusta and
were pushing into the future cotton country. West of the solid
line were three great detached island tracts, indicated respectively
by the Blue Grass of Kentucky, the valleys of East Tennessee, and
the Cumberland district of Middle Tennessee. The other isolated
settlements of even trifling density were small and unimportant,
but in scattered clearings there were beginnings of civilized life
over all the vast wedge of land that projects itself west from the
mountains, between southern Indiana and northern Alabama, to
the junction of the Ohio and the Mississippi. A rural economy prevailed over all the West even more markedly than elsewhere in the
Union. Lexington boasted 1797 inhabitants, and Frankfort 628;
Nashville reported 355, and Cincinnati 500; while Pittsburgh with
but 1565 had not yet realized its future place at the head of the
Ohio commercial area.

The social life of the frontier was as generally shaped by the
factor of separation as was the political, and the more so on this
transmontane border which the mountains cut off from their
social base. The rough and winding paths through the mountain

gaps forced the average migrant to abandon hope of quick return. The separation that induced self-reliance in government forced the pioneer to make his own furniture, build his own houses out of local materials, and get along with what his environment could supply him. The trails leading to the East were worse rather than better in 1800, for they had been heavily traveled without improvement. Where there were deep streams, private speculators conducted private ferries at extortionate rates. Elsewhere the rows of more or less parallel ruts that passed for roads forbade any traveler but the rider on horseback to make much progress. Wheeled vehicles for pleasure were hardly known, and the heavy farm wagons were moved only with disproportionate waste of strength. The leveling influence of frontier economy kept the well-to-do and the poor alike well fed but rough, in a world of simplicity.

Here and there, in the older parts of Kentucky and Tennessee, there was a house of stone or brick. Residences of sawed lumber were so rare as to attract attention. At Steubenville in 1807 a traveler counted one hundred and sixty houses — including a "gaol of hewn stone," a courthouse of squared logs, and a brick Presbyterian church. The typical home was the cabin built of logs, and limited by the shape of the material to small rooms, low ceilings, and single stories. In the cabin attic, reached by a ladder of saplings and restricted by the slope of a leaky roof, were pallets, and rough beds of log frame with rope or rawhide bottoms. The location of the home was generally determined by some natural spring, and the water that was carried for domestic use was heated in a swinging pot over an open fire, in a great fireplace. There were few artisans in the migration to the West, and the furniture proved it. What the axe, maul, and wedge could not produce was lacking from the ordinary home. Nails were too rare for common use, and wooden pegs did service for them. Mortar and plaster were beyond the domestic architect, but mud could and did stop the chinks between the logs.

By 1800 the external aspect of the landscape was changing, with the extension of cleared fields, and the gradual rebuilding of cabins over the older areas. But inside the cabins the family life still embraced the whole range of domestic manufactures. The frontier graveyards show how hard the early life was on the women of the family. The patriarch laid to rest in his family tract, beside two, three, or four wives who had preceded him, is much more common than the hardy woman who outlived her husbands. The housewife came to her new home young and raw, and found for neighbors other girls as inexperienced. She bore the children; and buried a staggering number of them, for medicine and sanitation, inadequate everywhere, were out of reach for the cabin on the border. She fed her men and raised her children, cooked their food and laid it by for winter. She was at once butcher, packer, and baker. The family clothes showed her craftsmanship, with skins playing a large part, and homespun or knitting revealing a luxury established. When one adds to the grinding and unavoidable labor, the anguish that came from sickness and danger, the frontier woman who survived becomes an heroic character, and the children who felt her touch become the proper material from which to choose the heroes of a nation.

1926 AWARD

ABOUT THE GENERAL
HISTORY OF THE UNITED STATES

BY

EDWARD CHANNING

Edward Channing (born on June 15, 1856, in Dorchester, Mass.) was graduated from Harvard University in 1880 and earned a doctorate in philosophy the same year. He first worked as instructor from 1883 to 1887, before he became assistant professor. In 1897 he was promoted to the rank of professor of history at Harvard University. From 1913 on Channing held the McLean professorship of ancient and modern history. He received honorary doctorates from the University of Michigan and from Columbia University in 1921 and 1926. In addition to this, he was member of the American Academy of Arts and Letters. Edward Channing was a very prolific author of book publications, among which count the following: *Town and County Government in the English Colonies of North America; The Narragansett Planters; The Navigation Laws; English History for American Readers*, which he wrote together with Thomas Wentworth Higginson; *The United States of America, 1765-1865; Students' History of the United States* and *First Lessons in United States History*. In 1926 the Pulitzer Prize for the best book upon history was awarded to Edward Channing for the sixth and last volume of *A History of the United States*, published one year earlier.

EARLY RAILROADS IN THE OHIO VALLEY REGION

[Source: Edward Channing: A History of the United States, Vol. 6: The War for Southern Independence, New York: The MacMillan Company, 1925, pp. 379 - 383; reprinted by permission of the Macmillan Publishing Company, New York, N.Y.]

The changes in routes of commerce from the Ohio Valley and the Northwest in the ten or dozen years... was due, of course, in a great measure to the changing demands of the markets of the East, of the South, and of the world. It was due also to the ability of the States of the Northwest to meet the demands that were made upon them by foreign buyers, and this grew out of the immigration of those years to the wheat-growing States, which made it possible for the farms of the Northern part of this area to supply the wheat required for export. As to the change in the course of the commerce of the Ohio Valley, that was due in part to an increased demand from the Northeastern markets for the products of that region, but this could not have been supplied and the course of commerce could not have changed in those years as it certainly did, had not the building of the railroads in that section been carried forward with a speed that, up to that time, had no parallel in the history of the world. In 1847, there were 660 miles of railroad in operation in the States of the Old Northwest, in Ohio, Indiana, and Illinois. In 1861 there were 7,653 miles of railroad in those three States. In January, 1848, there was not a railroad line connecting the Ohio River with the Lake. By the end of that year, the line connecting Cincinnati and Sandusky had been completed and was in operation; in 1850 there was not a single east to west line in those States connecting the Mississippi River system with the railroads of New York, Pennsylvania, and Maryland; in 1860 this had been accomplished. In other words, in 1850, the Ohio Valley had no easy connection with eastern markets, except by steamboat up the Ohio to Wheeling and Pittsburg and thence to the Atlantic seaboard, or by steamboat down the Ohio and Mississippi to New Orleans and thence by sail and steam through the Gulf and up the eastern coast.

Of course in any study of economic factors, great care must be taken not to exaggerate the influence of changing markets and changing routes of transportation on the minds of the people. It is undoubtedly true that few farmers and few immediate handlers of their products knew or cared where the goods went or how they went, as long as they received satisfactory prices for them. So we may conceive that the great mass of people of the

Ohio Valley was not immediately affected by the economic revolution that the railroad building of the 1850's had wrought: But it is undoubtedly true, although no statistics have been available, that the railroads that carried these products northward to the Lakes and eastward to New York, Philadelphia, and Baltimore, must have brought into the West large quantities of eastern and European manufactured goods in exchange and these must have been of a different quality from those produced on the farm and of a very different grade and price from similar goods that had been imported by the way of New Orleans, or had been produced in the factories of Cincinnati and Indianapolis. So we may suppose that something akin to a changing mental outlook and mode of living occurred, especially in the last years of the decade, in countless homes in southern Ohio, Indiana, and Illinois and in Kentucky, Tennessee, and western Virginia. But how far any such considerations may have altered political or social conceptions must always remain matter for debate. It is evident, however, that the influx of capital to build these railway lines and the coming in of railroad men from the

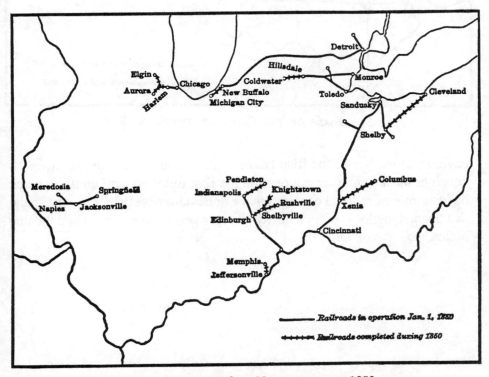

RAILROADS OF THE OLD NORTHWEST IN 1850

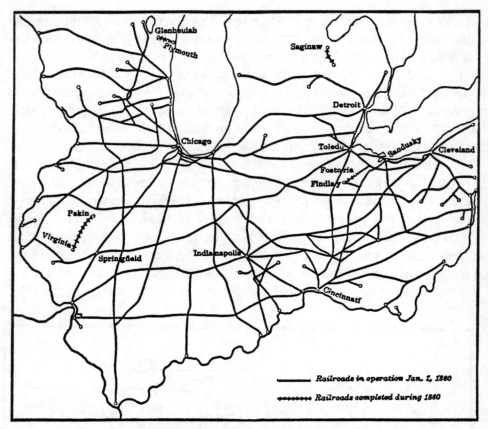

RAILROADS OF THE OLD NORTHWEST IN 1860

engineer of the line to the Irish laborer on the roadbed, and the facility with which news and communication with the East followed hard on the opening of each mile of railroad could not have done otherwise than upset the social and mental outlook of practically every man, woman, and child in that region.

1927 AWARD

ABOUT THE DISPUTES
ON THE MISSISSIPPI QUESTION

BY

SAMUEL F. BEMIS

Samuel Flagg Bemis (born on October 20, 1891, in Worcester, Mass.) was a student of early American diplomacy and Latin American relations in his native city at Clark University, where he also received the Master's degree in 1913. Bemis added Harvard's Master of Arts degree to that of Clark University in 1915 and earned the following year a doctorate in philosophy after a year of study in England and France on a fellowship. Still one year later, he began his teaching career as instructor in history at Colorado College. In 1918 he was promoted to associate professor. Samuel F. Bemis was appointed professor of history at Whitman College in Walla Walla, Washington. After one year as research associate with the Carnegie Institution of Washington from 1923 to 1924, he became professor of history at George Washington University. Following the death of Gaillard Hunt in March 1924, the editorship of the ten-volume work *The American Secretaries of State and Their Diplomacy* was taken over by Bemis. In 1927 he was named director of the European mission of the Library of Congress, a two-year appointment. He numbers among his books *Jay's Treaty; A Diplomatic History of the United States* and *The Latin American Policy of the United States*. His shorter writings have appeared in scholarly and general periodicals since 1916 as well as in collections of essays. Samuel F. Bemis won the Pulitzer Prize of 1927 for history for his *Pinckney's Treaty*, which had appeared the preceding year.

DIPLOMACY IN THE OLD AND THE NEW WORLD

[Source: Samuel Flagg Bemis: Pinckney's Treaty. America's Advantage from Europe's Distress, 1783-1800, Baltimore: The Johns Hopkins Press, 1926, pp. 7 - 10; reprinted by permission of Yale University Press, London, GB.]

The American Revolution immediately raised new problems for diplomacy in both the Old and the New World, and in some of these the Question of the Mississippi assumed increasing significance. The problems which will concern us here relate to the efforts of France and the United States to bring Spain into the war against Great Britain, if possible as the ally of the United States; the policy of Spain toward the United States following her actual intervention, in 1779, as the ally of France alone; and those issues pertaining to the Mississippi and the western and southern boundary of the United States which arose during the peace settlement at Paris in 1782, when it was the effort of French diplomacy to reconcile the diverging interests of Louis XVI's two separate allies.

The outbreak of hostilities between the American colonies and the mother country presented the opportunity for which many astute Frenchmen had been waiting ever since the humiliating Peace of Paris — of splitting apart the British Empire and of raising the power of France in the European scale proportionately to the abasement of Britain. The political religiosity of French public opinion toward the end of the eighteenth century beheld in American republican institutions the avatar of its own dreams and made it possible for French statesmen to direct their King and nation into the war against Great Britain as the ally of the United States with an enthusiastic popular support behind them. But at first, while the chances of ultimate success of the United States were so uncertain, the Count de Vergennes, able French Minister for Foreign Affairs after 1774, maintained a policy of watchful waiting, meanwhile furnishing (together with Spain) to the rebels secret aid in money and munitions to keep the war going in North America. After the capitulation of Saratoga in October, 1777, it was apparent that he might have to choose between recognition of the independence of the United States and a consequent treaty of alliance, with an excellent chance of winning the war, and witnessing the Americans, thanks to the prestige of the victory over Burgoyne's army, make an acceptable peace within the British Empire. Vergennes hastened to choose the former. France became the ally of the United States, and thanks to French intervention American independence was ultimately secured.

When the decision was made to recognize the United States, Vergennes thought, or certainly desired, that Spain would follow the French lead, but he did not wait for official Spanish approval for this new step.

In 1776 Spain, then under the administration of Grimaldi as Minister for Foreign Affairs, had been willing to consider intervening, with French alliance, in the war against Great Britain, because circumstances had then presented an opportunity to conquer Portugal, Britain's traditional ally, with whom a serious territorial dispute had evolved in South America. But at that time Vergennes was not sure enough of the chances of the United States for success against British armies to dare to intervene, nor did he wish by the Spanish acquisition of Portugal and Portuguese colonies to raise the power and prestige of Spain higher than that of France. By December of 1777 the Portuguese-Spanish issue had been settled and Spain was under the guidance of a new Foreign Minister, the able Count of Floridablanca, who was anxious above all things not to serve as a catspaw for French diplomacy. He refused to be wholly convinced by Vergennes' impressive arguments that it was indispensably necessary for Spain to join with France in a preventive war against Great Britain because of the danger to Spanish and French American islands and continental colonies, a conquest of which might conceivably serve to occupy British military forces after an Anglo-American reconciliation; nor was he willing to go to war solely on the theory that any kind of serious damage to the British Empire would redound sufficiently to the advantage of Spain to pay for the trouble of the war.

France therefore, to the intense chagrin of her family ally, precipitately entered the war alone. The affair called for a speedy decision at the close of 1777, and the opportunity appealed to Vergennes as too good to pass by. In the Franco-American alliance of February 6, 1778, a separate and secret article provided for the future adhesion of Spain, with the privilege of proposing other conditions analogous to the principal aim of the alliance and conformable to the rules of equality, reciprocity, and friendship.

From almost the first the Congress of the United States had been desirous of securing recognition from Spain of American independence, together with a treaty of friendship, commerce, and alliance, and had empowered its commissioners to the French Court to open negotiations to that end. In 1777 Arthur Lee, one of the three commissioners in Paris, had been sent by his colleagues, Benjamin Franklin and Silas Deane, on a mission to Madrid. For this purpose, Lee bore a letter of introduction from the Count de Aranda, Spanish Ambassador in Paris; but at Floridablanca's direction he was met at Burgos by the Minister Grimaldi, then just retired from the Council, who persuaded the American emissary to return to Paris, after giving him promises of financial assistance for the revolted colonies, promises which were soon fulfilled. Congress already, on January 1, 1777, had appointed Franklin as commissioner to Spain to negotiate a treaty of friendship, leaving the direction of the negotiation to Franklin's own discretion. Arthur Lee's recent experience and the advice of the Spanish Ambassador determined Franklin not to leave Paris, for it was certain that he would not be received by the Spanish Court. Spain already had furnished a million livres to put with another million with which the King of France was keeping alive the flames of rebellion in America. But even Grimaldi, an Italian by origin and francophil in all his conceptions of foreign policy, had hesitated about recognizing the independence of the United States. For an absolute monarchy with American colonies of her own thus to set a premium on insurrection was a dangerous precedent from which both he and his greater successor Floridablanca shrank with utmost abhorrence. For this reason the Spanish Council of State in 1776 had strongly advised against such recognition.

1928 AWARD

ABOUT THE ROMANTIC
REVOLUTION IN AMERICA

BY

VERNON L. PARRINGTON

Vernon Louis Parrington (born on August 3, 1871, in Aurora, Ill.) first attended Harvard University, later the College of Emporia, a Presbyterian institution, and was graduated in 1895. Already two years earlier, he had started to teach English and French at the College of Emporia. From 1897 to 1898 he was instructor in English and modern languages at the University of Oklahoma and was then promoted to the rank of professor of English. From 1903 to 1904 he spent fourteen months in Europe. There, he studied at the British Museum in London and at the Bibliothèque Nationale in Paris. After having lost his post at the University of Oklahoma in 1908, he became assistant professor of English and in 1912 professor of English at the University of Washington. The historian and philologist is in addition to this the author of several book publications, e.g. *The Cambridge History of American Literature*, volume 1; *The Connecticut Wits* and *Sinclair Lewis - Our Own Diogenes*. For the first and second tome of the three-volume work *Main Currents in American Thought*, published in 1927, Vernon L. Parrington received the Pulitzer Prize for history of the following year.

INDICATORS OF THE MIND OF THE SOUTH

[Source: Vernon Louis Parrington: Main Currents in American Thought, Vol. 2: The Romantic Revolution in America, 1800-1860, New York - London: Harcourt Brace Jovanovich, 1927, pp. 5 - 7; reprinted by permission of Harcourt Brace and Company, Orlando, Fla.]

THE history of the Old Dominion is an easy chapter in the text-book of economic determinism. It is a modern instance that exemplifies the law of land distribution and political control as laid down by James Harrington; it is another Oceana seated by the James River, that would not suffer a king to rule because gentlemen held the land and acknowledged no feudal dues or royal preroga-tives. On the surface its history seems little more than a bundle of paradoxes. From the raw materials of English middle-class stock it created a distinguished and capable aristocracy, that was re-strained from feudal tyranny by a vigorous yeomanry that held its land in fee simple and stoutly maintained its rights. Established on a slave economy, it adopted an agrarian economy, espoused a republic, and accepted the doctrine of democratic equalitarianism. It was generous, humanitarian, independent; parochial in its jealousies, yet farsighted in outlook; tenacious of its authority and quick to defend it, yet never mean or grasping. During the noonday of its power its influence was always on the side of local democratic freedom and the common well-being. It opposed the encroachments of the centralizing state and the spirit of capitalistic exploitation; yet its domestic economy rested on the most primitive of all exploitation.

But these paradoxes disappear when the history of Virginia is interpreted in the light of its land economy. By force of cir-cumstances the Old Dominion became broadly American in its social philosophy, the interpreter of America to herself. Native conditions created there a native psychology, and this native psychology spread widely through the frontier states where a like economics provided suitable breeding places. Virginia was the mother of the agrarian West, as New York, Philadelphia, and Boston were the progenitors of the mercantile and industrial

East; and in the frequent clashes between country and town, between agrarianism and capitalism, the ideas of Virginia have commonly opposed the ideas of the northern cities. Between the older colonial America and later industrial America, stand the ideals of the Old Dominion, more humane and generous than either, disseminating the principles of French romantic philosophy. and instilling into the provincial American mind, static and stagnant in the grip of English colonialism, the ideal of democratic equalitarianism and the hope of humane progress. The nineteenth century first entered America by way of the James River.

The renaissance in Virginia began with the transition from middle-class to plantation ideals that marked the last half of the eighteenth century; and it was given intellectual stimulus by the libertarian natural-rights philosophy that in England and France was undermining the old order. There were no cities either mercantile or social, in the Old Dominion, and no industrialism. Life everywhere centered in the plantation. The navigable rivers of the tide-water region were favorable to the development of a decentralized economics, and in spite of royal commands to create adequate seaports, and heavy taxes by the commonwealth, trading towns did not prosper. For two hundred years Virginia refused to create a native middleman group to handle its staples, but preferred to deal through British factors and ship directly, preferably in Dutch bottoms. Each planter insisted on putting his hogsheads of tobacco aboard ship at his own wharf, and receiving his merchandise direct from London. The system was wasteful, and Madison was active in an attempt to limit by law the ports of entry to two, in order to build up a middleman machinery; but the plan broke on the fixed prejudices of plantation masters who had come to share the old English dislike of tradesmen. Virginia stubbornly refused to adopt middle-class methods, even though refusal cost her dear. She preferred to be exploited by British factors rather than create a domestic class to devour her resources.

The system had grown up in earlier times when the merchant spirit was strong in Virginia. It is often assumed that the Virginia aristocracy was descended from emigrant Cavaliers who fled from

England during the commonwealth period; but the facts of history do not bear out such a theory. It was descended largely from vigorous middle-class stock—from men who had been merchants in England and in turning planters brought to the business qualities that had been developed in mercantile pursuits. In the seventeenth century Virginia society exhibited few of the usual characteristics of the Cavalier. It was frankly *bourgeois*, pushing, avaricious, keen in driving hard bargains, with no high sense of honor, canny rather than impulsive, preferring the law to the duel, hating war and only half-hearted in defense against the Indians—a little world of London burgesses new seated on the banks of the James and the Rappahannock. "Beyond doubt," concludes a recent student, "the most numerous section of the Virginia aristocracy was derived from the English merchant class" (Thomas J. Wertenbaker, *Patrician and Plebeian in Virginia*, p. 28), pretty much the same class that settled Boston and Philadelphia. For a hundred and fifty years these merchant ideals characterized Virginia society. Speculation in land was universal; exploitation was open and shameless; the highest officials took advantage of their positions to loot the public domain, resorting to divers sharp practices from tax dodging to outright theft. One gentleman added a cipher to a grant for two thousand acres, and although the fraud was commonly known, so great was his influence that no one disputed his title to twenty thousand acres. While governor, Alexander Spotswood issued patents for sixty thousand acres to dummy holders, who deeded the land to him after he had retired from office.

In the third quarter of the eighteenth century such practices came to an end. The merchant spirit died out among the Virginia planters, and the Cavalier spirit took its place. A high sense of personal and civic honor became the hall-mark of the landed aristocracy, and for upwards of a hundred years this common code gave to Virginia an enviable distinction.

1929 Award

ABOUT THE UNION
ARMY'S ADMINISTRATION

BY

Fred A. Shannon

Fred Albert Shannon (born on February 12, 1893, in Sedalia, Mo.) first attended the Indiana State Teachers College and earned the Master of Arts degree at Indiana University in 1918. After having worked as school teacher, he became professor of history at the Iowa Wesleyan College in 1919. Five years later, he earned his doctorate in philosophy and assumed the post of assistant professor of history at the Iowa State Teachers College. He stayed there until 1926 and changed then to the Kansas State College of Agriculture and Applied Science, where he was appointed associate professor of history. Shannon taught in the summer sessions of Cornell College in 1924 and of Ohio State University in 1929. Besides, he was member of the American Historical Association and was on the executive committee of the Mississippi Valley Historical Association. Moreover, he worked as editor and co-editor on several publications and made contributions to professional journals. As a specialist in research in American social and economic history, Civil War and antebellum period he wrote many books relating to these fields. In 1928 Fred A. Shannon wrote *The Organization and Administration of the Union Army, 1861-1865*, a work for which the Pulitzer Prize for history was awarded to him the next year.

FEEDING AND CLOTHING THE VOLUNTEERS

[Source: Fred Albert Shannon: The Organization and Administration of the Union Army, 1861-1865, Vol. 1, Cleveland: The Arthur H. Clark Company, 1928, pp. 53 - 57; reprinted by permission of the Arthur H. Clark Company, Spokane, Wash.]

Just as the states were entrusted with the recruiting and organization of the regiments for the army so, in like manner, they had to assume the responsibility of providing for the needs of the soldiers, until mustered into the service of the United States. The activities of states, corporations, and individuals in raising funds for this purpose has already been mentioned. Even for so small a force as 75,000, the Secretary of War was compelled to admit that the United States was not in a position to furnish camp equipage and clothing as rapidly as they were needed. Accordingly he advised the governors to furnish the material and present their bills. Though admitting that "clothing is sometimes issued to volunteers," he intimated that, since the soldiers received a monthly allowance for clothing in addition to their pay, it was up to them or to the states to see that they were provided with uniforms. The official correspondence of the period is replete with pleas from the governors to the War Department for everything from tincups to stables, and replies from that fountain head of chaos, courteously requesting said governors to help themselves and present their bills for payment.

It was not the intention that the state governments should be finally responsible for all such costs. The War Department simply confessed its inability to handle the situation and let it be understood from the first that the states would be reimbursed. Nor were its promises unfulfilled. Though the states assumed the risk of recovering these costs from the federal government, they were not the losers thereby. Congress, in its first rush of military legislation, made provisions for repaying to the states "the costs, charges, and expenses properly incurred by such State[s] for enrolling, subsisting, clothing, supplying, arming, equiping, paying, and transporting its troops. ..." The phraseology of the act itself shows the wide range of responsibilities which the governors were called upon to assume. Almost a month earlier, July 1, 1861, Secretary Cameron had estimated that $10,000,000 were due the states for advances already made. An appropriation act of February 25, 1862, set aside another $15,000,000 for the same purpose.

It is not to the discredit of the state governments that this abdication of authority on the part of the War Department resulted in confusion, graft on a wholesale basis, and untold hardships to the soldiers. The states did what they could. They purchased by contract and in the open market, at home and abroad, all manner of articles necessary for the armies. Legislatures were liberal and governors were zealous to hasten the work of organization. The result was that army contract business produced a windfall of profit to the omnipresent profiteer. The situation would have been bad enough if the federal government alone were in the market, buying up the scanty stores of the manufacturers and merchants. But the result produced by a score of states bidding against each other and against the federal government, was nothing short of deplorable.

The need for food, clothing, and shelter was immediate and urgent. Arms and ammunition might be supplied in more leisurely fashion, but food and clothing, especially food, must be had at once. Accordingly the first scandals concerning the army contract business were in connection with contracts for beef and clothing, and then in practically every line of military supply. An army of lobbyists, contractors, and speculators at once "hurried to the assault on the treasury, like a cloud of locusts. ... They were everywhere; in the streets, in the hotels, in the offices, at the Capitol, and in the White House. They continually besieged the bureaus of administration, the doors of the Senate and House of Representatives, wherever there was a chance to gain something." In a similar way, the same performance was repeated in practically every state capital.

Through haste, carelessness, or criminal collusion, the state and federal officers accepted almost every offer and paid almost any price for the commodities, regardless of character, quality, or quantity. The type of clothing, food, and munitions thus supplied will be considered separately, but, as an index to the kind of product commonly supplied the following, by comparison with numerous other accounts, does not seem exaggerated: "For sugar it [the government] often got sand; for coffee, rye; for leather, something no better than brown paper; for sound horses and mules, spavined beasts and dying donkeys; and for serviceable muskets and pistols, the experimental failures of sanguine inventors, or the refuse of shops and foreign armories."

War contractors became proverbially and notoriously rich. The $50,000,000 spent by the government in the first few months for arms alone went to enrich a dozen or more contractors. Poor men became rich and rich men became richer in a day. It was commonly reported that one man made two million dollars in a single year. Some made fortunes with practically no outlay or exertion of their own. Some received contracts at exorbitant figures and then sold them at a liberal discount to sub-contractors, thus making comfortable fortunes without turning a hand or a dollar or devoting any appreciable time to the process. Others made more, at slightly greater exertion, by filling contracts as poorly as possible. "The quality of the article they heeded little, provided it bore the name and the semblance of the thing, and could be had for almost nothing. ..." It is a notorious fact that many of the greatest fortunes of today had their origin in Civil War contracts. Many a millionaire who later sought so frantically to achieve respectability through alliance with foreign nobility might well have inscribed "Shoddy" as the legend on his costly coat of arms.

Necessity, haste, and carelessness can explain the acceptance of a great many of these contracts and a very great deal of inferior goods. But a large amount of blame must go to a horde of government-paid officials who, either through criminal negligence or criminal collusion, permitted or encouraged this robbing of the government treasury and cruelty to the American soldiers. The connection of General John C. Fremont and Secretary Simon Cameron with this sort of business is already widely known.

The army of lesser officials, inspectors and so on, who permitted such graft, came in for their full share of public censure at a time when General Fremont was considered a vicarious martyr — but few of them were ever punished. Accused inspectors passed the blame on to those letting the contracts, the latter blamed the contractors, and the contractors in turn contended that they furnished goods according to specifications.

1930 AWARD

ABOUT THE RESULTS
OF THE INDEPENDENCE WAR

BY

CLAUDE H. VAN TYNE

Claude Halstead Van Tyne (born on October 16, 1869, in Tecumseh, Mich.) started as a youth in the banking business and rose to the position of cashier. But instead of pursuing this career, he attended the University of Michigan and was graduated in 1896. During the years 1897/1898 he completed his studies in Leipzig, Heidelberg and Paris. Two years later, he earned his Ph.D. degree at the University of Pennsylvania, where he remained as senior fellow in history until January 1903. Then, after six months' work of investigation in Washington in connection with the Carnegie Institution, he came the fall of the same year to the University of Michigan as assistant professor. Three years later, Van Tyne was promoted to the rank of professor and was made head of the department of American history. In 1913/14 he was lecturer in the French provincial universities on the Fondation Harvard pour les relations avec les universités Françaises. In 1927 he occupied the Sir George Watson chair of American history, literature, and institutions in the British universities, an annual lectureship. Van Tynes scholarly publications were numerous, among them are *The Loyalists in the American Revolution; Guide to the Archives of the Government of the United States in Washington; The American Revolution; School History of the United States* and *England and America, Rivals in the American Revolution*. With *The War of Independence* Claude H. Van Tyne won the Pulitzer Prize of 1930 for the best book on history published the preceding year.

EUROPEAN COUNTRIES SUPPLY SECRET AID

[Source: Claude H. Van Tyne: The War of Independence, American Phase, Boston - New York: Houghton Mifflin Company/The Riverside Press, 1929, pp. 463 - 468; reprinted by permission of Houghton Mifflin Company, New York, N.Y.]

Soon after Lexington the public journals in America contained matter expressing faith in a French alliance. There was published a letter from an American in Paris who wrote that the French to a man were strongly in favor of America — on the 'principle of humanity.' Another thought France would wait until the breach between England and America was irreparable and then would come to aid. Zubly, of Georgia, declared in Congress, October 6, 1775, that a proposal had been made to apply to France and Spain. Though he believed that any one who would propose it would be torn to pieces like De Witt, yet it was only two months later when even Congress moved to explore the likelihood of French aid. The Committee of Secret Correspondence, Franklin, Dickinson, and Jay, wrote to Arthur Lee that Congress wished to know the disposition of foreign powers, but in learning it he must use 'impenetrable secrecy.' Franklin wrote to Dumas to inquire about among the many ambassadors at The Hague whether any power in Europe would enter into alliance with America for the sake of her commerce, amounting to some seven millions sterling per annum.

Meanwhile the popular imagination was pleased with delusions and anticipations. Early in 1775, colonial journals spread the tale of forty ships of war building in Sweden for the French Government with an eye to the quarrel between England and America. In May an imaginary French fleet had put to sea to give aid to American ships. By fall the papers carried the rumor that France and Spain had a greater sea force than the British could muster in a year; that superior French and Spanish fleets were in the West Indies; that Choiseul was again in favor and would lead France and Spain at once into war with England. Algiers was attacked, and Gibraltar besieged by the Spanish, ran the wild rumors. By midsummer of 1776, the daily press deluded Americans with a French general and an admiral in the West Indies ready to begin hostilities against England as soon as Congress decided upon Independence. Indeed, so alarmed was the British Ministry, late in June, 1776, that the Cabinet met to discuss the late intelligence, relative to menacing armament in the ports of France and Spain. They agreed to increase the guard-ships to twenty-four, the marines to one hundred per company, and to continue raising volunteer seamen for the fleet, and to impress them if necessary.

Nor were France and Spain the only hope. Soon after Bunker Hill, there were flying rumors of eight German general officers and a ship loaded with artillery and ammunition bound for America. Two months later, three German princes were said to be traveling *incognito* in New England hoping to aid America. There was joy everywhere over the report that the King of Prussia was about to invade Hanover to collect a British debt. In the hour of peril much comfort was derived from embracing these delusive phantoms of hope.

Against the growth of this American aspiration for aid from France, British pamphleteers and American Loyalists fought in vain. The Americans were reminded that 'the English are generous, brave mastiffs; the French have always been sly, ravenous foxes, the Spaniards cruel wolves.' A pamphlet circulated in the colonies at British Government expense offered friendly advice against reliance on France. If America wished the aid of France and Spain, no doubt it could be got. British felicity is the envy of all nations, the author insinuated. 'Slaves always hate the free.' But can Americans trust such aid? 'Will the despotism of France establish a new Empire of Liberty?' Will French armies conquer for America and not for themselves? 'Will the Inquisition of Spain make a Protestant cause independent?' asked the pamphleteer, appealing to New England prejudice. These dark hints were reenforced by Joseph Galloway's reminder of the 'danger, and all the horrors of French slavery and papish superstition.' In every way he tried to recall the old American hate of France. Her ambition is still alive, he warned. Her power is asleep, but will awake. With her aid America would win independence from England only to become the slave of arbitrary power — of popish bigotry and superstition. Beware of the miseries of a foreign yoke, he pleaded. Indeed, when John Adams first suggested in Congress application to Europe, he got only 'grimaces' and 'convulsions' from the members, for whose nerves it was too much. Paine and Sherman, of Connecticut, in fact, did not approve of employing 'Foreign Papists' in American service. But all warning and hesitancy were in vain. These imagined terrors were nothing compared with the dismay in the heart of every reasoning American as he contemplated war with England lacking the aid of France.

After the news of Lexington and Concord had spread in ever-widening circles over the sea and throughout Europe, the French Government felt pressure from every side to render some kind of aid to the Americans. It was the fashion in France in those days of absolutism for men of influence in the state to sit down and write to the monarch as publicists to-day write to the public in magazines or for the Sunday supplement of a great newspaper, long articles urging their political views. These *mémoires*, hundreds of them preserved in the French foreign archives, written by dukes, counts, nobles of every degree, great ministers of state, and intended solely for the eyes of the King and his Ministers, pressed at this time the argument that the prestige and the fundamental economic interests of the French nation were at stake in the outcome of England's struggle with her colonies. The Duke de Noailles, the Count de Broglie, the Count de Saint-Germain, the Chevalier d'Anemours, de Magnières, and many lesser persons offered the motives of historical example, of French safety, of right or of honor, decorous mantles for everything from secret aid to brutal assault. The sophisticated writers recalled that Carthage once had a navy, now England; that Carthage was destroyed, why not England? Others reminded the King that Queen Elizabeth gave aid to Holland in its struggle with the Duke of Alva. Like the Dutch provinces the Americans were republicans suffering impatiently and trying to shake off the yoke of domination, jealous to excess of their liberty, ready to sacrifice all to preserve it. England, on the other hand, was a nation rich, drunk with its success in the last war, impatient of the least resistance, resembling, indeed, the Romans dictating laws to their colonists.

1931 AWARD

ABOUT THE COMING
OF THE FIRST WORLD WAR

BY

BERNADOTTE E. SCHMITT

Bernadotte Everly Schmitt (born on May 19, 1886, in Strasburg, Va.) received his Bachelor's degree at the age of eighteen from the University of Tennessee. In 1905 he was chosen to go to Oxford as a Rhodes Scholar. He earned the Oxonian B.A. three years later. On his return to the United States Schmitt accepted a fellowship in history at the University of Wisconsin which he held from 1908 to 1909. He held an assistantship the next year, and in 1910 he received his Ph.D. degree and accepted an instructorship at Western Reserve University. At that time he did a great deal of lecturing on international politics. In 1913 the Master's degree was conferred upon him by Oxford University. The following year, Schmitt was made an assistant professor and in 1917 an associate professor. In 1925 he was appointed to the faculty of the University of Chicago as professor of modern history. At that time, Schmitt did a lot of traveling to Europe, the Balkans and the Far East. On these trips he did not only have the chance to augment his background, but also he met a great number of outstanding personalities of his times. Schmitt is also the author of the following book publications: *England and Germany, 1740-1914; Triple Alliance and Triple Entente* and *The Annexation of Bosnia, 1908-1909*. In 1931 Bernadotte E. Schmitt was awarded the Pulitzer Prize for history for *The Coming of the War, 1914*, which had been published one year earlier.

THE UNITED STATES AND MEDIATION IN PARIS

[Source: Bernadotte E. Schmitt: The Coming of the War, 1914, Vol. 2, New York - London: Charles
Scribner's Sons, 1930, pp. 477 - 481; reprinted by permission of the Macmillan Publishing Company,
New York, N.Y.]

On 28 July (1914) the American ambassador in Paris cabled to President
Wilson that the situation in Europe was regarded in Paris "as the gravest in
history." In his personal opinion, an "expression from our nation would
have great weight in this crisis": "I believe that a strong plea for delay and
moderation from the President of the United States would meet with the
respect an approval of Europe and urge the prompt consideration of this
question. This suggestion is consistent with our plea for arbitration and
attitude toward world affairs generally. I would not appear officious but
deem it my duty to make this expression to you."

Shortly after the receipt of this appeal, the secretary of state inquired of
the ambassador in London if there was "any likelihood that the good offices
of the United States if offered under Article 3 of the Hague convention
would be acceptable or serve any high purpose in the present crisis." The
sounding was made only in London. Sir Edward Grey expressed "his great
gratitude" for the suggestion, and said that he would be "only too delighted
if any opportunity in which the good offices of the United States could be
used." Thus encouraged, the President, who was "anxious to do everything
in his power to avert war," then inquired "if there is the slightest intimation
that such a suggestion might be effective elsewhere." Evidently Mr. Wilson
was unwilling to plunge uninvited into European politics, and wisely so.
The reply from London was the reverse of encouraging. Ambassador Page
telegraphed: "My very definite opinion is that there is not the slightest
chance of any result if our good offices be offered at any continental capital.
This is confirmed by the judgment of the British Foreign Office. We may
have a chance after the war has reached a breathing space."

President Wilson, however, did not wait for the war to reach a breathing
space — which in fact it never reached. On the next day he despatched the
following message to the heads of the five Great Powers then involved in
the war: "As official head of one of the powers signatory to the Hague
convention, I feel it to be my privilege and my duty under Article 3 of that
convention to say to you in a spirit of most earnest friendship that I should
welcome an opportunity to act in the interest of European peace, either now

or at any other time that might be thought more suitable, as an occasion to serve you and all concerned in a way that would afford me lasting cause for gratitude and happiness. WOODROW WILSON."

The first answer came from Russia. M. Sazonov replied: "Offer comes too late for Russia, should have been made earlier, Austria only country where it can help now." Mr. Poincaré declared that "the present circumstances give a new proof of that love of peace with which France is ever inspired," and continued: "For its preservation, the Government has made every sacrifice compatible with its dignity and its honor. Notwithstanding repeated provocations and numerous violations of territory, it has refused to be the aggressor. It was attacked at the same time that the territory of neutral powers was being violated." King George V "expressed most earnestly his thanks ... and the hope that an occasion would come when the President's offer of mediation might be accepted." The Emperor Francis Joseph thanked the President for "his friendly message which corresponds entirely with the peaceful sentiments which have guided me during my entire reign," but added: "Austria-Hungary will certainly accept with gratitude and in accord with its allies the mediation of your Government at such time as the honor of the flag will permit and when the objects of the war shall be attained."

The most interesting reply was that from the German Emperor. In the presence of the American ambassador, Mr. Gerard, he wrote out a long telegram in seven numbered paragraphs giving his version of the diplomatic negotiations preceding the war; for the rest he merely said, "I am most grateful for the President's message." Without exception, the replies made clear that mediation would not be welcome. One does not have to search long for the reasons. Each government, having proclaimed to its people and to the world that it had desired peace and had not been responsible for the war, was compelled, politically speaking, to continue the war in the hope of defeating and punishing its enemies; moreover, each government, declaring that it had been attacked, was in a position to realize certain national ambitions if the fortune of war went in its favor. The Germans, confident of victory, could not consider peace until their offensive had run its course, and the Entente Powers believed that ultimately their superior resources would enable them to achieve victory. In short, to discuss peace at the moment when the war had hardly begun, was out of the question for any belligerent. The Government of the United States was to offer its mediation more than once in the next two and a half years, only to discover that there was but one kind of effective mediation: armed intervention.

The crisis of July, 1914, was the most momentous event in the history of Europe since the Congress of Vienna a century before. If it culminated in a European war, this was partly because probably no diplomacy, however skilful, could have devised a compromise between the firm resolution of Austria-Hungary to make war on Serbia and the determination of Russia not to permit the crushing of that small state. But, as a matter of fact, much of the diplomacy exhibited was far from skilful. The Austro-Hungarian statesmen failed to foresee that Serbia might submit to their demands to so great an extent that their policy of war would be open to the charge of brutal aggression. The German Government, if it was to carry through its programme of localizing the war, needed to win the confidence of the Entente Powers in its professions of Austro-Hungarian disinterestedness; yet from the beginning it managed by its conduct to create only distrust and suspicion. The Russian diplomatists appear not to have appreciated sufficiently the probable effect of their military measures on the highly strung German general staff. The British cabinet found its action largely paralyzed because its members could not decide what course to take. The Germans miscalculated the attitude of Rumania, the Russians thought that they could dragoon Bulgaria to take their side, the British allowed themselves to be hoodwinked by Turkey. In one sense, therefore, Mr. Lloyd George was right when he exclaimed that the statesmen "staggered and stumbled" into the conflict. In another respect also diplomacy was found wanting. Although the immediate issue concerned only Austria-Hungary and Russia, the crisis was immediately viewed as a test of strength between the two rival groups of Powers, and it was the tragedy of Europe that among its many gifted statesmen there was no one of the caliber of a Canning or a Cavour to cut through the web of alliances and restore liberty of action to the states not directly interested.

1932 AWARD

ABOUT THE PERSONAL
EXPERIENCES IN WORLD WAR I

BY

JOHN J. PERSHING

John Joseph Pershing (born on September 13, 1860, in Linn County, Mo.) was graduated from the United States Military Academy in 1886. The same year he started serving in the Cavalry. He served in the Apache Indian campaign in New Mexico and Arizona in 1886, as well as in the Sioux campaign of 1890/91 in Dakota. Until August 1891 he commanded the Sioux Indian Scouts. During the following four years he worked as military instructor at the University of Nebraska. He joined the staff of the United States Military Academy as instructor in tactics in 1897. Four years later, Pershing became captain of the 1st U.S. Cavalry. From April 1902 to June 1903 he was in charge of the Moro Affairs and commanded military operations in Central Mindanao against the Moros. Afterwards he served on the General Staff for three years. As military attaché he came to Tokio, Japan, in 1905 and fought with Kuroki's army in Manchuria the same year. During the following years he carried out his duty on the Philippine Islands: He was commander of the Department of Mindanao and governor of the Moro Province. Pershing commanded successfully the military operation against hostile Moros terminating with their defeat at the battle of Bagsak on June 12, 1913. After the First World War, he was promoted to the rank of General of Armies of United States. He retired in 1924. Pershing received many military decorations among them the Distinguished Service Medal and the Grand Cross of the Legion of Honor. *My Experiences in the World War*, the only book that John J. Pershing ever wrote, earned him the Pulitzer Prize of 1932 for the best book on history published the preceding year.

THE U.S. COMMANDER AND THE ARMISTICE TALKS

[Source: John J. Pershing: My Experiences in the World War, Vol. 2, New York: Frederick A. Stokes Company, 1931, pp. 388 - 391; reprinted by permission of Harper Collins Publishers, New York, N.Y.]

AS the conference between Marshal Foch and the German delegates proceeded, and in anticipation of advices regarding the Armistice, telephone lines were kept constantly open between my headquarters and those of the First and Second Armies. When word came to me at 6 A.M. that hostilities would cease at 11:00 A.M., directions to that effect were immediately sent to our armies. Our troops had been advancing rapidly during the preceding two days and although every effort was made to reach them promptly a few could not be overtaken before the prescribed hour.

Between September 26th and November 11th, twenty-two American and six French divisions, with an approximate fighting strength of 500,000 men, on a front extending from southeast of Verdun to the Argonne Forest, had engaged and decisively beaten forty-three different German divisions, with an estimated fighting strength of 470,000. Of the twenty-two American divisions, four had at different times during this period been in action on fronts other than our own.

The enemy suffered an estimated loss of over 100,000 casualties in this battle and the First Army about 117,000. The total strength of the First Army, including 135,000 French troops, reached 1,031,000 men. It captured 26,000 prisoners, 874 cannon, 3,000 machine guns and large quantities of material.

The transportation and supply of divisions to and from our front during this battle was a gigantic task. There were twenty-six American and seven French divisions, besides hundreds of thousands of corps and army troops, moved in and out of the American zone. A total of 173,000 men were evacuated to the rear and more than 100,000 replacements were received.

It need hardly be restated that our entry into the war gave the Allies the preponderance of force vitally necessary to outweigh the tremendous increase in the strength of the Germans on the Western Front, due to the collapse of Russia and the consequent release of German divisions employed against her. From the military point of view, we began to aid the Allies early in 1918, when our divisions with insufficient training to take an active part in battle were sent to the inactive front to relieve French divisions, in order that they might be used where needed in the fighting line.

The assistance we gave the Allies in combat began in May with the successful attack of one of our divisions at Cantigny. This was followed early in June by the entrance into battle of the two divisions that stopped the German advance on Paris near Château-Thierry, and by three others that were put in the defensive line. In July two American divisions, with one Moroccan division, formed the spearhead of the counterattack against the Château-Thierry salient, in which nine of our divisions participated. There was a total of approximately 300,000 American troops engaged in this Second Battle of the Marne, which involved very severe fighting, and was not completed until the Germans were driven beyond the Vesle in August. In the middle of September an army of 550,000 Americans reduced the St. Mihiel salient. The latter part of September our great battle of the Meuse-Argonne was begun, lasting through forty-seven days of intense fighting and ending brilliantly for our First and Second Armies on November 11th, after more than 1,200,000 American soldiers had participated.

It was a time to forget the hardships and the difficulties, except to record them with the glorious history of our achievements. In praise and thanks for the decisive victories of our armies and in guidance for the future, the following order was issued:

"G. H. Q.
"American Expeditionary Forces.

"General Orders⎫
   "No. 203. ⎭   "France, Nov. 12, 1918.

"The enemy has capitulated. It is fitting that I address myself in thanks directly to the officers and soldiers of the American Expeditionary Forces who by their heroic efforts have made possible this glorious result. Our armies, hurriedly raised and hastily trained, met a veteran enemy, and by courage, discipline and skill always defeated him. Without complaint you have endured incessant toil, privation and danger. You have seen many of your comrades make the supreme sacrifice that freedom may live. I thank you for the patience and courage with which you have endured. I congratulate you upon the splendid fruits of victory which your heroism and the blood of our gallant dead are now presenting to our nation. Your deeds will live forever on the most glorious pages of America's history.

"These things you have done. There remains now a harder task which will test your soldierly qualities to the utmost. Succeed in this and little note will be taken and few praises will be sung; fail, and the light of your glorious achievements of the past will sadly be dimmed. But you will not fail. Every natural tendency may urge towards relaxation in discipline, in conduct, in appearance, in everything that marks the soldier. Yet you will remember that each officer and each soldier is the representative in Europe of his people and that his brilliant deeds of yesterday permit no action of to-day to pass unnoticed by friend or by foe. You will meet this test as gallantly as you have met the tests of the battlefield. Sustained by your high ideals and inspired by the heroic part you have played, you will carry back to our people the proud consciousness of a new Americanism born of sacrifice. Whether you stand on hostile territory or on the friendly soil of France, you will so bear yourself in discipline, appearance and respect for all civil rights that you will confirm for all time the pride and love which every American feels for your uniform and for you.

                                           "JOHN J. PERSHING,
"Official: "General, Commander-in-Chief.
  "ROBERT C. DAVIS,
    "Adjutant General."

The experience of the World War only confirmed the lessons of the past. The divisions with little training, while aggressive and courageous, were lacking in the ready skill of habit. They were capable of powerful blows, but their blows were apt to be awkward—teamwork was often not well understood. Flexible and resourceful divisions cannot be created by a few maneuvers or by a few months' association of their elements. On the other hand, without the keen intelligence, the endurance, the willingness, and the enthusiasm displayed in the training areas and on the battlefields, the decisive results obtained would have been impossible.

1933 AWARD

ABOUT THE SECTIONS
IN AMERICAN HISTORY

BY

FREDERICK J. TURNER

Frederick Jackson Turner (born on November 14, 1861, in Portage, Wis.) was graduated from the University of Wisconsin in 1884. After having taken his Master's degree in 1888, he gave up his original ideas of journalism and elocution and determined to start a career as professor of history. At the University of Wisconsin he became assistant professor of history in 1889. The following year, he earned his doctorate at Johns Hopkins. Still one year later, he was promoted to professor and in 1892 he received a professorship of American history. Furthermore, Turner took part in a deliberate attempt to erect a distinguished school of social studies at the University of Wisconsin. Until 1910 he declined all calls to other institutions, but then accepted a professorship at Harvard. He served as president to the inner council of the American Historical Association from 1909 to 1910 and during the period of 1910 to 1915, he was a member of the board of editors of the *American Historical Review*. After his retirement in 1924, the Huntington Library in Pasadena, Cal., welcomed him as research associate. Turner wrote only little. *Rise of the New West* and *Frontier in American History* count among his publications. Frederick J. Turner died on March 14, 1932. The same year *The Significance of Sections in American History* was published, a book for which the Pulitzer Prize for history was posthumously awarded to Turner in 1933.

STATE-MAKING IN THE REVOLUTIONARY ERA

[Source: Frederick Jackson Turner: The Significance of Sections in American History, New York: Henry Holt and Company, 1932, pp. 86 - 90; reprinted by permission of Harcourt Brace and Company, Orlando, Fla.]

The term "West" in American history is not limited to a single area. At first the Atlantic Coast was the West — the West of Europe; then the lands between tidewater and the Alleghenies became the West. In the second half of the eighteenth century the territory between these mountains and the Mississippi was occupied, and became the West of the Revolutionary era. In consequence of this steady march of the West across the continent, the term represents not only different areas; it stands also for a stage in American development. Whatever region was most recently reclaimed from the wilderness, was most characteristically Western. In other words, the distinctive thing about the West is its relation to free lands; and it is the influence of her free lands that has determined the larger lines of American development.

The country exhibits three phases of growth. First came the period of the application of European men, institutions, and ideas to the tidewater area of America. In this period of colonization, English traits and institutions preponderated, though modified by the new American conditions. But the constant touch of this part of the country with the Old World prevented the modifying influences of the new environment from having their full effect, and the coast area seemed likely to produce institutions and men that were but modified shoots from the parent tree. Even the physical features of the colonial Americans are described by travelers in colonial days as English: the ruddy complexions, without delicacy of features or play of expression; the lack of nervous energy. The second phase of our growth begins with the spread of this colonial society towards the mountains; the crossing of the Alleghenies, and the settlement upon the Western Waters. Here the wilderness had opportunity to modify men already partly dispossessed of their Old World traits. In adjustment of themselves to completely new conditions, the settlers underwent a process of Americanization, and as each new advance occurred, the process was repeated with modifications. In this reaction between the West and the East, American society took on its peculiar features. We are now in the third phase of our development: the free lands are gone, and with conditions comparable to those of Europe, we have to reshape the ideals and institutions fashioned in the age of wilderness-winning to the new conditions of an occupied country.

Not only is our own development best understood in connection with the occupation of the West; it is the fact of unoccupied territory in America that sets the evolution of American and European institutions in contrast. In the Old World, such institutions were gradually evolved in relation to successive stages of social development, or they were the outcome of a struggle for existence by the older forms against the newer creations of the statesman, or against the institutions of rival peoples. There was in the Old World no virgin soil on which political gardeners might experiment with new varieties. This, America furnished at each successive area of Western advance. Men who had lived under developed institutions were transplanted into the wilderness, with the opportunity and the necessity of adapting their old institutions to their new environment, or of creating new ones capable of meeting the changed conditions.

It is this that makes the study of Western statemaking in the Revolutionary period of peculiar interest. In the colonial era the task of forming governments *in vacuis locis* fell to Europeans; in the Revolution the task was undertaken by Americans on a new frontier. The question at once arises, How would they go about this, and on what principles? Would they strike boldly out regardless of inherited institutions? Would the work be done by the general government; by the separate states that claimed the jurisdiction of these unoccupied lands; or by the settlers themselves? To collect the principal instances of attempts at the formation of states in the West in this era, and briefly to consider the relations of the movement as a whole, is the purpose of this paper. An attempt will be made to interpret the movement from the point of view of the backwoodsmen.

Three types of colonial government are usually mentioned as having flourished on the Atlantic Coast: the charter colonies, outgrowths of the trading-company organization; the proprietary, modelled on the English palatinate; and the provincial colonies, which, having been established under one of the forms just mentioned, were taken under the government of the crown, and obliged to seek the constitutional law of their organization in the instructions and commissions given to the royal governor. In all these types the transformations due to the American conditions were profound. Colonial political growth was not achieved by imitating English forms, but by reshaping English institutions, bit by bit, as occasion required, to American needs. The product had many of the features of an original creation. But in one type of colonial organisations, which has usually been left out of the classification, the influence of the wilderness conditions was especially plain. The Plymouth compact is the earliest and best-known example of the organization of a colony by a social compact, but it is by no means exceptional. In Rhode Island, Connecticut, New Haven, New Hampshire, and elsewhere, the Puritan settlers, finding themselves without legal rights on vacant lands, signed compacts of government, or plantation covenants, suggested no doubt by their church governments, agreeing to submit to the common will. We shall have to recur to this important type of organization later on in our study.

When the tidewater colonial organization had been perfected and lands taken up, population flowed into the region beyond the "fall line," and here again vacant lands continued to influence the form of American institutions. They brought about expansion, which, in itself, meant a transformation of old institutions; they broke down social distinctions in the West, and by causing economic equality, they promoted political equality and democracy. Offering the freedom of the unexploited wilderness, they promoted individualism. One of the most important results of the rush of population into these vacant lands, in the first half of the eighteenth century, was the settlement of non-English stocks in the West. All along the frontier the Palatine Germans (Pennsylvania Dutch) and the Scotch-Irish Presbyterians ascended the rivers that flowed into the Atlantic, and followed the southward trend of the valleys between the Blue Ridge and the Alleghenies. These pioneers were of different type from the planters of the South, or the merchants and seamen of the New England coast. The Scotch-Irish element was ascendent, and this contentious, self-reliant, hardy, backwoods stock, with its rude and vigorous forest life, gave the tone to Western thought in the Revolutionary era.

1934 AWARD

ABOUT THE PRESIDENTS
AFTER GEORGE WASHINGTON

BY

HERBERT S. AGAR

Herbert Sebastian Agar (born on September 29, 1897, in New Rochelle, N.Y.) was graduated from Columbia University in 1919 and earned his Master's degree at Princeton University one year later. There, he received also his doctorate in 1922. From 1929 to 1934 he worked as London correspondent for the *Louisville Courier-Journal* and *Louisville Times*. Furthermore, Agar assumed the position of a literary editor for *The English Review* in London, England, during the period from 1930 to 1934. In New York, he was member of the National Arts Club and the Century Club, whereas in Washington, Agar joined the National Press Club. Throughout his career he was a very prolific author: Together with his second wife Eleanor Carroll Chilton and Willis Fisher he wrote *Fire and Sleet and Candlelight*. Eleanor Carroll Chilton was also his co-writer on *The Garment of Praise*. Other works of his are *Milton and Plato; Bread and Circuses* and *The Defeat of Baudelaire*, which is a translation. In 1933 Herbert S. Agar published *The People's Choice*, which earned the Pulitzer Prize on history the year after.

FROM WOODROW WILSON TO WARREN HARDING

[Source: Herbert Agar: The People's Choice. From Washington to Harding, a Study in Democracy, Boston - New York: Houghton Mifflin Company/The Riverside Press, 1933, pp. 268a, 305 - 309; reprinted by permission of Houghton Mifflin Company, New York, N.Y.]

Wilson, from his sick-bed looked forward to the election of 1920, when the people would have a chance to come to his support. His policies were sure to be the issue, and his old faith in the divine inspiration of the electorate was undimmed. He may have been a little daunted when his party nominated a hack politician from Ohio; nevertheless, the important point was that here was a plebiscite on the question of the League of Nations and the new reign of righteousness. Fortunately, the Republicans — as if to keep the issue clear — had nominated another hack politician from Ohio, a man who was nobody's superior. The people would declare for or against the Wilson policies. For the stricken Jeffersonian democrat in the White House not only a life's work but a life's faith was at stake. The people elected Warren Harding.

After his retirement, in March, 1921, Wilson lived quietly in Washington. He was a very sick man. On Armistice Day, 1923, he made a brief speech from the balcony of his house. This was his last public appearance. He died the following February.

Wilson had outlived President Harding, who succeeded him. He had lived long enough to see the country relapse into conditions as disgraceful as those of the seventies, and to see that the relapse was unlamented. It is not known whether this affected his views of democracy, or his faith in progress, whether, at the end, he would have subscribed to his statement made in the brave days before he first held public office: 'All through the centuries there has been this slow, painful struggle forward, forward, up, up, a little at a time, along the entire incline, the interminable way.'

Warren Gamaliel Harding was born in Ohio in 1865. His father was a farmer, and later became a physician. Harding attended the local school and the Ohio Central College — which was an ad-

WOODROW WILSON   WARREN GAMALIEL HARDING

vanced secondary school, not an institute of higher learning. After trying, and abandoning, the study of law, Harding got a job on one of the weekly newspapers in Marion, a town of about four thousand inhabitants. A little later he and a friend bought a moribund weekly paper for three hundred dollars, and within a few years Harding had made this a paying venture.

In 1891, Harding married Mrs. Florence Kling De Wolfe, a widow. Her father was a banker, and apparently a man of some discernment, for he opposed the match. Harding, by this time, was a strikingly handsome man — tall and strong-looking, good-natured, affectionate, and weak. He had a reputation for dissipation, but that is probably too strong a word to use for his activities. Shortly after his marriage, Harding transformed the *Star* from a weekly into a daily paper. It continued to prosper, and Harding became a man of some importance in the little town, and also in the local Republican Party. He was soon a director of the Marion County Bank, a trustee of the Baptist Church, a Mason, and an Elk.

In addition to his good looks, Harding had a strong, effective voice. As a result of these physical assets, and of the political position that his editorship gained him, he began to take part in local campaigns. At the close of the century, he was sent to the State Senate, and at about the same time he met Harry Daugherty — the man who was to make him President and then to ruin him. In 1902, Harding was elected Lieutenant-Governor of Ohio. In 1910, he was the Republican candidate for Governor, but was defeated. In 1914, with the help of Daugherty and his political 'gang,' he was elected to the United States Senate.

In the Senate, Harding was 'regular' and safe. He never said or did anything that attracted attention, but he was a friend of Big Business and a partisan anti-Wilson man. Also, he was a good friend of the Anti-Saloon League, supporting the Eighteenth Amendment (which was passed on the wave of moral uplift that accompanied the War) and the Volstead Act, and making useful suggestions for overcoming opposition to these measures. Aside from his official record, Harding was soon known to be an enthusiastic drinker and gambler, and a man of genuine good-nature who made friends quickly among the unexacting. What was not so well known was that in 1917 a woman named Nan Britton became his mistress, and that in 1919 Harding and Nan Britton had a daughter. This, however, is probably the reason why he was elected President a year later.

It was in 1919 that Harry Daugherty, political organizer, spoilsman, and head of the 'Ohio Gang,' began to push Harding for the Presidency. He had no popular support in the primaries, not even winning the entire delegation from his own State. Yet Daugherty insolently predicted that after a long deadlock in the Nominating Convention, at two o'clock some morning, a little group of the real Republican leaders would meet in a smoke-filled hotel room and would decide to make Harding the party's nominee. And this is exactly what happened. In the early ballots at the Convention, Harding was nowhere; but after a long struggle there was an early morning meeting in the hotel room of Colonel

George Harvey, and it was decided to give Harding the nomination. His qualifications were that he was good-looking, that he sounded significant, that he meant nothing, and that he came from Ohio. The last point was important. Grant, Hayes, Garfield, Harrison, McKinley, Taft — most of the Republican Presidents had come from Ohio. It is not, unhappily, that only Ohio can produce the typical President; it is simply that Ohio, since the Civil War, has been a crucial State. Farther east, the Republicans felt safe; farther south, the Democrats were invincible; the West voted chiefly on the price of wheat, which could not easily be changed for the sake of the election; but Ohio was fairly evenly divided between the two parties, so the Republicans usually chose a man who had shown that he could carry that State.

Before committing themselves to Harding, Harvey and his fellow-oligarchs showed their knowledge of Washington gossip by calling their prospective candidate before them and asking if there were any reason in his past life why he should not be nominated. Rightly considering that Nan Britton and her daughter belonged to his present rather than his past life, Harding answered no. He was nominated the same day. Harvey's comment was, 'He was nominated because there was nothing against him, and because the delegates wanted to go home.' In judging that there was nothing against Harding, Colonel Harvey showed the same acumen that had led him to pick Wilson as an easy man to use.

The League of Nations was the ostensible campaign issue. In fact, the League was a symbol for the high purpose, the whole atmosphere of effort and uplift, for which the Progressives had stood, and of which the nation was tired. The return to national isolation, which the repudiation of the League involved, was felt to mean a return to the old days of slackness and *laissez-faire* which had preceded Roosevelt. Senator Brandegee remarked that the time did not require 'first-raters.' Harding, with his one creative effort in the realm of the spirit, coined the word 'normalcy' to express the general desire. 'Back to normalcy' was the phrase that summed up the American temper. Harding was elected by a huge majority.

The new Cabinet contained some respected men, like Hughes, Mr. Hoover, and Mr. Mellon, and some cheap politicians like Daugherty and Fall. Below the Cabinet officers there were evil, disquieting figures, such as Charles R. Forbes, the head of the Veterans' Bureau, and Colonel Miller, the Alien Property Custodian. And below them there was a worse group still: hangers-on and go-betweens of whom the public as yet knew nothing. Within a month of Harding's inauguration, the whole atmosphere of Washington had changed. Both officially and socially, the tone became relaxed, care-free, abandoned.

The chief Administration policies were dictated by the Senatorial clique and by the three leading men in the Cabinet. The adoption of a National Budget — a reform which had been brought almost to completion under Wilson — and the Washington Conference are the achievements of which the Administration could be most proud. Meanwhile, behind the scenes, there was taking place a series of steals more wild, quick, brazen, and bizarre than anything that had yet happened in America. Harding, being a man without courage or character, was powerless. The 'Ohio Gang' owned him. With Daugherty as Attorney-General and Fall as Secretary of the Interior, and with Nan Britton and the baby to use in blackmailing Harding if, having learned too much of what was going on, he tried to interfere, they seemed safe. It is a sign of the grade of character these men possessed that they soon overplayed their hands so grossly that suicide, murder, or jail was the end of many of them.

1935 AWARD

ABOUT THE COLONIAL PERIOD OF NORTH AMERICA

BY

CHARLES M. ANDREWS

Charles McLean Andrews (born on February 22, 1863, in Wethersfield, Conn.) attended Trinity College in Hartford, Conn., and earned his Master of Arts degree there in 1890. Already one year earlier, he had received his doctorate of philosophy at Johns Hopkins University. Until 1907 he assumed first the position of associate professor of history, later that of professor of history at Bryn Mawr College in Pennsylvania. Then, he received a professorship at Johns Hopkins. During the years of 1910 to 1931 Andrews held the Farnam professorship of American history at Yale University. There, he was also responsible of the Yale Historical Publications. In October 1911 he delivered lectures at the University of Helsingfors, Finland. He was also invited by other institutions of higher education, among them the universities of Wisconsin, Iowa, Michigan and Chicago. Andrews retired in 1933. The list of his works is extensive, the following are among others part of it: *The River Towns of Connecticut; Contemporary Europe, Asia and Africa, 1871-1901; A Bibliography of History*, a project in which J. Montgomery Gambrill and Lida Lee Tall were his co-authors; *A Short History of England; The Colonial Period of American History; Journal of a Lady of Quality*, which he edited together with his wife Evangeline, and *The Colonial Background of the American Revolution*. In 1935 Charles McLean Andrews won the Pulitzer Prize in the category History for the first tome of his multi-volume work *The Colonial Period of American History*, which had been published one year earlier.

SOME ASPECTS OF EARLY MASSACHUSETTS LIFE

[Source: Charles McLean Andrews: The Colonial Period of American History, Vol. 1, New Haven - London: Yale University Press, 1934, pp. 506 - 509; reprinted by permission of Yale University Press, London, GB.]

The Puritan was not devoid of the spirit of inquiry and there were those both in Massachusetts and Connecticut who were anxious to know—in a semi or pseudo-scientific way—something of the phenomena of nature and to discover the causes of the woes of the flesh. Before the founding of the Royal Society, which marks a new era in the history of scientific inquiry, the older generations of Puritans were largely inhibited in their quest by their belief in God's responsibility for all that went right or wrong in human affairs. They had profound faith in the intervening hand of God, who blessed his people and brought them prosperity when they obeyed his will, or who showed his displeasure and wrath when they neglected their duty. Their God was the God of the Old Testament rather than of the New and he it was that kept watch upon scores of the incidental happenings of the Puritan's daily life. Accidents, failures, and deaths were traced not only to his disapproval of man's conduct on earth, but also to the successes of the devil, which were ascribed to God's own allowance, as a retribution for the sins of his people. It was practically impossible for anyone to pursue a strictly objective investigation into the operations of nature and the phenomena of the world about him or to concern himself seriously with the prevention of disease or the curing of the sick or injured, as long as he admitted the influence of such an uncertain factor as God's miraculous providence into his calculations. Winthrop tells the story of a child's injury—a piece of the skull being driven into the brain—and adds that the advice of one of the ruling elders, a layman and "an experienced and very skilful surgeon," prevailed over the opinion of seven other surgeons (some of the country and others of the ships that lay in the harbor), and the child was left to the mercies of God and prayers of the church for a recovery which, strange as it may seem, actually took place. Many other stories of the same sort could be related.

At the same time the general court could recommend to the authorities of Harvard College that such students as studied "physick or chirurgery" should have "liberty to reade anotomy and to anotomize once in four years some malefactor, in case there shall be such as the Courts allow of," and it sought to prevent epidemics by means of a quarantine at Castle Island in the harbor. In 1649 it ordered that no physician, surgeon, midwife, or others should presume to "put forth any act contrary to the knowne rules of art," in the way of using force, violence, or cruelty. Such a rule was particularly needed in the days before anesthesia was known and in cases of obstetrics, which were entirely in the hands of women, and had a prominent place in family experience on account of the early and frequent marriages and the large number of children born.

The credulity even of the intelligent leaders of the commonwealth is at all times conspicuous in the chronicles of the period, which show that belief in prodigies and portents was an everyday matter. Winthrop had no doubt that a calf was born at Ipswich with one head, three mouths, three noses, and six eyes. Mary Dyer gave birth to a woman child, so monstrous and misshapen as the like had never been seen, and even Mrs. Hutchinson was widely reported to have done the same, an event which signified to Cotton "her error in denying inherent righteousness." The Rev. John Wilson had no difficulty in interpreting a combat between a mouse and a snake as an allegory in which the snake was Satan and the mouse "a poor contemptible people, which God had brought hither." As the victory lay with the mouse so would God's people overcome the devil and dispossess him of his kingdom. Such analogies, allegories, and expositions had long been the stock in trade of the Puritans, whether in old or New England, and their presence in the Puritan writings does much to elucidate Puritan character and history. Once believe that the earth is the scene of an actual warfare between a personally present Christ on one side and a Satan equally present on the other, in a never ending conflict for the possession of the human soul; once become convinced that the Lord always intervenes to save his saints and to frustrate the designs of their enemies; once accept without questioning the view that the Puritan elect were the Lord's agents to carry out his purpose and to found a community and church in the place that he had chosen, and Puritan conduct becomes explicable. Under such conditions questions of toleration, liberty of thought and action, and even standards of human conduct become matters of secondary consideration, because the hand of God was everywhere and in everything.

The natural world was viewed with the eyes and understanding of a child, which is appalled at the mysteries and phenomena of the world about him. As Eggleston expresses it, "The sun, moon, and planets were flames of fire without gravity, revolved about the earth by countless angels; its God governed this our little world with mock majesty; its heaven, its horrible hell of material fire blown by the mouth of God; its chained demons, whose fetters might be loosed; its damnation of infants" were all characteristic of the medieval mind. Eclipses, parhelia, and comets were danger signals hung out in the heavens as warnings, the phases of the moon were factors to be reckoned with in performing the round of daily and weekly duties, and the signs of the zodiac were a regulating influence controlling man's future and the future of his children. The phenomena of nature were to the Puritan a never ending subject of speculation: comets were meteors sent by God to awaken a morally lethargic world and earthquakes were great and terrible expressions of God's wrath. That anything could happen in the physical universe uncontrolled by God was incomprehensible to the Puritan mind.

1936 AWARD

ABOUT THE CONSTITUTIONAL HISTORY OF THE UNITED STATES

BY

ANDREW C. MCLAUGHLIN

Andrew Cunningham McLaughlin (born on February 14, 1861, in Beardstown, Ill.) attended the University of Michigan and was graduated in 1885. Still within the same institution, he worked as instructor of Latin during the following two years. From 1887 to 1888 he taught history and then, was promoted to assistant professor. McLaughlin became professor of American history in 1891. Since 1898 he was associate editor of the *American Historical Review*, a position he assumed until 1914. The father of six children was also director of the Bureau of Historical Research at the Carnegie Institution in Washington from 1903 to 1905. From 1906 on, he taught at the University of Chicago, where he became head of the history department the same year. Six years later, he was awarded a honorary doctorate by the University of Michigan. McLaughlin went into retirement in 1927. Among his book publications count the following: *Lewis Cass; History of Higher Education in Michigan; Civil Government in Michigan; The Confederation and the Constitution; America and Britain; Steps in the Development of American Democracy; Foundations of American Institutionalism.* In 1935 Andrew C. McLaughlin published *A Constitutional History of the United States*, a work which earned him the Pulitzer Prize for history the year after.

THE FINAL ADOPTION OF THE U.S. CONSTITUTION

[Source: Andrew C. McLaughlin: A Constitutional History of the United States, New York - London: D. Appleton-Century Company, Inc., 1935, pp. 198 - 201; reprinted by permission of Irvington Publishers, New York N.Y.]

Congress received the Constitution with no unseemly expression of pleasure; indeed, as Bancroft says, it had been in reality invited "to light its own funeral pyre." No body can be expected to decree gladly its own demise; but there seems to have been no special desire on the part of the moribund Congress to prolong its own futile life. On the twenty-eighth of September, 1787, a resolution without words of commendation was unanimously adopted transmitting the Constitution to the several legislatures to be submitted by them to the state conventions.

The reception of the Constitution by the people at first appeared favorable. Gouverneur Morris wrote a characteristic letter to Washington: "The states eastward of New York appear to be almost unanimous in favor of the new Constitution, (for I make no account of the dissension in Rhode Island). . . . Jersey is so near unanimity in her favorable opinion, that we may count with certainty on something more than votes, should the state of affairs hereafter require the application of pointed arguments." He thought parties in New York were nearly balanced, but as the state was "hemmed in between the warm friends of the Constitution" there was ground for hoping that the "federal party" would prove successful. Of Pennsylvania he had fuller knowledge and entertained doubts. "True it is, that the city and its neighborhood are enthusiastic in the cause; but I dread the cold and sour temper of the back counties, and still more the wicked industry of those who have long habituated themselves to live on the public, and cannot bear the idea of being removed from the power and profit of state government. . . ."

Randolph reported favorable reception of the Constitution in Baltimore and Virginia, while Madison gathered a like impression concerning New York City and most of the eastern states. But the ratification had dangerous foes to meet, and as the days went by the contest became more serious. It will be remembered that Yates and Lansing, of New York, had left the Convention at an early day; and in a letter to Governor Clinton they forcibly expressed their objections to the proposed system of government, for they believed any general government, however guarded by declarations of rights, would be "productive of the destruction of . . . civil liberty. . . ." Clinton and his immediate retinue were particularly hostile and sought by correspondence with leaders of the opposition in some of the other states to create a coöperative resistance. Luther Martin of Maryland, who had declaimed vehemently against the new system, went home to attack it. Gerry played a similar rôle in Massachusetts; he declared in a letter to the legislature that the "liberties of America were not secured by the system. . . ." He believed that in many respects the Constitution had merits and by proper amendments might be "adapted to the 'exigencies of government, and preservation of liberty' "; the document as proposed had "few, if any, federal features," but was "rather a system of national government." George Mason proved a valiant opponent of the new system to which he had himself contributed. Randolph, who had labored earnestly in the Convention itself but had refused to sign, wrote the speaker of the Virginia house, not condemning the Constitution but suggesting its failings, the need of amendments, and the propriety of making changes "while we have the Constitution in our power. . . ." Fortunately, however, perhaps under the persuasion of Washington, he decided to favor adoption and worked to that end in the Virginia convention. It was soon evident that there would be strong opposition in three very important states, Massachusetts, New York, and Virginia, and without them a union would be useless and impracticable. A letter of Richard Henry Lee, written as early as October 16, expressed the opinion of one who was prepared to battle with unstinted persistence against ratification; a new convention ought to be summoned: "It cannot be denied, with truth, that this new Constitution is, in its first principles, highly and dangerously oligarchic. . . ."

In the course of the public discussion few portions of the Constitution escaped scathing criticism. Dangers were found lurking in one clause after another and they were gleefully brought to light to confound the friends of the new order. To meet such opposition naturally proved a difficult matter; for it appeared not infrequently that every power granted was certain to be abused and to involve the destruction of American liberties. The dread of granting power filled many minds with foreboding; this dread was the most formidable obstacle to be overcome. The new government seemed something extraneous and distinct, as if it were not to be in the hands of the same people as those choosing the state governments and not to be subject to popular control. The patience, wisdom, and skill with which objections were met call forth deep admiration as one reads to-day the pamphlets and debates of those trying years. Hamilton and Madison deserve the greatest credit, probably, for masterly management and skillful argument. But it is safe to say that the character of George Washington secured the adoption of the Constitution; there was one man known to be strongly in favor of the new system in whom the masses of men had faith. Some persons feared the presidential authority under the new government; as Patrick Henry said, "Your President may easily become King." Many foolish and extravagant attacks appeared in the newspapers. The delegates in the conventions appreciated the magnitude and solemnity of their task; and if the criticisms of the Constitution appear now to be the offspring of unnecessary fear of tyranny, the earnestness and the general intelligence of the discussion furnish marked evidence of political capacity. No mere analysis of the arguments can present the impression gathered by any thoughtful reader from the discussion, an impression of shrewdness and sagacity and common sense.

In some of the central states, conventions soon gathered and acted promptly. Before the first of the year, the Constitution was ratified by Delaware, New Jersey, and Pennsylvania, the two former unanimously giving a favorable vote. In Pennsylvania, though the final vote was two to one for acceptance, the debates lasted three weeks and were marked by the persistence of a determined opposition sufficient to call for the full strength of Wilson and McKean in advocacy of the new government.

1937 AWARD

ABOUT THE FLOWERING
OF THE NEW ENGLAND REGION

BY

VAN W. BROOKS

Van Wyck Brooks (born on February 16, 1886, in Plainfield, N.J.) entered Harvard University in 1904, where he became one of the editors of the *Harvard Advocate*. Although a member of the class of 1908, he took his Bachelor's degree one year earlier and went soon afterwards to London, England. There he was mainly employed as a journalist. He returned to the United States in 1909 and started working on the *Standard Dictionary* and *Collier's Encyclopedia*. In 1911 Brooks moved to California and taught English for the next two years at Leland Stanford University. In 1913 he revisited England, where he taught a class for the Workers' Educational Association at South Norwood. A few months after the outbreak of the First World War, Brooks went back to New York, entered the Century Company and began to translate French literature. He was also associate editor of *The Seven Arts* during the year of its existence 1917/18, and in 1920 he accepted the position of a literary editor of *The Freeman* for a four-year period. During the 1920's he became an influential critic. Due to mental illness he was unable to do much work from 1926 to 1931, but then resumed his work as a writer. The following titles number among his publications: The biography *John Addington Symonds; Ordeal of Mark Twain; Days of the Phoenix* and *Life of Emerson*. In 1936 Van Wyck Brooks started working on his five-volume study on American writers entitled *The Flowering of New England, 1815-1865*, of which the first volume won the Pulitzer Prize for history one year later.

EVENTS IN THE HISTORY OF HARVARD COLLEGE

[Source: Van Wyck Brooks: The Flowering of New England, 1815-1865, New York: E. P. Dutton & Co., Inc., 1936, pp. 33 - 37; reprinted by permission of New American Library, a division of Penguin Books USA, Inc., New York, N.Y.]

Harvard College was the heart of Cambridge. Seven generations before, every New England household had given the college twelvepence, or a peck of corn, or its value in unadulterated wampum peag. But those were the good old days when the Orthodox faith reigned in every mind. Established now on a Unitarian basis, — for the founding of the Divinity School, with Dr. Henry Ware as its chief professor, settled the character of the new regime, — the college was considered, in the country districts, dangerously lax and liberal. West of Worcester, and up the Connecticut Valley, the clergy, Calvinist almost to a man, united in condemning the Cambridge collegians, in the very words of Whitefield, as "close Pharisees, resting on head knowledge," — the same collegians who had called Whitefield "low." But as for this "head knowledge," no one denied that they possessed it. More than a few of the Orthodox admitted that it was what collegians ought to possess. Harvard still had an exalted prestige. The patrician families of Boston and Cambridge regarded it as more than a family affair. It was a family responsibility. They sent their sons to the college, as a matter of course. But they considered it a public duty, not only to endow and foster it, in the interests of the meritorious poor, but to maintain its standards and oversee it. They founded chairs that bore their names, the Boylston chair, the Eliot chair, the Smith professorship. They watched and brooded over its progress and welfare. Who would have respected wealth in Boston if wealth had not, in turn, respected learning? And, if the professors' salaries were very small, everyone knew they were partly paid in honour.

It was true that the standard of learning was not too lofty. In this, as in certain other respects, the well-known "Harvard indifference" resembled that of Oxford and Madrid. Intellectual things took second place. The object of study was to form the mind, but this was to form the character; and Massachusetts knew what its character was and took a certain satisfaction in it. Everyone was aware of the best Boston and Cambridge type, the type that Josiah Quincy represented, or the late Chief Justice Dana, formed on the classic models. A clear, distinct mentality, a strong distaste for nonsense, steady composure, a calm and gentle demeanour, stability, good principles, intelligence, a habit of under-statement, a slow and cautious way of reasoning, contempt for extravagance, vanity and affectation, kindness of heart, purity, decorum, profound affections, filial and paternal. A noble type, severely limited, which Boston celebrated in its marble busts. Comparing it, trait for trait, with half of Plutarch's characters, one might have felt that Boston deserved its busts. Moreover, beneath its cold and tranquil surface, burned, though the fires were low, the passions and convictions of the Revolution, ready to flame forth on a fresh occasion. But would the occasion ever recur? That was what a stranger might have asked, face to face with the marble busts. The surface, at least, seemed somewhat tame, suited for the merchant and the lawyer, and the man of God after the Boston fashion.

This was the type, and almost the only type, the curriculum of Harvard contemplated. Whatever studies favoured its formation, whatever were the best ways to form it, these were the ways and the studies that Harvard knew. Whatever studies did not favour it, or favoured the formation of other types that Boston did not like or had never heard of, these were no concern of Harvard, or its concern only to oppose them. Josiah Quincy was not enthusiastic. Why should Harvard be? Mr. Dana was eminently decorous. He had caused the arrest, for contempt of court, of a butcher who, appearing at the bar, had left his coat behind him. Decorum was a Harvard characteristic. Neither Mr. Quincy nor Mr. Dana cared a button for the German language, which had been spoken by the Hessian troops, a half-barbarous tribe of Europeans who had been hired out to the British king. German, from the point of view of Harvard, always excepting John Quincy Adams, who, as everyone knew, was a little queer, — German was an outlandish dialect; and, while it was not improper to speak French, the language of Lafayette, which it was quite improper not to know, more than a few felt that Bonaparte had destroyed its respectability. Greek was esteemed as the tongue of a group of ancient republics that possessed some of the virtues of New England. Greece had produced a number of orators who were more eloquent even than Samuel Adams. Search as one might, however, in Massachusetts, one could not find a play of Euripides; besides, compared with Latin, which everyone drank in with his mother's milk, Greek was a little dubious. The Roman word "convivium" meant "living together." "Symposium" had a similar sense in Greek, but what did "symposium" imply? "Drinking together." Was not this alone enough to prove that the Romans were more respectable than the Greeks? Cicero had made the point, and everyone knew that Cicero must be right.

These were the days of the genial President Kirkland, who, after conducting an examination, regaled the boys with a fine dish of pears. He was an easy-going man, a Unitarian minister, like most of the professors, sympathetic and of the gentlest temper, naturally frank and cordial, with all the delicate feeling for human behaviour that characterized the best New Englanders. It was said that he threw his sermons into a barrel, as the farmers threw their corn into the silo, and that on Sunday morning he fished out enough for a discourse and patched the leaves together. The story had a symbolic truth, at least. It signified the president's "Harvard indifference," which was accompanied by the best intentions and a notably warm heart. He never took the narrow view. Hearing that the flip at the Porter House had proved to be too attractive to the students, he dropped in to see the proprietor. "And so, Mr. Porter," he said, "the young gentlemen come to drink your flip, do they?" — "Yes, sir," said Mr. Porter, "sometimes." — "Well, I should think they would," the president said. "Good day, Mr. Porter." Any sort of illumination, physical or spiritual, might have taken place under his eye. He was kind to the rich young men whose fathers, at their graduation, gave them dinners in a great marquee, with five hundred guests and dancing in the Yard. He was kinder to the poor young men whose black coats were turning green. He was not a man to oppose any important change in the system of studies; and before the end of his long reign, in fact, certain changes were to occur that were eventually to transform the college. But he could not see why changes should occur. He thought the old ways were good enough, and he played into the hands of firmer men who thought that all other ways were bad. Four hours a day for study and recitation were quite enough for anyone. A library of twenty thousand books was certainly large enough. In fact, the Harvard library was a wonder. No other American library was larger, except perhaps one.

1938 AWARD

ABOUT THE ROAD
TO AMERICAN REUNION

BY

PAUL H. BUCK

Paul Herman Buck (born on August 25, 1899, in Columbus, Oh.) attended Ohio State University in Columbus for the Bachelor's degree, which was conferred to him in 1921. He received his Master of Arts degree from Ohio State one year later. That same year, his first book was published: *Evolution of the National Parks System.* He undertook further graduate study in history at Harvard University and was granted the Master's degree from Harvard in 1924. Under a Sheldon traveling fellowship he spent a year from 1926 to 1927 studying in France and Great Britain. In 1926 he also joined the staff of Harvard as an instructor in history. Buck earned his doctorate of philosophy in 1935 and was advanced to assistant professor of American history the following year. While teaching at Harvard, Paul H. Buck carried on extensive research at the university library and other libraries in the East and Southeast, which resulted in his study of Reconstruction years in the South, *The Road to Reunion, 1865-1900*, which was published in 1937. The following year, it received a Pulitzer Prize as the best book on history.

THE SITUATION OF BLACKS IN THE SOUTH

[Source: Paul H. Buck: The Road to Reunion, 1865-1900, Boston: Little, Brown and Company, 1937, pp. 283 - 285; reprinted by permission of Little, Brown and Company, Publishers, Boston, Mass.]

No question connected with the South rested more heavily and, it must be said, more wearily upon the American mind during the eighties than the problem of the Negro. For half a century the black man had been a symbol of strife between the sections. The chasm dug by the intemperance of the abolition attack against slavery and the Reconstruction crusade to give equality of status to the freedman had fortunately closed. But a line of demarcation still divided the nation. On one side lived a people faced with the menace of Negro domination, on the other a people committed by their intervention in the past to securing justice for the inferior race. Final reconciliation waited upon an adjustment that would quiet the apprehensions of the South and still the conscience of the North.

Southern whites had fought stolidly and unyieldingly for control over a problem they insisted was domestic in nature. They continued to resist without compromise any suggestion of outside pressure. Their minds were strong in the conviction that orderly society could exist only when the Negro was rigidly disciplined. The people of the North after 1877 were for the most part in substantial agreement that the Negro was not prepared for equality and that the South should be allowed to deal with the problem in its own way, "Henceforth," as one Northern journal observed, "the nation as a nation, will have nothing more to do with him [the Negro]." The South had won its major point. No longer would the black man figure as "a ward of the nation" to be singled out for special guardianship or peculiar treatment.

The discipline the South elaborated in the years following Reconstruction rested frankly upon the premise of the Negro's inferiority. Much was said about the South acting defensively to erect bulwarks against the threat of Negro domination. But actually the South moved aggressively to reduce the Negro's status to something comparable to serfdom. The intention openly averred was to give an inferior people an inferior rôle and to efface them as positive factors in the section's life. To this end the new discipline excluded the colored man from politics by disfranchising him, rendered him economically im- potent by making him a peon, and isolated him socially by an extensive practice of segregation. The net result was to deprive the Negro of more privileges than was necessary to keep him from becoming a menace and to make the South a "white man's country."

The methods of suppressing the Negro vote softened after the whites gained control of the machinery of state and local government, but they continued to be a mixture of fraud, trickery, intimidation and violence. Polling places were set up at points remote from colored communities. Ferries between the black districts and the voting booths went "out of repair" on election day. Grim-visaged white men carrying arms sauntered through the streets or stood near the polling booths. In districts where the blacks greatly outnumbered the whites, election officials permitted members of the superior race to "stuff the ballot box," and manipulated the count without fear of censure. Fantastic gerrymanders were devised to nullify Negro strength. The payment of poll taxes, striking at the Negro's poverty and carelessness in preserving receipts, was made a requirement for voting. Some states confused the ignorant by enacting multiple ballot box laws which required the voter to place cor- rectly his votes for various candidates in eight or more separate boxes. The bolder members of the colored race met threats of violence and, in a diminishing number of instances, physical punishment. When the black man succeeded in passing through this maze of restrictions and cast his vote there was no as- surance that it would be counted. Highly centralized election codes vested arbitrary powers in the election boards, and these powers were used to complete the elimination of the Negro vote.

These practices testified eloquently to the resourcefulness of the Southern whites, but they could not be considered as an adequate or permanent solution. So long as the South persisted by extra-legal and illegal methods to nullify the spirit of the Fifteenth amendment of the Federal constitution and to violate the letter of their own state constitutions framed in the Reconstruction era, there remained a potential danger of a Federal "force bill" or a refusal on the part of Congress to seat a congressman elected from a Southern district where the abuses seemed more than ordinarily flagrant. Furthermore the practices worked to the disadvantage of certain elements of the Southern whites. Fraud could not be used against the Negro without demoralizing the whole structure of politics. Walter Hines Page pointed to instances where a group in power used its control of the election machinery to "count out" white opponents who had polled a majority vote. The illiterate and impoverished white man frequently found himself enmeshed in the restrictions that had been framed to embarrass the Negro. But most serious was the fact that, so long as the constitutional provisions for universal suffrage remained unchanged, division among the whites might result in a recrudescence of Negro voting. When Benjamin F. Tillman led the dirt farmers of South Carolina in a common man's movement against the conservatives who had ruled the state since 1877 he found his opponents voting the Negroes of the Black Belt against him. The rise of Populism in the nineties accentuated the evil. Wherever the whites divided as Democrats and Populists, the rival factions courted the colored vote and some of the turbulence of Reconstruction came back again.

1939 AWARD

ABOUT THE HISTORY
OF AMERICAN PERIODICALS

BY

FRANK L. MOTT

Frank Luther Mott (born on April 4, 1886, in Keokuk County, Ia.) attended Simpson College in Indianola, Ia. from 1903 to 1906 and was graduated from the University of Chicago one year later. After graduation, he started working as a journalist and was first co-editor of the *Marengo Republican* from 1907 to 1914. Then, he joined the staff of the *Grand Junction Globe* as editor. In 1918 he became instructor at the Marquand School for Boys in Brooklyn, N.Y. The following year, he earned his Master of Arts degree at Columbia University and started teaching English as professor at Simpson College. Mott came as an assistant professor for English to the State University of Iowa in 1921, and was promoted to associate professor four years later. Also in 1925 he became joint editor and publisher of *The Midland*. Since 1927 he held a professorship of journalism and that same year became director of the School of Journalism at the State University of Iowa. Mott earned his doctorate of philosophy the following year. In 1930 he became editor in chief of *Journalism Quarterly* and from 1934 to 1938 he assumed the position of chairman of the National Council for Research in Journalism. Moreover, Mott is the author of quite a lot of book publications: e.g. *Six Prophets Out of the Middle West; The Man with the Good Face; The Literature of Pioneer Life in Iowa*. In 1939 Frank L. Mott received the Pulitzer Prize for history for the second volume of *A History of American Magazines* which had appeared the year before.

SKETCH OF THE UNITED STATES MAGAZINE

[Source: Frank Luther Mott: A History of American Magazines, Vol. 2: 1850-1865, Cambridge, Mass.: Harvard University Press, 1938, pp. 448 - 451; reprinted by permission of Harvard University Press, Cambridge, Mass.]

The *United States Magazine*, a dollar monthly, was founded in May 1854 by Alexander Jones, a New York journalist and financial writer. It was a quarto of thirty pages, printed on cheap paper, illustrated by a few woodcuts, and of a "useful, practical, instructive character." Its subtitle dedicated it to science, art, manufactures, agriculture, commerce, and trade; and its contents were even more varied than this catalogue would lead one to expect. "The publication of a single number has placed it on a paying basis," it boasted in June; and in August the company was reorganized to publish three periodicals. These were the *Magazine*; the *United States Journal*, a monthly newspaper selling for twenty-five cents a year; and the *United States Weekly Journal*, a paper which reprinted the matter in the *Magazine* and the monthly *Journal*. The new organization was called J. M. Emerson & Company and included, besides the printer and publisher Emerson, Jones, David Bigelow (elder brother of John Bigelow, managing editor of the *New York Evening Post*) and Franklin Woods, another journalist.

An editor was hired in the person of Seba Smith. Smith's chief claim to fame was the creation of the Yankee comic character, Major Jack Downing, whose shrewd comments on politics and personalities had amused many thousands of readers when copied into other papers from his own *Portland Courier* and his later magazine, the *Rover*. Smith did the editorial work on both the *Magazine* and the *Journal*, using the scissors more or less, writing a great deal himself, and getting some contributions from members of J. M. Emerson & Company and others. Elizabeth Oakes Smith, wife of the editor and well known as a poet, lecturer, and critic, did some articles on New York theaters. There was a well-illustrated series on "Our Manufactories," as well as biography, travel, ornithology, archaeology, and anecdotes. As might be expected of its editor, humor was notable in the magazine. Smith's "Democritus Junior" perpetrated some good satires, especially the one in which the Yankee sailor Solomon Swop, who accompanies Commodore Perry to Japan, lays down the law to the Japanese "rats." Later, in 1857-58, Smith reprinted in the magazine the first series of Downing letters, following them with the later series which had been appearing in the *National Intelligencer*, all under the title (itself a satire on Thomas H. Benton's autobiography) *My Thirty Years Out of the Senate*. There was much of the European war in 1854-55; and there were political articles, carefully nonpartisan, by the editor. Fiction was not prominent. Large woodcuts engraved by William Roberts and J. W. & N. Orr, and drawn by A. R. Waud and others, appeared, printed on colored stock.

In the middle of 1856, after missing a number, the *United States Magazine* changed to octavo size and raised its price to $2.00 a year. Mrs.

United States Magazine.

Vol. IV.]................JANUARY, 1857.................[No. 1.

THE CITY OF WASHINGTON.....No. VI.

THE SMITHSONIAN INSTITUTION.

AMONG the many magnificent public buildings and Governmental establishments in the city of Washington, perhaps none excites greater interest or attracts a larger share of attention from visitors at the national capital than the Smithsonian Institution. And yet this is not stictly a Government establishment, but a splendid monument of individual munificence and noble philanthropy, toward which the Government of the United States stands in the relation of perpetual trustee. The founder, an English gentleman of liberal culture, scientific attainments. and broad philanthropic views, it seems, had a stronger faith in the stability and permanence of the free institutions of our Republic than in the Governments and institutions of the Old World, and, therefore, when he determined to devote his princely fortune to establish an institution "for the increase and diffusion of knowledge among men," he chose the city of Washington as the locality, and appointed the Government of the United States as trustee to carry out his wishes.

The Smithsonian Institution is now firmly established, in successful operation, holding a high rank among the first scientific and intellectual establishments in the world, but differing in some respects from all of them. It is an honorable and imperishable monument to the memory of its founder, an ornament to the country, and a rich bequest to the world. To make our readers better acquainted with the history and objects of this noble Institution. and its successful progress thus far under the auspices of those who have so faithfully labored to carry out the expressed wishes of its founder. is the object of this article.

THE TESTATOR.

James Smithson was a native of England, a

Smith now became a leading contributor of poems, essays, and tales; there was better variety and better illustration; and an effort was made to compete with *Harper's*. The *United States Magazine* underbid Harper's, and for a time its illustration (which included fashions and comics) approached the *Harper* level; but it did not carry the popular English serials.

In October 1857 J. M. Emerson & Company took over *Putnam's Monthly*, a high-class periodical which had been founded the year before the *United States Magazine*, and which was now ready to give up the struggle to get the balance on the right side of the ledger. After the merger, the name was changed to *Emerson's Magazine and Putnam's Monthly*, which now claimed a circulation of 40,000. The editor's Downing letters, older tales and sketches by Mrs. Smith, now reprinted, and some serials translated from the French were among the leading features. Mrs. Smith also did dramatic criticism and wrote a life of Washington to the magazine. A serial description of the city of Washington was well illustrated. Advertising ran to ten or twelve pages.

The four sons of Seba and Elizabeth Oakes Smith joined their parents at the beginning of 1858, and under the name of Oaksmith & Company, bought the magazine from the Emerson group. Appleton Oaksmith, the eldest son, became publisher; and Edward wrote art criticism, while the other two sons, Sidney and Alvin, wrote on various subjects. But the lack of funds to bring writers of the first class into the pages of the magazine made a popular success impossible, and in November 1858 *Emerson's Magazine and Putnam's Monthly* suspended publication.

Smith thought that failure was owing to the fact that both *Emerson's* and *Putnam's* were moribund when the merger had been made, and announced immediately that a new magazine would be begun the following January to be called the *Great Republic Monthly*. It was to make a special effort to achieve national coverage and to be nonpartisan.

The new magazine was duly launched and was published for eleven months. The Oaksmiths conducted it, writing most of its articles, stories, and poems. Its chief feature was "Life and Travel in the Southern States," illustrated by woodcuts. Another travel series told of the West, and there were articles on the street life of New York: thus the magazine attempted to fulfill its promise. A serial history of America, Seba Smith's tedious three-part poems, musical and literary reviews, and fashions made up the contents. The periodical was in the form of a small quarto and left something to be desired in paper and presswork. With it the magazine publishing activities of the Oaksmiths ceased.

1940 AWARD

ABOUT THE WAR
YEARS OF ABRAHAM LINCOLN

BY

CARL A. SANDBURG

Carl August Sandburg (born on January 6, 1878, in Galesburg, Ill.) was the son of Swedish emigrants. Already at the age of eleven he helped to earn his keep with different jobs. When the United States declared war on Spain in 1898, he joined the army and served for eight months in Puerto Rico. After his discharge Sandburg enrolled at Lombard College in his native town, but he left college in 1902 without graduating and worked for a time as an advertising manager. During the following years he published his first two volumes of poems: *In Reckless Ecstasy* and *The Plaint of a Rose*. In 1907 Sandburg moved to Milwaukee to become district organizer for the Social Democratic party of Wisconsin. Since 1913 he worked as a newspaperman: For a time he worked as a reporter for a tabloid newspaper and in 1917 he joined the staff of the *Chicago Daily News*, where he remained for the following twelve years. During the early 1920's Sandburg started to make public appearances, giving lectures, reciting his poems and singing folk songs. Sandburg published many volumes of poetry, e.g. *Smoke and Steel* and *Good Morning, America*; he wrote a series of children's fairy tales, e.g. *Rootabaga Stories* and published *American Songbag*, a compilation of songs and ballads. In 1939 Carl A. Sandburg published the second volume of his Lincoln biography entitled *Abraham Lincoln: The War Years*, a work, in the study of which he had invested most of his time. It earned him the Pulitzer Prize for history the following year.

KILLING THE PRESIDENT IN FORD'S THEATER

[Source: Carl Sandburg: Abraham Lincoln: The War Years, Vol. 4, New York: Harcourt, Brace & Company, 1939, pp. 274, 277 - 281; reprinted by permission of Mrs. Helga Sandburg and of Harcourt Brace and Company, Orlando, Fla.]

From the upholstered rocking armchair in which Lincoln sits he can see only the persons in the box with him, the players on the stage, and any persons offstage on the left. The box on the opposite side of the theatre is empty. With the box wall at his back and the closely woven lace curtains at his left arm, he is screened from the audience at his back and from the musicians in the orchestra pit, which is below and partly behind him.

The box has two doors. Sometimes by a movable cross partition it is converted into two boxes, each having its door. The door forward is locked. For this evening the President's party has the roominess and convenience of double space, extra armchairs, side chairs, a small sofa. In the privacy achieved he is in sight only of his chosen companions, the actors he has come to see render a play, and the few people who may be offstage to the left.

This privacy however has a flaw. It is not as complete as it seems. A few feet behind the President is the box door, the only entry to the box unless by a climb from the stage. In this door is a small hole, bored that afternoon to serve as a peephole—from the outside. Through this peephole it is the intention of the Outsider who made it with a gimlet to stand and watch the President, then at a chosen moment to enter the box. This door opens from the box on a narrow hallway that leads to another door which opens on the balcony of the theatre.

Through these two doors the Outsider must pass in order to enter the President's box. Close to the door connecting with the balcony two inches of plaster have been cut from the brick wall of the narrow hallway. The intention of the Outsider is that a bar placed in this cut-away wall niche and then braced against the panel of the door will hold that door against intruders, will serve to stop anyone from interference with the Outsider while making his observations of the President through the gimleted hole in the box door.

At either of these doors, the one to the box or the one to the hallway, it is the assigned duty and expected responsibility of John F. Parker to stand or sit constantly and without fail. A Ward Lamon or an Eckert on this duty would probably have noticed the gimleted hole, the newly made wall niche, and been doubly watchful. If Lincoln believes what he told Crook that afternoon, that he trusted the men assigned to guard him, then as he sits in the upholstered rocking armchair in the box he believes that John F. Parker in steady fidelity is just outside the box door, in plain clothes ready with the revolver Pendel at the White House had told him to be sure to have with him.

In such a trust Lincoln is mistaken. Whatever dim fog of thought or duty may move John F. Parker in his best moments is not operating tonight. His life habit of never letting trouble trouble him is on him this night; his motive is to have no motive. He has always got along somehow. Why care about anything, why really care? He can always find good liquor and bad women. You take your fun as you find it. He can never be a somebody, so he will enjoy himself as a nobody—though he can't imagine how perfect a

Ford's Theatre

cipher, how completely the little end of nothing, one John F. Parker may appear as the result of one slack easygoing hour.

"The guard . . . acting as my substitute," wrote the faithful Crook later, "took his position at the rear of the box, close to an entrance leading into the box. . . . His orders were to stand there, fully armed, and to permit no unauthorized person to pass into the box. His orders were to stand there and protect the President at all hazards. From the spot where he was thus stationed, this guard could not see the stage or the actors; but he could hear the words the actors spoke, and he became so interested in them that, incredible as it may seem, he quietly deserted his post of duty, and walking down the dimly-lighted side aisle, deliberately took a seat."

The custom was for a chair to be placed in the narrow hallway for the guard to sit in. The doorkeeper Buckingham told Crook that such a chair was provided this evening for the accommodation of the guard. "Whether Parker occupied it at all, I do not know," wrote Crook. "Mr. Buckingham is of the impression that he did. If he did, he left it almost immediately, for he confessed to me the next day that he went to a seat, so that he could see the play." The door to the President's box is shut. It is not kept open so that the box occupants can see the guard on duty.

Either between acts or at some time when the play was not lively enough to suit him or because of an urge for a pony of whisky under his belt, John F. Parker leaves his seat in the balcony and goes down to the street and joins companions in a little whiff of liquor—this on the basis of a statement of the coachman Burns, who declared he stayed outside on the street with his carriage and horses, except for one interlude when "the special police officer [meaning John F. Parker] and the footman of the President [Forbes] came up to him and asked him to take a drink with them; which he did."

Thus circumstance favors the lurking and vigilant Outsider who in the afternoon gimleted a hole in the door of the President's box and cut a two-inch niche in a wall to brace a bar against a door panel and hold it against interference while he should operate.

The play goes on. The evening and the drama are much like many other evenings when the acting is pleasant enough, the play mediocre and so-so, the audience having no thrills of great performance but enjoying itself. The most excited man in the house, with little doubt, is the orchestra leader, Withers. He has left the pit and gone backstage, where, as he related, "I was giving the stage manager a piece of my mind. I had written a song for Laura Keene to sing. When she left it out I was mad. We had no cue, and the music was thrown out of gear. So I hurried round on the stage on my left to see what it was done for."

And of what is Abraham Lincoln thinking? As he leans back in this easy rocking chair, where does he roam in thought? If it is life he is thinking about, no one could fathom the subtle speculations and hazy reveries resulting from his fifty-six years of adventures drab and dazzling in life. Who had gone farther on so little to begin with? Who else as a living figure of republican government, of democracy, in practice, as a symbol touching freedom for all men—who else had gone farther over America, over the world? If it is death he is thinking about, who better than himself might interpret his dream that he lay in winding sheets on a catafalque in the White House and people were wringing their hands and crying "The President is dead!" —who could make clear this dream better than himself? Furthermore if it is death he is thinking about, has he not philosophized about it and dreamed about it and considered himself as a mark and a target until no one is better prepared than he for any sudden deed? Has he not a thousand times said to himself, and several times to friends and intimates, that he must accommodate himself to the thought of sudden death? Has he not wearied of the constructions placed on his secret night ride through Baltimore to escape a plot aimed at his death? Has he not laughed to the overhead night stars at a hole shot in his hat by a hidden marksman he never mentioned even to his boon companion Hill Lamon? And who can say but that Death is a friend, and who else should be more a familiar of Death than a man who has been the central figure of the bloodiest war ever known to the Human Family—who else should more appropriately and decently walk with Death? And who can say but Death is a friend and a nurse and a lover and a benefactor bringing peace and lasting reconciliation? The play tonight is stupid. Shakespeare would be better. "Duncan is in his grave . . . he sleeps well."

Yes, of what is Abraham Lincoln thinking? Draped before him in salute is a silk flag of the Union, a banner of the same design as the one at Independence Hall in Philadelphia in February of '61 which he pulled aloft saying, "I would rather be assassinated on this spot than surrender it," saying the flag in its very origins "gave promise that in due time the weights would be lifted from the shoulders of all men, and that all should have an equal chance." Possibly his mind recurs for a fleeting instant to that one line in his letter to a Boston widow woman: "the solemn pride that must be yours to have laid so costly a sacrifice upon the altar of freedom." Or a phrase from the Gettysburg speech: "we here highly resolve that these dead shall not have died in vain."

Out in a main-floor seat enjoying the show is one Julia Adelaide Shephard, who wrote a letter to her father about this Good Friday evening at the theatre. "Cousin Julia has just told me," she reported, "that the President is in yonder upper right hand private box so handsomely decked with silken flags festooned over a picture of George Washington. The young and lovely daughter of Senator Harris is the only one of his party we see as the flags hide the rest. But we know Father Abraham is there like a Father watching what interests his children, for their pleasure rather than his own. It had been announced in the papers he would be there. How sociable it seems like one family sitting around their parlor fire. Everyone has been so jubilant for days that they laugh and shout at every clownish witticism such is the excited state of the public mind. One of the actresses whose part is that of a very delicate young lady talks about wishing to avoid the draft when her lover tells her not to be alarmed 'for there is to be no more draft' at which the applause is loud and long. The American cousin has just been making love to a young lady who says she'll never marry but for love but when her mother and herself find out that he has lost his property they retreat in disgust at the left hand of the stage while the American cousin goes out at the right. We are waiting for the next scene."

And the next scene?

The next scene is to crash and blare and flare as one of the wildest, one of the most inconceivably fateful and chaotic, that ever stunned and shocked a world that heard the story.

The moment of high fate was not seen by the theatre audience. Only one man saw that moment. He was the Outsider. He was the one who had waited and lurked and made his preparations, planning and plotting that he should be the single and lone spectator of what happened. He had come through the outer door into the little hallway, fastened the strong though slender bar into the two-inch niche in the brick wall, and braced it against the door panel. He had moved softly to the box door and through the little hole he had gimleted that afternoon he had studied the box occupants and his Human Target seated in an upholstered rocking armchair. Softly he had opened the door and stepped toward his prey, in his right hand a one-shot brass derringer pistol, a little eight-ounce vest-pocket weapon winged for death, in his left hand a steel dagger. He was cool and precise and timed his every move. He raised the derringer, lengthened his right arm, ran his eye along the barrel in a line with the head of his victim less than five feet away—and pulled the trigger.

A lead ball somewhat less than a half-inch in diameter crashed into the left side of the head of the Human Target, into the back of the head, in a line with and three inches from the left ear. "The course of the ball was obliquely forward toward the right eye, crossing the brain in an oblique manner and lodging a few inches behind that eye. In the track of the wound were found fragments of bone, which had been driven forward by the ball, which was embedded in the anterior lobe of the left hemisphere of the brain."

For Abraham Lincoln it was lights out, good night, farewell and a long farewell to the good earth and its trees, its enjoyable companions, and the Union of States and the world Family of Man he had loved. He was not dead yet. He was to linger in dying. But the living man could never again speak nor see nor hear nor awaken into conscious being.

1941 AWARD

ABOUT THE CONTINUING
SETTLEMENT OF THE UNITED STATES

BY

MARCUS L. HANSEN

Marcus Lee Hansen (born on December 8, 1892, in Neenah, Wis.) obtained his Bachelor's and Master's degrees at the State University of Iowa in 1916 and 1917. He then went on for graduate study at Harvard University, where he began his investigations on the migration of people across the Atlantic. Hansen began persistent research in Europe in 1922, and served for two years as assistant professor at Smith College. In 1924 he received his doctorate. From 1925 to 1927 he was fellow of the Social Science Research Council in Europe. As research associate in Washington of the American Council of Learned Societies, during the following two years, he compiled data relative to the origins of the white American stock in 1790 for the new restrictive immigration quotas. His teaching career culminated at the University of Illinois, where he became associate professor in 1928 and full professor in 1930. He was historian for the A.C.L.S. committee on a linguistic atlas of the United States and Canada. In 1935 he delivered the Commonwealth Fund Lectures at the University of London. Untimely, Marcus L. Hansen died on May 11, 1938, in Redlands, Cal. Two years after his death, Arthur M. Schlesinger sen. published Hansen's *The Immigrant in American History*, while J. B. Brebner edited and completed *The Mingling of the Canadian and American Peoples*. The same year, Schlesinger also published *The Atlantic Migration, 1607-1860*, a work for which, posthumously, the Pulitzer Prize for history of 1941 was awarded to Marcus L. Hansen.

PIONEERS OF THE GREAT ATLANTIC MIGRATION

[Source: Marcus Lee Hansen: The Atlantic Migration, 1607-1860. A History of the continuing Settlement of the United States, Cambridge, Mass.: Harvard University Press, 1940, pp. 120 - 123, 269; reprinted by permission of Harvard University Press, Cambridge, Mass.]

A S EVIDENCE of the favor with which the United States was now regarded by Europeans, thirty thousand registered passengers entered the United States in 1828, a figure more than twice that of two years before. In 1832 over fifty thousand arrived, and henceforth on only two occasions did the annual total fall below that number. A new movement was under way which was to culminate in the tidal wave of the 1850's. But between the emigrant of 1830 and his successor of 1850 there were pronounced differences. The former migrated in considerable doubt. Though America stood on the threshold of a great period of development, the labor system for this expansion was not yet devised, and emigration in the hope of securing work still seemed a precarious step. The later emigrant crossed the ocean, knowing a system existed which would hire him, distribute him, train him and, finally, assure him a better economic and social status than the one he had left. The working out of this system by the newcomers in the 1830's makes it appropriate to call them the pioneers of the great mid-century migration.

The years after 1825 brought an increasing realization abroad of the labor shortage in America. The depression following 1819 had come to an end. Projects for canals and turnpikes, for warehouses and mills, were being launched. Willing hands were needed. Foreign ship captains spread the word when they tied up at their home ports; and contractors sent agents abroad to recruit workers. This appeal fell upon fertile soil, for times were hard in Europe. The bitter winter of 1825–1826 was followed by one of greater severity, lasting well into the spring of 1827. Prices kept within moderate bounds during 1826 because of the supplies still in storage, but with these exhausted, the second year of shortage witnessed a sharp rise. As was usual at such periods, southwestern Germany, which never produced an abundance of grain, suffered most. Moreover, the extreme cold had injured the vineyards, depleting the cash income with which food might have been bought.

The marked upturn in American immigration in 1827 and 1828 mirrors these new factors. Those leaving Ireland were described as "the small, but industrious and comfortable farmers. These, having tasted of independence, valued it, and prefer, to an uncertain elevation from poverty at home, the effort to secure a permanency in another country." Others were financed by relatives already established in Canada or the United States. The proportion of poverty-stricken Germans was probably greater. They created a serious problem at Le Havre where many of them were stranded, unable to obtain ocean passage within their means. Others became public charges in New York and Boston. The rush of newcomers proved so great as to cause a temporary glut in the labor market, and ship captains returning from the United States in the fall of 1828 spread pessimistic reports regarding the opportunities for work. As a result, the number of passengers declined the following season.

But the pause was only momentary. Two events account for the resumption of European interest in America. The first was the winter of 1829–1830, one of the coldest on record. Its later weeks caused bitter complaints among those who suffered from lack of fuel. The prices of all necessities of life rose sharply on the Continent, and June found Ireland in greater distress than in the famine summer of 1822. On

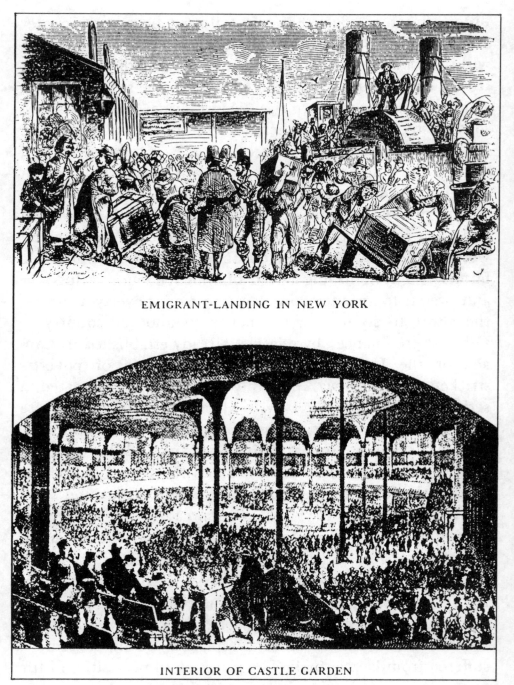

EMIGRANT-LANDING IN NEW YORK

INTERIOR OF CASTLE GARDEN

ARRIVING IN AMERICA

the earlier occasion men of means had aided the less fortunate; now they felt it prudent to conserve what they had. Before the summer was far advanced, a theme much more exciting than the price of rye or potatoes obtruded itself. The people of Paris (probably incited to violence by the high food prices) rose against the Bourbons, and from France the spirit of revolution spread to Belgium, Germany and Poland. These occurrences affected the emigration in a variety of ways.

As usual in Germany, students lent ready ear to the call of change. Forming secret societies, they studied constitutions and voiced radical theories. The authorities took stern measures to suppress such activities. Finally, on May 27, 1832, a great popular demonstration was held at Hambach to protest against the strict supervision. Thirty thousand visitors from all parts of southwest Germany collected in the village and listened to the spirited addresses. Many of the participants, returning to their homes, considered themselves apostles of the revolutionary gospel. Peasants who had gathered about the "liberty trees" refused in many communities to pay taxes and severely manhandled the officers who attempted to collect them. To cope with this situation, the government of Bavaria stationed soldiers through the Rhine districts, and presently peace returned to the countryside. An official investigation into the proceedings at Hambach led to many seizures and inquisitions, and scores of young enthusiasts recanted. Others, seeing the cause deserted by their companions and losing hope of ultimate success, fled the atmosphere of suspicion and espionage in which they lived for Switzerland.

In Zürich, Bern and Basel where they joined the Polish patriots they plotted new uprisings, or awaited a general European war, which would completely change the aspect of Continental politics. For a time they lived on the charity of the Swiss, the secret contributions of such of their fellow countrymen as retained faith in the cause, and the funds collected by committees of liberals in other lands. But the ardor of these benefactors presently cooled, and the German expatriates, chafing under the inaction and economic hardship, began to disperse to more distant countries. Of the large number who established themselves in France and England, many ultimately crossed the Atlantic and assumed positions of political and cultural leadership in German-American communities.

Numerically, however, this group was not great, and its influence on emigration was less than that exerted by other liberals whose protest had been expressed in a less violent manner. Many of these foes of reaction had long admired the government of the United States, and in addition usually had an interest in its economic opportunities. An uncertain future, dwindling property or growing families caused them to think of migration, but they were not living upon that ragged margin where any change would be for the better. A book published in 1829 by Gottfried Duden, a German who had settled in Missouri in 1824, was addressed to such persons. In this work, entitled *Bericht über eine Reise*, he proposed a plan. Let German initiative and capital, from both the United States and Germany, create a city in the American West to be a center of German-American culture and life; or let emigrants concentrate in one of the territories in sufficient numbers to control the organization of the new state government, and then by legislation establish the social customs and the language of the fatherland.

1942 AWARD

ABOUT THE CONCLUSIVE
PHASE OF LINCOLN'S PRESIDENCY

BY

MARGARET K. LEECH

Margaret Kernochan Leech (born on November 7, 1893, in Newburgh, N.Y.) attended Vassar College in Poughkeepsie and in 1915 received her Bachelor's degree. After graduation, she worked first for a publishing company, later she entered an advertising agency. Her publicity work in various World War I fund-raising organizations led to her joining the staff of the American Committee for Devastated France. While serving the committee in Europe, she contributed articles to American periodicals. During the 1920's, after she had returned to the United States, Margaret Leech was chiefly occupied with writing novels. In 1924 her first fictional work was published: *The Back of the Book*. In 1926 and 1928 *Tin Wedding* and *The Feathered Nest* followed. In 1927 she had turned temporarily from fiction to write in collaboration with Heywood Broun the biography *Anthony Comstock: Roundsman of the Lord*. On August 1, 1928, Margaret K. Leech was married to Ralph Pulitzer. Being herself an author and the wife of the publisher of the New York *World* she belonged to a distinguished literary circle that included publishers, playwrights, actors, journalists and other writers. Together with Beatrice Kaufman she wrote her only play *Divided by Three*, which was played for the first time in the fall of 1934. In 1935 she began a five-year investigation into life in Washington during the Civil War for *Reveille in Washington, 1860-1865*. The work was first serialized in the *Atlantic Monthly* magazine and in 1941 published in book form. The following year it earned Margaret K. Leech the Pulitzer Prize for history.

THE LINCOLN FUNERAL ARRANGEMENTS

[Source: Margaret Leech: Reveille in Washington, 1860-1865, New York - London: Harper & Brothers Publishers, 1941, pp. 399 - 403, 422 - 423; reprinted by permission of Harper Collins Publishers, New York, N.Y.]

Prudent secessionists hung mourning on their houses. Only a few reckless persons dared to oppose the popular feeling, and found themselves in jail. Among these were several women of Hooker's Division, charged with exulting over the murder of the President, and pulling mourning emblems from the windows of their neighbors. A warrant was issued for the arrest of Miss Mary Jane Windle, chronicler in prewar days of the doings of Washington society, who had recently returned after a long absence in the South. Miss Windle was accused of maliciously tearing down flags from her boarding-house, and throwing them into the street. At the Mission Church in the First Ward, a preacher made some slurring comment on Lincoln in the course of his Sunday sermon. Veteran Reserves in the congregation seized him, and dragged him from the pulpit. Outside the church, he was put under arrest.

For the most part, the capital's ministers, hastily revising their Easter sermons, exhorted their congregations to resignation to bereavement. The sun shone bright, and birds sang in the blossoming trees, as people trailed dejectedly to church to hear the soothing platitudes. One hospital nurse would remember the smell of the lilacs, and the weeping soldiers coming to ask for bits of crape and ribbon to fasten on their sleeves. At the New York Avenue Presbyterian Church, the President's pew was draped in black, and Dr. Phineas D. Gurley spoke of the chastening hand of a wise God. The Unitarians, however, heard a challenging discourse from their pastor, Dr. Willam H. Channing. He denounced the ruling class of the South, saying that they must either totally submit, or be brought as criminals before the law, and be condemned as guilty. His listeners repeatedly broke into applause, and several persons muttered "Hang them!"

The agitation was calmed by no official counsels of moderation and suspended judgment. In the despair and hysteria of Friday night, Mr. Stanton had grasped the reins of Government in his strong and trembling hands. He had been told of a prowler, skulking at his house on K Street, and believed that he, too, had been marked for assassination. Fearful of a vast murderous conspiracy, he had called Grant back to defend the capital. At the prisons he ordered special vigilance over rebel officers and soldiers. As though an invading army were marching on the city, he directed that the forts be alert and the guns manned. But, though the Secretary of War was frightened, he was not impotent. The wheels of Government turned, as he dictated his orders. All night, while Lincoln lay dying, mounted couriers had dashed from the boardinghouse to the War Department. With blanched faces, the telegraph operators had sent out Mr. Stanton's dispatches. They spread the terror of Washington over the nation, but they also carried the reassurance of authority in the crisis.

On Saturday morning, the Union had a new President. Andy Johnson, hastily inducted into office in his guarded rooms at the Kirkwood House, was a silent figurehead. Seward lay speechless on his bed. Stanton was still in power. He was convinced that the crimes had been deliberately planned by the rebels to avenge the South and aid the Confederate cause, and he would turn the great resources of the War Department into proving it.

Stanton's rage against the South was to become remarkable for its blind and passionate persistence; but on the day that Lincoln died it was representative of the wild revulsion of feeling that swept the capital and the nation. Even Grant was swayed by prejudice. On Saturday afternoon, he telegraphed to Richmond, "Extreme rigor will have to be observed whilst assassination remains the order of the day with the rebels." Although he later changed his mind, his first drastic order was to arrest the Confederate officials in Richmond, as well as all paroled officers who had not taken the oath of allegiance. The virulent reaction of the Federal army was reflected in a dispatch from General Horatio Wright, advising that rebel officers within control of the Army of the Potomac should be closely confined with a view to retaliation on their persons.

The frail shoots of good will to the defeated enemy had been blasted in a night. All over the Union, a hoarse cry of vengeance sounded a discordant requiem for Lincoln.

The preparations for the funeral were a somber diversion which served partially to abate the excitement in the capital. The services, set for noon on Wednesday in the East Room, were to be followed by a grand procession to the Capitol. The War Department issued orders for the military escort, and Lamon's office nominated the marshals for the civic procession of dignitaries, delegations, societies and clergy. Boswell's Fancy Store advertised its readiness to make up sable sashes, batons and rosettes. Shops sold quantities of black gloves, crape for hat and arms, and badges, adorned with Lincoln's portrait. Large supplies of mourning draperies had been rushed down from New York, and were offered at bargain prices. Every train disgorged a load of visitors. Tenth Street swarmed with sight-seers, staring at Ford's, which

BILLS FOR PRESIDENT LINCOLN'S FUNERAL

Paid by the Commissioner of Public Buildings

To Drs. Brown and Alexander
   To Embalming remains of Abraham Lincoln late President of
the United States .... $ 100.00
   To 16 Days services for self and assistant at $10.00 per day   160.00

                      $ 260.00

To Sands & Harvey
   To coffin covered with fine Broadcloth lined with fine white
Satin & silk trimmed with fine mountings heavy Bullion fringe &
tassells, Lead inside lining fine silver plate & walnut outside Box
for Abraham Lincoln, late President of U. S. $1,500.00
   700 Yds white silk at 3.75 pr. yd 2,625.00
   257 yds. black silk at 3.50 .... 899.50
   132 yds. white cambric at 1.00 .... 132.00
    90 boxes fine crape at 7.50 per box 675.00
    24 yds white swiss at 1.50 yd 36.00
   158 pair blk kid gloves at 3.00 .... 474.00
   126 pair white silk gloves at 1.00 .... 126.00
    84 pair black silk gloves at 1.00 .... 84.00
   170 boxes white thread at 3.25 per 552.50
       Removing remains of Willie 10.00
    23 days attendance 3 men at 5.00 per day each 345.00

                      $7,459.00

To John Alexander, Dr., Penna. Avenue, between 12th and 13th
Sts.
      Putting front of Presidents [House] in Mourning .... $ 50.00
      Putting East Room in Mourning 30.00
      Upholstering Catafalque in East Room 75.00
      Upholstering funeral Car 50.00
      Upholstering Rail Road Car 85.00

                      $ 290.00

Bought of George R. Hall
   To making Hearse body [and] Burnishing .... $ 350.00

To A. Jardin
   For flowers for the Funeral of the President April 18, 1865:
   Rose buds .... $ 9.00
   Other white flowers 1.00

                      $ 10.00

1865. To Phillip Ghegan Dr.
April 18th For Flowers for decorations for funeral of the President of the United States .... $ 20.00

OTHER INCIDENTAL BILLS

Also paid by Commissioner French

To James W. Callam 1865 April 14th.
Articles furnished on the occasion of the assassination of the late President viz.—

3 Packages Taylors Pat. Lint. .... $	3.00
2 Pounds Ground Mustard	2.00
6 Oz. Tinct. Camphor (ad)	.90
$	5.90

Bought of Harper & Mitchell [Mourning for Mrs. Lincoln]

1 Mourning dress & trimmings .... $	60.00
1 Mourning Shawl	25.00
1 Crape Veil	10.00
5 yds. Blk. Crape 4.00 per yd	20.00
Gloves & Hdkfs	7.50
5 pr. Hose	5.00
1 Crape Bonnet	15.00
$	142.50

To B. H. Stinemetz,
Apr. 18

2 Silk Hats for Coachmen at 8.00 each .... $	16.00
Mourning Bands for same	1.00
1 Silk Hat for Capt Robt Lincoln	10.00
Mourning Band for same	.75
Apr. 21	
1 Blk felt Hat for Tad Lincoln	4.50
Mourning Band for same	.50
$	32.75

To Elizabeth Kickey [Keckley]

To Services as first Class Nurse & attendant on Mrs. Lincoln from April 14th to May 26th, 1865. 6 weeks at $35.00 per week .... $	210.00
Traveling & incidental expenses in attending Mrs. Lincoln to her home in Chicago Ill & return trip to Washington	100.00
Amount expended in requisite mourning apparel	50.00
$	360.00

was guarded by soldiers, and invading the lodginghouse to see the room where Lincoln had died.

On Monday afternoon, the embalmers had finished, and Lincoln lay in his new black suit in the White House guest room. Officials came to bow beside the four-poster bed, whose pillow was strewn with flowers. Mrs. Lincoln did not leave her room. As though in death Lincoln belonged not to his family, but to the nation, the funeral arrangements were made with official impersonality. The total expenses amounted to thirty thousand dollars. Carpenters and costumers had come and gone past the military guard around the White House. In the middle of the East Room towered a catafalque, festooned with black silk. The domed canopy, lined in white, rose so high that it had been necessary to remove the central chandelier. The two remaining chandeliers were swathed in mourning. The frames of the mirrors were similarly darkened, and white material was stretched over the glass. A series of steps, which had been built around three walls of the room, were covered in black, as were also the chairs provided for the press. Black draperies, concealing the lace and crimson damask at the windows, gave the room the gloom of a vault. When all was ready, Lincoln's body was laid in the casket, braided and studded and starred with silver.

On Tuesday, Lincoln lay in state on the catafalque in the East Room, just as he had dreamed. Officers stood, rigid and severe, at his head and feet. The sepulchral light glinted on the veiled mirrors and the silver trimmings of the casket, as the people ascended the steps of the catafalque for a lingering look at his dim face. There were many soldiers and colored folk in the sorrowful procession which all day wound through the entrance, through the Green Room, slowly through the East Room, and over the black-draped platform which led from one of the windows. In the late afternoon, when the doors were closed, a long line was still waiting on the Avenue.

The hotels were as crowded as they had been for Lincoln's first inauguration, and it was said that six thousand persons spent Tuesday night in the streets and in depots and outbuildings.

At sunrise on Wednesday, a Federal salute awakened the capital to the most solemn day in its history. All places of business had been voluntarily closed, and nearly every house was deserted, as families, servants, boarding-house keepers and lodgers hurried to find vantage points from which to view the funeral procession. From the White House to the Capitol, the Avenue was bordered by two thick, dark stripes of humanity. Spectators gathered on roof tops, and weighted trees. Lafayette Square and the Treasury colonnade were packed. As the morning passed, fresh arrivals filled the town to overflowing—soldiers who had managed to slip away from the army, travelers by boat and train, and country people in hay wagons, donkey carts and dearborns.

The sun beamed from a cloudless sky, and a gentle breeze stirred the draperies on the buildings. The hush of the crowds was penetrated by the minor strains of the bands, as they took their places in line. Officers, with mourning knots on their sword hilts, led out the military escort. Black-gloved civilians were forming in every side street. Delegations from outside cities swirled around the City Hall. At noon, the church bells tolled, and the minute guns began to boom.

The press had arrived early in the fragrant stillness of the East Room. Flowers carpeted the platform of the catafalque, and were scattered on the coffin top. A cross of lilies stood at Lincoln's head, and an anchor of roses at his feet. General David Hunter silently paced the room, his buttons and twin stars and crape-hung sword faintly gleaming. Now and then he spoke to the other officers of the guard, before they all went to stand like statues beside the catafalque. The upholsterers softly drove the last nails, and smoothed the draperies, and the guests began to arrive. Tickets had been limited to six hundred, and the Treasury Department, which was in charge of the admissions, had been besieged. Clergymen, governors, mayors and councilmen, and the corporate authorities of Washington took their places on the tiers of steps, together with the Cabinet, the justices, senators and representatives, the diplomatic corps and many officers. President Johnson stood on the lowest step, facing the middle of the coffin, with his hands crossed on his breast. Grant, in white gloves and sash, was seated alone at the head of the catafalque. At the foot sat Robert and Tad and a few Todd relatives. In all the room, there were but seven ladies: Mrs. Welles, Mrs. Stanton, Mrs. Usher, the two daughters of Chief Justice Chase, and Mrs. Dennison and her daughter.

Dr. Gurley preached the funeral sermon, and, when the closing prayer had been spoken, the casket was closed. A detachment of Veteran Reserves carried it to the high, black-canopied hearse, drawn by six gray horses. Propped on the pillows of his bed near a window on Lafayette Square, a sick man vaguely saw the moving, plume-decked structure. Mr. Seward was too weak to understand its meaning, but he would keep a dreamy memory of those black, nodding plumes.

The dirges of the bands mingled with the tolling bells, and the minute guns repeated their methodical punctuation, as the military escort started down the Avenue. Regiments and battalions marched in slow time, with arms reversed and draped banners. Heavy artillery rumbled behind them. Hundreds of army and naval officers went on foot. There was one unforeseen change in the line of march. The Twenty-second Colored Infantry, just landed from Petersburg, found itself unable to proceed up the Avenue from

Seventh Street. Wheeling about, the Negro soldiers headed the procession to the Capitol.

Block after block, grief moved along the sidewalks at the sight of the casket, followed by Lincoln's horse, with his master's boots in the stirrups. Dignitaries, delegations and societies filled the wide street, on foot or in their carriages. Thirty thousand people took part in the funeral pageant, which ended with the colored lodges. When Welles drove back along the Avenue after the service at the Capitol, he met the broad platoons, still marching.

For one more day, Lincoln's corpse lay on view in a catafalque under the high dome. The walls were heavily draped, and the pictures and statues were covered, save only the figure of General Washington, on which a black sash was tied. From early morning until dark, soldiers marshaled the visitors into a double line which passed on either side of the casket.

At six on Friday morning, there was another brief service in the Rotunda. Stanton drove up in great haste, attended by Lincoln's guard of cavalry. Grant was present with his staff, and there were other officers, several members of Congress, and the Illinois delegation. Followed by this small cortege, the casket was removed to the railroad depot before Washington was well awake. It was placed on the funeral train, and Willie's smaller coffin, brought from the cemetery vault, was placed at its foot. The officers of the guard of honor, headed by General Hunter, took their places. The Illinois delegation and other friends and political associates climbed aboard. From the railroad yard came a melancholy clangor of engine bells. Crowds, which the early service at the Capitol had been designed to avoid, struggled to pass the lines of soldiers around the depot.

At eight o'clock, the funeral train pulled out of Washington on the slow and circuitous journey which would carry the prairie lawyer home to Springfield. By day and night, along the railroad tracks, in wayside stations and in the pomp and pageant of mourning cities, Lincoln's countrymen would pour forth to do him honor. Seven million people would gaze on his coffin. Over a million and a half would have a fleeting glimpse of his face. Back to the capital, for twelve days more, would come the noise of a nation's weeping. It would echo in a city distracted by changing events, by anger and excitement. On April 15, a new day had dawned in Washington and, after the lull of the obsequies, it blazed forth in noontide heat.

1943 AWARD

ABOUT THE UPCOMING
OF A FAMOUS BOSTON PIONEER

BY

ESTHER FORBES

Esther Forbes (born on June 28, 1891, in Westborough, Mass.) was graduated from Bradford Academy, Mass., in 1912. Thereafter, she continued her studies at the University of Wisconsin during the period from 1916 to 1918. Two years later Esther Forbes joined the staff of the Houghton Mifflin Company and stayed there until 1926, when she was married to Albert Learned Hoskins. This marriage lasted only for seven years. Mrs. Forbes was member of the American Academy of Arts and Sciences, the Society of American Historians and the first female member of the American Antiquarian Society. In the early 1940s she received honorary doctorates in literature from Clark University and the University of Maine. Her first historical novel *O Genteel Lady* was published in 1926. For *Johnny Tremain: A Novel for Young and Old* she received the John Newberry Medal, one of the most prestigious awards given for children's books. The book was later made into a television show as well as into a movie by Walt Disney. *The Running of the Tide*, a historical novel, won the Metro-Goldwyn-Mayer novel award and also became a movie. *The Boston Book*, which she wrote in cooperation with Arthur Griffin, *Paradise*; *The General's Lady*; *A Mirror for Witches* and *Rainbow on the Road* count also among her book publications. In 1943 Esther Forbes was awarded the Pulitzer Prize in American history for *Paul Revere and the World He Lived In*, which had been published the preceding year.

PAUL REVERE AND THE WORLD HE LIVED IN

[Source: Esther Forbes: Paul Revere and the World he lived in, Boston: Houghton Mifflin Company/The Riverside Press, 1942, pp. 353 - 355, third cover p.; reprinted by permission of Houghton Mifflin Company, New York, N.Y.]

THE American Revolution had begun as a flame of rebellion in Massachusetts, spread like a grass fire to all the other thirteen colonies, and by 1779 involved much of the world. As long as England held the sea power and could supply her own forces and cut off the rebels, she was sure of ultimate victory, but the entry of France into the war upset her control of the sea. She was without an ally in the world and at war with the principal marine powers of the day, France and Spain, as well as her own colonies. She was fighting desperately in the Orient, Europe, and America. At home, for the first time since the days of the Spanish Armada, she was in momentary danger of invasion. The French had fifty thousand troops concentrated at Havre and St. Malo, waiting the spring and summer of 1779 for an opportunity to jump the Channel and land at Falmouth. The fleet with which they could carry out this manoeuvre was almost twice as strong as the British.

In the face of the threat hanging over her at home, the wonder is she bothered as much as she did with that mere appendix to this fight for her life—the rebellion in America. But that June she landed a small garrison at Castine, Maine. General McLein had only parts of two regiments and three armed sloops. It was his duty to hold on, establish a naval base from which British ships could harass American privateersmen and French warships and merchantmen.

Maine was at this time part of Massachusetts and the threat was primarily against Massachusetts shipping. Nine days after McLein seized Castine, Massachusetts was organizing a large expedition to dislodge him. Colonel Revere was ordered 'to hold himself and one hundred of the Matrosses under his comand, including proper officers, in readiness at one hours notice to embark for the Defence of this State, and attack the Enemy at Penobscot.'

General Lovell, who had done extremely well on the Rhode Island expedition the year before, was to command the twelve hundred

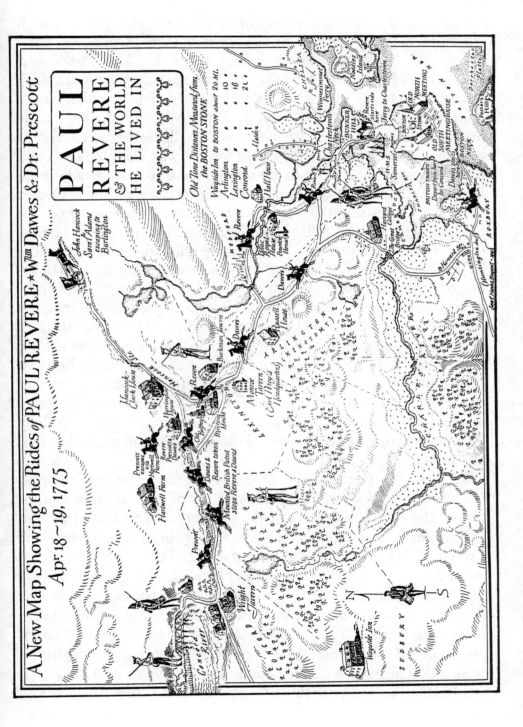

militiamen. Dudley Saltonstall, of the Continental Navy, was in charge of the very mixed fleet. There were three Continental ships taking part in the expedition (among them the sloop *Providence*, Captain Hacker, with whom Revere had recently been quarrelling over gunners) and Massachusetts' entire navy of three ships. In all there were nineteen armed ships and twenty-one transports, mostly privateersmen who were extremely loath for the service. It was only by threats and bribes that they were forced to go along at all. Their heart was not in it. Washington referred once to 'our rascally privateersmen.' They were accustomed to hunting alone and by their own methods. Organizing them into a regular expedition was about like harnessing so many seagulls. Incredibly brave, ferocious as wild hawks on occasion; on others they simply made sail and left. Commander Saltonstall probably had no control over them whatsoever. He belonged to the Connecticut branch of the already distinguished family. Before Penobscot and after he was an extremely good man, but rightly or not he has always been blamed for the failure of the expedition.

There was considerable delay in getting this flotilla to sea. They needed nine tons of flour, ten of rice and salt beef, twelve hundred gallons of rum, and an equal amount of molasses. These twelve hundred militiamen had but '500 stand of arms' among them. The three nine-pounders and four field pieces—not a very impressive 'artillery train'—were under Paul Revere. Besides these militiamen the ships had some eight hundred marines.

So they at last sailed from Boston and were as far as Townsend (Boothbay), Maine, on the twenty-first day of July. By this time, of course, the British had heard of the plan and sent to New York and Halifax for help, which they had no idea would arrive in time. At Townsend the Americans waited four days. The Reverend Mr. Murray entertained the General and his officers ('family' as it was called) in a 'much Genteeler seat than was by most persons expected in that part of the country,' for the coast of Maine was indeed wild enough in those days. Only at Townsend did General Lovell call for a review of his troops and there came off the ships (which were smart enough) and lined up on shore such a collection of 'scare crows' as even the American Revolution in its fourth year rarely brought together.

1944 AWARD

ABOUT THE GROWTH OF THOUGHT IN AMERICA

BY

MERLE E. CURTI

Merle Eugene Curti (born on September 15, 1897, in Papillion, Neb.) received his Bachelor's degree summa cum laude from Harvard University in 1920. The following year, he earned his Master's degree and became instructor in history at Beloit College. From 1924 to 1925 he pursued further studies at the Sorbonne in Paris, France. On his return to the United States he joined the staff of Smith College as assistant professor and received his doctorate in philosophy in 1927. The same year, Curti was promoted to associate professor and in 1929 to full professor. During the years of 1936/37 he held the Dwight Morrow professorship. Afterwards he became professor of history at the Teachers College of Columbia University. Since 1942 he was professor at the University of Wisconsin. Curti was a very prolific writer. The following are some of his works: *Austria and the U.S., 1848-1852; American Peace Crusade; Bryan and World Peace; Social Ideas of American Educators; The Learned Blacksmith: Letters and Journals of Elihu Burritt.* In 1943 *The Growth of American Thought* by Merle E. Curti was published, a work which - the year after - was chosen as the Pulitzer Prize-winning book on American history.

THE POPULARIZATION OF BUSINESS KNOWLEDGE

[Source: Merle Curti: The Growth of American Thought, New York - London: Harper & Brothers Publishers, 1943, pp. 345 - 349; reprinted by permission of Harper Collins Publishers, New York, N.Y.]

The expanding population and the rise of literacy which followed from the common school awakening resulted in a vast potential reading market. Business enterprise was quick to take advantage of this by providing the people with inexpensive reading matter designed to appeal to popular taste. New mechanical processes cheapened the cost of paper and of printing, and these improvements, the result in part of emerging needs, in turn facilitated the diffusion of knowledge.

Among the new literary fashions which proved a boon to publishers and authors no less than to the culturally ambitious among the middle class with money to spend, was the literary annual or gift book. In 1826, three years after the *Forget-me-not* saw the light of day in England, the *Atlantic Souvenir* appeared in Philadelphia. A plethora of gift books followed this venture—from 1846 to 1852 an average of sixty titles appeared each year. Made up of highly moral and sentimental verses, tales, proverbs, and admonitions to virtue, the gift book was "embellished" with engravings and color tints and bound ornately in embossed and decorated silk or gilded leather. It both met and created a demand for "better literature and art" among the rising middle classes. It provided such unknown writers as Hawthorne with their first tangible encouragement. It also familiarized a wide public with the names and at least fragments of the work of such writers as Byron, Southey, Scott, Wordsworth, Coleridge, Lamb, Ruskin, Dickens, Thackeray, Poe, Nathaniel P. Willis, Longfellow, Whittier, Emerson, Holmes, and a long list of others. Tokens of affection, of refinement, even of luxury, "these luscious gifts," in the words of one of their publishers, "stole alike into the palace and the cottage, the library, the parlor, and the boudoir" to create an ever-widening taste for purchasable culture, ornate, exquisite, sentimental, and uplifting.

For those who could not afford the expensive gift books, enterprising publishers found cheaper but no less profitable disseminators of knowledge and culture. The multiplication of lyceums, debating societies, and district school libraries created a wide market for new books. No sooner had the New York legislature enacted a law encouraging the establishment of district school libraries than an agent of Harper's obtained at Albany a contract to supply books for the new venture. Harper's District School Library was by no means the only uniformly bound and cheaply priced series which this enterprising firm sponsored. Harper's Boys' and Girls' Library, Harper's Family Library, which ran up to one hundred and eighty-seven volumes, and Harper's Library of Select Novels, reaching at length the six hundred and fifteenth title, all bore witness to the way in which an alert and profit-conscious publisher might take advantage of and contribute to the zeal for popularizing knowledge and culture.

What Harper's did others were quick to imitate. Publishers catered to the more serious intellectual aspirations of a public untrained in the foreign languages by bringing out an impressive range of translations of the writings of European philosophers, publicists, and men of letters. On a more popular level cheaply priced books of useful information, travel, history, biography, and religion appeared. Encyclopedias and popular "books of knowledge," ponderous or of pocket size, enjoyed an ever-growing vogue.

Pious folk distrusted the novel, but it had no real rival. Anxious to put prospective "best-sellers" on the market as speedily as possible, publishers sometimes dispatched messengers to incoming European packetboats and within a single day set up, printed, and bound in paper covers the most recent novel of Bulwer or Dickens. Newspaper boys sold for a half-quarter or a dime these "pirated" novels, the cheap cost of which was due to the fact that no international copyright existed. Thanks to new promotion methods, these inexpensive books quickly became available to travelers on canals and railroads and to dwellers in remote byways. Even more profitable than respectable novels was the sensational adventure story, frankly designed to appeal to the masses by exciting democratic prejudices, patriotic fervor, and sex interest (sugar-coated by highly moral sentiments). These paperback predecessors of the later Beadle Dime Novels enjoyed increasing popularity in the 'forties and 'fifties.

In consequence of such factors the domestic manufacture of books increased by leaps and bounds. Valued at three and a half million in 1830, it had by 1840 increased 60 per cent; in 1850 it was 125 per cent greater than it had been in 1840.

The older "high-brow" magazines did not enjoy all to themselves the field of periodical literature. New ventures, such as the *Magazine of Useful and Entertaining Knowledge, Grahams', Peterson's, Godey's Lady's Book, Parley's Magazine* and dozens of others sought and won through popular appeal a wider audience than the *North American* or *Port-Folio* had ever known.

No discussion of the role of the publisher in meeting and further stimulating the demand for the diffusion of information can properly neglect the rise of the penny newspaper, which, like so many American agencies of cultural life, was influenced by English example. Mass production and mass distribution in journalism resulted from the introduction of the steam rotary press and from the discovery that a new type of newspaper, frankly designed to appeal to the less well educated, was a profitable enterprise. While the discussion of party politics and political principles by no means disappeared, it was overshadowed by a different conception of news interest. Publishers and editors were increasingly willing to cater to the common man and his wife by filling the pages of their newspapers with the sensational doings of those in high or lowly walks of life—with the records of court trials, with stories of phenomenal successes and grim failures, with human interest stories of any and every type. Together with new methods for the rapid collection of news, this emphasis on sensationalism and on everyday matters virtually revolutionized journalism.

Since the common man could ill afford to buy the older and dearer papers, even if he could have relished their elevated if acrimonious discussion of politics, it was obviously necessary to lower the price of the new type of paper. The *New York Sun* appeared in 1833 as the first penny newspaper, and within a short time James Gordon Bennett of the *New York Herald* carried the penny paper further on its unique road than anyone had deemed possible. Frankly bent on tapping as wide a market as possible, Bennett offered, instead of the old type of serious, dull paper tied to a political faction, an organ which capitalized sensational news, vivacious gossip and prattle, and dramatic human interest stories. On a higher political and moral level and yet partaking of many of the features of the new journalism was Horace Greeley's *New York Tribune*. Its advocacy of reforms promising to elevate the common man to vast heights appealed to the self-interest and idealism of the plain people who subscribed to it in mounting numbers.

The agricultural press also developed rapidly in this period. The dirt farmer often complained that the contents of the agricultural journal were useless. Yet, in addition to hortatory and inspirational articles on the evils of the city and the glories of agriculture and on the need for temperance and schooling, it contained many pieces of an informational character. These included articles on soil, on state and federal aid to agriculture, on travel, politics, laws, and catastrophic events and accidents. The farm paper also contained household hints, rural poetry, and suggestions for the improvement of farm architecture.

All these ventures in the popularization of information, related as they were to an expanding business enterprise, both exemplified the widespread enthusiasm for the diffusion of knowledge and contributed to it.

At least one other development in the social and economic life of the period—improvement in communication and reduction of the cost of postage—was indirectly related to the rise of the common man. The law of 1825 lowered the postal charges that in the interest of additional revenues had been fixed at the close of the War of 1812. But even with these reductions the rates remained burdensome to the ordinary man who in his migration to the West and to cities found it costly to communicate with his home folk. Following the example of Rowland Hill in England, American reformers inaugurated a campaign to induce Congress, in face of the general opposition of the postal authorities, to eliminate the complex and burdensome practice by which the initial high cost of letters increased with the distance. The preservation of family affections, so the petitions ran, required cheaper postage; so too did the spread of the light reflected by the various crusades for moral reform. Business enterpises, especially the publishers of newspapers and magazines, added their voices to the hue and cry for cheaper rates. At length, in 1851, Congress responded by virtually adopting the principle of cheap and uniform postage rates; and the leader of the reform, Barnabas Bates, could maintain, as he had done at the beginning of the agitation, that the people had been aroused to demand revision in order that every avenue might be opened for the diffusion of useful knowledge. Nor did the movement stop here, for Elihu Burritt, "the learned blacksmith," determined to extend the idea to the international area. Although his motives were largely to enable immigrants to keep in touch with their people in the old home and to promote international good will, the argument was also advanced that "ocean penny postage" would diffuse more widely the knowledge of our free political institutions among "the misruled multitudes of the Old World."

1945 AWARD

ABOUT THE U.S. POLICY
AFTER THE FIRST WORLD WAR

BY

STEPHEN BONSAL

Stephen Bonsal (born on March 29, 1865, in Baltimore, Md.) was educated at the St. Paul's School in Concord, N.H., and studied also in Heidelberg and Bonn, Germany, as well as in Vienna, Austria. In 1885 he became special correspondent of the *New York Herald*. In this function he gave on-the-spot reports from all over the world, e.g. about the Bulgarian-Servian War, the Macedonian uprising in 1890, about the Chinese-Japanese War in 1895 and the Spanish-American War. During these years, he was also in the United States diplomatic service as secretary of legation and chargé d'affaires in Peking, Madrid, Tokio and Korea. Upon the outbreak of the Russo-Japanese War in 1904, he traveled for the *New York Herald* for six months in the Balkans, to Albania, Macedonia and Montenegro. Moreover, he was in Russia during the Revolutionary troubles of 1907 and visited all the West Indies and parts of South America. During the First World War Bonsal was major in the National Army. With the American Expeditionary Forces he went to France in 1918 and represented the United States in the Congress of Oppressed Nationalities. Also, as lieutenant colonel in the infantry, he was attached to the American mission to the Peace Conference after the armistice. In addition to this, Bonsal is the author of several book publications: e.g. *Morocco as It Is; The Real Condition of Cuba; The American Mediterranean*. Stephen Bonsal won the Pulitzer Prize for history of 1945 for *Unfinished Business*, which had been published the year before.

AMERICA'S POSITION AT THE PARIS CONFERENCE

[Source: Stephen Bonsal: Unfinished Business, Garden City, N.Y.: Doubleday, Doran and Company, Inc., 1944, pp. 8 - 13; reprinted by permission of Bantam, Doubleday, Dell Publishing Group, New York, N.Y.]

When House was leaving Washington to initiate the Armistice negotiations the President suggested Lausanne as the most suitable place for the Conference. He emphasized the fact that while undoubtedly the people of this Swiss town were pro-Ally in sentiment they were well behaved, unpleasant scenes would not take place, and besides the hotel accommodations were ample. By the time he reached Paris, House leaned personally toward Geneva and at his first meeting with Orlando he found that the Italian Premier was also in favor of the city of Calvin. In the midst of the Armistice discussions, on October 29th, Clemenceau announced that he hoped that Versailles would be chosen. House told him that Lloyd George, Orlando, and he himself were in favor of Geneva. It was agreed, however, that discussion was premature, it was, after all, not at all certain there would be a peace conference, and so the matter went over.

A few days later, when it appeared that Geneva had been definitely settled upon (when and if), a cable came from the President indicating that he had changed his mind and had reached a decision that later he was to regret most poignantly. In this cable, under date of November 8th, the President urged House to leave nothing undone to have Versailles chosen, and the reasons he advanced were as follows: "At Versailles friendly influences are in control, while Switzerland is saturated with every poisonous element, and open to every hostile influence."

While House confided to his diary that the President's second choice was a great mistake and that "he does not appreciate the influences we shall have to contend with in Versailles-Paris," he immediately set to work to carry out the President's wishes. Lloyd George for some days proved obstinate, but House overcame his opposition in a characteristically adroit manner. Knowing the dislike of the great press lord for the little Welshman, House induced Northcliffe to enter into the melee, and on November 11th the *Times* of London (his paper) announced, "The Conference must be held in Paris." The skirmishing continued for some days, but on November 20th House was able to cable the President that "his choice had prevailed."

The reasons why the President decided to take part personally in the Conference are more obscure. Undoubtedly, however, the President is mistaken in thinking that he came in response to the wishes of his friends. Many of them indeed ventured to dissuade the President from carrying out this purpose the moment they learned what was in his mind. As had been their custom during the last tense months of the war on every Wednesday afternoon the financial and economic advisors met with the President in the White House to confer with him on their current problems. On this particular Wednesday, three or four days after the Armistice, they were all on hand, and one after another they talked with Wilson. Vance McCormick had his talk, longer than usual, and Harry Garfield waited in a window embrasure with his memorandum in hand. "It was amazing, indeed magical it seemed to me, the way the President jumped from one problem to the next, always clearheaded and always with lucid thought and mind on the question presented," was the comment of the Fuel Dictator. On this day Garfield noticed that when McCormick left, the President looked out the window for a moment and then called him in. After the current fuel problems had been discussed Garfield lingered on until the President said, "What is on your mind, Harry?" (They had been professors together at Princeton and were on terms of close intimacy.) "I want to ask you not to go to Europe," said Garfield. "Not to take an active part in the Peace Conference. I and many of your other friends for whom I am speaking fear that if you do go you will have to descend from your present position of world arbiter. You will necessarily become a combatant in the hurly-burly. You will become a contestant in the struggle, in the struggle of which you are the only possible referee."

The President grew very thoughtful. "There is much in what you say, Harry. I am indeed confronted with a difficult decision. But now listen to me and weigh my thought. Here in America I understand what is going on throughout the country. I know even before the public what is likely to happen at the Capitol. But Europe is far away, and the voices that come to me from there are so confusing.

Half my time, and more, is occupied with decoding dispatches that come from Europe—and must come to me personally. So you see—at least I see—that by going abroad I would save time and would be helped by more direct contacts." Garfield bowed and was about to withdraw and then he blurted out, "May I say, Mr. President, how greatly I admire your ability to face alone all the problems we have to submit to you!" The President smiled and drawing Garfield to the window said, "I'll let you into a secret. Between each of the momentous interviews to which you refer I take, as you may have noticed, a peep out of the window. I watch the birds and the squirrels going about their daily tasks. I cannot tell you what refreshment there comes to me from watching them."

Downstairs Garfield found that McCormick was waiting for him. "What did you talk about so long with the President?" he asked.

"I begged him not to go to Europe—to remain here on top of the uneasy world," said Garfield.

"That is exactly what I talked to him about," answered McCormick, and there were many others who in these days expressed similar views and fears.

When the Colonel reached France (October 26th) he had not the remotest idea that the President had any thought of coming to Europe, but soon from many sources he learned that the idea was uppermost in his mind and also that it was being hotly debated in Washington. Under his instructions to make contacts with European leaders and to keep the President advised as to their views, it was impossible for House to hold himself aloof from the controversy, much as he would have liked to. So on November 14th he cabled:

"Americans here whose opinions are of value are practically unanimous in the belief that it would be unwise for you to sit in the Peace Conference. They fear it would involve a loss of dignity and deprive you of your commanding position. Clemenceau has just told me that he hopes you will not sit in the conference because no head of state should sit there. Cobb wires from England that Reading and Wiseman voice the same view. Everyone wants you to come over to take part in the preliminary talks. It is at these meetings that peace terms will be shaped, just as the informal conferences of last month determined the German and Austrian armistices."

A few hours later House cabled: "It is of vital importance, I think, for you to come as soon as possible for everything is being held in abeyance. Clemenceau assumes that the preliminary discussions will not last more than three weeks while he believes that the Peace Conference may take as long as four months. In announcing your departure I think it important that you should not state that you will sit at the Conference. That can be determined after you get here. The French, English, and Italian Prime Ministers will head their delegations."

Even for such a trained diplomatist as House, here was presented a most difficult situation. Any suggestion that the President should not come to Paris, or if he did come should not take an active personal part in the negotiations, meant that the chief responsibility for American representation would devolve on the shoulders of House. And it must be admitted that at this juncture even House's diplomacy failed to conciliate the President, and his reply, though cloaked in cable code, discloses his irritation. It ran:

"Your telegram upsets every plan we had made. I am thrown into complete confusion by the change of program (this is far from an accurate statement. No program had been settled upon, consequently none had been changed). The suggestion that I should not sit as a delegate but that I should be received with the honors due to the chief of state seems to me a way of pocketing me." Then with evidently rising indignation the President continued: "I infer that the French and British leaders desire to exclude me from the Conference for fear that there I might lead the weaker nations against them. I play the same role in our Government as the Prime Ministers do in theirs. The fact that I am head of the state is of no practical importance. I object very strongly to the fact that dignity must prevent us from securing the results we have set our hearts upon. It is universally expected and generally desired here (?) that I should attend the Conference, but I believe that no one would wish me to sit by and try to steer from the outside. I hope you will be very shy of their advice and give me your own independent judgment after reconsideration."

This cable put House in an even more difficult situation than before. He had been sent across the water to sound out the leaders of opinion in the countries with which we had been associated in the war and in conjunction with whom it was our task to make an honorable and durable peace. Now the President urged House to turn a deaf ear to their opinions and their advice and to send only his own independent judgment after reconsideration, which of course was tantamount to saying that his advice on the subject, hitherto expressed, had not been independently arrived at. Never had I seen the Colonel so perplexed, but with less than an hour's delay he handled the situation so loaded with dynamite with his accustomed wisdom. He had now no doubt as to the coming of the President, so he cabled:

"My judgment is that you should determine upon your arrival here what share it is wise for you to take in the proceedings." And then House sought to change the cable conversation into a field which he hoped would prove more advantageous, but here again he was unsuccessful. The illusion under which the President labored that all the European powers were banded together against America was, as the sequel shows, to become with him an obsession. "I do not note any signs of a reactionary conspiracy among the European powers," House cabled. "As far as I can see all the powers are trying to work with us rather than with one another. Their disagreements (among themselves) are sharp and constant."

After a short cooling-off period there came the following answer from Washington which as I decoded it with Gordon Auchincloss I found reassuring: "The President," it read, "will sail for France, immediately after the opening of the regular session of Congress, for the purpose of taking part in the discussions and the settlement of the main features of the Treaty of Peace. It is not likely that it will be possible for him to remain throughout the formal Peace Conference, but his presence at the outset is necessary in order to obviate the manifest disadvantages of discussion by cable in determining the larger outlines of the final treaty about which he must necessarily be consulted."

1946 AWARD

ABOUT THE AGE OF
PRESIDENT ANDREW JACKSON

BY

ARTHUR M. SCHLESINGER JR.

Arthur Meier Schlesinger Jr. (born on October 15, 1917, in Columbus, Oh.) completed his secondary education at Phillips Exeter Academy in New Hampshire, after which his education was rounded off by a world tour with his parents and his younger brother. On his return to the United States in 1934, he enrolled at Harvard University, where he specialized in American history and literature. He earned his B.A., summa cum laude, in 1938. Schlesinger spent a year at Cambridge University on a Henry Fellowship and then returned to Harvard for graduate school. In 1941, after two years of research, Schlesinger delivered a series of lectures on Andrew Jackson and his times at Boston's Lowell Institute. During World War II he spent one year working as a writer in the Office of War Information in Washington, D.C., and another one in the Office of Strategic Services. Schlesinger went overseas in the spring of 1944 and eventually became deputy chief of the O.S.S. reports board in Paris. After the war, he returned to Washington, where he established himself as a freelance writer specializing in political affairs. For about a year he contributed articles to the *Atlantic, Fortune, Life* and the *New Republic* and worked intermittently on a projected series of books about Franklin Roosevelt's administration. Schlesinger is also the author of *Orestes A. Brownson: A Pilgrim's Progress* and *The Age of Jackson.* The latter earned Arthur M. Schlesinger Jr., the 1946 Pulitzer Prize for the best book on history published the preceding year.

THE PRESIDENT'S FIRST YEAR IN OFFICE

[Source: Arthur M. Schlesinger Jr.: The Age of Jackson, Boston: Little, Brown and Company, 1945, pp. 45 - 47; reprinted by permission of Little, Brown and Company, Publishers, Boston, Mass.]

THE SHOUTING crowd on Inauguration Day, Daniel Webster noted sarcastically, really seemed to think "the country is rescued from some dreadful danger." Yet where was this danger? It was clear that Jackson had an impressive mandate, but it was not so clear what the mandate was for. Through the land, an excitement for change had welled up from profound frustration. But its concrete expressions were only slogans, epithets, meaningless phrases, the shout of crowds — not issues, programs, policies.

The new President's supporters in Congress had conspicuously failed to develop measures to meet the discontents which had toppled the previous administration. Their opposition to Adams and Clay had been confused and opportunistic, hiding a basic lack of ideas behind a smoke-screen of parliamentary obstruction and campaign invective. The campaign had reflected its shallowness. Hardly an issue of policy figured in the canvass, and, when Jackson triumphed, no one could be certain that his administration would not duplicate that of Madison or Monroe or even of Adams.

As for the new President, he was not only tired, sick and depressed by grief, but politically inexperienced. The problems he faced were new to him; and for a man who learned by dealing with actualities rather than by intellectual analysis this was a serious handicap. He had to feel his way and let things seep in before he could move with decision. In the meantime the demand for "reform" had to be met. The common man, too long thwarted by official indifference, had to be given a sense that the government was in truth the people's government. Jackson's answer was shrewd and swift: a redistribution of federal offices.

This measure served obvious political needs. It adapted to national purposes methods of political reward, long employed in some of the states, and became an invaluable means of unifying administration support. A party formed to aid special moneyed interests could depend on private contributions to pay the bills and keep the organization alive; but a party formed in the popular interest had no other resources save the offices at its disposal. "If you wish to keep up the party," a Pennsylvania politician told Van Buren, "you must induce them to beleive that it is their interest — Some few may adhere to the party from mere consciencious conviction of doing right but interest is a powerful stimulus to make them act energetically and efficiently."

But, while helping to build the party, the spoils system also contributed to the main objective of helping restore faith in the government. In the eyes of the people, the bureaucracy had been corrupted by its vested interests in its own power. "Office is considered as a species of property," as Jackson told Congress, "and government rather as a means of promoting individual interests than as an instrument created solely for the service of the people." Jackson believed that official duties could be made "so plain and simple that men of intelligence may readily qualify themselves for their performance." His quick action on this principle meant that the government was no longer "an engine for the support of the few at the expense of the many."

The doctrine of rotation-in-office was thus in large part conceived as a sincere measure of reform. Many professional reformers so regarded it. Robert Dale Owen hailed it enthusiastically in his radical New York sheet, the *Free Enquirer*, and Jeremy Bentham, the great English reformer, confided to Jackson, as one liberal to another, that he had held the doctrine of rotation himself since 1821.

In a larger context, which contemporary Americans could only have dimly apprehended, rotation-in-office possessed another significance. The history of governments has been characterized by the decay of old ruling classes and the rise of more vigorous and intelligent ones to replace them. This process had already begun in America. The "natural aristocracy" of Richard Hildreth — the class composed of merchant, banker, planter, lawyer and clergyman — had started to decline after the War of 1812. The rise of the military hero, a new "natural" aristocrat, hastened the time for a general breaking-up of the old governing elite. In extreme cases one ruling order succeeds another by violent revolution, but a democracy which preserves sufficient equality of opportunity may escape so drastic a solution. The spoils system, whatever its faults, at least destroyed peaceably the monopoly of offices by a class which could not govern, and brought to power a fresh and alert group which had the energy to meet the needs of the day.

Modern research has shown that legend, invented and fostered for partisan purposes, has considerably exaggerated the extent of Jackson's actual removals. The most careful estimate is that between a fifth and a tenth of all federal officeholders were dismissed during Jackson's eight years, many for good reason. Frauds to the amount of $280,000 were discovered in the Treasury Department alone. Jackson ousted no greater a proportion of officeholders than Jefferson, though his administration certainly - established the spoils system in national politics.

Until recent years, the study of the spoils system has been marred by a tendency to substitute moral disapproval for an understanding of causes and necessities. There can be small doubt today that, whatever evils it brought into American life, its historical function was to narrow the gap between the people and the government — to expand popular participation in the workings of democracy. For Jackson it was an essential step in the gradual formulation of a program for democratic America.

As the Jackson administration moved through its first year, two hostile factions began to emerge within the party, one pressing Vice-President John C. Calhoun's claims for the presidency in 1832, the other supporting Martin Van Buren, the Secretary of State.

1947 AWARD

ABOUT THE U.S. STRUGGLE
FOR SUPERIORITY IN WORLD WAR II

BY

JAMES P. BAXTER III

James Phinney Baxter III (born on February 15, 1893, in Portland, Me.) attended Williams College, majoring in history and was graduated summa cum laude in 1914. Afterwards, he worked for a year for the Industrial Finance Corporation in New York. But in the course of an illness, which lasted from 1915 to 1921, Baxter decided to make a career of history and, accordingly, joined the Colorado College faculty as an instructor in history in 1921. After further study at Harvard University he received his Master's degree in 1923. During the following two years he held a John Harvard Traveling Fellowship and earned his doctorate in 1926. The next year he became assistant professor at Harvard and in 1931 he was advanced to associate professor of history. Since 1932 Baxter has lectured at the Naval War College at Newport, R.I. He became full professor at Harvard in 1936, and the same year he lectured at Cambridge University, England. Forty-four-year-old, Professor Baxter became president of Williams College. During World War II he was first deputy on a parttime basis in the Office of Strategic Services and then became historian of the Office of Scientific Research and Development, with which he remained until June 1946. Since 1945 Baxter served also on the Navy Department board. That same year James P. Baxter III started working on *Scientists Against Time*, the first of a planned series entitled *Science in World War II*. This volume, published in 1946, earned him the Pulitzer Prize for American history the next year.

THE ANTIMALARIALS AND MILITARY MEDICINE

[Source: James Phinney Baxter 3rd: Scientists Against Time, Boston: Little, Brown and Company, 1946, pp. 299 - 303; reprinted by permission of Little, Brown and Company, Publishers, Boston, Mass.]

WHEN THE Office of Scientific Research and Development was organized in July 1941 there was established within it a Committee on Medical Research, whose function it was to initiate and support a research program "for the national defense." The committee was composed of Dr. A. N. Richards, of the University of Pennsylvania, Chairman; Dr. Lewis H. Weed of Johns Hopkins University, Vice-Chairman; Dr. A. R. Dochez of Columbia University, Dr. A. Baird Hastings of Harvard University, Brigadier General James Stevens Simmons, Rear Admiral Harold W. Smith, and Dr. L. R. Thompson of the United States Public Health Service. In contradistinction to NDRC, with which the previous chapters of this book have been concerned, it was the purpose of this Committee to save the lives of our troops; directly by improving methods for treating the sick and wounded, indirectly by preventing disease. In theory this function was easier of fulfillment than that of NDRC, for the prevention and cure of disease was a peacetime occupation of medical research. In practice the quantitative shift of emphasis, the dislocation of interest, was so great that much of the research had to be conducted practically *de novo*. The control of disease-bearing insects or even of malaria, for example, had been rather academic insofar as the health of the United States was concerned. It now became of controlling importance. Similarly the necessity of flying aircraft at unprecedented heights and at unprecedented speeds introduced quite new problems.

There was grave need for the establishment of such an official agency as the CMR. For more than a year, since war had seemed possible and more than possible, committees of the Division of Medical Sciences of the National Research Council had been meeting in Washington to answer questions posed by the Army and Navy and to recommend procedures to them. In July 1941 there were 41 such committees, each composed of eminent men in the medical and surgical specialties, but many of the questions put to them could not be answered from existing knowledge and many of the procedures recommended were obviously susceptible of improvement. On both accounts research was essential but, aware as the committees were of this necessity, there were no funds at their disposal with which to conduct investigation. The Committee on Medical Research was able to implement with Government funds the research programs which these committees had planned. It continued throughout the war to utilize their advice upon proposals for specific investigations. Upon its own initiative and upon advice of its service members the Committee amplified these programs and extended them into other fields, utilizing its knowledge of the investigative and personnel resources of the country to do so. It was never hampered by lack of funds. It was hampered by the lack of a considered national policy to maintain highly trained technical personnel in their proper sphere: the laboratory and hospital. During its existence the Committee expended some $24,000,000 — a sum which would have supported our share in the war for only four hours — in approximately 600 contracts with 133 universities, foundations, and commercial firms. Over 1500 doctors of medicine, science, and philosophy and 4000 other laboratory personnel were engaged in these researches on scores of subjects.

From these subjects, five have been selected for description in the subsequent chapters of this book: research upon malaria, transfusions, penicillin, insecticides, and aviation medicine. They were selected because they lend themselves to nontechnical exposition better than do many of the others. Each of them in its own fashion contributed to winning the war. In each it will be observed that one or several years intervened between recognition of the problem and the discovery and development of its solution. This lag in time is unavoidable because the problems are complicated ones. If these chapters carry any moral it lies in this very observation: the time for the conduct of research in military medicine is before and not after the war starts.

"Malaria is an acute and chronic febrile disease, its onset often marked by chills, which is present in countries lying between 45° North and 40° South latitude." There are several million GI's who would have found that statement not only meaningless but uninteresting four years ago.

Today the sentence does not seem meaningless to them. Either from their own experience or from the recollection of their friends the word "malaria" means chills and fever and sweating in bashas or tents pitched in far places. They are wise in the habits of mosquitoes, in the use of repellents and mosquito bars, in the types of Plasmodium, and the color of atabrine.

Maps designed to show the distribution of malaria picture a black band of heavy incidence round the belly of the world. A grayish mottling in the southern part of the United States indicates our light infestation. But North Africa and Sicily are in black, and India and all of Burma and Southern China are in black, as are the West Pacific islands and Panama. In these areas and in the regions of Western Africa and South America where malaria is common, it is estimated that there are 300,000,000 cases a year and 3,000,000 deaths. These were the areas to which, in December of 1941, it became clear our armies must go.

MALARIA

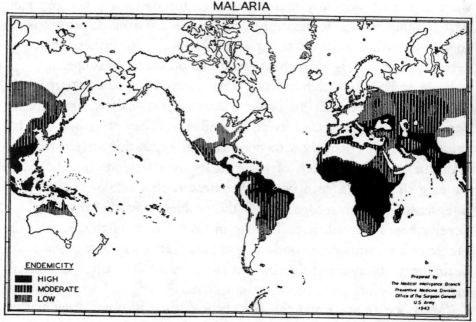

U.S. Army Medical Museum

MAP SHOWING MALARIAL ENDEMICITY

At the outbreak of the war, although not one out of a hundred of the doctors who were to enter the services had seen a case of malaria, they were familiar with the essential features of the disease: that it was caused by organisms called Plasmodia, that it was spread by mosquitoes, that its acute symptoms were relieved by quinine. All of these points had been known for many years. In point of time, the discovery of quinine had come first. Back in 1638 when the Spanish Count Cinchon was Governor of Peru, his wife, falling sick of an "intermittent fever," was treated with brew made from the bark of a native tree and promptly recovered. In recollection of this Countess, the tree was named cinchona and when one of the bark's active principles was isolated in 1820 it was called quinine. Taken to Europe and known there as Jesuit bark because of its use by the monks, it provided the first rational and specific treatment of an acute disease. For a long time of course it was not clear why certain cases of fever were cured by quinine and others unaffected by it. The mystery was only partly solved by calling those which were cured malaria, only completely solved in 1880 when the Frenchman Leveran demonstrated organisms which he called Plasmodia in the red blood cells of patients infected with the disease. These organisms were absent from the blood of patients with other fevers, they could reproduce the disease when they were injected into other patients, and they disintegrated and disappeared under treatment with quinine. As the name of the disease implies it had been attributed to "bad air" or, more specifically, to noxious vapors, miasmas, arising from swamps in the evenings. This conception was a little fuzzy but fundamentally sound. It became more precise in 1898 when the Englishman Ross proved that mosquitoes, rather than air, arising from swamps in the evenings transmitted the disease. He demonstrated Plasmodia in mosquitoes and showed that men develop malaria when bitten by them. By the turn of the century the fundamental information was thus in hand.

The information has been amplified. It was found that only the *Anopheles* mosquito transmitted malaria, indeed only some 60 of its 200 species which have been recognized in various parts of the world. The Plasmodia spend a portion of their life cycle within the stomach wall of these carrier-species and then migrate to the salivary gland where they are in an ideal position for transmission to man when the mosquito bites. In man the Plasmodia grow in the tissues for from seven to fourteen days and then, reaching the blood stream, produce an acute attack of the disease. When the structure of the Plasmodia was studied as they developed in the mosquito stomach and in human blood, it was found that they were not all alike but had to be divided into four species, anatomically distinguishable one from the other. This species difference explained the different clinical types of malaria which had already been observed, for a different Plasmodium was found to be associated with each type of the disease. Only two species are sufficiently common to warrant mention: *P. vivax*, which produces *vivax* malaria (synonym benign tertian), and *P. falciparum*, which produces *falciparum* malaria (synonym malignant tertian, subtertian, estivo-autumnal). A great majority of cases in the African theater were to be of the *falciparum* type; in the Pacific and CBI theaters distribution between the two was to be nearly equal. The two types of malaria are not unlike in their clinical onset. In both instances, approximately two weeks after being bitten by an infected mosquito, the patient begins to feel ill, usually quite suddenly. He develops chilly sensations which may increase to a bed-shaking chill and within a matter of hours his temperature has risen to 102–105°. His head aches, his back aches, he is nauseated, he feels sick, he looks sick, he is quite uninterested to hear that he will be better in a day or so. In both instances, if the patient receives no treatment, the disease will last for from several weeks to several months, gradually subsiding as he gains some immunity to the infection. In both instances, though more commonly in the *vivax* type, if the patient is treated and recovers from his initial attack he shows a tendency to relapse.

1948 AWARD

ABOUT THE CROSSING
OF THE MISSOURI RIVER

BY

BERNARD A. DEVOTO

Bernard Augustine DeVoto (born on January 11, 1897, in Ogden, Ut.) served - at the young age of twenty - as lieutenant in the United States Army during the First World War. Thereafter, he enrolled at Harvard University, where the Bachelor's degree was conferred upon him in 1920. As an instructor and assistant professor of English he was member of the staff of Northwestern University from 1922 to 1927. Two years later, he returned to Harvard to work there as an instructor and tutor. He was promoted to lecturer in 1934. DeVoto was a very prolific writer. He contributed stories, articles, historical essays and reviews to various magazines. During the 1930's he was first the editor of *Americana Deserta* and *Harvard Graduates' Magazine*, then of *The Easy Chair* and since 1935 of *Harper's Magazine*. From three institutions of higher education he received honorary doctorates: Middlebury College, Kenyon College and the University of Colorado. The following book titles count among his publications: *The Crooked Mile*; *The House of Sun-Goes-Down*; *Mark Twain's America*; *We Accept with Pleasure*; *Minority Report; Mark Twain at Work*; *The Year of Decision: 1846*; *Mountain Time*. Bernard A. DeVoto published *Across the Wide Missouri* in 1947, which brought to him the Pulitzer Prize for history in the following year.

PIONEER TIMES OF THE CITY OF ST. LOUIS

[Source: Bernard DeVoto: Across the Wide Missouri, Boston: Houghton Mifflin Company/The Riverside Presse, 1947, pp. 15-17; reprinted by permission of Houghton Mifflin Company, New York, N.Y.]

In 1833 St. Louis had a population of something over seven thousand and its steamboat age was beginning to roar toward the flush times. The town was mistress of the western waters, had been long before there were steamboats, when the traffic of those waters was by keelboat, flatboat, pirogue, and mackinaw. It was a river town, but if it was Huck Finn's town it was also Mike Fink's, who was not only a keelboatman but a fur-hunter. The rivers had made it more cosmopolitan than other places in America. It looked eastward to Pittsburgh and beyond, southward to New Orleans and the Gulf, northeastward to the Great Lakes and the St. Lawrence, and northward as far as boats of any kind could go. Here, more plentifully than anywhere else, the continental mind was showing itself.

But 'St. Louis — mixture of French & American character — French billiard room — market-place where some are speaking French, some English,' Washington Irving had jotted in his notebook last September, putting up at the Union Hotel and going out at once to check impressions against what he knew of Europe and New York. For of all the rivers that were destiny to St. Louis, those that flowed from the wilderness counted most, the French had pioneered them, and the town polarized innumerable energies from the eastward in order to direct them west. Here was the headland from which the nation overlooked the West. The Ohio and the lower Mississippi were important, but the upper Mississippi meant more and the Missouri most of all. The Indians and trappers and voyageurs who brought a barbaric color to the cobbled streets were of the West, and an old and rich aristocracy, dating back long before Mr. Jefferson's Purchase, were borne on their shoulders. The Chouteaus, Bertholds, Prattes, Cérrés, Cabannés, and the like ruled the city by birthright, they got their wealth from the West, and they had led their own parties West to bring it back.

The wharves of the steamboat age multiplied along the river. Just above them, on a flat bench sometimes flooded by the June rise, stood the warehouses where the goods carried by the steamboats were stored for distribution and transshipment. Most conspicuous of all buildings on this bench, however, were large structures of gray and yellow stone which always smelled to heaven. These were the warehouses of the fur companies, the core of the town's economy. Here from all the northern and western rivers the pelts for which the trappers risked and lost their lives came down, and hence they went out to New York, Montreal, London, Leipsic, Lyons, St. Petersburg, Canton, Athens, Constantinople — to all the world. Some of the companies went back to a time when St. Louis was a Spanish town, some of them beyond that to the poignant, dimming days when it was the farthest outpost of Louis XVI — and even then was thrusting up Chouteaus. Almost from the beginning the dugouts had moved up the Mississippi and Missouri to the Indian country, after furs. In 1833 there were few businesses in St. Louis that did not somehow impinge on the fur trade. And John Jacob Astor had some kind of tie-up with most companies in the fur trade and was the principal force to be taken into account by all the rest.

Three and a half weeks after the *Christian Advocate* published Mr. Disoway's letter, on the morning of March 24, 1833, the steamboat *Paragon*, from the Ohio River, docked at St. Louis. Among the passengers who streamed down her gangplank was a thin, worn man of fifty, excitable, choleric, with a gift of invective. He spoke English by main force, through an unleavened Prussian accent, and the effect was not made more intelligible by the fact that years of military service and geographical exploration had cost him his teeth. He was traveling as Baron Braunsberg but he was Maximilian, Prince of Wied-Neuwied. He had with him the young Swiss artist, Charles Bodmer, and a servant whose improbable name, Dreidoppel, could hardly have been bettered among the Indians whom the Prince intended to visit. For he was in St. Louis to begin a scientific journey to the Indian country.

Maximilian had fought in the Prussian army against Napoleon, had been a prisoner of war, had fought again, had been promoted major-general and decorated with the Iron Cross, had ridden at the head of his division when the Allies entered Paris. This distinguished military career had been forced on him against his will by Napoleon's world war. For the Prince wanted a career in science and, after his patriotic obligations were discharged, embarked on one. He spent two years in Brazil, exploring its wilderness, studying the natives and the flora and fauna, and making a large natural-history collection which he took back to Wied. A book embodying his studies was published in 1820; like the one he was to write about the Indians it was accompanied by an atlas of illustrations. It won him a distinguished reputation and he prepared to engage in a similar study of North America. In the great spring morning of nineteenth-century science a man did not have to be a specialist and Maximilian had something of Humboldt's versatility, being a botanist, a zoologist, a geologist, a meteorologist and climatologist, something of a paleontologist, but mostly what we would today call an ethnologist. He wanted to use all his tools in a study of the West, but mainly he wanted to compare the Western Indians with the Indians he had studied in South America.

He had reached the United States on July 4, 1832, and after a brief tour of the seaboard had gone to New Harmony, Indiana.

1949 AWARD

ABOUT THE DISRUPTION
OF AMERICAN DEMOCRACY

BY

ROY F. NICHOLS

Roy Franklin Nichols (born on March 3, 1896, in Newark, N.J.) was graduated from Rutgers University in 1918 and earned his Master of Arts degree there the year after. From 1920 to 1921 he was fellow at Columbia University, where he also received his Ph.D. degree in 1923. Already the year before he had joined the staff of Columbia as an instructor in history. In 1925 Nichols came to the University of Pennsylvania to assume there the position of assistant professor of history. He was promoted to full professor five years later. In 1944/45 he returned to Columbia University as visiting professor and in 1948/49 he held guest lectures at the University of Cambridge, England. In addition to this, he received several honorary doctorates amongst them one from Rutgers University. Nichols is the author of quite a number of book publications, e.g. *The Democratic Machine (1850-54)*; as joint author he worked on *Syllabus for History of Civilization*; *America Yesterday and Today*, a work on which C.A. Beard and W.C. Bagley were his co-authors; in cooperation with his wife, Jeannette P. Nichols, *Growth of American Democracy*; *The Republic of the United States: a History* and *A Short History of American Democracy* were published. The 1949 Pulitzer Prize for history was awarded to Roy F. Nichols for *The Disruption of American Democracy*, which had appeared the year before.

MAIN ASPECTS IN THE SPLIT OF THE REPUBLIC

[Source: Roy Franklin Nichols: The Disruption of American Democracy, New York: The MacMillan Company, 1948, pp. 502 - 504; reprinted by permission of the Macmillan Publishing Company, New York, N.Y.]

THE DISRUPTION of the American Democracy was complete in 1861. Secession had split the Republic, and the guns of civil war were thundering. The breakup of the Democratic party and the beginning of armed conflict were almost simultaneous; they were intimately related phenomena. The shattering of the party of Jackson was the bursting of a dike which unloosed an engulfing flood.

On the reasons for the Civil War there has been a vast amount of theorizing. Writers have been prone to select patterns—economic, cultural, political, racial, moral, and others—and to devise and emphasize theories in conformity with them. Long arguments as to whether the conflict was repressible or irrepressible, whether the war was inevitable or might have been avoided, have preoccupied historians. As they have unearthed more and more "causes," as they have introduced into the picture more and more elements, they have not altogether succeeded in answering the moot question: Why a civil war? Most of the principal "causes"—ideological differences, institutional differences, moral differences, cultural differences, sectional differences, physiographic differences—have existed in other times and places, without necessarily causing a war. Then why should they set the people of the United States to killing one another in 1861?

People fight under the stress of hyperemotionalism. When some compelling drive, whether it be ambition, fear, anger, or hunger, becomes supercharged, violence and bloodletting, thus far in human history, seem "inevitable." Now why was emotion in the United States in 1861 supercharged?

The basic reasons for this hyperemotionalism cannot be neatly formulated and weighted. Fundamentally the process was an illustration of what Macchiavelli describes as the "confusion of a growing state." The population of the United

States was rapidly multiplying, partly by natural increase and partly by foreign immigration, at the same time that it was arranging itself in rapidy changing patterns. Many Americans were creating new communities, others were crowding together into older urban centers. In old and new, change was continual, with a ceaseless moving out and coming in. The rate of growth, however, could not be uniform; for it was determined in large part by physiographical considerations and the Republic extended from the temperate into the semitropical zone. In the semitropical-to-temperate agricultural South, enterprise was less active, mobility less noticeable. In the northerly states, on the other hand, the variety of realized and potential wealth was greater, the stimulus from climate was sharper, the interest in projects of all sorts was more dynamic. There the vision of wealth and of the needs of the growing society continually inspired the creation of new and more powerful interests, under zealous and ambitious leaders.

So rapid and uneven a rate of social growth was bound to inflict upon Americans this "confusion of a growing state." Characteristic of it and dominant in it were pervasive, divisive, and cohesive attitudes which, as Whitman put it, were "significant of a grand upheaval of ideas and reconstruction of many things on new bases." The social confusion in itself was the great problem confronting statesmen and politicians. Turn where they would, they could not escape it; they themselves were confused by it, and yet they must wrestle with it.

The political system which was in the process of evolving reflected their predicament. They knew that they were operating a federal system, but they oversimplified their problem by believing that it was only a political federalism. They did not grasp the fact that it was a cultural federalism as well. Not only were they dealing with a political federation of states, they must understand this cultural federation of attitudes. The inability to understand contributed much to their failure to organize partisanship and to create political machinery which would be adequate to deal with the complexities of this cultural federation.

This lack of understanding was accompanied by a deep-seated enjoyment of political activity by Americans which proved dangerous. They gave themselves so many opportunities to gratify their desire for this sport. There were so many elections and such constant agitation. Contests were scheduled automatically by the calendar, at many different times and seasons; there were thirty-three independent state systems of election. Within each state the parties, despite their national names, were really independent, each a law unto itself, and none was subjected to much if any central direction; there were nearly eighty such party organizations. A great disruptive fact was the baneful influence of elections almost continuously in progress, of campaigns never over, and of political uproar endlessly arousing emotions. The system of the fathers might possibly bear within itself the seeds of its own destruction.

This constant agitation certainly furnishes one of the primary clues to why the war came. It raised to ever higher pitch the passion-rousing oratory of rivals. They egged one another on to make more and more exaggerated statements to a people pervasively romantic and protestant, isolated and confused. The men and woman exhibiting these different attitudes were not isolated and separated by boundaries—they dwelt side by side, and the same person might be moved by more than one attitude at a time, or by different attitudes at different times.

1950 AWARD

ABOUT THE ART AND
LIFE IN THE UNITED STATES

BY

OLIVER W. LARKIN

Oliver Waterman Larkin (born on August 17, 1896, in Medford, Mass.) was already as a youth interested in painting, drawing and dramatics. While an undergraduate at Harvard he won several scholarships and was elected to Phi Beta Kappa in his senior year. During the First World War he served as a private in the Medical Corps of the Infantry of the United States Army. In 1919 he obtained his Master of Arts degree from Harvard, to which he returned as an assistant in fine arts two years later. At this time, too, he directed plays and designed scenery for Lincoln House, a settlement house in Boston. At the age of twenty-eight, he was made assistant professor of art at Smith College, in Northampton, Mass. Promoted to associate professor in 1926, he became full professor in 1931. For a time during 1925 and 1926, he also taught at Iowa State University; and in 1950 he lectured on American Art at the Harvard Student Council's American Seminar Studies for European students in Salzburg, Austria. That same year he became head of the art department at Smith College. Larkin has contributed numerous articles and book reviews to various periodicals, including *Theatre Arts, Magazine of Art, Saturday Review of Literature* and the *College Art Journal*. Oliver Larkin's book *Art and Life in America* was published in the fall of 1949; the following year it earned him the Pulitzer Prize in history.

ARCHITECTURE OF CULTURAL INSTITUTIONS

[Source: Oliver W. Larkin: Art and Life in America, New York: Rinehart & Company, Inc., 1949, pp. 337 - 340; reprinted by permission of Henry Holt and Company, Inc., New York, N.Y.]

The Putnams published in 1900 a volume with a pompous title which gave a more impressive account of what the nation had achieved in medicine and military science, in life insurance and libraries, in gold production, steel, women's rights, and psychic research than in the arts. Russell Sturgis was one of the contributors to *The Nineteenth Century, A Review of Progress during the Past One Hundred Years in the Chief Departments of Human Activity*; and Sturgis, the scholarly critic and historian of architecture, declared that new problems and new materials had found few architects intelligent enough to cope with them. This faithful Ruskinian knew his first principles and could never accept the clever plan on paper as a substitute for designing in three dimensions; he had written on an earlier occasion that no building could be judged by its outline on the ground, since it would never be looked into from above by a disembodied spirit to whom the roof was transparent. Now he saluted Sullivan's effort to design the exteriors of lofty steel-framed structures in accordance with their nature; but his report closed with a question: Would a community whose best energies were given to making money apply those energies in the next hundred years with serious purpose to architecture as an art? The nation's artistic mind, he concluded, had outgrown its callow, ill-bred youth, but in 1900 had not reached maturity.

Nothing could have been more immature, for example, than the country's attitude toward the planning and replanning of its towns. Nearly a century before, Owen's New Harmony had implied the value and beauty of a community whose life could proceed as an integrated whole; and in the mid-century there had been groups of cooperatively owned houses in the outskirts of American cities, like John Stevens' Industrial Homes Associations. No real effort had been made, however, to stem the tide of speculation and reckless concentration which had made the larger town a shapeless mass of factories, commercial buildings, residential oases, and shabby, depressing slums. It was now too late to do more than modify these features of the older cities; the alternative was to plan new ones. Ebenezer Howard had shown how this could be done in *Garden Cities of Tomorrow*, with its small industrial units surrounded by well-spaced homes and greenbelts, and

McKim, Mead, & White, Columbia University Library, New York City

the garden city of Letchworth in England rose in 1903 to demonstrate his principles. Six years later Raymond Unwin devoted his *Town Planning in Practice* to civic art as an expression of the total life of the community, surveying the history of that notion from Egypt to Sir Christopher Wren.

This book and Patrick Geddes' *City Development* of 1904 would be a challenge and an inspiration to the few American designers of vision in the nineteen twenties; but meanwhile what passed for "planning" in the century's first few years was a shallow solution on the aesthetic level, a tactful mitigation of a disorder which had its roots in the national attitude toward private property and the inalienable right to speculate with land.

There was a flurry of municipal planning in the first decade of the century: a scheme for Los Angeles with an avenue a mile long and two hundred feet wide ending in a plaza. Olmsted and Cass Gilbert were trying to restore order out of chaos at New Haven; Burnham drew a plan for Chicago and another for Cleveland, in the latter case assisted by Carrère and Arnold Brunner. San Francisco failed to adopt a Brunham scheme. When the Columbus, Ohio, Commission discovered that a new skyscraper stood on the edge of its proposed long mall to the state house, it recommended that a companion be built for the sake of symmetry. Such planners did their best to plant a miniature version of the Chicago Exposition in the midst of some urban tangle and thus to present as dignified a front as possible to the world.

No one could complain in the early nineteen hundreds that architecture was not taken seriously. Up and down the land courses were being given in colleges and universities; the Society of Beaux-Arts Architects conducted extension courses and organized ateliers; every important structure was described, illustrated, and criticized in the professional periodicals. The *American Art Annual* published in 1900 a directory of architects which was far from being complete, since it was drawn from the membership lists of seven professional societies, yet the roster had nearly twelve hundred names and in 1910 had risen to over twenty-six hundred.

The work of most of them suffered not so much from what Sturgis called immaturity as from premature senility. The shingled "Richardsonian" of Babb, Cook, and Willard, for example, and the railway stations of the dead master's partners and pupils were thin variations on his sturdy theme; without his instinct for unity, their contrasts of light and dark stone defaced the solid wall, their careful asymmetry became a loose jumble of parts. Their failure was written large and sprawling in schools, libraries, town halls, and courthouses in what Ralph Adams Cram calls a "love-feast of cavernous arches, quarry-faced ashlar, cyclopean voussoirs and seaweed decorations." Frank E. Case, a prosperous manufacturer of dental equipment, was one of countless citizens who built in this fashion, and whose mansion at Canton, Ohio, in the nineties bristled with gables, with turrets poked into angles, with monstrous chimneys erupting from sandstone façades, and with porte-cocheres huddling against them.

Large and small, in country and in suburb, thousands of competent men rang endless changes on the Romanesque, the Queen Anne, and a "Colonial" which reproduced the low ceilings, the boxlike rooms, the small windows of the age of fireplaces. In cities where the human stream wore deeper among man-made canyons with every year of "progress," firms like George Browne Post and Sons committed themselves to no one dialect but spoke loudly and fluently in all, clinging to the old three-part formula for the skyscraper which Sullivan had long since discarded. In the same years which saw Sullivan's Bayard Building in Bleecker Street praised by Montgomery Schuyler as architecture "founded on the facts of the case," the Posts raised New York's tallest structure, the St. Paul, whose twenty-two stories apologized garrulously for being so high. Their Prudential Insurance Building in Newark was lined with Caen marble, and Blashfield's *Prudencia* graced the ceiling of its board room; their huge hotels at Detroit and Cleveland in the century's second decade established a type but not a style.

As the states outgrew their old capitols the pattern of Thornton, Latrobe, and Walter on the Potomac was let out to fit them. The ungainly national dome was on McKim's state house at Providence in 1903, with four tourelles at its base which recalled the more florid ones on Madison Square Garden; it rode the crossing of the Posts' capitol at Madison, Wisconsin, and reared itself as the climax of the Wilder and White group in faraway Olympia in the State of Washington.

All these were monuments to the Easiest Way, like Francis Henry Kimball's Manhattan Life, the Metropolitan Life by Le Brun with its Venetian campanile, the pedimented Stock Exchange in New York by Post and Sons, the châteaulike St. Luke's Hospital by Ernest Flagg, the Waldorf-Astoria of Henry J. Hardenbergh — to choose at random among their kind. There were plan-and-elevation men in all cities, many of whom took their cue from McKim, Mead, and White, who had no peers in the art of the polished quotation. Having conquered the Chicago Exposition, the McKim idea proceeded to conquer the country. The firm produced another Pantheon with a dim reading room beneath its dome, the Columbia Library, and its Herald Building of 1894 was an exquisite near replica of the Consiglio Palace at Verona. Three years later the palazzo formula was used again in the University Club where H. Siddons Mowbray plagiarized the Pintoricchio murals at Rome and Siena. The Baths of Caracalla became the Pennsylvania Station in 1903, its huge waiting hall of Roman travertine dwarfing the human passenger, the naked steel trusses of its concourse more impressive than the veneered tepidarium behind it.

The McKim example, in the words of Pope, "filled half the land with imitating fools;" and when Mr. Morgan's library in 1906 was housed behind the Palladian motif of the Villa Medici, Rochester copied it in the Art Gallery of Foster, Gade, and Graham.

McKim's young men had already been heard from when Cass Gilbert placed the dome of St. Peter's on his St. Paul capitol in 1896, and when John Merven Carrère and Thomas Hastings designed a public library in New York which was only a little better adapted to its purpose than the Boston one. Carrère and Hastings had been fellow students at the Beaux-Arts before they worked together for McKim and became partners on their own, designing a more or less Spanish hotel for Henry Flagler at St. Augustine. They rebuilt the Palace of Fontainebleau at Lakewood, New Jersey, as the Hotel Laurel-in-the-Pines. The rear façade of their New York Public Library suggested the life within as its three Roman arches on Fifth Avenue did not; their Frick house in the Louis XVI manner was as expensively simple as the Morgan pile; they made the Senate and House Office Buildings discreetly subordinate companions to the Washington Capitol.

In the century since Latrobe, America had always had its partisans of the crocket and the finial. Now Upjohn and James Renwick were dead, leaving Trinity, Grace Church, and St. Patrick's to remind younger men of their fine strength and independence. Charles Coolidge Haight designed the General Theological Seminary in the eighties, and his sober charm in these and his Yale buildings seemed the proper scholastic note. New Yorkers praised the skill with which J. Stewart Barney's massive tower — in fact, a five-story office building — rode the nave of his Broadway Tabernacle. What the Gothicists needed was a scholar-designer who could speak this language as authoritatively as McKim spoke another, and who could justify the flying buttress in the age of Bryan. This man was Ralph Adams Cram, whose Gothic quest had begun in the eighties.

Neither of Cram's partners shared his concern with the values beneath forms. The practical mind of Frank W. Ferguson occupied itself with problems of business, construction details, and efficient specifications, which he organized into systematic office files. Bertram G. Goodhue's mind was pictorial; dissatisfied with the hard, ruler-drawn lines of architectural rendering, and perhaps inspired by the brilliant pen-and-ink methods of Pennell and the illustrators, he made ingratiating sketches of the firm's projects. In the Goodhue drawings, details were tactfully suppressed to intimate how a structure would look when the sun played over its forms and patterned them with shadows. He had learned his Gothic from Renwick and practiced it with an eye for the handsome general effect. He built a church at Havana with the lush detail of an authentic Spanish mission, launched the California Renaissance with his Gillespie villa at Santa Barbara, and gave the Romanesque a new twist in the brick vaults of St. Bartholomew's in New York. The gigantic reredos of St. Thomas' on Fifth Avenue was his, and much of the firm's work at West Point had his flair for the handsome site handsomely built upon.

1951 AWARD

ABOUT THE PIONEER
PERIOD OF THE NORTHWEST

BY

R. CARLYLE BULEY

R. Carlyle Buley (born on July 8, 1893, in Georgetown, Ind.) was graduated from Indiana University in 1914 and earned his Master of Arts degree there two years later. At the same time, he joined the staff of Delphi and Muncie (Ind.) high schools as a history teacher. After having served as a private advancing to the rank of sergeant with the United States Army during World War I, he became head of department and assistant principal of Springfield (Ill.) High School, as well as principal of the Knights of Columbus evening schools in 1919. Four years later, Buley started working as an assistant instructor at the University of Wisconsin, where he also earned his doctorate of philosophy in 1925. Thereafter, he came as an instructor to Indiana University, being promoted to professor of American history in the course of the years. In addition to this, he was member of the American Mississippi Valley historical associations and the Ohio historical societies. Buley was the editor of *The Indiana Home. The Political Balance in the Old Northwest* and *The American Life Convention - A Study in the History of Life Insurance*, a work in two volumes, number among his publications. Moreover, he worked as co-author on *The Midwest Pioneer - His Ills, Cures and Doctors*. In 1950 R. Carlyle Buley published his two-volume work *The Old Northwest, Pioneer Period 1815-1840*. The year after, it was selected by the Advisory Board on the Pulitzer Prizes as the best book on American history.

MEDICAL AND HEALTH-RELATED CONDITIONS

[Source: R. Carlyle Buley: The Old Northwest, Pioneer Period 1815-1840, Vol. 1, Indianapolis: Indiana Historical Society, 1950, pp. 240 - 243; reprinted by permission of Indiana University Press, Bloomington, Ind.]

NOTHING was more vital in the conquest of the wilderness than health, but over none of the factors involved did the settlers seemingly have less control. Active life in the open did not suffice to counteract the effects of exposure, decaying vegetation, swamps, poor food habits, lack of sanitation and hygiene, and inadequate knowledge and facilities for prevention and cure. The sallow complexions and jaundiced looks of the firstcomers, so often noted by the travelers, bore ample witness to the fact that all was not well within, and for a generation or longer sickness was a thing certainly to be expected. The reputation of the West for unhealthfulness was the one important factor to be weighed in the balance against the powerful appeals of fortune and freedom.

"The principal objection I have to this country is its unhealthiness the months of August and September are generally very sickly," wrote Gershom Flagg in 1819 from Edwardsville, Illinois, after he had been ill of fever and ague for two months, and he decided if another season did not bring improvement, to sell out and leave the country. The *Spectator* announced that its hands had been so disabled by the influenza, that it could issue only half a sheet. Conditions remained much the same for years. Fifteen years later, during the exceptionally dry, hot summer of 1834, there was much sickness in this same region. "It ought not to be concealed that . . . there are many sick people; and we believe that there are many situations, some of which have been noticed, that may properly be denominated sickly . . . ," wrote Thomas of the Wabash country in 1816. He listed the prevailing ills as bilious, intermittent, and remittent fevers, with some liver complaints.

Around the new settlement at Indianapolis toward the end of the summer and during the fall of 1821 epidemic intermittent and remittent fevers and agues assailed the people to such an extent that the few unafflicted were employed night and day ministering to the sufferers, and one eighth of the population was swept away. "Out of one thousand souls in town on the donation and the farms surrounding the town, at least 900 sickened during the prevailing epidemic." At Vevay, where rapid influx of settlers resulted in congestion and two or three families to the house, one in six died of bilious fevers during the summer and fall of 1820. The next autumn the sluggish, green, putrid waters of the Wabash and White rivers affected towns in Indiana and Illinois. "The situation of this town is at present truly deplorable," wrote the Vincennes *Western Sun*. "Nearly one-third of the population appears to be confined on beds of sickness, while the houses of the humane farmers in the vicinity are crowded with our fugitive convalescents." "Last season has been unprecedented in the annals of the Western States for malignant diseases," wrote Dr. Asahel Clapp of New Albany in January, 1823.

In the middle 1830's the people of Elkhart County had an epidemic of typhoid and pneumonia and in 1838 almost half the population was affected with bilious disorders. The wave of erysipelas which enveloped the whole Northwest in the early 1840's struck this county with unusual severity; also Evansville and southern Indiana. Dysentery, scarlatina, phthisis, pneumonia, bronchitis, occasionally yellow and spotted fevers, whooping cough, and diphtheria appeared in many parts of the state. The year 1845 was a "disastrous and melancholy sickly season" in the Wabash country; the South Bend *St. Joseph Valley Register* noted that it was the seventh year from the last bad outbreak, as if that explained it.

In Michigan as soon as the land was plowed "and the malarial gases set free, . . . the country became very sickly. . . . There were ten all down at once, my mother, the only one able to minister the cup of cold water and care for the sick. Crops went back into the ground, animals suffered for food, and if the people had not been too sick to need much to eat they, too, must have gone hungry. The pale, sallow, bloated faces of that period were the rule; there were no healthy faces except of persons just arrived." Bilious diseases were very prevalent in Detroit in the autumns of 1819, 1823, and 1826. Filth in the streets and filthy drinking water scooped up from the river shore were partly blamed. As late as 1839 whole villages were laid out temporarily, but after a few days people would crawl about like yellow ghosts, fortunate if they got enough to eat, for appetites were ravenous, but food digested little easier than stones.

> Don't go to Michigan, that land of ills;
> The word means ague, fever, and chills.

Even in Ohio the most distressing sickness generally prevailed and great mortality, particularly from bilious fevers and cholera morbus. Said James Kilbourne, prominent journalist and legislator: "Respecting the healthfulness of this country, I have to repeat that it is in fact sickly in a considerable degree." He reported the presence of bilious fever:

Almost all were sick, both in towns and country, so that it became difficult, in many instances, to get tenderers for the sick. In many instances whole families were down at a time and many died. . . . What seems strange to me is that the Indians who were natives of the country are as subject to the disorder as the whites. Of the few who remain in the territory some are now sick with it and they say it has always been so, and that they have often been obliged to move back from the meadows and bottoms where they always lived, into the woods and uplands during the sickly season to escape it.

The autumn of 1819 was bad along the Scioto bottoms, "whence deleterious exhalations arise."

1952 AWARD

ABOUT THE GREAT
MIGRATIONS IN AMERICA

BY

OSCAR HANDLIN

Oscar Handlin (born on September 29, 1915, in Brooklyn, N.Y.) attended Brooklyn College, where he majored in history. He completed the undergraduate course in three years, taking his B.A. degree in 1934 and winning the Union League Award for history. The following year he received his Master of Arts degree in history at Harvard University. A Frederick Sheldon Traveling Fellowship enabled him to devote a year to research in England, France, Italy and Ireland. On his return to the United States, he taught history at Brooklyn College before, in 1939, he returned to Harvard as an instructor in the History Department and as candidate for the Ph.D. degree. He received the doctorate the following year. In 1941 Handlin published his first book, *Boston's Immigrants, 1790-1865*, which won for him the J.H. Dunning prize of the American Historical Association. He is also the recipient of the 1942 Brooklyn College Alumni Award of Honor. Handlin held an assistant professorship of history at Harvard and was later transferred to the newly formed Department of Social Science. In 1948 he returned to the History Department as an associate professor. Handlin, who frequently contributed articles to scholarly and general periodicals, is also the compiler and editor of *This was America*. He and his wife are the co-authors of *Commonwealth*. Oscar Handlin won the Pulitzer Prize for history of 1952 for his work entitled *The Uprooted*, which had been published the preceding year.

GHETTOS IN SEVERAL METROPOLITAN AREAS

[Source: Oscar Handlin: The Uprooted. The Epic Story of the Great Migrations that Made the American People, Boston: Little, Brown and Company, 1951, pp. 144 - 148; reprinted by permission of Little, Brown and Company, Publishers, Boston, Mass.]

In the United States, the newcomers pushed their roots into many different soils. Along the city's unyielding asphalt streets, beside the rutted roads of mill or mining towns, amidst the exciting prairie acres, they established the homes of the New World. But wherever the immigrants went, there was one common experience they shared: nowhere could they transplant the European village. Whatever the variations among environments in America, none was familiar. The pressure of that strangeness exerted a deep influence upon the character of resettlement, upon the usual forms of behavior, and upon the modes of communal action that emerged as the immigrants became Americans.

The old conditions of living could not survive in the new conditions of space. Ways long taken for granted in the village adjusted slowly and painfully to density of population in the cities, to disorder in the towns, and to distance on the farms. That adjustment was the means of creating the new communities within which these people would live.

Although the great mass of immigrants spent out their days in the great cities, there was always an unorganized quality to settlement in such places that left a permanent impress upon every fresh arrival. Chance was so large an element in the course of migration, it left little room for planning. The place of landing was less often the outcome of an intention held at the outset of the journey than of blind drift along the routes of trade or of a sudden halt due to the accidents of the voyage. Consequently the earliest concentrations of the foreign-born were in the chain of Atlantic seaports: Boston, Philadelphia, Baltimore, New Orleans, and most of all New York, the unrivaled mart of Europe's commerce with America. For the same reasons, later concentrations appeared at the inland termini, the points of exchange between rail and river or lake traffic — Cleveland, Chicago, Cincinnati, Pittsburgh, and St. Louis.

In all such places the newcomers pitched themselves in the midst of communities that were already growing rapidly and that were therefore already crowded. Between 1840 and 1870, for instance, the population of New York City mounted by fully 50 per cent every ten years; for every two people at the start of a decade, there were three at its end. (In all, the 312,000 residents of 1840 had become 3,437,000 in 1900.) Chicago's rise was even more precipitate; the 4000 inhabitants there in 1840 numbered 1,700,000 in 1900. Every ten-year interval saw two people struggling for the space formerly occupied by one.

These largest cities were representative of the rest. The natural increase through the excess of births over deaths, with the additional increase through the shift of native-born population from rural to urban areas, and with the further increase through overseas immigration, all contributed to the enormous growth of American municipalities. To house all the new city dwellers was a problem of staggering proportions. Facilities simply did not keep pace with the demand.

To house the immigrants was more difficult still. For these people had not the mobility to choose where they should live or the means to choose how. Existing on the tenuous income supplied by unskilled labor, they could not buy homes; nor could they lay out much in payment of rent. Their first thought in finding accommodations was that the cost be as little as possible. The result was they got as little as possible.

The willingness to accept a minimum of comfort and convenience did not, however, mean that such quarters would always be available. Under the first impact of immigration, the unprepared cities had not ready the housing immigrants could afford. The newcomers were driven to accept hand-me-downs, vacated places that could be converted to their service at a profit.

The immigrants find their first homes in quarters the old occupants no longer desire. As business grows, the commercial center of each city begins to blight the neighboring residential districts. The well-to-do are no longer willing to live in close proximity to the bustle of warehouses and offices; yet that same proximity sets a high value on real estate. To spend money on the repair or upkeep of houses in such areas is only wasteful; for they will soon be torn down to make way for commercial buildings. The simplest, most profitable use is to divide the old mansions into tiny lodgings. The rent on each unit will be low; but the aggregate of those sums will, without substantial investment or risk, return larger dividends than any other present use of the property.

Such accommodations have additional attractions for the immigrants. They are close to the familiar region of the docks and they are within walking distance of the places where labor is hired; precious carfare will be saved by living here. In every American city some such district of first settlement receives the newcomers.

Not that much is done to welcome them. The carpenters hammer shut connecting doors and build rude partitions up across the halls; middle-class homes thus become laborers' — only not one to a family, but shared among many. What's more, behind the original structures are grassy yards where children once had run about at play. There is to be no room for games now. Sheds and shanties, hurriedly thrown up, provide living space; and if a stable is there, so much the better: that too can be turned to account. In 1850 already in New York some seven thousand households are finding shelter in such rear buildings. By this time too ingenuity has uncovered still other resources: fifteen hundred cellars also do service as homes.

If these conversions are effected without much regard for the convenience of the ultimate occupants, they nevertheless have substantial advantages. The carpenter aims to do the job as expeditiously as possible; he has not the time to contrive the most thorough use of space; and waste square feet leave luxurious corners. There are limits to the potentialities for crowding in such quarters.

There were no such limits when enterprising contractors set to work devising edifices more suitable for the reception of these residents. As the population continued to grow, and the demand with it, perspicacious owners of real estate saw profit in the demolition of the old houses and the construction, between narrow alleys, of compact barracks that made complete use of every inch of earth.

Where once had been Mayor Delavall's orchard, Cherry Street in New York ran its few blocks to the East River shipyards. At Number 36, in 1853, stood Gotham Court, one of the better barrack buildings. Five stories in height, it stretched back one hundred and fifty feet from the street, between two tight alleys (one nine, the other seven feet wide). Onto the more spacious alley opened twelve doors through each of which passed the ten families that lived within, two to each floor in identical two-room apartments (one room, 9 x 14; one bedroom, 9 x 6). Here without interior plumbing or heat were the homes of five hundred people.

1953 AWARD

ABOUT THE YEARS OF
PRESIDENT JAMES MONROE

BY

GEORGE B. DANGERFIELD

George Bubb Dangerfield (born on October 28, 1904, in Newbury, Berkshire, England) entered Hertford College at Oxford University in 1923. He received his Bachelor of Arts degree with honors in English literature in June 1927. Beginning his career as a poet, Dangerfield taught at the English Institute in Prague, Czechoslovakia, and subsequently at the English College in Hamburg, Germany. In 1930 he settled in the United States and served as a reader and editor for the New York publishing house of Brewer, Warren and Putnam during the following two years. From 1933 to 1935 he held the post of literary editor of *Vanity Fair* magazine. During World War II Dangerfield served with the 102nd Infantry Division of the United States Army and while stationed at Paris, Texas, in April 1943, he became an American citizen. Dangerfield has lectured widely throughout the United States and has contributed numerous book reviews and articles on such writers as Strachey, E.M. Forster, Archibald MacLeish and Rosamond Lehmann to various periodicals. He is the author of the following books: *Bengal Mutiny: The Story of the Sepoy Rebellion*; *The Strange Death of Liberal England*; *Victoria's Heir: The Education of a Prince*. After the Second World War George B. Dangerfield wrote his first book dealing with American history. In January 1952 it was published under the title *The Era of Good Feelings* and earned him the Pulitzer Prize for history of the following year.

THE PRESIDENT'S BACKGROUND AND PLANS

[Source: George Dangerfield: The Era of Good Feelings, New York: Harcourt, Brace and Company, 1952, pp. 97 - 100; reprinted by permission of Mr. Anthony Dangerfield, Santa Barbara, Cal., and of Harcourt Brace and Company, Orlando, Fla.]

He was in his sixty-first year when he became President, a tall man, of a rather venerable appearance, who wore the knee-length pantaloons and white-topped boots of an earlier day. Men looked up and took their fill of his obvious presence. It was easy to recall the fact that he had fought with credit in the Revolutionary War; indeed, everything about him was a reminder of a time sufficiently distant for everyone to be proud of it. He was a Virginian, but not an aristocratic Virginian like Jefferson and Madison: he was more awkward and more formal than they; he was also less subtle, original, and intelligent. On the whole, people preferred it that way. The Virginia Dynasty had been noted hitherto rather for complexity than for simplicity, and if the new President had to be a Virginian, which some northern people did not think a necessity, at least it was a consolation to know that he was an understandable one.

Two weeks before his inauguration, Monroe received a letter from Boston which has at least the merit of foreshadowing the course of events. His correspondent, William Tudor, Jr., was editor of the *North American Review*, a periodical which became so extremely sectional under his brief sway that it was sometimes called the *North Unamerican*. After congratulating the President-to-be on the "feeling of sovereignty," Tudor—who was, needless to say, a Federalist—went on to suggest that the time had come for a conciliation between Massachusetts and the national government. "I have heard in more than one instance solid respectable citizens express their belief in your magnanimity & generous feelings." These solid respectable citizens were all, oddly enough, Federalists also. As for the Democrats in Boston, they were "utterly contemptible . . . cringing & subservient . . . in reality ready to betray those who have fostered them." In Monroe's case, the writer had it on the best authority that they were determined that he should not enjoy a second term, and that they proposed to unite with the "sorry factions" of Pennsylvania and New York for this purpose. The Federalists, on the other hand, were now ready to support and not oppose the national government. "I think on the principles now acted upon at Washington that they have no dispute to maintain. If it were possible for you gradually to bring about an exchange, take the support of the Federalists and abandon their opponents you would be a prodigious gainer."

Such were the beguilements of Mr. William Tudor. Whether a Jeffersonian President would care to be congratulated upon a "feeling of sovereignty," or whether he would repose much confidence in a party that had delivered the electoral vote of Massachusetts to his rival in the recent election, were questions Mr. Tudor—who can hardly be accused of being over-sensitive—seems not to have pondered very deeply. What is more to the point is that the letter revealed, in an irritating but useful manner, both the tactics and sentiments of the Federalist minority.

When the news of peace reached Washington in February 1815, the commissioners from the Hartford Convention, who had come to present their somewhat secessionist resolutions, departed from the capital city as unobtrusively as possible, but pursued by the gibes of their countrymen. With them they carried the ruin of the Federalist Party. It was just strong enough in 1816 to carry the states of Massachusetts, Connecticut, and Delaware against Monroe, but that was the end. Thereafter it clung, in a rather fungoid manner, to certain localities, but as a national party it had ceased to exist.

The Federalist Party might roughly, very roughly, be described as the party of the mercantile, manufacturing, and investing interests. The future of these interests in the nineteenth century was to be a glowing one; and since the party that had hitherto served them had been so factious and disloyal as to lose all influence in the country, it was natural enough for them to look for another one. They looked around. There was no choice but a choice between discredited Federalism and triumphant Republicanism; towards Republicanism, therefore, they gravitated. They were not generally so crude as Mr. William Tudor; they did not suppose that the President would openly seek their support; but they were sure that they could seek the support of the President. For indeed, as Mr. Tudor had so unkindly put it, there was nothing in recent events at Washington to indicate that their ideas would be unwelcome there.

Thomas Jefferson was not a party man. He believed that political parties had to some extent a physiological foundation—that they represented rather a variety in nature than a validity of principle. "The terms of whig and tory," he said, "belong to natural as well as to civil history. They denote the temper and constitution of mind of different individuals." Certainly parties were useful, but how easily did they cease to embody principles and degenerate into factions! "If we can hit on the true line of conduct which may conciliate the honest part of those who are called federalists," he wrote in 1801, ". . . I shall hope to be able to obliterate, or rather to unite the name of federalists & republicans." But Jefferson grew alarmed at the amount of union, or obliteration, that took place under his successor. Before he left office in 1817, James Madison seemed almost to have adopted the program of his adversaries—seemed only to have saved himself, by a last veto, from becoming a convert, by total immersion, to the Federalist Church. True, that church as a physical structure was in ruins; but its spirit was everywhere. When the Republicans, under Madison, chartered a Second Bank of the United States; when their newspapers recited in support of this Second Bank the very arguments Alexander Hamilton had adduced to prove the constitutionality of the First; when they showed a marked solicitude for manufactures, for tariffs, for an army and a navy—where was it all to end?

Where indeed? James Monroe, so susceptible to influences, was not the man to resist the drift away from old agrarian Republicanism. The inferences Mr. Tudor had drawn from the late proceedings of Mr. Madison and his Administration were, no doubt, crudely drawn, but who was to say that they were not correct?

President Monroe assumed office under conditions very nearly unique. Every man who hoped to better his interests—it scarcely mattered what those interests were—had begun to call himself a Jeffersonian Republican. A social democracy can survive under, or even require, a one-party government; but a political democracy cannot. Thomas Jefferson had predicted this state of affairs long before, and had outlined also the dangers that might arise from it. "I had always expected," he told Thomas Cooper in 1807, "that when the republicans should have put all things under their feet, they would schismatize among themselves. I always expected, too, that whatever names the parties might bear, the real division would be into moderate & ardent republicanism. In this division there is no great danger. . . . It is to be considered as apostasy only when they purchase the votes of federalists, with a participation in honor & power."

But Jefferson did not take into consideration the fact that "moderate" republicanism might apostatize to the Federalists not by purchasing their votes but by assimilating their views; in short, that it was not political apostasy that was to be feared, but political osmosis. Apostasy had been thrust under Monroe's nose in the letter from William Tudor; and, several months later, was thrust under it again in a letter from George Sullivan, one of the leaders of the Boston bar, who blandly suggested that his intimate friend, Mr. Daniel Webster, could readily be induced to come into Monroe's Administration as Attorney-General, and that if he did so he would prove to be "a rock, on which your administration might rest secure against the violence of almost any faction." Otherwise, said Mr. Sullivan, "your administration will be overthrown; because your Cabinet is weak & discordant."

Monroe was proof against such offers. What confronted him was a more alluring possibility: that inaction might become wisdom. To let things slide; to observe and modify but not actually attempt to shape the course of events; all Monroe's instincts urged him to such a course. It had, it is true, some distressing results. It meant the death of the old—the "ardent"—Republican Party as a national force, and its transfiguration into a sectional one. It meant that Monroe must drift, at a slightly increasing tempo, along the stream of neo-Federalist ideas which had already captured his predecessor. It meant that the clash of parties would give way to the clash of personalities. It meant the most vicious quarrels at the top, and the most peculiar incoherence underneath. But the one-party government of James Monroe gave this very incoherence a chance to develop a shape, however vague, and a direction, however veering.

1954 AWARD

ABOUT THE CIVIL WAR
IN THE STATE OF VIRGINIA

BY

C. BRUCE CATTON

Charles Bruce Catton (born on October 9, 1899, in Petoskey, Mich.) attended Benzonia Academy and entered Oberlin College in 1916. He left college during World War I to enlist in the Navy. After two years' service he returned to Oberlin, but at the end of his junior year he left to become a professional newspaper man. From 1920 to 1926 he reported for the Cleveland *News*, the Boston *American* and the Cleveland *Plain Dealer*. In 1926 he joined the Newspaper Enterprise Association service - writing editorials and book reviews, running a Sunday section or acting as a Washington correspondent. Catton became a government man in 1942, serving as director of information for the War Productive Board and holding similar posts after the war with the Department of Commerce and the Department of the Interior. Since 1952 he has devoted his entire time to the production of his literary works such as *U.S. Grant and the American Military Tradition* and *The War Lords of Washington*. In 1953 *A Stillness at Appomattox* by C. Bruce Catton was published. It is the third of a trilogy on the Union Army, including *Mr. Lincoln's Army* and *Glory Road*. This third volume made Catton the winner of the 1954 Pulitzer Prize in the category History.

A BATTLE NEAR THE APPOMATTOX RIVER

[Source: Bruce Catton: A Stillness at Appomattox, Garden City, N.Y.: Doubleday & Company, Inc., 1953, pp. 164 - 167; reprinted by permission of Bantam, Doubleday, Dell Publishing Group, New York, N.Y.]

Life began with the darkness. All day long the men out in front huddled close to the ground, dust in their teeth, a glaring sun pressing on their shoulders. To peer over the rim of earth that lay between the firing line and the enemy was to ask for a bullet, and it was almost certain death to try to go to the rear for any reason at all—to have a wound dressed, to get food, to fill a canteen with muddy warm water, or to attend to a call of nature. Death was everywhere, its unspeakable scent in every breath men drew, the ugly whine of it keening through the air over the flat whack of the sharpshooter's rifle. On distant elevations, obscure in the quivering haze, there were the guns, cleverly sited, and the gunners were prompt to fire at anything that moved. From one end of the army to the other, men endured heat and thirst and nameless discomforts and waited for night.

At night the front came alive. Along the lines men took the shovels and picks and axes which details brought out to them and worked to make their trenches deep and strong. Where there were trees, they cut them down, put the slashed branches out in front for an abatis, and used the logs to make the breastworks solid. They dug their trenches deep, so that a man could stand erect in them without being shot, and they cut zig-zag alleyways through the earth back toward the rear, so that they might go to and from the front without being killed.

Being very human, the soldiers on both sides often dug their trenches so deep that while they offered almost perfect protection against enemy fire they were quite useless for fighting purposes. In each army it was found that there were long stretches of trench in which a man could not possibly point his musket toward the enemy, and from both blue and gray headquarters orders went out to front-line commanders warning that there must always be fire steps on which riflemen could stand to shoot their foes.

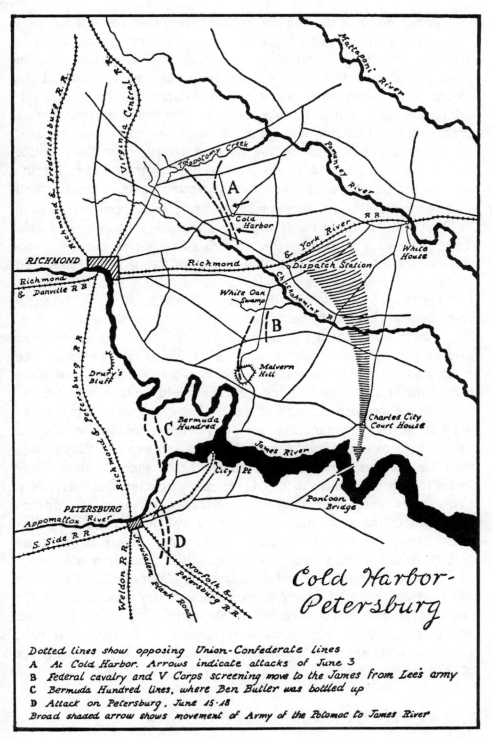

*Cold Harbor-
Petersburg*

Dotted lines show opposing Union-Confederate lines
A   At Cold Harbor. Arrows indicate attacks of June 3
B   Federal cavalry and V Corps screening move to the James from Lee's army
C   Bermuda Hundred lines, where Ben Butler was bottled up
D   Attack on Petersburg, June 15-18
Broad shaded arrow shows movement of Army of the Potomac to James River

Along much of the line the trenches were so close that the men could hear their enemies chatting together. In many places the lines were not far enough apart to give the pickets proper room, and in these places there was constant skirmishing all the way around the clock. Even where there was a decent distance, the lines were seldom quiet. Half a dozen shots from the skirmish lines could bring great rolling salvos from the guns, so that at times it sounded as if an immense battle were rocking back and forth over the desolate bottomlands. Most of this cannonading did no great harm, for the men in the deep trenches were well protected against missiles fired with relatively flat trajectory, and fuses were so imperfect that even the best gunners could rarely explode a shell directly over a trench. To get around this difficulty the artillerists brought up coehorn mortars—squat little jugs of iron that rested on flat wooden bases and pointed up toward the sky, which could toss shells in a high arc so that they might fall into a distant slit in the earth. At night the fuses from these shells traced sputtering red patterns across the sky.

The infantry hated the mortars, regarding them, as one veteran said, as "a contemptible scheme to make a soldier's life wretched." The weapons were usually out of sight behind a bank of earth, and when they were fired the men in the trenches could neither hear the report nor see the flash and puff of smoke. They had no warning: nothing but the hissing spark that rose deliberately, seemed to hang in the air high overhead, and then fell to earth to explode. Even more than the mortars, however, the soldiers hated sharpshooters. They had a feeling that sharpshooters never really affected the course of a battle: they were sheer malignant nuisances, taking unfair advantages and killing men who might just as well have remained alive. One artillerist wrote that the sharpshooters would "sneak around trees or lurk behind stumps" and from this shelter "murder a few men," and he burst out with the most indignant complaint of all: "There was an unwritten code of honor among the infantry that forbade the shooting of men while attending to the imperative calls of nature, and these sharpshooting brutes were constantly violating that rule. I hated sharpshooters, both Confederate and Union, and I was always glad to see them killed."

1955 AWARD

ABOUT THE RIO GRANDE IN NORTH AMERICAN HISTORY

BY

PAUL HORGAN

Paul Horgan (born on August 1, 1903, in Buffalo, N.Y.) attended the New Mexico Military Institute at Roswell, N.M., where he edited the school literary journal and where he already demonstrated a great interest in dramatics, music and art. After his father's death in 1922 the family moved back East and for three years Paul Horgan studied at the Eastman School of Music in Rochester, N.Y. There, he also worked at the school's theatre. In 1926 Horgan returned to the New Mexico Military Institute as the institute's librarian, a job compatible with writing and historical research. When the U.S. entered World War II, Horgan became chief of Army Information with the Department of War in Washington, D.C., a post in which he reached the rank of lieutenant colonel and received the Legion of Merit. On his discharge from the Army, he received the first of two Guggenheim grants. After lecturing for a semester in the Graduate School of Arts and Letters of the University of Iowa, he returned to Roswell to resume his research and writing. Horgan was a very prolific writer: His first historical book, *Men of Arms*, which was illustrated by himself, was published in 1931. His first Southwestern novel *No Quarter Given* was followed by a whole lot of fictional works e.g. *Main Line West*; *A Lamp on the Plains*; *The Return of the Weed* and *The Habit of Empire*, as well as the play *Yours, A. Lincoln* and the libretto to the folk opera *A Tree on the Plains*. Fourteen years of research and composition went into Paul Horgan's *Great River: The Rio Grande in North American History*, published in 1954. The following year it earned him the Pulitzer Prize for history.

AMERICAN AND MEXICAN RIVER SETTLEMENTS

[Source: Paul Horgan: Great River: The Rio Grande in North American History, New York - Toronto: Rinehart & Company, Inc., 1954, pp. 614, 888 - 890; reprinted by permission of Farrar, Straus & Giroux, Inc., New York, N.Y.]

In 1860, as though re-enacting in miniature an earlier pattern of conquest, a small party of Americans passed through the Mexican settlements of the San Luis Valley and followed the Rio Grande out of sight into the mountains of the source. They were looking for gold in the San Juan. Their search took them through summer and autumn, until they were caught in the snows of winter. In the following spring they were joined by other prospectors and all spent the next summer in the San Juan Mountains, but without finding gold. Before another winter could trap them they returned eastward to Fort Garland, where they heard that the Civil War had broken out; and the leader of the prospectors hurried to Virginia to enlist.

At the end of the decade other attempts were made to find the riches of the San Juan, and scattered strikes led to the establishment of mines on the western slope of the continental divide. By 1870 there was enough traffic along the headwaters of the Rio Grande to call alive the town of Del Norte as a supply point, at the gateway of the river between the San Luis Valley and the mountains. In the same year gold was found at Wightman's Gulch and other sites in the Del Norte region, the most thriving of which was Summitville to the southwest. The population of the district grew to six hundred. Stamp mills were set up at the largest camps. During the short summers pack trains bringing ore came from over the divide by way of Stony Pass which was over twelve thousand feet above sea level. On the eastward road out of the mountains a new town was founded in 1878—Alamosa.

It came as the new western terminus of the Denver and Rio Grande Western Railroad. The town itself came by rail, for from the old terminus of Garland City houses, churches, stores and other buildings were hauled on flat cars to be set up at the new end of the line. With heavy transportation now available, a new commercial interest was developed in the San Luis Valley that soon overshadowed mining as the main business of the region. Large-scale irrigation projects were organized and supported by foreign capital—principally British. Between Alamosa and Del Norte a huge grid of irrigation canals reached out from the Rio Grande for thirty or forty miles north and south. A land boom resulted. Speculation in land values and water rights went wild. As in so many other Western localities toward the end of the nineteenth century, company promoters preached a new paradise and trainloads of colonists came in response to the dazzling promise. For a little while, so long as competition was fresh and vigorous, the San Luis prospered in the vision of a future nourished by inexhaustible resources. Monte Vista, a third railroad town, was founded in 1887. But within a decade the vision bagan to pale, for what ended so many other organized Western dreams elsewhere presently took effect in southern Colorado—there was not enough water. Sapped by the greatly overextended system

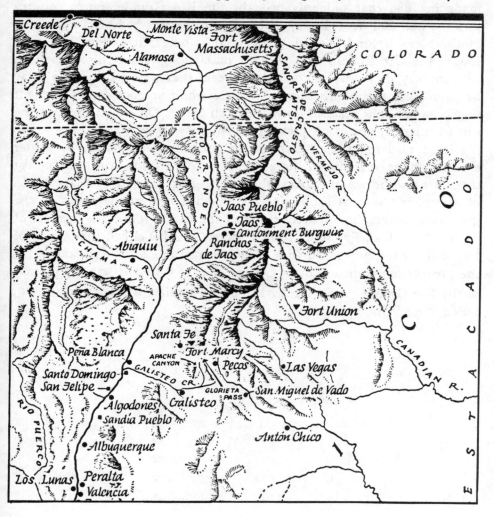

of canals, the river could not supply all. The euphoria of the pioneer faded, many immigrants abandoned their hopes and went away, and those who remained came to a regulated sharing of the waters whose stabilized flow was made possible by the building of reservoirs at the head of the valley. In the same period the mining ventures of the San Luis Valley began to lose energy. The camptowns of the Summitville region were left to the weather, and turned into silvered ghosts. Raw pine boarding turned gray, and weeds climbed the rusting machinery, and the character of the wide valley became wholly agricultural, supplied and drained by the railroad in a stabilized economy.

But farther up the river a major find of precious minerals was made in 1889 that suddenly brought the Rio Grande source country into the national news. For several years prospectors had been scratching at the rocks beyond Wagon Wheel Gap—where Kit Carson had once fought the Ute Indians—but without making significant discoveries. In that country they saw diamond clear creeks that were shadowed all day by narrowing mountains but for a little while at noon, when straight fingers of sunlight reached down through forest. On slopes open to the sun in summer, groves of quaking aspens showed here and there, creating little gardens of their own within immense wild parks. In winter the only green was that of the evergreens, solemn and frowning amidst the silver and brown of lichens—the colors of age—set off by heavy banks of snow. Far above, at timberline, like fixed images of the winds on the inhumane peaks, the last trees clutched the naked rock with gestures of agonized survival. Emerging from between two flat-cliffed mountains of flesh-colored stone streaked with olive lichens came a little stream which the prospectors named Willow Creek. They saw that it was a tributary of the Rio Grande, and that it had its own smaller tributary which they called West Willow Creek.

1956 Award

ABOUT THE AGE OF
REFORM IN THE UNITED STATES

BY

RICHARD HOFSTADTER

Richard Hofstadter (born on August 6, 1916, in Buffalo, N.Y.) studied at the University of Buffalo, majoring in history and philosophy. He received his Bachelor's degree in 1937 and was elected to Phi Beta Kappa. Hofstadter enrolled for graduate study at Columbia University, where he earned his M.A. degree in history in 1938. Thereafter, while writing his doctoral dissertation, he began his teaching career as an instructor in history at Brooklyn College. In 1941 he held an instructorship at the College of the City of New York. Columbia University awarded him the William Bayard Cutting Travelling Fellowship for 1941/42; during this time he completed his requirements for the Ph.D. degree which he received in 1942. That same year Hofstadter became assistant professor of history at the University of Maryland. Two years later his doctoral dissertation, entitled *Social Darwinism in American Thought, 1860-1915* won the Albert J. Beveridge Memorial Prize. In 1946 he returned as assistant professor of history to Columbia University. He rose to the rank of associate professor in 1950 and in 1952 attained a full professorship. In the summer of 1950 the historian taught at the fourth summer session of the Salzburg, Austria, Seminar in American Studies. In 1952 Richard Hofstadter was invited to the University of Chicago to give the Charles R. Walgreen Foundation Lectures. It was out of these lectures that *The Age of Reform* developed. Published in 1955, it was chosen the following year by the Pulitzer Advisory Board as the best book on American history.

PROGRESSIVE IMPULSE IN THE URBAN SCENE

[Source: Richard Hofstadter: The Age of Reform, from Bryan to F.D.R., New York: Alfred A. Knopf, 1955, pp. 173 - 176; reprinted by permission of Alfred A. Knopf, Inc., New York, N.Y.]

FROM 1860 to 1910, towns and cities sprouted up with miraculous rapidity all over the United States. Large cities grew into great metropolises, small towns grew into large cities, and new towns sprang into existence on vacant land. While the rural population almost doubled during this half century, the urban population multiplied almost seven times. Places with more than 50,000 inhabitants increased in number from 16 to 109. The larger cities of the Middle West grew wildly. Chicago more than doubled its population in the single decade from 1880 to 1890, while the Twin Cities trebled theirs, and others like Detroit, Milwaukee, Columbus, and Cleveland increased from sixty to eighty per cent.

The city, with its immense need for new facilities in transportation, sanitation, policing, light, gas, and public structures, offered a magnificent internal market for American business. And business looked for the sure thing, for privileges, above all for profitable franchises and for opportunities to evade as much as possible of the burden of taxation. The urban boss, a dealer in public privileges who could also command public support, became a more important and more powerful figure. With him came that train of evils which so much preoccupied the liberal muckraking mind: the bartering of franchises, the building of tight urban political machines, the marshaling of hundreds of thousands of ignorant voters, the exacerbation of poverty and slums, the absence or excessive cost of municipal services, the co-operation between politics and "commercialized vice"—in short, the entire system of underground government and open squalor that provided such a rich field for the crusading journalists.

Even with the best traditions of public administration, the complex and constantly changing problems created by city growth would have been enormously difficult. Cities throughout the industrial world grew rapidly, almost as rapidly as those of the United States. But a great many of the European cities had histories stretching back hundreds of years before the founding of the first white village in North America, and therefore had traditions of government and administration that predated the age of unrestricted private enterprise. While they too were disfigured and brutalized by industrialism, they often managed to set examples of local administration and municipal planning that American students of municipal life envied and hoped to copy. American cities, springing into life out of mere villages, often organized around nothing but the mill, the factory, or the railroad, peopled by a heterogeneous and mobile population, and drawing upon no settled governing classes for administrative experience, found the pace of their growth far out of proportion to their capacity for management. "The problem in America," said Seth Low, "has been to make a great city in a few years out of nothing."

The combination of underdeveloped traditions of management and mushroom growth put a premium on quick, short-range improvisation and on action without regard for considered rules—a situation ideal for the development of the city boss and informal government. The consequences were in truth dismal. Lord Bryce thought that the government of cities was "the one conspicuous failure of the United States." Andrew D. White asserted in 1890 that "with very few exceptions, the city governments of the United States are the worst in Christendom —the most expensive, the most inefficient, and the most corrupt."

One of the keys to the American mind at the end of the old century and the beginning of the new was that American cities were filling up in very considerable part with small-town or rural people. The whole cast of American thinking in this period was deeply affected by the experience of the rural mind confronted with the phenomena of urban life, its crowding, poverty, crime, corruption, impersonality, and ethnic chaos. To the rural migrant, raised in respectable quietude and the high-toned moral imperatives of evangelical Protestantism, the city seemed not merely a new social form or way of life but a strange threat to civilization itself. The age resounds with the warnings of prophets like Josiah Strong that the city, if not somehow tamed, would bring with it the downfall of the nation. "The first city," wrote Strong, "was built by the first murderer, and crime and vice and wretchedness have festered in it ever since."

In the city the native Yankee-Protestant American encountered the immigrant. Between the close of the Civil War and the outbreak of the first World War, the rise of American industry and the absence of restrictions drew a steady stream of immigrants, which reached its peak in 1907 when 1,285,000 immigrant entries were recorded. By 1910, 13,345,000 foreign-born persons were living in the United States, or almost one seventh of the total population.

1957 AWARD

ABOUT THE EARLY
SOVIET-AMERICAN RELATIONS

BY

GEORGE F. KENNAN

George Frost Kennan (born on February 16, 1904, in Milwaukee, Wis.) attended Princeton University, majoring in history and received his B.A. degree in 1925. The following year, he entered the U.S. Foreign Service and subsequently was assigned as vice-consul to Geneva, Hamburg, Berlin and Tallin (Estonia). From 1929 to 1931 Kennan pursued studies on the Russian language and culture under a State Department's program at the University of Berlin. When the United States reopened its embassy in Moscow in 1933, he was called to the Soviet capital. The posts that Kennan filled during the next few years included vice-consul in Vienna, second secretary in Moscow, second secretary and later consul in Prague. At the outbreak of World War II, he was sent as second secretary to Berlin, where he was promoted to first secretary the following year. When the Americans joined the war in 1941, Kennan was interned by the Nazis at Bad Nauheim. After his repatriation, he became counselor of the American delegation to the European Advisory Commission and then returned to Moscow as minister-counselor in 1944. In spring 1947 he was named director of the policy planning staff of the Department of State. Briefly during 1952 he was U.S. Ambassador to the Soviet Union, but then, in 1953, left the Foreign Service to become member of the Institute for Advanced Studies at Princeton, where, at the school of historical studies, he has been professor since 1956. In 1957 George F. Kennan won the Pulitzer Prize in history for his *Russia Leaves the War: Soviet-American Relations, 1917-20*, which had been published one year earlier.

THE MAJOR STATESMEN IN THAT PROCESS

[Source: George F. Kennan: Russia Leaves the War: Soviet-American Relations, 1917-1920, Princeton, N.J.: Princeton University Press, 1956, pp. 27 - 32, 114 - 115; reprinted by permission of Princeton University Press, Princeton, N.J.]

The major statesmen involved in the initial stages of Soviet-American relations—Wilson and Lansing on the American side, Lenin and Trotsky on the Russian—need no general introduction to the reading public. Their respective reactions to the problems of Russian-American relations will best be left to reflect themselves in the happenings that make up the body of this narrative. There are, however, a few observations concerning the respective experiences and personalities of these men that might be in order at this point.

Although Woodrow Wilson has received extensive attention in American historical literature ever since his death, the full pattern of his complicated and subtle political personality is only now beginning to emerge in the light of the more intensive and detached scrutiny to which it has recently been subjected. It is the writer's hope that the glimpses of Wilson in his confrontation with the Russian problem, as they emerge in this narrative, will contribute something to the fullness and richness of this pattern.

Two points are worth bearing in mind as we observe the reactions of President Wilson to the problems posed by the Russian Revolution.

First, Wilson was a man who had never had any particular interest in, or knowledge of, Russian affairs. He had never been in Russia. There is no indication that the dark and violent history of that country had ever occupied his attention. Like many other Americans, he felt a distaste and antipathy for Tsarist autocracy as he knew it, and a sympathy for the revolutionary movement in Russia. Precisely for this reason, the rapid degeneration of the Russian Revolution into a new form of authoritarianism, animated by a violent preconceived hostility toward western liberalism, was a phenomenon for which he was as little prepared, intellectually, as a great many of his compatriots.

Secondly, while Wilson was largely his own Secretary of State insofar as the formulation of policy in major questions was concerned, he shared with many other American statesmen a disinclination to use the network of America's foreign diplomatic missions as a vital and intimate agency of policy. Nothing was further from his habit and cast of mind than to take the regular envoys into his confidence, to seek their opinions, or to use their facilities for private communication with foreign governments as a vehicle for achieving his objectives of foreign policy. Seldom did it occur to Wilson to pursue his objectives by the traditional diplomatic method of influencing the attitudes of foreign governments through private persuasion or bargaining; in the rare instances where this was done, it was mainly an irregular agent, Colonel Edward M. House, and not the permanent envoys, whose services were employed. In general, the President's taste in diplomacy ran rather to the direct appeal to foreign opinion, for which American diplomatic representatives were not required.

In these circumstances, individual diplomatic envoys, such as Ambassador Francis in Petrograd, had no sense of intimacy with the President, and no opportunity to feel that they were the special repositories of his confidence and the vehicles of his will. . .

Of Robert Lansing it need only be said that while he, too, had experienced no special interest in Russian affairs prior to the Russian Revolution, he had had a unique preparation for the responsibilities of statesmanship in twenty-two years of practice as an international lawyer and nearly three years of grueling responsibility as Counselor and Secretary of State. Not only had he gained in this way an exceptional understanding of the diplomatic process as such, but he had acquired in high degree those qualities of thoroughness and precision that lie at the heart of the diplomatic profession. The same experiences had rendered him sensitive to the importance of international forms and amenities as reflections of the deeper realities of foreign affairs. These qualities were to stand him in good stead as he confronted the ordeals of statesmanship brought to him by the Russian Revolution and its consequences.

For his own contemporaries, Lansing's light was somewhat obscured by the contrast between his quiet, unassuming nature and
the President's overriding personality. His task was not eased by the
President's innate secretiveness and tendency to act on his own
without consulting or informing his Secretary of State. The two men
grated on each other in their official habits. Foreign diplomats were
quick to sense this relationship and to exploit it by taking their problems directly to the President.

In these circumstances it is not surprising that there was a tendency
to underrate Lansing, and sometimes to ridicule him. George Creel
charged, contemptuously, that he "worked at being dull." But this
is a charge to which orderly and methodical natures must expect to
be exposed in the more strident periods of history. It would be wrong
to assume that Lansing's plodding meticulousness of method, his de-
ficiency in showmanship, and his lack of personal color rendered
unimportant the contribution he was capable of making to the
formulation of America's response to Soviet power. Behind this
façade of stuffy correctness and legal precision there lay powers of
insight that might have been envied by the more boisterous natures
with which wartime Washington then abounded.

Of Lenin we need say little by way of introduction. He had had as
little interest in America as Wilson or Lansing had in Russia. Insofar
as he thought about the United States at all, he probably identified
it with the England he knew from his periods of exile in London. If
his impression of Anglo-Saxon civilization differed from the image
of continental capitalism on which his outlook of life had been
formed, it was not enough to affect his thinking in any important
way. It was Lenin, after all, who had corrected Marx's sloppiness and
tidied up the symmetry of the doctrine by overriding Marx's admission that in the Anglo-Saxon countries the socialist revolution *might*
conceivably occur by means short of revolutionary violence. In this
way he had made it possible to lump all capitalist countries neatly
together, and had avoided the hideous necessity of recognizing a
world of relative values. For Lenin, quite obviously, America—at the
time of the Bolshevik seizure of power—was just one more capitalist

Le Commissaire du Peuple

aux affaires étrangères

Petrograde.

le 7 Novembre 1917

Transmitted as Document No 3 to Despatch No. 1386, dated July 15, 1919.

800

Received at Embassy 11 P.M. Nov. 8/21. 1917

Monsieur

l' Ambassadeur des États Unis

Avec la présente j'ai l'honneur de Vous informer,Monsieur l'Ambassadeur,que le Congres National des Conseils des Députés des ouvriers et des soldats a établie le 26 du mois d'octobre a.c. un nouveau gouvernement de la République Russe sous la forme du Conseil des Commissaires du Peuple.Le Président de de gouvernement est M-r Vladimir Ilych Lénine et la direction de la politique extérieure fut confié à moi, en qualité du Commissaire du Peuple des affaires étrangeres.

En attirant Votre attention au texte de la proposition de l'armistice et de la paix démocratique sans annexions ni contrubitions, fondée sur le droit des peuple de disposer d'eux mêmes ,-propositionsapprouvés par le Congrés des Conseils des ouvriers et des soldats.- J'ai l'honneur de Vous prier,Monsieur l'Ambassadeur,de bien vouloir regarder le document susmentionné comme une proposition formelle d'une armistice sans délai sur tous les fronts et de l'ouverture sans retard des négociations

Page 1 of the first communication from the Soviet Government
to the U.S. Government, signed by Trotsky

country, and not a very important one at that. (The Decree on Peace, drafted by Lenin himself in the fall of 1917, significantly failed to mention the United States and referred to England, France, and Germany as "the three mightiest States taking part in the present war.")

Of the four leading statesmen, Trotsky was the only one to have visited the other country concerned in the Russian-American relationship. He had been in the United States in the winter of 1917 (January 13 to March 27). He had lived in what he called a "working-class district" on New York's upper east side—162nd Street. He had worked at the editorial offices of the Russian-language socialist newspaper, the *Novy Mir,* near Union Square. Altogether, he had led, for this brief period, the peculiarly narrow and restricted life that Russian political exiles have so often tended to create for themselves in foreign capitals. As he himself put it: "My only profession in New York was the profession of a revolutionary socialist."

Trotsky relates that he studied American economic life in the New York Public Library. Whatever this study amounted to, it would be a mistake to conclude that he gained from it any rich or accurate picture of the nature of the civilization he was touching on its eastern fringe. The flesh-and-blood America, with all those subtle peculiarities of spirit and custom that have done so much more than political or economic institutions to determine the values of its civilization, remained for him—fortunately for the peace of his brilliant but dogmatic mind, unfortunately for the course of Soviet-American relations—a closed book.

1958 AWARD

ABOUT THE AMERICAN BANK POLICY SINCE THE REVOLUTION

BY

BRAY HAMMOND

Bray Hammond (born on November 20, 1886, in Springfield, Mo.) started at the age of 21 a career as assistant cashier at the State Bank in New Sharon, Iowa. There, he worked until 1909 and then enrolled at Stanford, where he earned his Bachelor of Arts Degree in 1912. For the following three years Hammond held an assistant professorship at the State College in Pullman, Wash. During the First World War he served in the United States Army advancing from second lieutenant to captain. After his discharge from the Army, he invested his entire time into writing, research and private business. It was in 1930 that he joined the Federal Reserve Board, where he assumed the position of assistant secretary from 1944 to 1950. That same year, as well as in 1955, he received a Guggenheim grant. Hammond, who contributed several articles on historical subjects to different periodicals, is also the author of *Sovereignty and an Empty Purse*. In 1958 Bray Hammond's *Banks and Politics in America* was awarded the Pulitzer Prize for the best book on American history published during the preceding year.

THE GROWTH OF MAJOR BANKING INSTITUTIONS

[Source: Bray Hammond: Banks and Politics in America. From the Revolution to the Civil War,. Princeton, N.J.: Princeton University Press, 1957, pp. 145 - 147; reprinted by permission of Princeton. University Press, Princeton, N.J.]

In 1791, when the Bank of the United States was chartered, the Federalists, a monied minority of the population, were in control of the government, and there were three banks in operation. In 1811, when the Bank of the United States was let die, the Federalists were disintegrated, the Jeffersonians had long been in power, and banks, which were one of that party's principal traditionary aversions, had multiplied from three to ninety. In the next five years the number increased to nearly 250; by 1820 it exceeded 300—an increase of more than a hundred-fold in the first thirty years of the federal union. It is hard to imagine how banking could have been propagated more under its sponsors than it was under its "enemies."

That banking flourished with the decline of Hamilton's party and the ascendancy of Jefferson's connotes the fact that business was becoming democratic. It was no longer a select and innumerous aristocracy—business opportunities were falling open to everyone. The result was an alignment of the new generation of business men with the genuine agrarians, whose rugged individualism constituted the Jeffersonian democracy's professed faith and required very little alteration to fit enterprise as well. The success of the Republican party in retaining the loyalty of the older agrarians while it recruited among the newer entrepreneurial masses was possible, Professor Beard has explained, because Jefferson's academic views pleased the one group and his practical politics propitiated the other. It was also because equality of opportunity in business and the principle of *laisser faire* could be advocated with a Jeffersonian vocabulary.

The number of banks grew from 6 to 246 in the twenty-five years between establishment of the Bank of the United States in 1791 and establishment of a new Bank of the United States in 1816. This growth was not the multiplication of something familiar, like houses or ships or carriages, but a multiplication of something unfamiliar or even mysterious. Had banks been thought to be merely depositories where savings were tucked away—as came to be thought in time—there would have been nothing remarkable about their increase. But they were known to do more than receive money. They were known to create it. For each dollar paid in by the stockholders, the banks lent two, three, four, or five. The more sanguine part of the people were happy to have it so, no matter if they did not understand how it could be. The more conservative, like John Adams, thought it a cheat. Since the Republican party had both its agrarian wing and its speculative-entrepreneurial wing, it came to include both the conspicuous opponents of banking and the conspicuous advocates of it.

The Jeffersonian impetus in banking may well have begun in reaction to the Federalist character of the first banks, all of which were conceived and defended as monopolies. The surest procedure for any new group that wished to obtain a bank charter from a Jeffersonian state legislature was to cry out against monopoly in general and in particular against that of the Federalist bankers who would lend nothing, it was alleged, to good Republicans. The argument was persuasive. Jeffersonians, if they could not extirpate monopoly, could at least reduce its inequities by seizing a share of its rewards. So Jefferson himself seems to have thought. "I am decidedly in favor of making all the banks Republican," he wrote Gallatin in July 1803, "by sharing deposits among them in proportion to the dispositions they show." Dr Benjamin Rush wrote to John Adams in 1810 that though Federalist and Democratic principles were ostensibly at issue between the parties, "the true objects of strife are a 'mercantile bank' by the former and a 'mechanics bank' by the latter party." The State Bank of Boston solicited federal deposits in 1812, following the demise of the Bank of the United States, with the assurance to the Republican administration that the State Bank was "the property of sixteen hundred freemen of the respectable state of Massachusetts, all of them advocates of the then existing federal administration, associated not solely for the purpose of advancing their pecuniary interests but for the more noble purpose of cherishing Republican men and Republican measures against the wiles and machinations" of the rival political party. The same course could be followed by any sort of special interest—geographic, economic, or what not—which wanted credit and was dissatisfied with the existing banks. So the number grew. Each borrowing interest wanted a bank of its own. Soon, as Dr Rush said, banks were serving not only merchants but "mechanics," on whose skills the Industrial Revolution was progressing, and farmers. The charter of the Washington Bank, Westerly, Rhode Island, June 1800, solicited both interests. It recited that "added to those common arguments in favour of bank institutions, such as promoting punctuality in discharge of contracts, . . . and extending commerce by accumulating the means of carrying it on, there are also arguments in favour of such establishments, as promoting the agricultural and mechanical interest of our country." It declared that "those banks which at present are established in this state are too remote or too confined in their operations to diffuse their benefits so generally to the country as could be wished." It mentioned the embarrassments into which "the farmer is frequently drove for the want of means of stocking his farm at those seasons of the year when money is obtained with the greatest difficulty"; and it expressed the belief that "in a place peculiarly fitted by nature to encourage the industry and ingenuity of the mechanic by holding out the sure prospects of a profitable return for his enterprise, nothing is wanting but those little assistances from time to time which banks only can give."

1959 AWARD

ABOUT THE HISTORY OF THE U.S. ADMINISTRATIVE SYSTEM

BY

LEONARD D. WHITE / D. JEAN SCHNEIDER

Leonard Dupee White (born on January 17, 1891, in Acton, Mass.) obtained his Master of Arts degree at Dartmouth in 1915. That same year he became instructor in government at Clark College in Worcester, Mass. In 1918 he joined the staff at Dartmouth as an instructor in political science and was later promoted to assistant professor. Twenty-nine years old, White became associate professor at the University of Chicago, and later full professor. From 1931 to 1933 he was member of the Chicago Civil Service Commission, and from 1934 to 1937 he was on the Civil Service Commission and Central Statistics Board in Washington, D.C. Two years later he joined the President's Committee on Civil Service Improvement, where he stayed until 1941. During 1948/49 he worked as an investigator in the Personnel Policy Committee of the Hoover Commission and from 1953 to 1955 White was member of the personnel task force of the Second Hoover Commission. White was a very prolific author. The following works count among his book publications: *The Status of Scientific Research in Illinois*; *Evaluation of the System of Central Financial Control of Research in State Governments*; *Introduction to Study of Public Administration*; *Trends in Public Administration*; *Politics and Public Service*. Leonard D. White died on February 23, 1958. That same year *The Republican Era: 1869-1901*, which he had written with the assistance of *Donna Jean Schneider* (born on September 2, 1935, in Vancouver, Wash.), was published. The next year the Pulitzer Prize for history was posthumously awarded to Leonard D. White.

GLANCES OF THE POST OFFICE DEPARTMENT

[Source: Leonard D. White/Jean Schneider: The Republican Era, 1869-1901. A Study in administrative History, New York: The MacMillan Company, 1958, pp. 259 - 262; reprinted by permission of the Macmillan Publishing Company, New York, N.Y.]

Most administration settles into established routine. The Post Office Department was par excellence the home of routine so far as its central task of collecting, transporting, and delivering the mail was concerned. Collections were made at stated times at specified places on specified routes in the cities; mails were closed at specified hours in the small country offices, were put on the railroad for transportation, sorted and put in the hands of carriers for delivery at regular intervals. Innovation occurred in better equipment, in speeding up deliveries, in extending free delivery, in introducing stamp books, and in other improvements in details.

Functions. The principal additions to the basic functions of collecting, transporting, and delivering the mail occurred before Grant's administration. The postal money order system, the only major new activity, had been authorized in 1864. In 1900–1901 its business exceeded 294 million dollars. Free delivery in the largest cities was inaugurated in 1863 and extended to smaller communities from time to time, but this was only an improvement in service. So with rural free delivery, the early experiments in which occurred in the 1890's. Special delivery was inaugurated in 1885. Apart from the banking business of the Post Office, the Department continued in a well-established pattern.

Postmaster General John Wanamaker was not content with these ancient functions. He made three major recommendations for the extension of service: Post Office delivery of telegrams in the larger cities by contract with the telegraph companies; postal savings banks; and parcel post. None of these innovations appealed to Congress.

The Postmasters General. The political overhead of the Post Office Department comprised primarily the Postmaster General, the four Assistant Postmasters General, and on the local scene over 75,000 postmasters. No one should suppose, however, that a reasoned line was drawn between this group of officials and the mass of employees.

Until 1883 the latter was as vulnerable as the former. At the clearly political level, which had the final authority for management, much time had to be given to relations with Senators and Representatives, to "recognition" of competing factions, and to strengthening the party organization. Since Jackson's time the Department had been a powerful asset in winning elections.

Postmasters General were appointed normally with political considerations in view, but occasionally (as in the case of Cleveland's law partner, Wilson S. Bissell) for personal reasons. The practice of appointing the chairman of the National Committee to the Post Office was not established, however, until the choice of George B. Cortelyou in 1905. A few Postmasters General had sufficient prominence to induce full-length biographies.

For one reason or another incumbency of the office was seldom more than two years. Grant and Arthur each had four Postmasters General, one of whom, John A. J. Creswell, served Grant for five years; otherwise only Harrison retained the same man for four full years, the Philadelphia merchant, John Wanamaker. The administrative impact of Postmasters General was thus necessarily curtailed—for better or for worse—except in the field of appointments.

The organization of the Department in itself was enough to minimize innovation by its head, since endless detail flowed into Washington for decision. Wanamaker quickly recognized this handicap, and in proposing a remedy, wrote an able and unique exposition of the proper function of the Postmaster General.

The Postmaster-General thus relieved of the dead-weight of numberless details, which would be left to the equally safe and prompt action of experienced and less occupied assistants, could intelligently exercise the functions of an administrative officer. He could apply the inventive and creative power of a mind freed from minor things, to the larger work of executive management of greater organization. He would do the planning, originate new ideas and inaugurate new methods, revise and make more practical and effective the regulations, study the systems of other countries, superintend the heads of departments, and give constantly the touch of life to the entire system, making it more representative of the commercial energies and social requirements of the American people. He would ascertain by investigation, study, and experiments, and by encouraging invention, possible improvements that would make the postal organization an agency of larger service and greater convenience. Many of the newer and more useful discoveries in applied science might be utilized and fashioned into a quicker and more satisfactory service than the present agencies, which are now plainly proving themselves too slow. He would secure transit for mail on faster schedules; provide quicker collections and distributions in cities and towns by pneumatic tubes or other improved and more rapid couriers than now exist; push forward American mails as the forerunner of the extension of American commerce; lift the entire service into a larger usefulness for the people and a larger increase for itself.

These and other possible improvements would all be open to the research of a Postmaster-General. His would be the duty and opportunity to study them and the power of the Government, and the interest of the people would aid and stimulate him to lead in enterprise, departures, and experiments. . . . The expanding energies of the human mind, the rapid progress and practical achievements of science, should be seen first rather than last in the conduct of the Government business.

The venerable clerk who is always with us, faithful to tradition and proudest of all in remembering precedents, should not worry and retard a progressive Department in this progressive age by making a wall of an opinion delivered in 1823 or citing a precedent that governed in 1848. And especially should the postal service utilize in this advanced time of the world everything that can make the mails anticipate the wishes and expectations of the people. The one man who should be expected to ascertain and apply to the postal service all possible better agents, whether they be thus employed in the business world or developed in science, is the Postmaster-General, who under the present methods is allowed no time for studying such great questions or for dealing with anything more than the passing subjects of every day.

Few indeed were the Postmasters General from Grant to McKinley who understood such a function or accepted such a responsibility. All were diligent, signing a never-ending stream of documents and papers that came to their desks; some had considerable business experience, notably Wanamaker; some sought to curtail the influence of politics, such as Marshall Jewell during Grant's brief experiment with examinations and David M. Key, Hayes' first head of the office.

1960 AWARD

ABOUT THE TWENTY-FIFTH
PRESIDENT OF THE UNITED STATES

BY

MARGARET K. LEECH

Margaret Kernochan Leech (born on November 7, 1893, in Newburgh, N.Y.) attended Vassar College in Poughkeepsie and in 1915 received her Bachelor's degree. After graduation, she worked first for a publishing company, later she entered an advertising agency. Her publicity work in various World War I fund-raising organizations led to her joining the staff of the American Committee for Devastated France. While serving the committee in Europe, she contributed articles to American periodicals. During the 1920's, after she had returned to the United States, Margaret Leech was chiefly occupied with writing novels. In 1924 her first fictional work was published: *The Back of the Book*. In 1926 and 1928 *Tin Wedding* and *The Feathered Nest* followed. In 1927 she had turned temporarily from fiction to write in collaboration with Heywood Broun the biography *Anthony Comstock: Roundsman of the Lord*. On August 1, 1928, Margaret K. Leech was married to Ralph Pulitzer. Together with Beatrice Kaufman, she wrote her only drama *Divided by Three*, which was played for the first time in the fall of 1934. In 1935 she began a five-year investigation into life in Washington during the Civil War for *Reveille in Washington, 1860-1865*. The work was first serialized in the *Atlantic Monthly* and in 1941 published in book form. The following year it earned Margaret Leech the Pulitzer Prize for history. After twelve years of work, her next book, *In the Days of McKinley*, was published in November 1959. The year after, it was this work that made Margaret K. Leech for the second time the winner of the Pulitzer Prize for the best book on American history.

MCKINLEY AS A CHAMPION OF PROTECTIONISM

[Source: Margaret Leech: In the Days of McKinley, New York: Harper & Brothers Publishers, 1959, pp. 34 - 36, 246a; reprinted by permission of Harper Collins Publishers, New York, N.Y.]

McKINLEY had entered elective office in a spirit of dedication to the principles of the party of Lincoln. Twelve years after the war, the basis of a Union soldier's political allegiance was already open to challenge. The doom of civil rights for the Negro was foretold in the necessity for conciliating the South. The voice of Lincoln was drowned in the unrest of financial depression, the demand for currency inflation, the uproar against the monopolies, and the strife between capital and labor. But McKinley's loyalty was not confused by changing issues. He stood on the Republican platform, satisfied that its declarations embodied the noblest expression of American patriotism and promised the highest fulfillment of the national welfare.

During McKinley's service in Congress, scattered protests arose and swelled that representative government had become the rule of plutocracy, that both major parties fattened on the subsidies of business, and that courts and legislatures bowed to the will of the corporations. These were still the protests of the few. The danger of the relationship between government and big business was not generally apprehended, and such strictures seemed to McKinley a passing phase of minority opinion, subversive or misguided. As the foremost exponent of the high protective tariff, he played a major role in leading the Republican party to its eventual identification with the moneyed interests. He acted in the belief that he was serving all the people by promoting American prosperity.

The national veneration for private enterprise was not proof against the flagrant abuses of the railroads and the trusts. Appeals for their regulation became a demand on which the Republicans felt obliged to act. McKinley voted with his party to pass the first timid, though precedent-breaking measures of federal control, the Interstate Commerce and Sherman Antitrust Acts; but his primary concern was always the encouragement, not the curtailment of business. He said very little on the question of the trusts, and obviously had not yet recognized its importance. The postwar revolution in American industry was too cataclysmic for the ready comprehension of men who had grown to maturity in a simple economy and formed their political ideas in the service of the Union. The march of the new issues left them in the rear, clinging devoutly to the standards of a bygone day. Yet Congressman McKinley was not classed with the Old Guard of reaction. Young Robert La Follette of Wisconsin, who saw much of him on the Ways and Means Committee, thought that he "represented the newer view." Within the framework of his basic, fixed beliefs, McKinley was exceedingly flexible in his opinions. His critics called him changeable and lacking in convictions, but McKinley's adaptability was a political advantage. It denoted a ready sympathy with contemporary trends which counterbalanced his rigid position on the tariff. "Of course, McKinley was a high protectionist," La Follette wrote, "but on the great new questions as they arose he was generally on the side of the public against private interests."

McKinley's supreme political talent was his identification with the people. In a time of ferment and transition, Americans longed for a voice of resolute affirmation which would appease their qualms of conscience and assure them that they were the noblest, as they were fast becoming the richest people in the world. This was the voice with which McKinley spoke, not only to the wealthy and privileged few, but to the rank and file

The young Congressman—
listening more than he talked

Congressman and Mrs. McKinley
during a visit to San Francisco in 1881

of Republicans, small manufacturers and merchants, farmers and workingmen. In brain and heart, he was himself the average middle-class American, abounding in optimism, proud of the national efficiency and enterprise; respectful of self-made success, and pious in devotion to the past. It was the faith of the fathers that McKinley invoked in every crisis; and in nothing was he more typical of his countrymen than in his willingness to turn that faith to the cause of material betterment.

Congress was the school of McKinley's education. It made him a preeminently "practical" politician, always ready to concede and take as much as it was possible to get. "We cannot always do what is best," he once told a gathering of his comrades at Canton, "but we can do what is practical at the time." A deliberate man with infinite resources of patience, he was content to progress by easy stages toward the millennium. Some private legerdemain must have reconciled him to the "practical" methods that were employed. The struggles in the "dusty arena" of Ohio were notorious. Medieval knight or not, McKinley fought shoulder to shoulder with highly irregular partisans. He scrupulously shunned the bribe and the bargain, but his purity must have involved an intricate self-deception, a timely looking away and convenient forgetfulness.

Political life confirmed McKinley in an excessive cautiousness. The inner minds of few public men have been so well concealed. He left almost no personal papers. He rarely wrote a private letter. Apart from his public utterances, the record of the spoken word is small. He sometimes obscured his views by a fog of phraseology, conventional or oracular. Often in private conversation, it seems that he merely listened sympathetically. People, convinced that he agreed with them, were at a loss to remember what he had said. Even his intimates frequently had to guess what he was thinking. Yet McKinley did not seem an enigma to the men who knew him. Everyone found it easy to describe his simple character. Many people called him pliant and amiable. Close associates were surprised to learn that he always contrived to have his way. A very few saw stubborn, secret strength.

1961 AWARD

ABOUT THE AMERICAN
POSITION AT THE POTSDAM CONFERENCE

BY

HERBERT FEIS

Herbert Feis (born on June 7, 1893, in New York, N.Y.) graduated from Harvard University with the B.A. degree in 1916, and after having served in World War I as a lieutenant in the U.S. Navy, he returned to Harvard for graduate study. During 1920/21 Feis was an instructor in economics at Harvard as well as a student. He received his doctorate in economics in 1921. From 1922 to 1925 he taught as an associate professor economics at the University of Kansas. He held a Guggenheim Fellowship in 1926 and for the next three years was head of the department of economics at the University of Cincinnati. Meanwhile, during various periods from 1922 to 1927, he also served as adviser on American industrial relations at the International Labor Office of the League of Nations in Geneva. In 1931 Feis accepted an appointment as economic adviser in the Department of State in Washington, D.C. He remained with the department for twelve years, holding from 1937 to 1943 the position of adviser on international economic affairs. Then, he moved as a special consultant to the War Department and in 1946 was a member of an observation group in the Far East. Beginning in 1948, Feis was intermittently over a period of more than ten years a member of the Institute for Advanced Study in Princeton. He was the author of many book publications, e.g. *Europe, the World's Banker, 1870-1914*; *Sinews of Peace*; *The Road to Pearl Harbor*; *The China Tangle*. Herbert Feis received the 1961 Pulitzer Prize in American history for his *Between War and Peace: The Potsdam Conference*, which had been published one year earlier.

ROOSEVELT'S AND TRUMAN'S POLAND POLICY

[Source: Herbert Feis: Between War and Peace: The Potsdam Conference, Princeton, N.J.: Princeton University Press, 1960, pp. 31 - 35; reprinted by permission of Princeton University Press, Princeton, N.J.]

The three Heads of Government at Yalta, in February 1945, had agreed on the ways whereby the Polish Provisional Government, formed by disciples of Moscow, was to be reorganized so as to qualify for recognition by the United States and Great Britain, and on the general location of the new Polish frontiers. But the accord was ambiguous in the first respect, and incomplete in the second.

On what should be done about the government, the formula, to which Churchill and Roosevelt had given their resigned approval, read (in the Declaration on Poland): "The Provisional Government which is now functioning in Poland should . . . be reorganized on a broader democratic basis with the inclusion of democratic leaders from Poland itself and from Poles abroad." Whether Churchill realized that Stalin believed he and Roosevelt were assenting that groups loyal to Moscow would have dominant influence in the made-over government is hard to tell; in his memoirs the thought is not expressed. But Roosevelt knew it. His misgivings had been eased by the affirmation in the same declaration that the reorganized Provisional Government "shall be pledged to the holding of free and unfettered elections as soon as possible on the basis of universal suffrage and secret ballot." Any chance left that the Polish people might be free to choose their own government and fix their national policies depended on the honest fulfillment of this pledge. It had been arranged that Molotov and the American and British Ambassadors in Moscow (Harriman and Clark Kerr) should meet as a group to work out the steps by which this accord was to be carried out.

About frontiers the sustained argument at Yalta had been only partially resolved in that part of the Declaration which read: "The three Heads of Government consider that the Eastern frontier of Poland should follow the Curzon Line with digressions from it in some regions of five to eight kilometres in favour of Poland. They recognize that Poland must receive substantial accessions of territory in the North and

West. They feel that the opinion of the new Polish Provisional Government of National Unity should be sought in due course on the extent of these accessions and that final delimitation of the Western Frontier of Poland should thereafter await the Peace Conference."

Stalin had been determined to extend Soviet territory westward to the so-called Curzon Line. He had insisted that the whole eastern segment of Poland, which he wanted, was not only Russian by habitation and historical heritage, but also vital for the protection of the Soviet Union. Churchill, whatever regrets he may have had that a former British Prime Minister had proposed this line as a just and suitable Soviet-Polish frontier, had not opposed it. Roosevelt had agreed to it, in the belief that it was futile to try to deny to the Soviet Union what its armies could take and hold whether or not he and Churchill consented. But the Polish Government in Exile, resident in London and still regarded by the British and American governments as the only legitimate government of Poland, had been bitter about this turnover of territory to the Soviet Union. So had been the commanders of the valiant Polish armed forces who were fighting side by side with western soldiers and airmen.

Both Churchill and Roosevelt had been disposed to make up to Poland for this severance of its estate in the east. It would be amply compensated, they judged, if Poland received from Germany that part of East Prussia south of the Königsberg line, plus Upper Silesia and the area up to the line of the Oder River. Thus bounded, the new Poland, it was reckoned, would be almost as large as the old and have a longer seacoast on the Baltic and greater sources of raw materials, especially coal. But at Yalta the President and Prime Minister had been faced by a claim for more by the Provisional Polish Government, backed strongly by Stalin and Molotov. Stalin urged that Poland's western frontier be carried to that Neisse River (there was another of the same name further to the east) which flows south from the Oder River where that stream turns off to the southeast.

Several million Germans lived in this large additional area, almost no Poles. These, presumably with the other six million or so Germans who lived east of the Oder, would be compelled to find new homes in the rest of Germany. That vulnerable country would be the more exposed to Soviet influence if Poland came under Communist control. Most significantly, it was foreseen that sooner or later this frontier might have to be defended by force. For these reasons Churchill and Roosevelt firmly refused to accede to this enlarged claim.

The issue had remained open. But the situation had not waited upon the consultations of the statesmen. During the spring many of the Germans had fled before the advancing Red Army and the Poles; and most of those who tried to stay were expelled.

In Moscow the Commission of Three had met many times. Their talks tore the Yalta accord apart, by distortion. The story of the tiring and repetitive arguments that wore out the patience of the American and British members has been told elsewhere. Harriman and Clark Kerr concluded that the Soviet government would not permit the emergence of any Polish government that might not be securely subject to its will; and that it was seeking to make Poland merely a protective and submissive projection of Soviet power.

After this failure Churchill and Roosevelt had sent distressed appeals to Stalin, and submitted several proposals that would allow the Commission to go on with its task. Stalin had answered them sternly. The Soviet position, he had alleged, conformed with the Yalta accord. It was they who were now trying to void it, by seeking to get rid of the Provisional Government in favor of a wholly new one. He had charged them with wanting to use persons who were known to be against all main points of the Yalta accord. Among those he had in mind was Mikolajczyk, the former Prime Minister of the Polish Government in Exile, who despite his resignation was its leading political figure. Why should they not, Stalin and Molotov had urged, adopt for Poland the same terms on which a new government for Yugoslavia had been formed? Why not? Of the twenty-seven top places in that government, twenty were held by Tito's subordinates and only six by men of other groups and parties; and this minority were finding out that they had no influence and could not protect their supporters.

As a way of marking his displeasure at this resistance to his will, Stalin—on a pretext—had sent notice that Molotov would not be able to attend the San Francisco conference. The many Americans whose longings were centered on that venture in international creation were dismayed. But then, on an evening when he and Harriman spoke of Roosevelt's death, Stalin had relented. As a gesture he had said he would

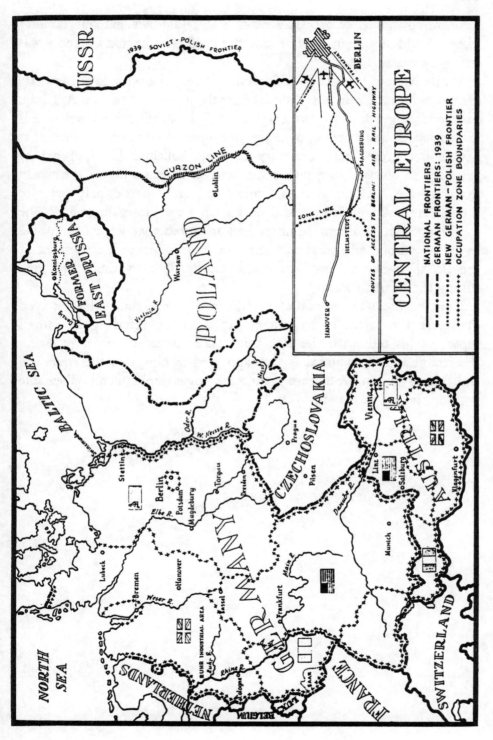

CENTRAL EUROPE

NATIONAL FRONTIERS
GERMAN FRONTIERS: 1939
NEW GERMAN – POLISH FRONTIER
OCCUPATION ZONE BOUNDARIES

USSR

1939 SOVIET - POLISH FRONTIER

CURZON LINE

oLublin

POLAND

FORMER EAST PRUSSIA

oKoenigsburg

Vistula R.

Warsaw

Danzig

BALTIC SEA

NORTH SEA

NETHERLANDS

BELGIUM

LUX.

SWITZERLAND

FRANCE

GERMANY

CZECHOSLOVAKIA

AUSTRIA

Vienna

Linz o

Salzburg

Klagenfurt o

Munich o

Danube R.

Pilsen o

Prague o

Dresden o

Torgau o

Oder R.

W. Neisse R.

Neisse R.

Stettin o

Berlin

Potsdam

Magdeburg o

Elbe R.

Lubeck o

Bremen o

Hanover o

Weser R.

Frankfurt o

Main R.

Kassel o

RUHR INDUSTRIAL AREA

Ruhr R.

Cologne o

Rhine R.

SAAR

BERLIN

TO HAMBURG

TO MARIENBORN

MAGDEBURG

ROUTES OF ACCESS TO BERLIN: AIR · RAIL · HIGHWAY

ZONE LINE

HELMSTEDT

HANOVER o

let Molotov go after all. The news that Molotov's flat but familiar visage would be among those around the head table at that assembly was strangely reassuring.

While Molotov was in Washington, not only the officials of the State Department but President Truman himself, in a blunt talk on April 23, had tried to get him to give ground on Poland. They had failed. All his responses had been akin to the one given to Stettinius when that affable but often inept Secretary of State solicited his approval of language to be used in a public announcement indicating to the world that "we are working in collaboration and unity particularly prior to the solemn task just facing us of setting up a world organization." The coral-like Soviet Foreign Minister had answered that we could "prove to the world our collaboration" when we had "achieved a settlement of the Polish question," but this could not be done "without first consulting the Warsaw Poles."

None of the later entreaties by Churchill and Truman had swayed Stalin. In the rejoinder he sent on April 24, on receiving Molotov's report of his talk with the President, Stalin asserted, after reviewing the record and the equities as they appeared to him, that the American and British governments were putting the Soviet Union in an unbearable position, trying to dictate to it.

1962 AWARD

ABOUT THE PRE-REVOLUTION YEARS IN AMERICA

BY

LAWRENCE H. GIPSON

Lawrence Henry Gipson (born on December 7, 1880, in Greeley, Col.) received the A.B. degree in 1903 from the University of Idaho. In the following year he successfully competed for the first Rhodes scholarship to be granted in Idaho. In 1907 he was awarded the B.A. degree from Oxford University, England. On his return to the United States, Gipson worked as a professor of history for three years at the College of Idaho. He continued his studies at Yale University as a Farnham fellow in history in 1910/11. At Wabash College in Crawfordsville, Ind., Gipson became professor and head of the department of history and political science in 1911 and in 1918 he received his doctorate from Yale. It was in 1924 that he became the head of the department of history and government at Lehigh University. A grant from the Social Science Research Council, that Gipson received in 1929, enabled him to visit Ireland, Scotland, England and France. Transferred in 1946 to the Lehigh Institute of Research, Gipson became a research professor in history. The historian occupied the Vyvyan Harmsworth Chair in American History at Oxford University in 1951 and 1952. Also in 1952, he was given emeritus status at Lehigh University. Since 1927 he worked on an eight volume work entitled *The British Empire Before the American Revolution*. Others of his works are: *Studies in Colonial Connecticut Taxation* and *The Moravian Indian Mission on White River*. In 1961 *The Triumphant Empire: Thunder-Clouds gather in the West, 1763-1766* by Lawrence H. Gipson was published and one year later, it was selected by the Pulitzer Advisory Board as the best book on history.

NEWSPAPERS IN SOME METROPOLITAN AREAS

[Source: Lawrence Henry Gipson: The Triumphant Empire: Thunder-Clouds gather in the West, 1763-1766, New York: Alfred A. Knopf, 1961, pp. 8 - 11; reprinted by permission of Alfred A. Knopf, Inc., New York, N.Y.]

Although there was no press in New France (*La Gazette de Quebec* was not due to appear until 1764), it is true that there had been printing in Mexico a century before the first English press was set up in the colonies at Cambridge in 1638, and that presses had been established in Spanish South America long before that date. Even in the seventeenth century there was issued the so-called *relaçion*, a type of Spanish news-sheet, and subsequently other publications corresponding to newspapers began to appear. They were, however, held to strict censorship by state and ecclesiastical authorities and therefore were not independent organs for the creation of public opinion, free to take the government or church to task, as was the case with the British colonial press, especially after 1763.

As early as 1690 an effort was made to launch an American newspaper in Boston, called *Public Occurrences;* this was unsuccessful as the result of the restraints placed upon it by public authority. However, in 1704, the same town saw the appearance of the *News-Letter,* "Published by Authority," which through a studied policy of circumspection continued in existence for over seventy years and only ceased publication in the course of the War for American Independence. This was followed by the founding of other newspapers along the Atlantic seaboard. The colonial press, especially after the outcome of the famous Peter Zenger trial in New York in 1735, was in most respects a free press — outside the risk that undue criticism of the local government might-result in the loss of profitable public printing. In addition to printing and disseminating news items it also voiced ideas that might be highly critical of both government and church. Herein lies the uniqueness of the press in the British colonies.

Quite logically, for a variety of reasons, the presses that printed newspapers in the British continental colonies in 1763 were located in the chief centres of population. While there was in that year no newspaper to be found in New Jersey, the Lower Counties on the Delaware, or North Carolina, Massachusetts Bay could boast of four papers: the *Massachusetts Gazette, and Boston News-Letter* (1704–76), which, starting as the *Boston News-Letter*, had become the *Boston News-Letter, and the New-England Chronicle* by January 1763 and by April 7 of that year had changed to the title given above; the *Boston-Gazette, and Country Journal* (1719–98); the *Boston Post-Boy & Advertiser* (1734–75); and the *Boston Evening-Post* (1735–75). Pennsylvania could claim the same number: two English-language papers, the *Pennsylvania Gazette* (1728–1815) and the *Pennsylvania Journal and Weekly Advertiser* (1742–93); and two printed in German, the *Germantowner Zeitung* (1762–77) – a continuation of the senior Christoph Saur's (Sauer, Sower) earlier papers – and *Der Wöchentliche Philadelphische Staatsbote* (1762–79). In New York there were three: the *New-York Gazette; or, the Weekly Post-Boy* (1747–73); the *New-York Gazette* (Weyman's) (1759–67); and the *New-York Mercury* (1752–83). Rhode Island, Connecticut, and South Carolina each supported two newspapers: in Rhode Island these were the *Newport Mercury* (1758–1820) and the *Providence Gazette; and Country Journal* (1762–1820); in Connecticut they were the *Connecticut Gazette* (1755–68), published in New Haven, and the *New-London Gazette* (1763–1820), immediate successor to the *New-London Summary* (1758–63); and in South Carolina the newspapers were the *South-Carolina Gazette* (1732–75) and the *South-Carolina Weekly Gazette* (1758–64, but published until 1781 as the *South Carolina and American General Gazette*). New Hampshire, Maryland, Virginia, and Georgia could each claim but one; they were the Portsmouth *New-Hampshire Gazette, and Historical Chronicle* (1756–1820), the Annapolis *Maryland Gazette* (1745–1820), the Williamsburg *Virginia Gazette* re-established by William Hunter (1751–78), and the Savannah *Georgia Gazette* (1763–76).

With the coming of the Anglo-American crisis, after 1763 the number of newspapers sharply increased, although some of them, it is true, came and went. In Massachusetts Bay starting with 1767 there appeared the *Boston Chronicle* (1767–70), the *Essex Gazette*

(1768–75), the *Massachusetts Spy* (1770–5), *The Censor* (1771–2), and the *Essex Journal* (1773–7). In Pennsylvania the *Pennsylvania Chronicle* (1767–74) made its bow to the public the same year as the *Boston Chronicle* and was followed by the *Pennsylvania Packet* (1771–90) and in 1775 the short-lived *Pennsylvania Mercury, and the Universal Advertiser*. As for New York, the *New-York Journal* (1766–75) was added to the list, to be followed by the *New-York Chronicle* (1769–70) and by *Rivington's New-York Gazetteer* (1773–5). Connecticut added a third newspaper when the *Connecticut Courant* (1764–1820) began publication at Hartford; it should also be added that when the New Haven *Connecticut Gazette* was on the eve of ceasing publication the *Connecticut Journal* (1767–1820) took its place in that town. James Davis, who had published the first newspaper in North Carolina at New Bern in 1751, also produced its next paper, the *North-Carolina Magazine; or, Universal Intelligencer* (1764–8), while the *North-Carolina Gazette and Weekly Post Boy* (1764–6) was published at Wilmington. Neither was destined to survive long, but Davis at New Bern revived the *North Carolina Gazette* (1768–78), which he had originally published as *The No^{th} Carolina Gazette* (1751–9), and the following year Wilmington acquired the *Cape-Fear Mercury* (1769–75). South Carolina likewise came into possession of a third newspaper under the name of the *South-Carolina Gazette; And Country Journal* (1765–75). New Hampshire saw the appearance of its second newspaper called the *Portsmouth Mercury, and Weekly Advertiser* (1765–7). Maryland did not come into possession of a second newspaper until the publication in Baltimore of the *Maryland Journal, and the Baltimore Advertiser* (1773–97). Finally, with respect to the Old Dominion, by the spring of 1775 the number of newspapers had increased from one in 1763 to four. Curiously enough, three were published at Williamsburg and all carried the same name: the *Virginia Gazette*. The first of these, a revival in 1751 by William Hunter of the paper founded by William Parks in 1736, was in 1775 published by Dixon and Hunter; the second, founded in 1766 by William Rind, was in 1775 published by John Pinkney; and the third, established in February of that year, was published by Alexander Purdie. The fourth newspaper was published in Norfolk by William

The PENNSYLVANIA GAZETTE

NUMB. 1923

October 31, 1765.

Containing the Freſheſt Advices, Foreign and Domeſtic.

NOW in the Preſs, to be ſpeedily publiſhed, in one Volume Octavo, neatly bound and lettered, and ſold by DAVID HALL, in Philadelphia, and JAMES PARKER, in Burlington.

Juſt imported in the Philadelphia Packet, Captain Budden, from London, and to be ſold by RANDLE MITCHELL, [...]

AS the Partnerſhip of FRANKLIN and HALL, Printers of this Paper, is now very near expired, [...]

* 1924

No Stamped Paper to be had.

BOSTON, October 28.

WE hear from Halifax, in the province of Nova-Scotia, that on Sunday, the 13th inſt. in the morning, was diſcovered hanging on the gallows behind the Citadel Hill, the effigies of a ſtampman, accompanied with a boot and devil, together with labels ſuitable to the occaſion (which we cannot inſert, not being favoured with the ſame) this we are informed gave great pleaſure and ſatisfaction to all the friends of liberty and their country there, as they hope from this inſtance of their zeal, the neighbouring colonies will be charitable

George the Third, to the crown of Great-Britain, &c. upon which occaſion the ſaid freemen unanimouſly, and with one voice declared,

FIrſt. That they have at all times heretofore, and ever would bear true allegiance to his Majeſty King George the Third, and his royal predeceſſors, and wiſhed to be governed agreeable to the laws of the land, and the Britiſh conſtitution, to which they ever had, and for ever moſt chearfully would ſubmit.

Secondly. That the ſtamp act, prepared for the Britiſh colonies in America, in their opinion, is unconſtitutional; and ſhould the ſame take place, agreeable to the [...]

Pennsylvania Gazette mastheads of the last issue (October 31, 1765) before and the first (November 7, 1765) after the effective date of the Stamp Act.

Duncan & Company and was called the *Virginia Gazette, or Norfolk Intelligencer* (1774–5).

Between 1763 and 1775 there were some forty-three newspapers in existence for brief or fairly long periods in the older British North American colonies. Each followed its own devices. Some sought to stir the public into action against the constituted authorities as was the case with Edes and Gill's highly inflamatory *Boston Gazette, and Country Journal;* others were inclined to calm the public, as was the case with Richard and Samuel Draper's *Boston News-Letter, and the New-England Chronicle,* which in 1769 changed its name to the *Massachusetts Gazette; and the Boston Weekly News-Letter;* still others, although only a few, attempted to take the popular leaders to task as did Mein and Fleming's *Boston Chronicle* and *Rivington's New-York Gazetteer.* As was to be expected, most of these newspapers reflected local, popular feeling on public issues and helped mightily — as Professor Schlesinger, in his recent book, *Prelude to Independence,* has so strikingly brought out — to create after 1763 a common American public opinion.

Nor does this tell the full story of the significance of the free American press toward that end. During the period from the beginning of 1763 to the end of 1774 there appeared some 4,467 distinct publications. Besides the newspapers, counting each year's issue only by title, there were many books, including those printed by authority as well as privately, pamphlets, and broadsides, making an average of 372 each year, with 239 issuing from the press in 1763, and 694 in 1774.

1963 AWARD

ABOUT THE EMERGENCE
OF THE U.S. CHIEF NATIONAL CITY

BY

CONSTANCE M. GREEN

Constance Winsor McLaughlin Green (born on August 21, 1897, in Ann Arbor, Mich.), daughter of the 1936 Pulitzer Prize winning historian Andrew C. McLaughlin, earned her Bachelor's degree at Smith College in 1919. In 1921 she enrolled at Mount Holyoke College, where she obtained her M.A. degree in history in 1925. From 1925 to 1932 Mrs. Green taught part-time as an instructor at Mount Holyoke, in the meanwhile raising a family. In 1937 she received her Ph.D. degree in history from Yale University. The following year she returned to Smith College as an instructor in the history department and in 1939 became head of the Smith College Council of Industrial Relations. During the Second World War she joined the U.S. Army Ordnance Department as historian at the Springfield Armory, where she remained until 1945. The next year she became consulting historian for the American National Red Cross and in 1948 chief historian of the Army Ordnance Department. It was in 1952 that Mrs. Green became historian at the research and development board, Office of the Secretary of Defense. She is the author of several book publications, including *Eli Whitney and the Birth of American Technology* and *American Cities in the Growth of the Nation*. In 1954, under a six-year grant from the Rockefeller Foundation, Constance W. McLaughlin Green was named head of the Washington history project, an undertaking that culminated in the publication of *Washington, Village and Capital, 1800-1878*. It is this work that earned her the Pulitzer Prize of 1963 for the best book on history published during the preceding year.

214

THE VILLAGE AND CAPITAL OF WASHINGTON

[Source: Constance McLaughlin Green: Washington, Village and Capital, 1800-1878, Princeton, N.J.: Princeton University Press, 1962, pp. 364 - 365, 383 - 386; reprinted by permission of Princeton University Press, Princeton, N.J.]

WASHINGTONIANS after 1800 had thought of themselves as residents of a national city. Other Americans, including a majority of members of the first forty-four congresses, had not. At times senators and representatives had paid lip-service to the concept; and in authorizing new public buildings to replace those destroyed by the British during the War of 1812 they had revealed a readiness to give reality to the idea. Gradually, however, the idea had faded, recapturing a slight bloom in the late 1840's with the founding of the Smithsonian Institution, and then withering during the period antecedent to the irrepressible conflict, the war, and its aftermath. In that interval Washington had become a focus of northern antagonisms, more nearly an embodiment of the enemy than the city that represented national ideals and strength. The community again and again had endeavored to build up a vigorous economy able to survive without federal patronage, only each time to encounter frustration or disaster. For nearly three quarters of a century Washington had had neither recognized standing as an independent American municipality nor any whole-hearted acceptance as a capital for whose well-being the entire nation was concerned. Now that Congress was taking full control, the city, already visibly improved by Alexander Shepherd's work, might at last look forward to assuming the honored place her eighteenth-century founders had intended.

The contentment born of such hopeful, albeit still vague, notions unhappily was shaken by the deepening of the depression that had come in the wake of the panic of 1873. The federal

"Image of the City," 1852. Aquatint by E. Sachse & Co.

payroll and an appropriation of $75,000 for the back wages of laborers whom the board of public works had not paid tempered distress in Washington during the last half of 1874, but a drastic reduction in the number of District jobs, followed by a cut in laborers' wages to a dollar a day, left hundreds of families in want by the summer of 1875. The Navy Yard had curtailed operations—there was talk of closing it altogether—and the Treasury had dismissed 400 employees. A brief flurry of strikes proved as useless as the series of clerks' advertisements offering a hundred dollars for a government post. The next year, after lengthening office hours from six to seven a day, the executive departments sliced the number of clerkships. The shutting down of the Bureau of Engraving brought 700 women to "the ragged edge of starvation," most of them too impoverished to journey home to their own states. Although the District commissioners pointed out that over 1,100 new buildings had gone up in Washington and Georgetown within the year and that crowds of visitors to the Centennial Exhibition in Philadelphia had stopped off in Washington to see the sights, people who had expected the federal government to make the capital as depression-proof as in 1837 and 1857 were discouraged.

Worse lay ahead. During the next winter beggars and tramps swarmed into the District. The citizens' committee in charge of dispensing relief reported funds nearly exhausted in January and an average of 300 applications for help coming in daily. No one dared guess at the number of families who, unwilling to have their neighbors know of their poverty, were starving in quiet gentility. Necessities had always been notoriously high in Washington. Bread rose in price from six to seven cents a loaf. When spring appeared to bring an upturn in business to other sections of the country, it was "not very satisfactory to the people of non-commercial cities like Washington, as it simply amounts to a speculative rise in the price of provisions without supplying any additional occupation or increase in wages to enable the poor or unemployed to pay the increased price." The District commissioners, their hands tied by a new law making it a penal offense to increase the District debt, eventually got permission to borrow from the United States Treasury in anticipation of taxes, but the lengthening relief rolls were alarming. While bank failures all but wiped out the funds of several charitable organizations, individuals who had long been mainstays of local philanthropy were themselves in financial straits. The closing of the Freedmen's Bank swept away the savings of hundreds of colored families. In speaking for a bill to provide $20,000 for the destitute, Representative Adlai Stevenson of Illinois testified to the "absolute starvation in this city," where suffering was acute "not only among the laboring classes, but among people who have never known penury until now." Congress voted the $20,000.

The year 1877 was grim throughout the United States. Hungry men looking for work walked the city streets and the country lanes. That summer the most violent labor revolt the nation had ever known swept across the continent from the freight yards in Baltimore to San Francisco; and sympathetic strikes in a dozen industries followed upon the railroad strike. Washington had no industrial proletariat, but neither had her working classes reason to hope for prompt easing of pressures when industry and commerce elsewhere revived. The $20,000 from Congress constituted only a stopgap. Talk of developing the water power of the Potomac to bring factories to the area had stopped altogether, and plans for improving the harbor facilities to stimulate commerce dimmed to shadow. During the tense weeks of the national railroad strike the lack of open violence in the District of Columbia appeared to be due not to better conditions here than elsewhere but to the despairing conviction of workingmen that action would not improve their lot.

In the upper brackets of society, however, where hunger was generally a word rather than a gnawing reality, faith in a make-work policy slowly strengthened. In the fall of 1877 a newly appointed District commissioner, Thomas B. Bryan, a Chicago lawyer and real estate dealer, called a citizens' mass meeting to discuss ways and means of launching a Labor Exchange. His threefold proposal called, first, for shipping some of the unemployed out of the District to sections of the country that needed workmen, second, for opening a kind of public pawnshop where people could get an advance on their "jewelry" without paying interest, and, third, a public works program. Enthusiastic endorsers of his plan shut their eyes to the fact that labor surpluses apparently existed in every part of the United States; no one remarked on the resemblance of the loans on jewels to Marie Antoinette's nostrum; and optimists forgot that public works would need congressional approval. The *Star* cheerfully remarked that the first people the Exchange would send out of the area would be "the plantation hands who came here during the war . . . found employment to some extent while the extensive system of public works was going on, but who are now stranded here." The scheme did not work that way.

1964 AWARD

ABOUT THE FORMATION
OF A NEW ENGLAND SPOT

BY

SUMNER C. POWELL

Sumner Chilton Powell (born on October 2, 1924, in Northampton, Mass.) was graduated from Taft School in 1942. During World War II he served for three years as lieutenant in the United States Naval Reserve. Meanwhile he enrolled at Amherst College, where he received his Bachelor of Arts degree in 1946. From 1953 to 1954 he assumed the position of vice president of the Ewen Knight Electronic Research Corporation in Cambridge, Mass. In 1954 he became instructor in English and history at the Choate School. After having been president of the Powell Associations in New Haven from 1960 to 1962, he joined the staff of the Barnard School for Boys in Riverdale, N.Y., as an instructor in history. Powell was member of the American Historical Association and of the American Academy of Political and Social Science. *From Mythical to Mediaeval Man* and *Venture of Windward* count among his book publications. *Puritan Village: The Formation of a New England Town* won Sumner C. Powell the Pulitzer Prize for history of 1964; it had been published one year earlier.

THE MASSACHUSETTS VILLAGE OF WATERTOWN

[Source: Sumner Chilton Powell: Puritan Village: The Formation of a New England Town, Middletown, Conn.: Wesleyan University Press, 1963, pp. 60a, 74 - 76; reprinted by permission of the University Press of New England, Hanover, N.H.]

WHEN the Goodnows, the Noyeses, and the Rices landed in Watertown about 1637–1638, they found, indeed, a "select society," and a vigorous spirit of dissent. There were many yeomen and artisans but no archdeacons or bishops and, most important, no landlords. Everyone hoped that there would be no poor, and Watertown had made special provisions to exclude them.

Noyes must have been one of the first to sense that he was surrounded by East Anglians. Or, at least, he knew that these were the men who were quickly obtaining large grants of land in the new town. A rough survey of those granted meadow in Watertown in June, 1637, shows that 60 per cent of the total number of grantees had come from Essex, Suffolk, and Norfolk.

Even more important, all the first selectmen of Watertown but two had emigrated from East Anglia. As might be expected, these men were establishing the land habits they were familiar with. The 4625 acres which had been granted to 120 men in 1636 were to be rectangular sections, laid out "successively one after another," in four "great dividends." Although the town law gave the alternative, "for them to enclose or feed in common," it was obvious what these East Anglians hoped to do. (See map.)

Each man was obtaining from twenty-five to fifty acres of uncleared land, by a freehold grant, to be made into arable, hay ground, and pasture. Houses had been constructed around a village common, to be sure, and a few "plowlands" were being tilled in common for the first years, but each farmer was shifting to individual management as quickly as he could.

This posed a serious dilemma for West Country men like the Goodnows, the Haineses, and others. They were not able or willing to change farming habits which went back "till the memory of man runneth not to the contrary." Few of them had brought over enough equipment to run a whole farm. Just as serious was the fact that the Watertown men were not granting any more lots after 1634–1635. The center was crowded, and Watertown was considered one of the most populous settlements in the Bay Colony. Any newcomer was ordered to obtain his land by purchase, and no one could settle in the town without the express permission of the Watertown freemen.

Peter Noyes was fortunate. Although he had arrived after the cessation of the free allotments, he either bought, or wheedled, twelve acres of plowland,

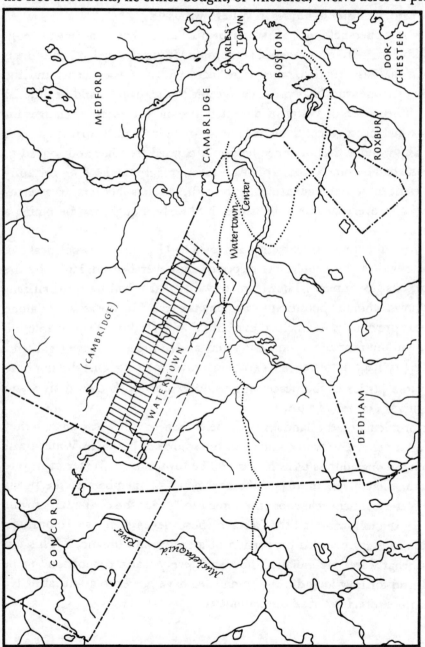

Watertown, Massachusetts, and its Neighbors, about 1638

twelve acres of meadow, eighteen acres of upland, and lot number nineteen in the first dividend, a seventy acre piece of land. But it was all distant from the town center — the plowland and the upland were on "the further plaine"; the pasture was in "the remote meadow"; and his grant lot was about five miles from the central cluster of houses in Watertown itself.

His fellow open-field men in Watertown in 1638 were in a difficult position. Unable to get free allotments, perhaps unwilling to buy land and to settle among the East Anglians, they were faced with tax assessments and the threat that anyone who "may prove chargeable to the town" could be ordered to leave. The leaders of Watertown wanted to avoid the excessive charges for the poor which every one of them had known in their English parishes.

Is it any wonder that the open-field folk banded together and looked to Noyes, who had become a citizen of Watertown, to help them? They certainly did not want to become tenants, or worse still, landless laborers, in a settlement in which everyone else, if he had arrived early enough, was becoming a landlord.

But these unhappy residents in Watertown had learned a key political fact — that the will of the people was respected, however begrudgingly, by the Massachusetts government. They learned swiftly that it had been the citizens of Watertown who, in opposition to a colony tax levied by the assistants alone a few years previously, had helped establish that basic English principle, no taxation without representation. Laws were also in process to give legal sanctity to the privilege of raising one's voice in a town meeting. One did not have to apply to a justice of the peace; one could express one's own desires and claim rights as a citizen of a town.

The problem for the landless open-field men in 1638 was clear — they needed allotments. But who constituted the source of power in Watertown? To whom did one address pleas for land? The townsmen of Watertown were not certain themselves. In 1634, "the Freemen," or members of the newly formed Watertown church, chose three men to "order the civil affairs in the Town." In the following fall the freemen chose eleven men, as a committee, to "divide to every man his proportion of meadow and upland." This was fine, but what were "civil affairs," how was "every man's proportion" to be decided, and for how long did the committee have power to grant land? No one was quite sure, least of all the committee.

1965 AWARD

ABOUT THE DEVELOPMENT
OF AMERICAN FINANCE POLICY

BY

IRWIN UNGER

Irwin Unger (born on May 2, 1927, in Brooklyn, N.Y.) attended the City College of New York, majoring in social sciences and earned his Bachelor's degree there in 1948. For graduate study he enrolled at Columbia University, where he obtained his Master of Arts degree in 1949. During the following two years he studied at the University of Washington and from 1952 to 1954 he served in the United States Army. Unger became instructor at Columbia University in 1956 and in 1959 he came as an assistant professor to the Long Beach (Cal.) State College. As an associate professor he joined the staff of the University of California in Davis in 1962. He was member of the American Historical Association, the Organisation of American Historians, and the Economic History Association. In 1964 his book *The Greenback Era* was published, it made Irwin Unger the recipient of the Pulitzer Prize for history in the following year.

ASPECTS OF POST-CIVIL WAR MONEY DEBATE

[Source: Irwin Unger: The Greenback Era. A social and political History of American Finance, 1865-1879, Princeton, N.J.: Princeton University Press, 1964, pp. 3 - 8; reprinted by permission of Princeton University Press, Princeton, N.J.]

SINCE the seventeenth century, financial questions have often been the distinctive form social conflict has taken in America. Periodically, from the earliest colonial difficulties in finding a sufficient circulating medium to the most recent dispute over a balanced budget, differences over currency and the related subject of banking have expressed basic American social and political antagonisms. It is not surprising, then, that the Civil War, initiating sweeping financial change, made the problems of money and banking of extraordinary national concern. In the decade and a half following Appomattox, national finance absorbed more of the country's intellectual and political energy than any other public question except Reconstruction. The debate over paper money, debt repayment, the national banks, and silver remonetization reflected the ambitions, aspirations, and frustrations of the most active and vigorous men of the republic and set the terms of American political conflict for the remainder of the century.

The passion and drama surrounding the post-Civil War money debate are enough to justify its description. Yet more important is the light the conflict sheds on the question of national political power in the momentous postwar era. The pushes and pulls of competing groups, local and national, in the unfolding of federal financial legislation, identify the locus of control in emerging modern America.

The interest in American *Realpolitik* is, of course, not new. For the last half-century, scholars have sought to peel away the opaque surface of post-Civil War political life to reveal its inner workings. In particular, Charles A. Beard, J. Allen Smith, and their disciples, have been concerned with the question: who ran the United States? And their conclusions have long since become part of the accepted historical canon. To the Beardians, the formal politics of the late nineteenth century were an elaborate ritual designed to disguise the blunt truths of domestic power politics. Beneath the day-to-day intrigues for place and perquisite, they argued, one could discern a raw struggle between the older agrarian America and the emerging, assertive, industrial America.

The key to our nineteenth-century history, the Beardians claimed, was the confrontation of farmer and capitalist along a broad front of vital public issues. The Civil War itself was the culmination of eighty years of economic rivalry between the plantation South and the business-dominated Northeast, allied at the end with the grain-producing West. But while the nation's agricultural heartland poured out its blood and its wealth in the common cause, Union victory in the "Second American Revolution" was a triumph of the "investing section" alone. Acting through their servile instrument, the Republican Party, eastern businessmen crammed through Congress a legislative program which subordinated public interest to private profit and ushered in a reign of predatory capitalism. Tariff protection, federal subsidies for railroads, government-sponsored rivers and harbors improvements, and, finally, "sound money," the story goes, all testified to the postwar capture of the national government by the "business interests." Although bemused for a while by appeals to northern solidarity against a resurgent South, the western farmer finally rose against the dominant Northeast. The Granger movement, Greenbackism, the free silver and Populist crusades, were in turn all manifestations of agrarian resistance to capitalist control and exploitation.

The Beardian story is so familiar that we tend to overlook the assumptions that underlie it. As a picture of American history it is fundamentally dualistic. Capitalist versus farmer, debtor versus creditor, East versus West, conservative versus radical, hard money versus soft money—these appear as successive guises of the same inherent division. The nation's story is a battle of two great antagonists who, although their names may vary, always remain essentially the same. As two disciples of Beard have recently written, "a single basic cleavage can be distinguished as running through most of our history." ". . . the 'two major complexes of interest' which have been arrayed against one another time and again are the agricultural interest on the one hand and the mercantile and financial interests, together with the industrial interest which grows out of them, on the other. Primarily this dualism may be defined as a contest between wealth in the form of land and wealth seeking outlets in commerce and industry."

As the quotation implies, along with the dualism the Beardians also accepted the central role of economic drives in our history. Both contenders in the power struggle are interest groups propelled by the acquisitive instincts appropriate to their role in the economy. It is true that the disciples of Beard and Smith, political liberals to a man, displayed far greater tenderness for the agrarian than for the capitalist, but if they were partial to the farmer or the "little man," they had no illusions about his altruism. Like the capitalist, his primary concern was for his livelihood.

This economic emphasis, of course, parallels that of Marx, and it is clear that Beard was aware of the most ambitious and challenging analysis of historical forces that the nineteenth century produced. Nevertheless, Beard was not a Marxist. He owed far more to the very agrarian tradition he so sympathetically described. Beard was a neo-Populist, and his version of post-Civil War America leaned heavily on the interpretation accepted by the contemporary leaders of agrarian dissent. There is little in Beard's "Second American Revolution" thesis that cannot be found in the reform polemics of the Granger era, the Populist revolt, and most immediately, the Progressive movement. The Manichaean view of the basic struggle, the belief in conspiracy, even the economic determinism, all belong to the Jacksonian antimonopoly thread connecting all three movements. It is this native neo-Populism, rather than an exotic European Socialism, that is responsible for both the dualism and the determinism of the Beardian philosophy.

In what follows it is this neo-Populist picture of post-bellum America that I am seeking to evaluate. This is primarily a political, not a financial history. Although fixed to a skeleton of financial events, my story is largely concerned with the decision-making process in American society. I do not wish to compete with the existing excellent surveys of financial history. I shall examine the politics of money between the end of the Civil War and the resumption of specie payments in 1879, but I shall emphasize the events of the 1870's. A recent study of the immediate postwar half-decade by Dr. Robert Sharkey of Johns Hopkins University enables me to limit my work. It has also made my task more challenging. Though we share similar conclusions, we do disagree on several important points. Briefly, Dr. Sharkey remains convinced that the governing forces in America after 1865 were economic; he disputes Beard's implied "monolithic" business, labor, and agricultural interests, but adopts an economic determinism even more complete. I cannot accept this conclusion. The events of our lifetime seemingly have revealed how weak in crisis are social and ethical restraints. Yet we must not in our despair read our own attitudes and experiences into the past. Implanted values and controls were, I believe, tougher then than now. In the matter of post-Civil War finance men indeed marshaled principle to rationalize expediency, but they also rejected perceived interest for conscience' sake. In general, most men tried to strike a balance between their pocket books and their duty. This mixture of ethics and interest, this very human attempt to serve both God and Mammon, must be recognized if we hope to understand the events of these years.

Unfortunately, adding ethics to interest greatly complicates any attempt to analyze the postwar money question. When economic self-interest is made the prime mover of human events, profit or loss will explain any historical happening. This simplification is all the more appealing since it becomes possible to deal with measurable quantities which may be summarized on a balance sheet. We record changing price per bushel, the rise and fall of interest rates, miles of track built, tons of iron produced, annual bankruptcy rates, and perform the appropriate additions and subtractions; history loses its human complexities and becomes a form of social accountancy.

1966 AWARD

ABOUT THE LIFE
OF THE MIND IN AMERICA

BY

PERRY G. MILLER

Perry Gilbert Eddy Miller (born on February 25, 1905, in Chicago, Ill.) earned his Bachelor of Philosophy degree at the University of Chicago in 1928. Three years later, he added to this degree his doctorate and joined the staff of Harvard University as an instructor. In 1939 he was promoted to associate professor. During the Second World War Miller served successively as a captain and as a major in the United States Army. Since 1946 he held a full professorship in American literature. In 1952 he came as visiting professor to the seminar in American studies at the University of Tokio, Japan, and in the following year, as well as in 1962/63, he was member of the Institute of Advanced Study. He became Powell M. Cabot professor of American literature in 1960. Miller, who received honorary doctorates from several institutions of higher education, e.g. the Northeastern University and Syracuse University, was also the author of the following book publications: *Orthodoxy in Massachusetts*; *Roger Williams*; *The New England Mind: From Colony to Province*; *Consciousness in Concord* and *The Raven and the Whale*. Perry G. E. Miller died on December 9, 1963. Posthumously, the 1966 Pulitzer Prize for American history was awarded to him for his work *The Life of the Mind in America*, which had been published one year earlier.

ORIGINS OF CHURCH AND STATE SEPARATION

[Source: Perry Miller: The Life of the Mind in America. From the Revolution to the Civil War, New York: Harcourt, Brace & World, Inc., 1965, pp. 36 - 40; reprinted by permission of Harcourt Brace and Company, Orlando, Fla.]

It was clear from the beginning of the American Revolution that the achievement of national independence would confirm the long colonial struggle for separation of church and state. The Virginia Ordinance of 1785 was revered by all churches as the codification of the victory and the First Amendment aroused no opposition. In Connecticut an established order was maintained until 1818, and in Massachusetts until 1833, but these were vestigial remains and eventually their abolition was greeted with full satisfaction by all parties.

A fact of great importance in the religious mentality of the early Republic is that nobody regarded this principle as having been violently or suddenly promulgated by the Revolution itself. Every denomination saw it as the logical culmination of native experience. American apologists were particularly annoyed by European notions that it had been embraced in a "revolutionary spirit." After his ten years in America, Philip Schaff returned to Germany to explain that the process had been one of natural growth. "Christianity proceeds in an altogether conservative spirit and with the tenderest regard for all existing institutions." Perhaps other groups might not put quite so much stress as Schaff upon the adjective "conservative," but there were few in Jacksonian America who saluted the First Amendment as a "radical" measure.

Nor would the religious allow Thomas Jefferson the credit he took unto himself. Jefferson may have boasted that his Ordinance reduced Christianity to the level of Mohammedanism or Hinduism, a bland pronouncement which "the arch-infidel" may well have uttered with a chuckle; but, insisted Robert Baird, the act itself "contains nothing to which a friend of full and equal liberty of conscience would perhaps object." As proof Baird quoted the act, with its preamble, "Whereas Almighty God hath created the mind free. . . ." Schaff was not convinced that separation was the perfect or final solution, but he much preferred the American way "to the territorial system and a police guardianship of the church." America proposed no such civil equality of atheism with Christianity as some members of the Frankfort Parliament advocated in 1848; for, as Justice Story explained in 1833, the object of the First Amendment is not to countenance or advance infidelity, but simply "to exclude all rivalry among Christian sects, and to prevent any national ecclesiastical establishment, which should give to a hierarchy the exclusive patronage of the national government." Though there were many in the country who disliked the tenor of Story's thinking, there was still universal agreement with his legalistic premise that the rights of conscience are beyond the just reach of any human power, and cannot "be encroached upon by human authority without a criminal disobedience of the precepts of natural as well as of revealed religion." The evangelical crusade to make and keep America Christian had to be conducted upon this explicit premise.

Those European theologians who listened skeptically to Schaff were invincibly persuaded that a state which officially declared itself neutral on ecclesiastical policy was *ipso facto* infidel, or at least non-Christian. Schaff and Baird stoutly fought this delusion. The Constitution, Baird patiently recounted, was intended for a people already Christian, and the fact that its authors enunciated nothing positive on the subject speaks "more loudly than if they had expressed themselves in the most solemn formulas on the existence of the Deity and the truth of Christianity." Such protestations, however, bespeak an inner uneasiness. In this period begins that silent conspiracy of ignoring the deistic propensities of the Founders and the legendary version of Washington's pietism. Baird admitted that he did regret that the Constitution had not specifically mentioned God and Christ; there were sporadic movements to get up a Christian amendment, but the more astute of the evangelicals gradually learned that the wisest policy, in terms of self-interest, was to leave well enough alone.

If they needed time to learn this lesson, the Jacksonian regime hastened their education. In the 1790's, while the churches were girding for the fight against French atheism, they could assume that the federal government was on their side because both Washington and Adams, following the example of the Continental Congress during the war, proclaimed days of thanksgiving or of fasting on emergent occasions, thus tacitly implying that the regime was sensible of standing in a Christian posture. But the need for serious thought as to just where they stood was thrust upon the pious in 1802 when President Jefferson, taking advantage of an awkward address from the Danbury Baptist Association (which minority in Connecticut was balking at being obliged to observe fasts appointed by the still-standing order), refused any longer to designate such holy festivals. In a much-quoted letter of 1808 he said that the federal government was strictly interdicted from meddling with religious institutions, and even to "recommend" a fast would be to assume religious authority. Many ministers might growl, but they were deterred from vehemence by the fact that a large number of the most devoted people (such as these same Connecticut Baptists) were grateful for Jefferson's restraint. Despite his sharing Jefferson's scruples, Madison did appoint a day of humiliation in 1812, but the effect was blunted because the Federalists denounced it as a ruse to force their support of his foreign policy. Monroe genially observed the custom, but in 1832 Henry Clay, in a misguided effort to embarrass Jackson, forced the issue to the floor of the Senate, and so compelled the conscience of the country to recognize, once and for all, that the state really was separated from all the churches.

In June of that year news of a cholera epidemic in Europe reached America, and fears that it would spread across the Atlantic amounted to panic. Revivalists, of course, improved the occasion, but the Synod of the Dutch Reformed Church requested Jackson to appoint a day of national humiliation, in the ancient manner. Jackson restated Jefferson's stand: he believed in the efficacy of prayer, but could not appoint such a day without disturbing "the security which religion now enjoys in this country in its complete separation from the political concerns of the General Government." Clay thought he saw his chance, and so introduced a resolution that Congress call upon the President to act. Betraying that this was a purely political, not to say cynical, maneuver, Clay confessed that he was not a church member, but that even so he had "a profound respect for christianity, the religion of my fathers, and for its rites, its usages, and its observances." Carefully he guarded against seeming to violate the canons of Justice Story by insisting that the Presidential recommendation "would be obligatory upon none," that it would be grateful "to all pious and moral men, whether members of religious communities or not."

Most Whigs supported Clay. Theodore Frelinghuysen recalled Madison's proclamation of 1812—an ineffectual gambit, since he had at that time, along with his fellow-Federalists, sneered at Madison's trickery. The Democrats, many of whom *were* church members, affirmed the principles of Jackson's letter. Tazewell of Virginia flatly declared that Congress has no power to make any resolutions concerning religious matters, and Davis of South Carolina effectively torpedoed the proposal by calling the custom of official fasts something "derived from our English ancestors." Jackson was preparing to veto the resolution, but the end came when so good a Whig, and also an ex-Federalist, as Verplanck agreed with the Democrats (and with Story) that pollution and degradation must be the result "of every attempt to draw religion from her seat in the hearts and consciences of men, and to associate her with power, or parade her before the world."

Jackson was at the same time arousing cries of anguish by insisting that the mails be carried on Sundays. Whigs made what propaganda they could by denouncing his administration as infidel, and in 1838 Frelinghuysen (he was generally supposed the author) painted pictures of ruin in *An Inquiry into the Moral and Religious Character of the American Government* by solemnly asserting, "Without religion, law ceases to be law, for it has no bond, and cannot hold society together." There can be no doubt that many of the more articulate Whig clergy denounced Jackson, even from their pulpits, and demanded that orthodox Christianity regulate legislation, virtually going so far as to make a stand for some direct union, if not of church and state, then of piety and politics.

But it is a mistake to suppose that all revivalists, or even a majority of them, were opposed to Jackson, or that they were deceived by Whig propaganda into misinterpreting the Jacksonian attitude toward the fast. There was a vital thrust in the very heart of revivalism which made it welcome the freedom to organize its own days of penance within localities where the "work" was alive. Furthermore, a great many "conservatives," of Verplanck's complexion, were satisfied to let things be. The "Old School" of Princeton Presbyterianism positively rejoiced in 1832 at being able to give up its "Utopian ideas" of a great national church with perfect consistency of character. "Neither the state of the country nor the temper of the age will admit of it. Theological peculiarities, and sectional feeling call for separate institutions." And Philip Schaff, who out of his European experience knew more thoroughly than his American colleagues what it was to be really "conservative," startled his Prussian audience by informing them that, with the blessings of separation of powers and full religious liberty, there were two hundred and fifty well-attended churches, "some of them quite costly and splendid," in New York, for a population of six hundred thousand, whereas in Berlin, a city of four hundred and fifty thousand, there were only forty. He could safely, and proudly, assert, "The United States are by far the most religious and Christian country in the world; and that, just because religion is there most free." Though he disapproved of revivalism, yet he had no fears about freedom. No one of the present confessions can ever become exclusively dominant in America, he said, "but rather . . . out of the mutual conflict of all something wholly new will gradually arise." In this he spoke the evangelical hope—nay, the expectation—which was a mainspring of the Revival. In 1800 the churches may have thought that all their concern lay in repelling deism and saving souls, but bit by bit, and by the 1830's entirely, they learned that they were vindicating a radical thesis unprecedented in the history of Christendom: they were proving that a wild diversity of churches within a single society could survive and prosper.

1967 AWARD

ABOUT THE EXPLORERS
OF THE AMERICAN WEST

BY

WILLIAM H. GOETZMANN

William Harry Goetzmann (born on July 20, 1930, in Washington, D.C.) enrolled at Yale University and earned his Bachelor of Arts degree there in 1952. In 1955 he joined the staff of Yale as an assistant in instruction, was promoted to instructor and finally assumed the position of associate professor. During his time at Yale University he also earned his Doctor of Philosophy degree. In 1964 Goetzmann became member of the faculty of the University of Texas, where he has held the Stiles professorship of American studies since 1967. In addition to this, he was professor of history and director of the department of American Studies at the University of Texas. A recipient of the John Addison Porter Prize of 1957, Goetzmann was awarded an honorary doctorate from St.Edwards University in Austin, Tex. *Army Exploration in the American West* and *When the Eagle Screamed: The Romantic Horizon in American Diplomacy* count among his works. William H. Goetzmann's *Exploration and Empire: The Explorer and the Scientist in the Winning of the American West* was published in 1966. It was this book which won for him the Pulitzer Prize for history the year after.

SOME LEADING FIGURES OF THAT REGION

[Source: William H. Goetzmann: Exploration and Empire: The Explorer and the Scientist in the Winning of the American West, New York: Alfred A. Knopf, 1966, pp. 169 - 173; reprinted by permission of Alfred A. Knopf, Inc., New York, N.Y.]

By the end of the 1830's a turning point had been reached in Western history. The Oregon Trail had been clearly established. Forts Laramie, Hall, and Boise existed as points of respite along the way, and within a few years Fort Bridger would be added to their number. In 1835 the Rocky Mountain Fur Company collapsed, and by 1839 the yearly rendezvous was a thing of the romantic past. The free trappers were all company men working out of trading posts, or else they had begun to put their knowledge to work in the most important enterprise of the next decade—guiding the countless wagon trains westward to Oregon and California over trails which they themselves had helped to establish. The final opening of practical emigrant trails to California was in fact the climax of the "mountain man" era of Western exploration. It demonstrates more clearly than anything else the ultimate utility of their knowledge, and their settler-oriented point of view.

The first important emigrant party to take the trail to California was the Bartleson-Bidwell company of 1841. Organized by John Bidwell, a frontier schoolteacher and farmer who had recently been robbed of most of his worldly possessions by a band of Missouri gunmen, the party was captained, at least for ceremonial purposes, by wealthy John Bartleson, who refused to go at all unless he was voted to command. It was guided as far as Soda Springs on Bear River by the mountain veteran Thomas "Broken Hand" Fitzpatrick, who taught the settlers most of what they came to know about the plains and the mountains, and then pointed them with vague geographical directions toward the Great Basin and California. From that point they were on their own.

A comparatively youthful group, the Bartleson-Bidwell party had had no real experience in the Far West with its mountains and deserts, but it did number a family of Kentucky hunters, a few frontier veterans, and some border adventurers. It also included five hardy women and ten children. Setting out into the unknown with no maps, no familiarity with landmarks, and only vague hearsay directions to guide them, they nevertheless persevered through heat and thirst and near-starvation, to blaze a first crude emigrant trail into California.

From Soda Springs they followed the Bear River south almost to Great Salt Lake and then turned west into the barren desert-like country north of the lake. Guided by Indians, they swung south at a point just below the Idaho border and reached Rabbit Spring, a forlorn spot. There the real hardships began as they failed to find the headwaters of Ogden's River, their only guide to California. When they reached Pilot Peak, a prominent landmark due west of Salt Lake, they had begun to abandon their wagons and supplies, and by the time they crossed the Ruby Mountains, which jutted up out of the desert south of Ogden's (Humboldt) River, they had left all their wagons behind and converted to pack mules.

In mid-September, however, they reached Ogden's River, and from that point on followed it as far as the Sinks forty miles east of the Sierras. Their trail across the mountains was via Sonora Pass and the Stanislaus River into central California, a difficult and dangerous route that proved to be generally impractical for anything but pack trains. Finally, however, on October 30, 1841, worn out by the mountain country and much reduced by a starvation diet of mule meat, coyote, and acorns, they came at last to the Valley of the San Joaquin and their destination—Marsh's Ranch. They were the first emigrant party to reach California, proving, with incredible perseverance and hardship, that it could be done.

The experience of the Bartleson-Bidwell party proved valuable. J. B. Chiles, one of the group, headed back East the following year, determined to lead another party to California. His return route took him via Tejon and Walker's Pass across the southern flank of the Sierras into the Great Basin, then north to the Humboldt River. He followed the Humboldt as far as he could, then struck out overland to Fort Hall in Idaho. From Fort Hall he made a personal exploration of the Rocky Mountain West on a grand scale, heading due south to the headwaters of Bear River, then across to the Green, and then to the Old Spanish Trail, which he followed into Santa Fe. He reached Independence, Missouri, via the Santa Fe Trail, which by 1842 had become a well-marked avenue of commerce.

In 1843 Chiles made use of the experience he had gained as he led another emigrant party West to California. However, when he got as far as Fort Hall he abandoned the Humboldt River–Great Basin route and continued on to Fort Boise in western Idaho. From there he blazed a trail due west via the Malheur River of Oregon and the forbidding country which surrounded it, to the Pit River country of northern California. By the time he and his party reached the coastal province, they too had been forced to abandon their wagons. With great hardship, they made their way, sometimes hopelessly lost, across the lava beds and through the rough timbered country around Mt. Shasta, down into the Sacramento Valley. In attempting to turn the northern flank of the Sierras, Chiles had not been much more successful than had the leaders of the Bartleson-Bidwell party in their march to the south.

Also in 1843, however, the mountain veteran Joseph Walker led a party on a more direct route to the Humboldt River via Thousand Springs Creek. Continuing south past the Humboldt Sinks, the Walker party entered Owens Valley and successfully crossed over Walker Pass into the San Joaquin Valley. However, despite Walker's great experience and unsurpassed knowledge of the country, this party too was forced to abandon its wagons and hence could not claim the distinction of being the first to lay out a true emigrant trail to California.

This objective was attained by the Stevens-Murphy party in 1844 in what could be called the most important of all the overland trail explorations of the early emigrant period. The party, which formed at Council Bluffs, Iowa, in the spring of 1844, was composed of twenty-three men, eight women, and fifteen children. More than half of this number consisted of the numerous members of the family of Patrick Murphy, a Missouri farmer. But, most important, it also included at least three experienced mountain men: Caleb Greenwood, who had been to Oregon with the Astorians; Isaac Hitchcock, a veteran of forty years in the fur trade, who may have been one of Bonneville's men; and Elisha Stevens. Stevens was chosen the leader, and his knowledge and resourcefulness seems to have been chiefly responsible for the success of the expedition.

They left Council Bluffs on about May 18, taking what was later called the Mormon Trail north of the Platte River. By the fourth

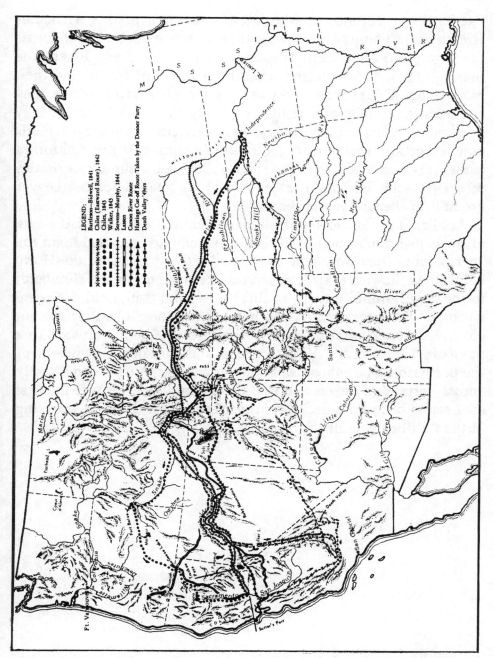

of July they had passed Fort Laramie and reached Independence
Rock in time for an appropriate celebration. After they crossed
South Pass and descended the Little Sandy, which flows to the

Pacific, Isaac Hitchcock, who knew something of this particular stretch of the country, persuaded them to strike out due west across the sage plain of western Wyoming toward the Green River (see map, p. 239). This required several days of hard travel, and then more difficult days from the Green to the Bear River, where they again struck the Oregon Trail. In making this forced march, they had laid out what came to be known as Sublette's Cut-off. A famous and important variation of both the Oregon and the California trails, this was essentially the track followed by numerous parties of early Rocky Mountain trappers as they headed for the beaver grounds of the Green and Bear rivers.

At Fort Hall, Stevens and his party learned nothing of the fate of the expeditions, such as Walker's, which had preceded them the year before. They were able to follow Walker's tracks to the Humboldt River, however, after which they coursed down the Humboldt to the now familiar Sinks. On this part of the trail, neither Greenwood nor Hitchcock was much help, but at the Sinks they met an old Indian chief named Truckee who directed them westward to a pass over the Sierras. With Stevens and two other members of the party riding out ahead as scouts, the emigrants headed directly across Forty Mile Desert and into the mountains. This was the first of a series of crucial decisions that resulted in the final breaking of the California Trail.

1968 Award

ABOUT THE IDEOLOGICAL
BACKGROUND OF THE REVOLUTION

BY

Bernard Bailyn

Bernard Bailyn (born on September 10, 1922, in Hartford, Conn.) served from 1943 to 1946 in the United States Army. At the same time he enrolled at Williams College, where he received his Bachelor's degree in 1945. For graduate studies he came to Harvard University and earned there his M.A. degree two years later. In 1953 he was granted his doctorate of philosophy and in the same year he joined the staff of Harvard as an instructor. He stayed at Harvard University and was advanced to full professor of history in 1961. The following year Bailyn became editor-in-chief of the John Harvard Library. Since 1966 he has held the Winthrop professorship of history. The historian received honorary doctorates from Lawrence University and Bard College and he is the author of several book publications, including *New England Merchants in the 17th Century*; *Massachusetts Shipping*, a book on which his wife Lotte was the co-writer; *Education in the Forming of American Society* and *Pamphlets of the American Revolution, 1750-1776*. 1967 was the publishing year of *The Ideological Origins of the American Revolution*, which earned Bernard Bailyn the Pulitzer Prize for the best book on history the following year.

THE LITERATURE AS A DISCUSSION PLATFORM

[Source: Bernard Bailyn: The Ideological Origins of the American Revolution, Cambridge, Mass.: The Belknap Press of Harvard University Press, 1967, pp. 1 - 4; reprinted by permission of Harvard University Press, Cambridge, Mass.]

WHATEVER deficiencies the leaders of the American Revolution may have had, reticence, fortunately, was not one of them. They wrote easily and amply, and turned out in the space of scarcely a decade and a half and from a small number of presses a rich literature of theory, argument, opinion, and polemic. Every medium of written expression was put to use. The newspapers, of which by 1775 there were thirty-eight in the mainland colonies, were crowded with columns of arguments and counter-arguments appearing as letters, official documents, extracts of speeches, and sermons. Broadsides — single sheets on which were often printed not only large-letter notices but, in three or four columns of minuscule type, essays of several thousand words — appeared everywhere; they could be found posted or passing from hand to hand in the towns of every colony. Almanacs, workaday publications universally available in the colonies, carried, in odd corners and occasional columns, a considerable freight of political comment. Above all, there were pamphlets: booklets consisting of a few printer's sheets, folded in various ways so as to make various sizes and numbers of pages, and sold — the pages stitched together loosely, unbound and uncovered — usually for a shilling or two.

It was in this form — as pamphlets — that much of the most important and characteristic writing of the American Revolution appeared. For the Revolutionary generation, as for its predecessors back to the early sixteenth century, the pamphlet had peculiar virtues as a medium of communication. Then, as now, it was seen that the pamphlet allowed one to do things that were not possible in any other form.

The pamphlet [George Orwell, a modern pamphleteer, has written] is a one-man show. One has complete freedom of expression, including, if one chooses, the freedom to be scurrilous, abusive, and seditious; or, on the other hand, to be more detailed, serious and "highbrow" than is ever possible in a newspaper or in most kinds of periodicals. At the same time, since the pamphlet is always short and unbound, it can be produced much more quickly than a book, and in principle, at any rate, can reach a bigger public. Above all, the pamphlet does not have to follow any prescribed pattern. It can be in prose or in verse, it can consist largely of maps or statistics or quotations, it can take the form of a story, a fable, a letter, an essay, a dialogue, or a piece of "reportage." All that is required of it is that it shall be topical, polemical, and short.

The pamphlet's greatest asset was perhaps its flexibility in size, for while it could contain only a very few pages and hence be used for publishing short squibs and sharp, quick rebuttals, it could also accommodate much longer, more serious and permanent writing as well. Some pamphlets of the Revolutionary period contain sixty or even eighty pages, on which are printed technical, magisterial treatises. Between the extremes of the squib and the book-length treatise, however, there lay the most commonly used, the ideally convenient, length: from 5,000 to 25,000 words, printed on anywhere from ten to fifty pages, quarto or octavo in size.

The pamphlet of this middle length was perfectly suited to the needs of the Revolutionary writers. It was spacious enough to allow for the full development of an argument — to investigate premises, explore logic, and consider conclusions; it could accommodate the elaborate involutions of eighteenth-century literary forms; it gave range for the publication of fully wrought, leisurely-paced sermons; it could conveniently carry state papers, collections of newspaper columns, and strings of correspondence. It was in this form, consequently, that "the best thought of the day expressed itself"; it was in this form that "the solid framework of constitutional thought" was developed; it was in this form that "the basic elements of American political thought of the Revolutionary period appeared first." And yet pamphlets of this length were seldom ponderous; whatever the gravity of their themes or the spaciousness of their contents, they were always essentially polemical, and aimed at immediate and rapidly shifting targets: at suddenly developing problems, unanticipated arguments, and swiftly rising, controversial figures. The best of the writing that appeared in this form, consequently, had a rare combination of spontaneity and solidity, of dash and detail, of casualness and care.

Highly flexible, easy to manufacture, and cheap, pamphlets were printed in the American colonies wherever there were printing presses, intellectual ambitions, and political concerns. But in their origins most of them may be grouped within three categories. The largest number were direct responses to the great events of the time. The Stamp Act touched off a heavy flurry of pamphleteering in which basic American positions in constitutional theory were staked out; its repeal was celebrated by the publication of at least eleven thanksgiving sermons, all of them crowded with political theory; the Townshend Duties led to another intense burst of pamphleteering, as did the Boston Massacre and the precipitating events of the insurrection itself — the Tea Party, the Coercive Acts, and the meeting of the first Continental Congress.

1969 AWARD

ABOUT THE ORIGINS
OF THE FIFTH AMENDMENT

BY

LEONARD W. LEVY

Leonard Williams Levy (born on April 9, 1923, in Toronto, Ont., Canada) enrolled at Columbia University after having served with the United States Army during World War II. He earned his Bachelor of Science degree in 1947 and received his M.A. degree the following year. From 1950 to 1951 he worked as a research assistant at Columbia University. On a University fellowship Levy wrote his doctoral thesis in 1951. That same year, he joined the staff of Brandeis University in Waltham, Mass., as an instructor. There, he assumed successively the position of assistant professor and associate professor, before he was advanced to full professor. In 1957 he became the first incumbent of the Earl Warren chair of constitutional history. From 1958 to 1963 he was dean of the Graduate School of Arts and Sciences and became then dean of the faculty of arts and sciences. Being a prolific author, Levy has published a large number of books: *The Law of the Commonwealth and Chief Justice Shaw*; *Legacy of Suppression*; *Freedom of Speech and Press in Early American History*; *Jefferson and Civil Liberties* and *The Darker Side*. In 1969 the Pulitzer Advisory Board chose *Origins of the Fifth Amendment* by Leonard W. Levy as the best book on modern American history published during the preceding year.

THE BASIC RIGHT AGAINST SELF-INCRIMINATION

[Source: Leonard W. Levy: Origins of the Fifth Amendment. The Right against Self-Incrimination, New York: Oxford University Press, 1968, pp. 368 - 372; reprinted by permission of the author, Ashland, Or.]

The right against self-incrimination was but shakily or unevenly established in America by the close of the seventeenth century. But a perceptible change was occurring in the legal development of all the colonies: the English common law was increasingly becoming American law. The degree to which that was true varied from colony to colony, and the pace was not the same in each. But in all, as their political and economic systems matured, their legal systems, most strikingly in the field of criminal procedure, began more and more to resemble that of England. The consequence was a greater familiarity with and respect for the right against self-incrimination.

In the eighteenth century the legal profession, which in the early years of every colony was virtually nonexistent and distrusted, rapidly grew in size, competence, social status, and political power. The rise of a substantial propertied class and the growing complexity and prosperity of colonial business required the services of a trained legal profession; the colonial governments also found an increasing need for the special skills of lawyers, both on and off the bench. Although lay judges still dominated the colonial bench at the time of the American Revolution, they increasingly included men who, though self-educated in the law, were highly knowledgeable and respectful of professional standards. Bench and bar resorted more and more to English law and English procedure as their guide. The complex, highly technical common-law system required well-trained lawyers to administer it, and they looked to Westminster, to the English law reports and legal treatises, for their rules and even for their training. There were more and more Americans educated at the Inns of Court with each passing decade, about sixty before 1760, triple that number by 1776. They became the leaders and teachers of the American bar and had a prodigious effect in making American law imitative of the English, by making English cases and English legal treatises the measure of competence, the fount of inspiration, and the precedent for emulation. Although law books, especially in the seventeenth century, had been in short supply in the colonies, there were always enough to provide instruction, especially in matters of criminal law and procedure. Michael Dalton's *Countrey Justice* was the universal handbook. It was one of the books, along with Coke's works, ordered by the General Court of Massachusetts in 1647 "to the end that we may have better light for making & proceeding about laws." Rhode Island relied heavily on Dalton in framing her criminal code in 1647; Maryland in 1678 required that all her judges keep copies of Dalton at hand, and in 1723 added Hawkins's *Pleas of the Crown* and Nelson's *Justice of the Peace* to the required list. In Virginia, where the assembly also prescribed Dalton for the courts, gentlemen increasingly read law books as part of their general education. A seventeenth-century Virginia lawyer named Arthur Spicer had a private library of fifty-two law books. In the eighteenth century the supply of law books became more and more plentiful as their importation increased and as American printers took to issuing local editions.

The experience of New York is a good indication of the trend of the time. Beginning in 1683 the criminal law of New York became an extremely sophisticated duplication of the "practices and forms of the English central courts." From the beginning of the eighteenth century, according to Goebel and Naughton, New York's criminal courts were peopled by men with excellent legal training who conducted their work as skillfully as their counterparts in England. Because their "intellectual home . . . centered in the dingy streets about the Inns of Court, they read and cited what lawyers did at home." They prized English law books, "because it was from English precedent that provincial law was built." The standard of practice in the highest court of the colony became "really comparable" with that in King's Bench, while the inferior criminal jurisdiction was "administered in much the same way as . . . in English Quarter Sessions." Goebel and Naughton also said, with reference to the "malignant ferocity" of the judges, "If the case of Penn and Mead at Old Bailey was typical the proceedings were exactly similar," and presumably, therefore, they illustrate the sessions trials in colonial New York. It is to the point, then, to repeat that at that trial, Mead, on being asked an incriminating question, replied: "It is a maxim in your own law, 'Nemo tenetur accusare seipsum,' which if it be not true Latin, I am sure it is true English, 'That no man is bound to accuse himself.' And why dost thou offer to insnare me with such a question?" "Sir, hold your tongue," replied the judge, "I did not go about to insnare you," and he dropped the question.

Goebel and Naughton heavily stressed the influence of English law books on the development of New York law generally and that colony's criminal procedure in particular. They pointed out that James Alexander, William Smith, Joseph Murray, John Tabor Kempe, and other New York attorneys "collected every [law] book they could lay their hands on" and subscribed to new ones as they were published. Alexander's collection of 152 law books as of 1721 was probably the largest in the colonies at the time, and he generously loaned them, making his, in effect, the first circulating library in New York. William Smith's library in 1770 contained three times as many law titles as Alexander had had. "No one," says Goebel and Naughton, "who has examined the memoranda and citations of any first-rate New York lawyer of the 1730's can doubt the general availability or spread of these sources or the competency to use them." For nearly everything done in the New York Supreme Court, precedent could be found in Hawkins's *Pleas of the Crown*, while the New York City Sessions Court trod "as closely as it may the path of the superior court," and the local justices of the peace found some manual like Dalton or Nelson to be the magistrate's vade mecum. Because the "patterns of practice were cut after the designs of Hawkins, Hale, and the *Crown Circuit Companion*," defiance of these tutelary geniuses was "exceptional." "The course of the typical criminal trial in New York during the eighteenth century," Goebel and Naughton concluded, "can be plotted with the Office of the Clerk of Assize or the *Crown Circuit Companion* in one hand and with Hawkins' *Pleas of the Crown* in the other. . . ."

In view of the fact that the right against self-incrimination had by then become entrenched and respected in England, its existence in New York and in the other colonies should be expected, its absence would be an astonishing departure from the general reception of the common law's accusatorial system of criminal procedure. Because England provided the model, English history, English law books, and English criminal practice are at the source of any understanding of the right in New York and the other colonies. And since the colonial bar so avidly followed the English treatises and precedents, Goebel and Naughton would be justified in concluding that a strong prima facie case against the existence of the right could be constructed *if* it were passed over in those books and cases. As noted earlier, Goebel and Naughton unequivocally stated that the right was unknown in colonial New York. And they added that, "It is obviously idle to imagine that a 'principle' which even Baron Gilbert forbears to mention, should have been cosseted in our own courts."

The existence of the right against self-incrimination in English case law, especially that of the central courts at Westminster, has already been established in earlier chapters. That the right was scarcely unnoticed by English law writers might be taken for granted had not a distinctly contrary impression been spread by such impressive authority as the authors of *Law Enforcement in Colonial New York*. Baron Gilbert, as a matter of fact, by no means forbore to mention the "principle," nor was it ignored by other writers or in the law books that were relied upon by the colonial lawyers of New York or of the other colonies.

Geoffrey Gilbert's *Law of Evidence*, published in 1756, was, as Goebel and Naughton say, the first work on the subject with any analytic merit. Gilbert, whose words have been fully quoted earlier, observed that while a confession was the best evidence of guilt, it must be voluntarily made because "our Law . . . will not force any Man to accuse himself; and in this we do certainly follow the Law of Nature. . . ." Gilbert's statement of the right against compulsory self-incrimination reflected the age-old English phrasing which, by his time, required no explanation. His *Law of Evidence* was used in New York even before it was published in England. On February 5, 1753, William Smith, Jr., one of the luminaries of the New York bar, received from John McEvers, a fellow attorney, a manuscript volume "supposed to be done by Baron Gilbert." Smith copied 173 pages of the manuscript, including the passage against self-accusing, and in the margin later wrote, "Note this book is now printed under title Law of Evidence in 8 vo. 1 June 1756." Smith, by the way, not only knew of the right from many sources, in addition to Gilbert, but as an historian, councilor, and lawyer, he respected the right.

Gilbert's book has been singled out for special consideration only because its alleged silence on the subject has been offered by Goebel and Naughton as proof that the right was not even known in New York's English-minded courts. Yet almost any law book that touched criminal law might be used to prove that information about the right was available to the colonists. In the most widely used English law dictionary of the eighteenth century, written by Giles Jacob, the broad proposition is stated under "Evidence" that "the witness shall not be asked any Question to accuse himself." Jacob cited Coke's *Institutes*, Hobbes's *Leviathan*, and the *State Trials* as his authorities. He restated the proposition in his popular guidebook, *Every Man His Own Lawyer*, the seventh edition of which was published in New York in 1768.

1970 AWARD

ABOUT THE EXPERIENCES
IN THE STATE DEPARTMENT

BY

DEAN G. ACHESON

Dean Gooderham Acheson (born on April 11, 1893, in Middletown, Conn.) entered Yale University at the age of 18 and earned his Bachelor of Arts degree in 1915. Thereafter, he enrolled at the Harvard University Law School, but his studies were interrupted, when he served with the United States Navy during World War I. He completed his law course in 1918 and was granted his LL.B. degree. From 1919 to 1921 he worked as private secretary to Associate Justice Louis D. Brandeis. From this post he went to the Washington law firm of Covington, Burling and Rublee, where he practiced corporate and international law from 1921 to 1933. President Roosevelt appointed Acheson Under Secretary of the Treasury on May 19, 1933, but Acheson was replaced in late 1933, after having criticized the President's program for raising prices. In 1934 he returned to his law firm, now called Covington, Burling, Rublee, Acheson and Schorb. It was in 1941, that Roosevelt requested him to return to Government service as Assistant Secretary of State. Acheson became Under Secretary of State in 1945. After six and a half years in the State Department, he resigned in 1947 to return to private practice. At that time President Truman bestowed on him the Medal of Merit for his services. Acheson returned to the State Department in 1949, when he was the fiftieth American to be appointed Secretary of State. He remained in this position until 1953 and returned then to private practice for good. Dean G. Acheson, the author of *A Citizen Looks at Congress* and *A Democrat Looks at His Party*, published *Present at the Creation: My Years in the State Department* in 1969. This work made him the winner of the Pulitzer Prize for history the year after.

TOP GOVERNMENT OFFICIALS IN WORLD WAR II

[Source: Dean Acheson: Present at the Creation: My Years in the State Department, New York: W. W. Norton & Company, Inc., 1969, pp. 9 - 11; reprinted by permission of the W. W. Norton & Company, Inc., New York, N.Y.]

IN FEBRUARY 1941 the Department over which the Secretary of State presided was less than a quarter of its present size, made up at home and abroad of twelve hundred officers and twenty-nine hundred other American employees. With the Bureau of the Budget it shared the old State, War, and Navy Building on Pennsylvania Avenue, across West Executive Avenue from the White House, and had bureaus scattered all over town. "Old State," a well-known Washington architect has maintained, was built from the same basic plan as the Treasury on the other side of the White House, although it was erected half a century later and thus, in accordance with the architectural style of the period, has pillared porticoes and a mansard roof instead of the classic simplicity of the Treasury. Only a few years ago it was regarded as a horror. Now Congress has appropriated a staggering sum to restore the much-cut-up interior, which houses the Executive Office of the President, to the spacious dignity it had when, after the Civil War, it was built to accommodate three whole departments of government. It is to be preserved as a "national monument." Congress does not entertain the same sentiment about those who have inhabited it.

Cordell Hull was a handsome man. He looked like a statesman in the classic American tradition—the tradition of the great Virginia dynasty, of Henry Clay, of Daniel Webster (but much handsomer, more like Warren Harding). His well-structured face was sad and thoughtful, his speech slow and gentle, except when he was aroused, as over the duplicity of the Japanese emissaries at the time of Pearl Harbor. Suspicious by nature, he brooded over what he thought were slights and grievances, which more forthright handling might have set straight. His brooding led, in accordance with Tennessee-mountain tradition, to feuds. His hatreds were implacable—not hot hatreds, but long cold ones. In no hurry to "get" his enemy, "get" him he usually did.

Mr. Hull's feuds grew out of his relations with President Franklin Roosevelt. The natures of the two men being what they were, their relations were bound to have been difficult. The Secretary—slow, circuitous, cautious—concentrated on a central political purpose, the freeing of international trade from tariff and other restrictions as the prerequisite to peace and economic development. With almost fanatical single-mindedness he devoted himself to getting legislative authority, and then acting upon it, to negotiate "mutually beneficial reciprocal trade agreements to reduce tariffs" on a basis of equal application to all nations, a thoroughly Jeffersonian policy. These often-enunciated words, due to a speech impediment, emerged as the "wecipwocal twade agweement pwogam to weduce tawiffs."

Mr. Hull's amazing success with this important undertaking, a reversal of a hundred years of American policy, was due both to his stubborn persistence and to his great authority in the House of Representatives and the Senate, in each of which he had served. It is all the more remarkable that, unlike almost all the New Deal economic legislation once regarded as radical, the executive power to negotiate trade agreements has not been permanently incorporated in American legislation, but only extended from time to time for short periods with alternating contractions and expansions of scope.

While the Secretary had concentrated on external trade in the prewar administration, the President's interest was absorbed by the effects of the Great Depression on the internal economy. Neither man—in common with most of his fellow citizens—was aware of the catastrophe building up in Europe and Asia, which would dwarf the preoccupations of both. When, later on, the President's quicker perception awakened to it, he got little help from the Secretary and turned elsewhere for it. At the outset, however, economic problems strained their relations.

The strains began with the debacle of the London Economic Conference of July 1933, torpedoed by the President with the Secretary on the bridge. Looking back on that unhappy episode, it seems to have been caused primarily by divided counsel within the Administration and sloppy preparation, which obscured for both the President and the Secretary the relation between the foreign and domestic issues involved and the essential connection between foreign trade policy and international monetary arrangements. Eleven years later, in 1944—the last year of Mr. Hull's long tenure—these issues had been resolved, and brilliant results were achieved at the International Monetary Conference at Bretton Woods. Ironically, this conference was presided over by the Secretary's arch rival for the President's favor, Secretary of the Treasury Henry Morgenthau.

In 1933 Mr. Hull did not fix blame for the disaster upon the ineptness of a new and disorderly administration, nor would loyalty permit him to place it upon the President. However, a satisfactory villain was at hand. Raymond Moley, a professor of economics at Columbia University and a member of Governor Roosevelt's campaign "brain trust," had been made an Assistant Secretary of State. The appointment would not have been made over the Secretary's objection, but he accepted and resented it. Years later he wrote: "Mr. Roosevelt, without much ceremony, appointed Raymond Moley as one of my Assistant Secretaries of State. . . . I . . . concluded that Mr. Roosevelt was placing him in this position, not to render regular service as Assistant Secretary of State, but to continue to stay close around the President. . . . In any event, I was not at all enthusiastic about this sort of appointment, and I grew less enthusiastic until the London Economic Conference was over and Moley retired from the State Department."

Mr. Moley's flamboyant part in the collapse of the conference humiliated Mr. Hull. Before long, other duties were found for Mr. Moley, and he returned, disgruntled, to Columbia. Mr. Hull cut a notch in his rifle stock.

Trouble, however, continued. The President chose to raise prices as the principal method of stimulating American agriculture and industry. To accomplish this he set about depreciating the dollar by monetary devices. This campaign conflicted sharply with Mr. Hull's principal aim, the freeing and stimulation of international trade. If American prices were artificially raised, they would attract foreign goods, which would defeat the price rise. Accordingly, these goods must be excluded. The Agricultural Adjustment Act, the brain child of Secretary of Agriculture Henry Wallace, gave the President power to do so should he find that imports threatened to imperil domestic prices. Where foreign markets were of great importance, as they were to farm products, such men as George N. Peek, former Administrator of the Agricultural Adjustment Administration, advocated bilateral, practically barter, deals with selected nations, a deathblow to the most-favored-nation principle. Mr. Hull was constantly fighting the President's favorites for the very life of his basic policy.

More and more the President turned to other, more energetic, more imaginative, more sympathetic collaborators—General Hugh Johnson, "Old Ironpants" of the NRA; Henry Wallace and Rexford G. Tugwell for agriculture and housing; Harry Hopkins and Harold Ickes to create employment; Morgenthau and Jesse Jones to rehabilitate finance; Frances Perkins to do the same for labor. Except for the secretaries for the armed services, whom the President dealt with directly as Commander in Chief, the Secretary of State—the senior Cabinet officer—became one of the least influential members at the White House. It was neither the first nor the last time this has happened.

1971 AWARD

ABOUT THE THIRTY-SECOND
PRESIDENT OF THE UNITED STATES

BY

JAMES M. BURNS

James MacGregor Burns (born on August 3, 1918, in Melrose, Mass.) entered Williams College in Williamstown, Mass., in 1935, majoring in political science. He was graduated in 1939 magna cum laude, receiving his B.A. degree. The following year, Burns studied at the National Institute of Public Affairs. He returned to Williams College in 1941 as an instructor in political science. After the United States entered World War II, however, he became the executive secretary of the nonferrous metals commission of the National War Labor Board. In 1943 he joined the Army with the rank of private, and during the next two years he served as combat historian with the 1st Information and Historical Service and eventually advanced to master sergeant. At the end of the war, Burns studied at Harvard University, which in 1947 awarded him both the M.A. and Ph.D. degrees, and in 1949 he took further graduate courses at the London School of Economics. Meanwhile, in 1947, he had resumed teaching at Williams College, as an assistant professor in political science. He was promoted to associate professor in 1950 and to full professor in 1953. Burns worked as a local and county leader of the Democratic party. He was a member of the Berkshire County delegation to the Massachusetts state convention in 1954 and a member of the Massachusetts delegation to the Democratic National Convention in 1952, 1956, 1960 and 1964. Burns is the author of quite a number of books, including *Guam: Operations of the 77th Infantry Division*; *Congress on Trial*; *Roosevelt: The Lion and the Fox*; *John Kennedy: A Political Profile* and *Presidential Government: The Crucible of Leadership*. James M. Burns' volume *Roosevelt: The Soldier of Freedom* was published in 1970 and won the Pulitzer Prize in history the following year.

THE REELECTION OF FRANKLIN D. ROOSEVELT

[Source: James MacGregor Burns: Roosevelt: The Soldier of Freedom, New York: Harcourt Brace Jovanovich, Inc., 1970, pp. 22 - 27; reprinted by permission of the author, Williams College, Williamstown, Mass.]

Two days after the election Franklin Roosevelt's train rolled slowly south along the Hudson River, was shunted through New York City, and then bore him through the long night to Washington. In the morning Eleanor Roosevelt, Vice President-elect Henry A. Wallace, and several thousand Washingtonians greeted him at Union Station. Two hundred thousand people lined Pennsylvania Avenue. The returning hero, back from the wars like some conqueror of old, jubilantly doffed his familiar campaign fedora as the limousine inched its way to the White House. Thousands followed the car, poured through the open White House gates, swarmed over the lawn, and chanted "WE WANT ROOSEVELT!" until the President and the First Lady appeared on the north portico.

And now the daily routine, fashioned during eight years in office, began again in the famous old mansion. Around 8:30 A.M. the President, a cape thrown around his shoulders, breakfasted in bed while he skimmed rapidly through dispatches and newspapers—usually the New York *Times* and the *Herald Tribune* (especially flown from New York), the Washington papers, the Baltimore *Sun*, and the Chicago *Tribune*—his eyes lighting with radar speed on presidential and political items. Eleanor might come in at this point with an urgent plea, and then presidential aides—Hopkins, Watson, Early, McIntyre, the old White House hand William D. Hassett, presidential physician Ross T. McIntyre for a brief check-up. Around 10:00 A.M. the President's valet, Arthur Prettyman, trundled him into the White House elevator in his small armless wheel chair, lowered him to the ground floor, and wheeled him through the colonnade to his office, now accompanied by Secret Service men with baskets of presidential papers. Fala might meet his master on the way and receive a presidential caress. After the President's return to his study around 5:30 came a relaxed and garrulous cocktail hour, as the President painstakingly measured out the liquor and dominated the conversation at the same time. Usually he dined with immediate members of his family and staff, and in the evening variously worked on speeches, leafed through reports, reminisced with his secretaries, or toyed with his collections of stamps and naval prints.

Friday was usually Cabinet day; on the Friday after the election the President met with his official family for the first time since he had left for the campaign battles. The Cabinet of November 1940 was ripe in years, experience—and disagreements. The members with the greatest political weight, measured either by formal authority or by easy access to the President and *his* influence, were (along with Morgenthau) Secretary of State Cordell Hull, courtly, conspicuously patient and long-suffering until the point when he could explode under pressure with a mule skinner's temper and damn his enemies, foreign and domestic; Secretary of War Henry L. Stimson, no intimate of the President, but a man of such moral stature in American politics and strong and plain opinions that he exerted a constant, if unseen, influence on his chief; Secretary of Labor Frances Perkins, the first woman Cabinet member in American history, utterly loyal to the President and to Eleanor Roosevelt, a sweet-talking conciliator of rival politicians and labor leaders, her official mien hardly concealing a sensitive feminine personality; and, oddly, Secretary of the Interior Harold L. Ickes, the Eeyore of the Cabinet if Morgenthau was its Rabbit, a prowling defender of his bureaucratic turf, prickly and petty but insufferably right-minded on the big issues, a host to his chief for poker and a grumpy guest of the President for fishing.

The Cabinet was a brier patch of rivalries and differences. Stimson and most of the others fretted over Hull's procrastinations and precautions; Hull, for his part, suspected, sometimes rightly, that certain of his colleagues would be happy to take over some of his department's responsibilities; Morgenthau, in moving ahead on aid to Britain, jousted with both the State and War Departments; Ickes had battled with virtually all his colleagues, and pursued his most passionate determination, next to thwarting Hitler, to filch the Forest Service from the Department of Agriculture.

But the Cabinet was broadly united on the cardinal issue of 1940. Hull had warned Latin-American diplomats of a wild runaway race by "certain rulers" bent on conquest without limit. Stimson was gradually becoming convinced that war was not only inevitable but also necessary to clear the field for a decisive effort. Morgenthau feared and hated the Nazis and yearned to help Britain as fully as American resources allowed. Ickes for years had been publicly reviling Hitler and for months urging a full embargo against Japan. The others were strong interventionists.

Every ounce of the Cabinet's talent and militance was needed in the fall of 1940. It was clear that Britain faced a crisis of shipping, supply, and money. There were rumors of mighty strategic decisions being made in enemy capitals. Interventionists were demanding action; the President had a mandate for all aid to Britain short of war—why didn't he deliver? But nothing seemed to happen. When Lord Lothian, the British Ambassador, returned from London late in November with a warning that his nation was nearing the end of its financial resources, Roosevelt told him that London must liquidate its investments in the New World before asking for money.

While official Washington waited for marching orders, the President took a four-day cruise down the Potomac to catch up on his sleep. Then he upset press predictions by making no changes in his Cabinet, tried unsuccessfully to persuade the aged General John J. Pershing to serve as ambassador to Vichy France, asked Librarian of Congress Archibald MacLeish to find out if the Cherable Islands, which he had once told reporters he would visit, could be found in poetry or fiction (they could not), and called for an annual Art Week under White House sponsorship. The President made it clear that he would not ask for repeal or modification of the Neutrality Act, which forbade loans to belligerents, or of the Johnson Act, which forbade loans to countries that had defaulted on their World War I debts.

At a press conference, the President fended off reporters who were looking for big postelection decisions on the war. It was all very good-natured. Asked by a reporter whether his economy ban on civilian highways included parking shoulders for defense highways, the President could not resist the opening.

"Parking *shoulders?*"

"Yes, widening out on the edge, supposedly to let the civilians park as the military go by."

"You don't mean necking places?"

The reporters roared, but they got precious little news. The administration seemed to be drifting. Then on December 3 the President boarded the cruiser *Tuscaloosa* for a ten-day cruise through the Caribbean. Besides his office staff he took only Harry Hopkins.

While Roosevelt fished, watched movies, entertained British colonial officials—including the Duke and Duchess of Windsor—and looked over naval bases, Cabinet officers back in Washington struggled with the dire problem of aid to Britain. Production officials

January 8, 1941, Ernest
H. Shepard

FULL PRESSURE

agreed that American industry could produce enough for both
countries, and army chiefs were happy to supply British as well as
American needs, for this would require an enormous expansion of
defense production facilities, but what about the financing? The
British in Washington contended that they could not possibly pay
for such a huge program. Morgenthau asked Jesse Jones, head of
the Reconstruction Finance Corporation, if he could legally use
its funds to build defense plants. For the War Department, yes,
said Jones, but not for the British. Stimson argued that the administration must no longer temporize, but present the whole issue to
Congress, and the others agreed. But this seemed a counsel of despair; everyone could imagine the explosion on Capitol Hill if the
issues were clearly drawn. And would the President risk a legislative defeat of this magnitude?

A thousand miles south, Navy seaplanes were bringing the President daily reports on these anxious searchings. Then, as the *Tuscaloosa* sat off Antigua in the bright sun, a seaplane arrived with
Churchill's fateful postelection letter. No one remembered later

that Roosevelt seemed especially moved by it. "I didn't know for quite a while what he was thinking about, if anything," Hopkins said later. "But then—I began to get the idea that he was refueling, the way he so often does when he seems to be resting and care-free. So I didn't ask him any questions. Then, one evening, he suddenly came out with it—the whole program. He didn't seem to have any clear idea how it could be done legally. But there wasn't a doubt in his mind that he'd find a way to do it."

The "whole program" was Lend-Lease—the simple notion that the United States could send Britain munitions without charge and be repaid not in dollars, but in kind, after the war was over.

This was no rabbit pulled out of a presidential hat. Churchill's letter had acted merely as a catalyst. A British shipbuilding mission had recently arrived in Washington to contract for ships to be built in the United States. For weeks, perhaps months, the President had been thinking of building cargo ships and leasing them to Britain for the duration. Why not extend the scheme to guns and other munitions? This apparently simple extension, however, represented a vast expansion and shift in the formula. There was no way that Britain could return thousands of planes and tanks after the war; there was no way that Americans could use them if it did. Maritime Commission officials had opposed even the leasing of ships, on the ground that the United States would not need a large fleet after the war and would be stuck with a lot of useless vessels. If this was true of ships, it was doubly true of tanks and guns. But so adroitly and imaginatively did Roosevelt handle the matter that for a long time its critics made every objection except the crucial one.

Armed with his formula, restored and buoyant after his trip, the President returned to Washington on December 16 and plunged into a series of conferences with his anxious advisers. The next two weeks were one of the most decisive periods in Roosevelt's presidency. His foxlike evasions were put aside; now he took the lion's role.

1972 AWARD

ABOUT THE COMPARISON
OF RACE RELATIONS IN AMERICA

BY

CARL N. DEGLER

Carl Neumann Degler (born on February 6, 1921, in Orange, N.J.) earned his Bachelor's degree from Upsala College, New Jersey, in 1942. Thereafter, he served with the United States Army in World War II. In 1945 he enrolled at Columbia University for graduate study and received his M.A. degree there in 1947. That same year he joined the staff of Hunter College as an instructor. During the following years he also taught at the New York University, at Adelphi College and at the College of the City of New York. In 1952 the Ph.D. degree was conferred upon him by Columbia University and Degler became member of the faculty of history at Vassar College. He was promoted to full professor of history in 1962 and, in 1966, he became chairman of the department. Meanwhile Degler taught as visiting professor at Columbia Graduate School in 1963/64 as well as in Stanford during the summer term of 1964. In 1968 he accepted a professorship of American history at Stanford University. The historian has published a large number of books including *Age of Economic Revolution*; *Affluence and Anxiety* and *Out of Our Past*. Degler was the editor of *Pivotal Interpretations of American History*; *Women and Economics* and *The New Deal*. In 1971 *Neither Black Nor White* by Carl N. Degler was published. It won the Pulitzer Prize for history the year after.

STATUS OF BLACKS IN BRAZIL AND U.S.A.

[Source: Carl N. Degler: Neither Black nor White. Slavery and Race Relations in Brazil and the United States, New York: The MacMillan Company, 1971, pp. 3 - 6; reprinted by permission of the Macmillan Publishing Company, New York, N.Y.]

Actually, Negroes have always constituted a larger proportion of the population in Brazil than they ever have in the United States. Indeed, until the 1880's, when large numbers of European immigrants began to enter the country, the majority of the Brazilian population was colored—that is, Negro or mulatto. During the colonial era, as far as can be estimated, most of the population of Brazil was both colored and slave. Even during the nineteenth century, visitors immediately were made aware of the preponderance of blacks. At Santos, Rio de Janeiro, and other ports it was not unusual for ships' passengers to be literally carried ashore through the shallow water and mud in the arms of black slaves. And, if that startling introduction were not enough to proclaim the importance of Africa in Brazil, the first walk through the crowded streets would. One English visitor to Rio de Janeiro in 1829 remarked that "my eye really was so familiarized to black visages that the occurrence of a white face in the streets of some parts of the town, struck me as a novelty." In the midst of talking about the number of free people in Brazil, Henry Koster, an English planter who spent many years in Brazil, inadvertently testified to the great number of colored people in the country. "In none of these districts which I saw, do I conceive that the slaves outnumbered the free people in a greater proportion than three to one." Also in the early years of the nineteenth century, another English visitor, Maria Graham, estimated that in the city of Recife, "not above one third are white; the rest are mulatto or Negro."

In the United States, on the other hand, Negroes have never constituted more than 19 per cent of the population at any time (1790), and for the last one hundred years the proportion has been always around 10 per cent. Even in Mississippi, which has long been the state with the highest proportion of blacks, the ratio has never been above 60 per cent. Thus, Brazil in the nineteenth century was known as the country of blacks and mixed bloods, but the United States has always been dominated by whites and so perceived by outsiders.

Undoubtedly the most obvious measure of white dominance in the United States has been the institution of legal and customary segregation—that is, the separation of whites and blacks in the activities of daily life. Although historians have now made it clear that elaborate *legal*, as distinguished from *customary* segregation, is a relatively recent phenomenon in the history of the United States, dating principally from the late nineteenth century, the *practice* of excluding Negroes from theaters, hotels, parks, and segregating them on street cars, trains, and other major public institutions runs far back into the nation's history. As we shall see later, Brazilian colonial laws often discriminated against blacks, too, but the systematic separation of the races, whether legally or customarily, is a North American phenomenon. It has no analog in Brazil. Today Brazil lacks a tradition of formal separation of the races.

The difference in attitudes and practices toward blacks in Brazil is positive as well as negative. Not only are there no laws that stigmatize Negroes as inferior, but the history of Brazil offers many examples of Negroes or mulattoes who achieved relatively high status in church and state. Travelers from the United States, for example, were struck by the sight of Negroes in high positions in nineteenth century Brazil. "I have passed black ladies in silks and jewelry, with male slaves in livery behind them," wrote Thomas Ewbank in 1856. "Today one rode past in her carriage, accompanied by a liveried footman and a coachman. Several have white husbands. The first doctor of the province is a 'colored man'; so is the President of the Province." The Brazilian acceptance of miscegenation always forcefully attracted the attention of North Americans.

Then, as now, Brazilians have been aware of the dramatic difference between their attitudes and practices and those of the United States. For example, Joaquim Nabuco, the great abolitionist of Brazil, made the contrast explicitly in a book published just before slavery ended there in 1888. In the United States, he observed, during slavery and after, a sharp and rigid line was drawn between the races with relatively little mixing. "In Brazil, he went on, "exactly the opposite took place. Slavery founded on the differences between the races never developed the color line and in this Brazil was infinitely wiser. The contacts between the races, from the first colonization of the *donatario*, up to today, has produced a mixed population . . . and the slaves who were granted a letter of manumission, also received induction into citizenship. Thus there were not among us perpetual social castes; there was not even any fixed division of classes. . . . This system of absolute equality certainly opened a better future to the Negro race than was suggested by his horizon in North America."

Modern Brazilian commentators have echoed Nabuco's praise of the Brazilian solution to the problem of race, miscegenation. "The problem of racial assimilation and absorption among whites and blacks," Nelson de Senna wrote in 1938, "is a solved problem in Brazil, without conflict or hatred; it differs radically from the more serious North American Negro problem, where there still exists a racial block of twelve million 'coloured people'; the pure Negroes and their more direct descendants isolated and separated from the racial mass of whites, by an impenetrable barrier of prejudice."

1973 AWARD

ABOUT THE ORIGINS
OF AMERICAN CIVILIZATION

BY

MICHAEL G. KAMMEN

Michael Gedaliah Kammen (born on October 25, 1936, in Rochester, N.Y.) was graduated from George Washington University and elected to Phi Beta Kappa in 1958. During the following year he attended Harvard University, where he earned his Master of Arts degree. Thereafter, he started working on his doctoral dissertation and in 1964 he received the Ph.D. degree. That same year he joined the staff of Harvard as an instructor. Since 1965 he taught history at Cornell University, where he became full professor of American history in 1969. Kammen, who became member of the board of editors of Cornell University Press in 1971, is the author of the following book publications: *A Rope of Sand: The Colonial Agents, British Politics and the American Revolution*; *Politics and Society in Colonial America: Democracy or Deference*; *Deputyes and Libertyes: The Origins of Representative Government in Colonial America* and *Empire and Interest: The American Colonies and the Politics of Mercantilism. People of Paradox: An Inquiry Concerning the Origins of American Civilization* was published in 1972. It made Michael G. Kammen the winner of the Pulitzer Prize for the best book on American history in the following year.

SOME PARADOX ASPECTS OF THE PEOPLE

[Source: Michael Kammen: People of Paradox: An Inquiry Concerning the Origins of American Civilization, New York: Alfred A. Knopf, 1972, pp. 290 - 294; reprinted by permission of the author and of Alfred A. Knopf, Inc., New York, N.Y.]

Americans have managed to be both puritanical and hedonistic, idealistic and materialistic, peace-loving and war-mongering, isolationist and interventionist, conformist and individualist, consensus-minded and conflict-prone. "We recognize the American," wrote Gunnar Myrdal in 1944, "wherever we meet him, as a practical idealist."

Throughout our history we find, all too often, ironic contrasts between noble purposes and sordid results. One need only look at Reconstruction after the Civil War, or at World War I. Americans have experienced many disappointments because prospects for realizing national purposes have presented themselves but have often gone unfulfilled. There is a profound contradiction in the American ethos which commands men to seek worldly goods while warning them that the search will corrupt their souls. Those who aspire to middle-class membership will be thrifty on the way up and then extravagant upon arrival. The co-ordinate of Yankee ingenuity is resourceful wastefulness. We seek efficiency through labor-saving devices and then squander the savings through thoughtless exploitation.

The American passion for movement and change has been matched by an equally strong sense of nostalgia and inertia. Our garden has produced abundance but not fulfillment. Our cities have produced slum tenements as well as sanitary hospitals, ideas, music, and culture in addition to filth, disease, and misery. The National Commission on the Causes and Prevention of Violence reported in 1969 that "paradoxically, we have been both a tumultuous people and a relatively stable republic." Hannah Arendt has suggested that America is more likely to erupt into violence "than most other civilized countries. And yet there are very few countries where respect for law is so deeply rooted." Perhaps the explanation is partially historical, for in the colonial era law had to be built everywhere as a bulwark against lawlessness, a process repeated on the moving frontier in the nineteenth century and the urban frontier of the twentieth. Even our anti-militarists have become violent about their pacifism.

Americans expect their heroes to be Everyman and Superman simultaneously. I once overheard on an airplane the following fragment of conversation: "He has none of the virtues I respect, and none of the vices I admire." We cherish the humanity of our past leaders: George Washington's false teeth and whimsical orthography, Benjamin Franklin's lechery and cunning. The quintessential American hero wears both a halo *and* horns.

Because our society is so pluralistic, the American politician must be all things to all people. Dwight Eisenhower represented the most advanced industrial nation, but his chief appeal rested in a naïve simplicity which recalled our pre-industrial past. Robert Frost once advised President Kennedy to be as much an Irishman as a Harvard man: "You have to have both the pragmatism and the idealism." The ambivalent American is ambitious and ambidextrous; but the appearance of ambidexterity — to some, at least — suggests the danger of double-dealing and deceit. The story is told of a U.S. senator meeting the press one Sunday afternoon. "How do you stand on conservation, Senator?" asked one panelist. The senator squirmed. "Well, I'll tell you," he said. "Some of my constituents are for conservation, and some of my constituents are against conservation, and I stand foursquare behind my constituents."

Raymond Aron, the French sociologist, has remarked that a "dialectic of plurality and conformism lies at the core of American life, making for the originality of the social structure, and raising the most contradictory evaluations." Americans have repeatedly reaffirmed the social philosophy of individualism, even making it the basis of their political thought. Yet they have been a nation of joiners and have developed the largest associations and corporations the world has ever known. Nor has American respect for the abstract "individual" always guaranteed respect for particular persons.

There is a persistent tension between authoritarianism and individualism in American history. The genius of American institutions at their best has been to find a place and a use for both innovators and consolidators, rebellious dreamers and realistic adjudicators. "America has been built on a mixture of discipline and rebellion," writes Christopher Jencks, "but the balance between them has constantly shifted over the years." Our individualism, therefore, has been of a particular sort, a collective individualism. Individuality is not synonymous in the United States with singularity. When Americans develop an oddity they make a fad of it so that they may be comfortable among familiar oddities. Their unity, as Emerson wrote in his essay on the New England Reformers, "is only perfect when all the uniters are isolated."

How then can we adequately summarize the buried historical roots of our paradoxes, tensions, and biformities? The incongruities in American life are not merely fortuitous, and their stimuli appear from the very beginning. "America was always promises," as Archibald MacLeish has put it. "From the first voyage and the first ship there were promises." Many of these have gone unfulfilled — an endless source of ambiguity and equivocation. More than that, "Jacobethan" travelers and settlers discovered that the various images projected of America could be contradictory. The New World turned out to be hospitable to radically different expectations. If America seemed to promise everything that men had always wanted, it also threatened to obliterate much of what they had already achieved. Critics and intellectuals throughout our past have recognized not only the gap between national aspirations and numbing realities, but also ambiguities endemic in the actual configuration of American goals.

Guilt and insecurity have played a major part in keeping contradictory tendencies inherent in our style. First we wiped out the Indians whose land this was; then we emasculated the Africans brought to work the land. Few cultures in history have had to bear this kind of double collective culpability.

There are also paradoxes of freedom in this country. There seemed to be no limits to what America and Americans, beginning *de novo*, could become. Consequently, the American way is so restlessly creative as to be essentially destructive: witness our use of natural resources. Because achievement seems so accessible, Americans are competitive and competition is a major source of inner conflict. Because unlimited competition is not good for either individuals or the public interest, we seek restraints; but the restraints themselves involve irreconcilable antagonisms. Mutual exercise of complete freedom by rulers and subjects alike is impossible; but only recently, and very painfully, have we begun to learn that there must be limits placed upon democratic resistance to democratic authority. Above all other factors, however, the greatest source of dualisms in American life has been unstable pluralism in all its manifold forms: cultural, social, sequential, and political.

1974 AWARD

ABOUT THE DEMOCRATIC EXPERIENCE IN THE UNITED STATES

BY

DANIEL J. BOORSTIN

Daniel Joseph Boorstin (born on October 1, 1914, in Atlanta, Ga.) entered Harvard University at the age of fifteen, majoring in history and English literature. Being awarded his B.A. degree summa cum laude in 1934, he enrolled as a Rhodes scholar in Balliol College, Oxford University, where he studied law and earned two degrees, a B.A. in jurisprudence in 1936 and a Bachelor of Civil Laws in 1937. Still inclined toward a legal career, he returned to the United States and started studying at the Yale University Law School under a Sterling fellowship. Boorstin obtained his Doctor of Juridical Science degree in 1940 and was admitted to the Massachusetts bar in 1942. Meanwhile he had begun to teach American history and literature at Harvard. Afterwards he became assistant professor of history at Swarthmore College, but after two years moved on to the University of Chicago. Boorstin remained there for twenty-five years, rising through the academic ranks from assistant professor of history to the endowed chair of Preston and Sterling Morton Distinguished Service Professor of American History. He also spent considerable time abroad as a visiting lecturer at the Universities of Rome, Puerto Rico, Kyoto, Paris and Cambridge. In 1969 he left Chicago to become director of the National Museum of History and Technology of the Smithsonian Institution in Washington, D.C. Boorstin has written many books, including *The Lost World of Thomas Jefferson* and *The Genius of American Politics*. In 1973 the third and concluding volume of *The Americans* subtitled *The Democratic Experience* was published. The year after it earned Daniel J. Boorstin the Pulitzer Prize in American history.

SOME KEY FOUNDERS OF DEPARTMENT STORES

[Source: Daniel J. Boorstin: The Americans: The Democratic Experience, New York: Random House, 1973, pp. 113 - 115; reprinted by permission of the author and of Random House, Inc., New York, N.Y.]

"GOODS SUITABLE for the millionaire," R. H. Macy's advertised in 1887, "at prices in reach of the millions." The fixed price had helped democratize the marketplace, and the new impersonal way of pricing had far-reaching effects on the consumers' world. Consumers with money to spend were eager to find something to buy. But they were more uncertain than ever about what they "needed," what was really essential to their style of life or to their station in life.

New classes of merchandise came into being, characterized not by their quality or function, but by their *price*. One of the most spectacular careers in American history and some of the nation's most distinctive institutions were built on this simple new notion.

TO CALL the five-and-ten-cent store the poor man's department store tells only part of the story. The department store was a consumers' palace; the five-and-ten was a consumers' bazaar. Both were places of awakening desire. The department store displayed items of all prices and shapes and sizes and qualities; and the five-and-ten displayed a tempting array of items which one could buy for the smallest units of cash. If an attractive item was offered at a low enough price, the customer would buy it if he needed it—but if the price was low enough and in convenient coin, perhaps the customer would buy it anyway on the spur of the moment, whether or not he "needed" it. In a world where the fixed price and the public price were only beginning to be known, where haggling was still a social pastime, it required a bold imagination to conceive the five-and-ten way of merchandising. If the fixed price was low enough, could people somehow be induced to buy *because of* the fixed price? Even before the fixed price was a firmly established institution, a clever merchant built an empire on this experiment.

The man who, more than any other, helped give commodities this price-focused quality was F. W. Woolworth. He conjured up a new world of five-cent items and ten-cent items. Hating the drudgery on his father's farm in upstate New York, young Woolworth had found work in the general stores of neighboring country towns. But, significantly, he had no knack as a salesman. In one of his early jobs his salesmanship was so poor that his employer reduced his wages from $10 to $8.50 a week. He did have a flair for display. His first success, in a small dry-goods store in Watertown, New York, was in using remnants of red cloth to make an attractive window display. His employer, hearing of another merchant's success in selling handkerchiefs at five cents apiece, decided to try a "five-cent counter," and bought a hundred dollars' worth of miscellaneous five-cent items: crocheting needles, buttonhooks, watch keys, safety pins, collar buttons, baby bibs, washbasins and dippers, thimbles, soap, and harmonicas. Woolworth arrayed them on a long table surmounted by a placard advertising the price. On the first day they were all sold.

Profiting from this experience, in 1879 Woolworth went off on his own (first in Utica, New York, then in Lancaster, Pennsylvania), trying out the idea of a "Five and Ten Cent Store." His first problem was finding enough different items to sell at his price. In the long run Woolworth would secure a large enough stock of five-and-ten-cent items by multiplying his stores and increasing his volume. By 1886 Woolworth controlled seven stores; by 1895 there were twenty-eight; by 1900, fifty-nine. Even though each store was small, with a chain of them he could buy on a large scale. He attracted new kinds of merchandise, he invented some items himself, and he bought in large quantities. In this way he gave to all buyers, even in small towns, the advantages of membership in a vast consumption community.

"Price lining"—the production of items to sell at a predetermined price—expressed a new way of thinking. And it expressed a new extreme of buyer passivity, perhaps the last stage in making shopping into a spectator sport. In the new world of the fixed price, Woolworth gave modern form to the traditional notion of a "fair price," long since elaborated by Aristotle and the medieval moralists. Was price somehow not a product of individual bargaining, but a quality of the commodity itself?

Woolworth from the beginning was bold in using red and he showed lots of red jewelry. In 1900 he standardized on the brilliant-carmine-red storefront (probably borrowed from The Great Atlantic & Pacific Tea Company), with gold-leaf lettering and molding.

For his advertising, Woolworth relied not on the newspapers or magazines, but on architecture and on the self-advertising qualities of his merchandise, which had not been widely exploited until the recent improvements in plate-glass manufacturing. "No, you don't have to bark for customers," Woolworth advised his store managers near the beginning of the century. "That method is too ancient for us. But you can pull customers into your stores and they won't know it. Draw them in with attractive window displays and when you get them in have a plentiful showing of the window goods on the counters. . . . Remember our advertisements are in our show windows and on our counters."

Goods that carried a tag announcing their price actually "sold" themselves. The only function of salesclerks was to wrap packages and make change. This helped Woolworth keep costs and prices low, since he could conduct his business successfully by employing young girls at low wages. In the early days they received $1.50 a week. "We must have cheap help," he wrote his store managers in 1892, "or we cannot sell cheap goods. When a clerk gets so good she can get better wages elsewhere, let her go—for it does not require skilled and experienced salesladies to sell our goods . . . one thing is certain: we cannot afford to pay good wages and sell goods as we do now, and our clerks ought to know it." Following the examples of John Wanamaker and Marshall Field, who would not allow a clerk to approach a customer, Woolworth boasted that his managers "make their stores Fairs and a person can go entirely through them without once being pressed to buy anything."

And Woolworth's flourished. By 1900 his volume was over $5 million a year; in another five years it had trebled. For more customers he reached up into the middle classes. Then he crossed the Atlantic and opened a chain in England. By 1913 F. W. Woolworth, who made a fetish of simplicity and directness, who believed his five-and-ten-cent merchandise should be its own advertisement, had built the most spectacular piece of architectural advertising in history. President Woodrow Wilson pressed the button in Washington which lit up in New York City the tallest habitable building in the world, the Woolworth Building.

1975 AWARD

ABOUT THE TIME AND
LIFE OF THOMAS JEFFERSON

BY

DUMAS MALONE

Dumas Malone (born on January 10, 1892, in Coldwater, Miss.) earned two Bachelor's degrees, one from Emory University in 1910 and another one from Yale University in 1916, before he served during the First World War with the United States Marine Corps advancing from private to second lieutenant. After the war he enrolled at Yale for graduate study and received his A.M. degree in 1921, to which he added a doctorate in 1923. Meanwhile he had started to work as an instructor in history. In 1923 he joined the staff of the University of Virginia as an associate professor and was promoted to full professor in 1926. Three years later he became one of the editors of the Dictionary of American Biography and in 1931 editor in chief. From 1936 to 1943 he was director of Harvard University Press. Malone accepted a professorship of history at Columbia University in 1945, a post in which he stayed until 1959. In 1962 he returned to the University of Virginia to assume there the position of a biographer-in-residence. The historian is also the author of many book publications, including *The Public Life of Thomas Cooper*; *Saints in Action*; *Edwin A. Alderman - A Biography*; *The Story of the Declaration of Independence* and *Thomas Jefferson as Political Leader*. From 1948 to 1974 the five volumes of *Jefferson and His Time* were published. It was this work that earned Dumas Malone the Pulitzer Prize in history one year after the publication of the concluding volume.

BEGIN OF THE PRESIDENT'S SECOND TERM

[Source: Dumas Malone: Jefferson and His Time, Vol. 5: Jefferson the President. Second Term, 1805-1809, Boston: Little, Brown and Company, 1974, frontispiece, pp. 3 - 7; reprinted by permission of Little, Brown and Company, Publishers, Boston, Mass.]

WHEN Thomas Jefferson was inaugurated as President of the United States for the second time — on Monday, March 4, 1805 — the echoes of the impeachment trial of Justice Samuel Chase, which ended on the previous Friday, had not yet died away. And the capital city was still talking of the extraordinary valedictory of Aaron Burr on Saturday, which had reduced the senators to breathless silence and left many a strong man in tears. The acquittal of the Justice was far more dramatic and the exit of the Vice President much more moving than the re-entry of the President, which had so long been taken as a matter of course. Though he had received, only a few months before this, an electoral majority that was not to be matched by any successor of his for upwards of a century, he entered upon his second term under rather unpropitious circumstances. His inauguration would have been a more triumphal occasion if it had occurred in January, as is the case today. Apart from the inaugural address, the occasion and the meetings in celebration of it in other places received relatively little attention in the newspapers, which continued for weeks to be filled with details of the Chase trial.

The President could hardly have wished that his inauguration should be thus overshadowed, but, disliking ceremony as he did, he undoubtedly wanted it to be unpretentious — as it unquestionably was. He did not walk to the Capitol from his nearby lodgings as he had done four years before, but on his ride from the President's House a mile away, he was accompanied by only his secretary and a groom. He took the oath of office from Chief Justice Marshall and delivered his address in a crowded Senate chamber, but no quorum of either House was present. By or shortly before half past nine on the previous night, Congress had adjourned *sine die* after the stormiest and most unproductive session of his administration thus far. At its end the President himself, according to his custom, was in a committee room in the North Wing signing bills. Before noon on Monday the congressional exodus was well under way.

There was no spectacle to miss and little to hear, for Jefferson's second inaugural address, like his first, turned out to be only partly audible. Commentators should have made some allowance for the poor acoustics of the chamber, but the President spoke in a low voice. He had once expressed satisfaction at being able to pursue a noiseless course; he was virtually doing that now, wittingly or unwittingly. But the address, printed in advance of its delivery by the *National Intelligencer* as his first one had been, was quickly available, and it was better read than listened to anyway. No doubt it was read afterwards by many of the President's auditors, but in the meantime everybody proceeded by common accord to the big house at the other end of the unpaved road known as Pennsylvania Avenue to pay him compliment. A young British diplomat, more sympathetic than his superior, Anthony Merry, noted with apparent approval that Jefferson was dressed in black, with black silk stockings, and was in high spirits. But this aristocratic and by no means uncritical observer described the company as very mixed and some of it as uncouth, while in his view the procession on the road was composed of "low persons." This had been formed in the Navy Yard by the mechanics there, who presented the President with an address of congratulation. They expressed gratitude that they lived in a land "where the honest industry of the mechanic is equally supported with the splendor of the wealthy." The support of such "low persons," who regarded the President as the symbol and champion of the liberty and equality they prized, undoubtedly gratified him far more than the grudging plaudits of a foreign observer could have.

Outside Washington the details of the day's happenings may have been little known, for they were not extensively reported. More was said, in newspapers and private letters, about the inaugural address, but this attracted no such attention as the one delivered by Jefferson four years earlier, and it has no such historical significance. The author himself described it as an account of performance, rather than a statement of profession and promise. His critics now taunted him, as in fact they had long been doing, with failure to live up to his own declaration that his fellow citizens were all republicans, all federalists — a saying they interpreted as a promise that no member of their own party should be removed from office except for malfeasance. The justice or injustice of this allegation can be determined only in the light of the policy of removals and appointments, which we have discussed at

length in the previous volume and which should be viewed on the
background of the intense political partisanship of the times on both
sides. It seems safe to say that on the whole the President, harassed by
both friends and foes, had conducted himself with wisdom and moderation while maintaining high standards of administration.

That he had reduced taxes and practiced economy while preserving
the peace could not be denied. He touched on foreign affairs only
lightly in his address, and could not have been expected to admit that he
had been lucky. We can now see that his luck had already begun to
turn, though few of his political enemies appear to have recognized the

THE "MEDALLION PROFILE" OF JEFFERSON
Portrait by Gilbert Stuart, 1805

trend as yet. The maintenance of peace with honor was to prove more difficult and more costly in his second term than in his first. He did not boast of the acquisition of Louisiana, as he would have been warranted in doing. Instead, he recognized the apprehensions of some that the enlargement of the nation's territories would endanger the Union. "But," he asked, "who can limit the extent to which the federative principle may operate effectively? The larger our association, the less will it be shaken by local passions; and in any view, is it not better that the opposite bank of the Mississippi should be settled by our own brethren and children, than by strangers of another family?" He spoke as a nationalist against the localists, making no attempt to foresee the ultimate effect of the settlement of the trans-Mississippi region on the position and power of the old states. Actually, he was trying to facilitate settlement east of the river by encouraging the Indians to move to the west of it.

In this address he devoted what he himself recognized as disproportionate attention to the Indians. His policies with respect to them cannot be divorced from considerations of national defense and the interests of white settlers, and they may seem irreconcilable with his claim that the sad history of the aborigines had inspired in him commiseration for them. But few of his American contemporaries were so deeply interested in the Indians over so long a period as he, if indeed anybody was; and, while seeking to effect the peaceful removal of as many of them as he could before the irresistible tide of white settlement should engulf them, he had followed a supplementary policy aimed at preparing them for the settled agricultural life he regarded as necessary for their survival. He wanted to make citizens of them in the end and was seeking to "humanize" his fellows toward them. In discussing their plight and problems on this occasion, however, he had an ulterior motive. By condemning hostility to them and obstructions to their progress toward civilization, he sought by inference to condemn antisocial and unprogressive attitudes of which he disapproved but which he preferred not to attack directly. This oblique approach may not commend itself to the present-day reader, but the end result was one of the most striking condemnations of the ultra-conservative mind he ever penned, and as such it marks a contrast with his customary public moderation. Speaking of "crafty individuals" who, to maintain their own position in the existing order, imposed obstacles to necessary changes in Indian society, he drew a pen picture which approaches timelessness and universality:

These persons inculcate a sanctimonious reverence for the customs of their ancestors; that whatsoever they did, must be done through all time; that reason is a false guide, and to advance under its counsel, in their physical, moral, or political condition, is perilous innovation; that their duty is to remain as their Creator made them, ignorance being safety, and knowledge full of danger; in short, my friends, among them [the Indians] is seen the action and counteraction of good sense and bigotry; they, too, have their anti-philosophers, who find an interest in keeping things in their present state, who dread reformation, and exert all their faculties to maintain the ascendency of habit over the duty of improving our reason, and obeying its mandates.

This passage, in which he set reason above tradition and appeared as a thinly disguised champion of progressive change, created little noise, but the contrast between Jefferson's bold words and prudent actions was not lost on his political enemies of that time, and it offered them ground to charge him with hypocrisy. To resolve all the apparent contradictions in this complicated man would be difficult indeed, and he would lose much of his fascination if reduced to stark simplicity, but a distinction can be made between what John Marshall referred to as the "general cast" of his political and social theory and his working philosophy as a responsible statesman. The latter he well summed up in a private observation at the beginning of his presidency, that "no more good must be attempted than the nation can bear." His zeal for reform and progress was tempered by his assessment of the actualities of a particular situation. By the same token, he has been described as both a visionary and an opportunist. Since both of these terms are in ill repute we hesitate to apply either of them, but they suggest qualities commonly found in elected officials in varying proportions. Like others, Jefferson oscillated between the two extremes. Mistakes in judgment were to be expected of him as of everybody else, and in the pursuit of immediate objectives he may at times have lost sight of long-range goals. Interpreters may be expected to differ about the precise proportions in the mixture, but his statecraft was marked on the one hand by rare vision and on the other by unusual sensitivity to public opinion and by extraordinary patience.

1976 AWARD

ABOUT THE ACTIVITIES
OF A MISSIONER IN AMERICA

BY

PAUL HORGAN

Paul Horgan (born on August 1, 1903, in Buffalo, N.Y.) attended the New Mexico Military Institute at Roswell, N.M. Starting in 1922 Paul Horgan studied for three years at the Eastman School of Music in Rochester, N.Y. In 1926 Horgan returned to the New Mexico Military Institute as the institute's librarian. When the U.S. entered World War II, Horgan became chief of Army Information with the Department of War in Washington, D.C., a post in which he reached the rank of lieutenant colonel and received the Legion of Merit. On his discharge from the Army, he received the first of two Guggenheim grants. After lecturing for a semester in the Graduate School of Arts and Letters of the University of Iowa, he returned to Roswell to resume his research and writing. In 1959 Horgan became senior fellow of the Center of Advanced Studies at Wesleyan University and was promoted to its director in 1962. Until his retirement in 1971 he was in succession senior fellow in letters and adjunct professor of English. Horgan, who afterwards was a writer in residence, published quite a number of books; his works include *Men of Arms*; *No Quarter Given*; *Main Line West*; *A Lamp on the Plains*; *The Return of the Weed* and *The Habit of Empire*, as well as the play *Yours, A. Lincoln*. Fourteen years of research and composition went into Paul Horgan's *Great River: The Rio Grande in North American History*, published in 1954. The following year it earned him the Pulitzer Prize for history. Paul Horgan was awarded another Pulitzer Prize in this category in 1976. His winning work, *Lamy of Santa Fe*, had been published the year before.

THE MOUNT VERNON TIME OF LAMY OF SANTA FE

[Source: Paul Horgan: Lamy of Santa Fe. His Life and Times, New York: Farrar, Straus and Giroux, 1975, cover p. 2, pp. 36 - 37; reprinted by permission of Farrar, Straus & Giroux, Inc., New York, N.Y.]

IN 1840 LAMY SET ABOUT the building of a small brick church in Mt Vernon. Its substance began with his creation of a sense of community among the people there. Someone gave land, another was to take the lead in bringing timber, others worked to use the roads and canals of Ohio to gather other materials. As resident pastor of Danville, Lamy could not give all his time to Mt Vernon—or even to Danville itself— for he was charged with mission duties also in Mansfield, Ashland, Loudonville, Wooster, Canal Dover, Newark, and Massillon, in addition to even less coherent communities by the waysides.

In the hot, white, diffused mists of summer, and the cracking and often howling winters alike, he and Machebeuf both had to forward their home parishes and attend to their missions. As Lamy wrote to Purcell, "I have bought a horse, and I am now a great 'traveller'; for I have many places to attend, and I don't stay more than two Sundays a month in Danville."

Machebeuf, too, had acquired a horse—"beau et excellent"—from a German priest at the exorbitant rate of one hundred dollars. His letters home were full of lively details about the life of the missioner— typical of what Lamy, too, was experiencing, and all the other young Auvergnats who had come away with them.

In their own parishes they wore their cassocks, but travelling they put on their oldest clothes, and when they came to towns they dressed more neatly in order not to invite scornful comments from entrenched Protestants. They used a long leather bag in which to carry vestments, Mass vessels, and other supplies, and the bag was thrown over the saddle. Where roads permitted, a four-wheeled wagon served the missioners and then they could carry a travelling trunk. In the very beginning, they had to "preach by their silence" but it was not long before they were able to get along in English, to the delight of their listeners. Sometimes it was so cold that the ink froze in its bottle as they wrote at night by firelight. The visitor often had to sleep next to his horse to keep warm. Coming to a house where he would spend the night, the missioner was given a bed, "sometimes very good, sometimes only passable." In the morning, children would be sent in every direction to tell other remote homesteaders that the priest had come, and, so soon that it was amazing, the people came gathering, settlers from Germany, Ireland, France, and the eastern states, and it was time for the sacraments and the Mass and the sermon. The listeners were "not savages, but Europeans who are coming in crowds to clear off the forests of America." And then on again to the next cluster of those waiting for what the visitor alone could bring them. It was a matter of literally

TRAVELS OF
LAMY
AND
MACHEBEUF
IN AMERICA
1839~1884

282

keeping the faith, at whatever cost to the traveller—on one occasion Machebeuf used the frozen Toussaint River as his highway, until the ice broke and he went through into water five feet deep.

Danville and Tiffin were eighty to ninety miles apart and there were few occasions when Lamy and Machebeuf could see each other. Sometimes they would converge at Cincinnati on visits to the bishop. Now and then they were prevented by illness from visiting each other— Lamy was ill several times, once "dangerously for several days," but when he was well enough he joined Machebeuf for a visit to the Irish canal workers on the Maumee River, and exclaimed over American enterprise which was constructing a canal forty feet wide. One day Lamy heard that Machebeuf was dead of cholera, and "heartbroken" went to bury his oldest friend. When he arrived, he found instead that Machebeuf was simply recovering from a fever. There was joy all around, and another of the French missioners referred to the invalid who had deceived death as "Monsieur Trompe-la-Mort."

Loving all which they were overcoming in the name of what they believed, they were content. Machebeuf wrote to Riom, "I declare to you that for all the gold in the world I would not return to live in Europe," and Lamy in one of his letters written from abroad some years later, said he was preparing himself "to return to my Beloved Ohio." Still, the call of their early home was strong in their early days in the Middle West. They had fine plans for a visit to Auvergne. They knew how they would go—the Lake Erie steamboat from Sandusky to Buffalo, the great canal to the Hudson River and down to New York, and from there, no such antiquated an affair as a ship under canvas but a steamer, which would reach Liverpool in fourteen days. "From Liverpool to Paris by railroad and the Straits of Dover, two days would be enough," wrote Machebeuf to his father. "Then from Paris to Riom is but a hop-step-and-a-jump for an American. This is the way Father Lamy and I have fixed up our plan." Yet there was a condition which had to be met first. "But it cannot be carried out until we have each built two churches, [Lamy] at Mt Vernon and Newark, I, at my two Sanduskys [then known as Upper and Lower Sandusky]. So, if you can find some generous Catholic who can send us at least eighty thousand francs for each church, we can leave within a year. *Merci. . . .*"

1977 AWARD

ABOUT THE IMPENDING
CRISIS IN THE UNITED STATES

BY

DAVID M. POTTER

David Morris Potter (born on December 6, 1910, in Augusta, Ga.) attended Yale University, where he earned his Master of Arts degree in 1933. From 1936 to 1938 he taught history at the University of Mississippi. Thereafter, he worked for four years at the Rice Institute in Houston, meanwhile writing his doctoral thesis. From 1942 to 1961 Potter was on the teaching staff of Yale University. Advancing from assistant professor to full professor, he became Coe professor of American history in 1950. From 1949 to 1951 he assumed also the position of the editor of the *Yale Review*. In the meantime he visited several other universities as a guest lecturer, amongst them the University of Delaware, the University of Wyoming, Stetson University and the State University of New York. In 1961 he accepted the Coe professorship of American history at Stanford University. He was author or editor of several books, including *Lincoln and His Party in the Secession Crisis*; *Trail to California: The Overland Diary of Vincent Geiger and Wakeman Bryarly* and *People of Plenty: Economic Abundance and the American Character*. In 1977 David M. Potter was posthumously awarded the Pulitzer Prize in history for *The Impending Crisis, 1848-1861*, published one year earlier.

THE BASIC FUNCTION OF THE 1860 ELECTION

[Source: David M. Potter: The Impending Crisis, 1848-1861, New York - Evanston - San Francisco - London: Harper & Row, Publishers, 1976, pp. 270 - 271, 405 - 408; reprinted by permission of Harper Collins Publishers, New York, N.Y.]

B Y 1860, the United States had completed the development of a series of arrangements, both formal and informal, by which a president is chosen every four years. Some of these arrangements, though commonly taken for granted, are singular in the extreme, and make American presidential elections unique as a way of choosing a head of state.

Under the Constitution, the president was chosen by electors, rather than by voters, with each state having a number equal to the total of its senators and representatives. The mode of choosing electors was left by the Constitution entirely to the state legislatures, which might have proceeded in any of several ways: They might have chosen the electors themselves, which all of the thirteen original states except Virginia did at one time or another, and which eight states were still doing as late as 1820. Or they might have provided for choice by popular election, which is what all states except South Carolina were doing by 1832. In the process of popular election, a state might have given to each candidate electoral votes in proportion to the popular votes received in the state, but no states have ever done this. They might have chosen electors by district, and in fact, ten states, at various times between 1788 and 1832, used this method. But in general, the states were jealous of the political power they could wield by casting their vote as a block, and by 1836 every state (again, except South Carolina) was holding a popular, "general ticket" election, by which it cast its total electoral vote for whoever won a majority or even a plurality in the state election. Although conducted simultaneously throughout the nation, the November election was not a national election, but a multiplicity of statewide elections, in which popular votes had no value toward an electoral total unless the candidate receiving them carried the state in which they were cast. In short, election depended not upon winning popular votes but upon winning a combination of states which held a majority of electoral votes. In 1860, as it turned out, 39 percent of the vote was enough to provide such a combination.

These electoral arrangements are well known, but they have had profound effects not always recognized. Since, at the state level, a vote for a candidate was "wasted" unless he had some realistic chance of winning more votes than any other candidate, minor candidates tended to be squeezed out, and elections tended to resolve themselves into contests between two leading candidates. This was true both within a state and among the states, for it did a candidate no good to win popular votes unless they might be converted into electoral votes, and it did a state no good to give a candidate electoral votes unless he stood a good chance of winning enough electoral votes in other states to constitute a majority.

The iron logic of these circumstances tended, from a very early time, to make the American political system a bipartisan one and the party structure a federated one. In a situation in which minority votes were "wasted," third parties had short lives and supporters who often wanted merely to express a protest or to help defeat one of the major candidates by drawing away some of his votes. Thus, even when there were three or more parties in the race, the election in any given state tended to become a two-way contest, as in 1856, when the effective rivalry was between Buchanan and Frémont in the northern states and between Buchanan and Fillmore in the southern states. At the same time, every state political organization, while jealous of its own autonomy, was anxious that its party counterparts in other states should be strong enough to provide favorable prospects for winning the "national" election. In the 1830s, the national conventions, first of the Democrats and then of the Whigs, had been instituted, thus giving each state party a chance to express its voice in national party councils, and even more to see visible proof of the vigor and compatibility of the party organizations in other states.

Once the system of conventions and elections had been established, devices had to be developed for instructing and arousing the electorate. Party candidates were not expected to participate in this process, for the office was supposed to seek the man and not the man the office. But there were swarms of editors, officeholders, and

Cloth banner promoting the Republican ticket, 1860. By H. C. Howard.

party leaders available to publicize the issues, to organize supporters, and to galvanize the electorate with glee clubs, marching clubs, and other such activities for voters who responded to excitement more than to reason. By 1860, the colors were set. The quadrennial choosing of a president was accomplished in the context of a ritualized "campaign," which began in the summer with the national conventions and ended in November with the election.

It was part of the ritual that the Democrats should make their nominations first, and in 1860 they prepared to do so at Charleston, South Carolina. Just when it needed bisectional harmony more than ever before, the party met in the city least likely to support the cause of bisectional harmony. The atmosphere of Charleston—physically a miserable place for such a large convention—heightened the tensions within the party. Less than a year later, military warfare between North and South would begin in this same city where, in April 1860, some of the party leaders were seeking to avert political warfare.

The Democratic convention of 1860 remained in session for ten days in Charleston and then adjourned for six weeks, to convene again at Baltimore on June 18 for another six-day session. No American party convention has exceeded it in length except the Democratic convention of 1924, and none has been the scene of such a bitter and complicated contest. Altogether, the convention took fifty-nine ballots on the nomination of a presidential candidate, in addition to many votes on parliamentary issues, and it witnessed two major scenes of disruption by the withdrawal of delegates from the South. It ended with a schism which not only destroyed the last remaining party with a nationwide constituency, but also foreshadowed with remarkable accuracy the schism that appeared in the Union itself less than a year later.

Despite all the elaborate maneuvering for advantage in the convention, and all the hairbreadth votes which seemed so crucial at the time, the basic situation was fairly simple: Douglas had the support of a bare majority of the delegate votes. With this majority, he could prevent the adoption of a platform calling for a congressional slave code such as the Davis resolutions had demanded; but, because of the two-thirds rule (which had blocked the nomination of another northern candidate, Martin Van Buren, in 1844), he could not gain the nomination. Further, neither side was prepared for the kind of concessions which so commonly resolve the deadlock in party conventions. As the southern rights supporters saw it, the Supreme Court, in the Dred Scott decision, had validated their claims, and they were not going to barter them away in an equivocating platform. But Douglas could reply that he was not insisting on a divisive doctrinal test—it was the South which took a rigid attitude. And as for the two-thirds rule, he felt that his majority placed the opposition under a moral obligation to acquiesce in his nomination; he had twice stepped aside, first for Pierce in 1852 and then for Buchanan in 1856, though he could definitely have blocked Buchanan; now, he would not let a minority deny him the nomination by creating a deadlock.

The convention assembled in an atmosphere of acute tension and excitement, for the participants all sensed that a disruption was imminent. Delegates from the Northwest were determined to resist southern demands for a platform with a plank calling for a slave code, and Henry B. Payne of Ohio had written to Douglas in the month preceding the convention that if such a platform were adopted the Ohio delegation would "be prepared to retire from the convention. I have no reason to doubt that this will be the course of seven Northwestern States."

1978 AWARD

ABOUT THE MANAGERIAL REVOLUTION IN U.S. BUSINESS

BY

ALFRED D. CHANDLER JR.

Alfred Dupont Chandler Jr. (born on September 15, 1918, in Guyencourt, Del.) was graduated from Harvard University in 1947. From 1950 to 1951 he worked as a research associate at the Massachusetts Institute of Technology. Then, Chandler became instructor at Johns Hopkins University, where he stayed until 1971, having been advanced to full professor of history in 1963. In addition to this, he was director of the Center for Study of Recent American History from 1964 to 1971 and chairman of the history department at Johns Hopkins from 1966 to 1970. In 1971 he got the Straus professorship of business history at Harvard Business School. As visiting professor he lectured at All Souls College of Oxford University, England. Chandler received an honorary doctorate from the University of Leuven, Belgium, in 1976. Being the editor of *Papers of Dwight D. Eisenhower*, Chandler has written the following books: *Henry Varnum Poor*; *Strategy and Structure*; *Giant Enterprise* and *The Railroads*. In 1977 *The Visible Hand: The Managerial Revolution in American Business* was published. In the following year, this work made Alfred D. Chandler Jr. the recipient of the Pulitzer Prize for the best book on American history.

EARLY RAILROADS AS THE KEY ENTERPRISES

[Source: Alfred D. Chandler Jr.: The Visible Hand: The Managerial Revolution in American Business, Cambridge, Mass. - London: The Belknap Press of Harvard University Press, 1977, pp. 81 - 86; reprinted by permission of Harvard University Press, Cambridge, Mass.]

Modern business enterprises came to operate the railroad and telegraph networks for both technological and organizational reasons. Railroad companies were the first transportation firms to build and to own rights-of-way and at the same time to operate the common carriers using those rights-of-way. Telegraph companies also both built the lines and ran the messages through them. The enterprises, both public and private, that constructed and maintained the canals and turnpikes rarely operated the canal boat companies, stage lines, or mail routes that used them. Even when they did, their rights-of-way were used by many other independent transportation companies.

On the railroad, however, the movements of carriers had to be carefully coordinated and controlled if the goods and passengers were to be moved in safety and with a modicum of efficiency. The first railroads—those using horses for motive power—were often able to allow common carriers operated by other individuals and companies to use their rails. But as soon as the much faster steam locomotive began to replace the horse-drawn vehicles, operations had to be controlled from a single headquarters if only to prevent 'accidents. Considerations of safety were particularly compelling in the United States, where nearly all railroads relied on a single line of track. For a time railroad managers experimented in hauling cars owned by local merchants and freight forwarders. However, the coordination of the movement of cars and the handling of charges and payment proved exceedingly difficult. By 1840 the railroad managers found it easier to own and control all cars using their roads. Later, express companies and other large shippers operating on a national scale came to own their own cars; but only after the railroads had devised complex organizational arrangements to handle the movement of and charges for such "foreign" cars.

Because they operated common carriers, railroads, unlike the major canal systems, became privately rather than publicly owned enterprises. In the early years of the Republic, American merchants and shippers gave strong support to government construction and operation of costly rights-of-way. On the other hand, these businessmen rarely, if ever, proposed that the government operate the common carriers. Only a small number of American railroads were initially operated by the state, and by 1850 with very few exceptions these had been turned over to private business enterprises. These same merchants and shippers who distrusted government ownership were also fearful of private monopoly. Therefore, the charters of the early roads generally provided for close legislative oversight of these new transportation enterprises.

The railroads did not begin to have a significant impact on American business institutions until the nation's first railroad boom which began in the late 1840s and 1850s. Before that time railroad construction did not fundamentally alter existing routes or modes of transportation, since the first roads were built in the 1830s and 1840s to connect existing commercial centers and to supplement existing water transportation. The lines from Boston to nearby towns (Lowell, Newburyport, Providence, and Worcester); from Camden to Amboy in New Jersey (the rail link between New York and Philadelphia); from Philadelphia to Reading, Philadelphia to Baltimore, and Baltimore to Washington, were all short, rarely more than fifty miles.

This was also true of those lines connecting the several towns along the Erie Canal. In the south and west, railroads were longer because distances between towns were greater, but they carried fewer passengers and smaller amounts of freight. Until the 1850s, none of the great lines planned to connect the east with the west were even close to completion. Before 1850 only one road, the Western, which ran from Worcester to Albany, connected one major regional section of the country with another. Except for the Western, no railroad was long enough or busy enough to create complex operating problems.

During the 1840s the technology of railroad transportation was rapidly perfected. Uniform methods of construction, grading, tunneling, and bridging were developed. The iron T rail came into common use. By the late 1840s the locomotive had its cams, sandbox, driver wheels, swivel or bogie truck, and equalizing beams. Passenger coaches had become "long cars," carrying sixty passengers on reversible seats. Boxcars, cattle cars, lumber cars, and other freight cars were smaller but otherwise little different from those used on American railroads a century later.

As technology improved, railroads became the favored means of overland transportation. They not only quickly captured the passenger and light-weight and high-value freight traffic from the canals and turnpikes but also began soon to compete successfully as carriers of textiles, cotton, grain, coal, and other more bulky products. Indeed, some of the first roads in the north, such as the Boston and Lowell and the Reading, were built by textile manufacturers and anthracite coal mine owners to replace canals they had already constructed to carry their products to market; while railroads in the south and west were constructed specifically to carry cotton and grain. In the decade of the 1840s, only 400 miles of canals were built to make the nation's total mileage at the end of the decade just under 4,000. In that same decade, over 6,000 miles of railroads went into operation providing a total of 9,000 miles of track by 1850.

As the country pulled out of the long economic depression of the late 1830s and early 1840s, railroad building began in earnest. The railroad boom came in the mid-1840s in New England and then in the late 1840s in the south and west. In the decade of the 1850s, when more canals were abandoned than built, over 21,000 more miles of railroad were constructed, laying down the basic overland transportation network east of the Mississippi River. As dramatic was the almost simultaneous completion between 1851 and 1854 of the great intersectional trunk lines connecting east and west (the Erie, the Baltimore and Ohio, the Pennsylvania, and the New York Central) and the building of a whole new transportation network in the old northwest. In 1849 the five states of the old northwest, a region endowed with a superb river and lake system, had only 600 miles of track. By 1860 the 9,000 miles of railroad covering the area had replaced rivers, lakes, and canals as the primary means of transportation for all but bulky, low-value commodities.

The reason for the swift commercial success of the railroads over canals and other inland waterways is obvious enough. The railroad provided more direct communication than did the river, lake, or coastal routes. While construction costs of canals on level ground were somewhat less than for railroads, the railroad was cheaper to build in rugged terrain. Moreover, because a railroad route did not, like that of a canal, require a substantial water supply, it could go more directly between two towns. In addition, railroads were less expensive to maintain per ton-mile than canals. They were, of course, faster. For the first time in history, freight and passengers could be carried overland at a speed faster than that of a horse. The maps emphasize how the railroad revolutionized the speed of travel. A traveler who used to spend three weeks going from New York to Chicago, could by 1857 make the trip in three days. The railroad's fundamental advantage, however, was not in the speed it carried passengers and mail but its ability to provide a shipper with dependable, precisely scheduled, all-weather transportation of goods. Railroads were far less affected by droughts, freshets, and floods than were waterways. They

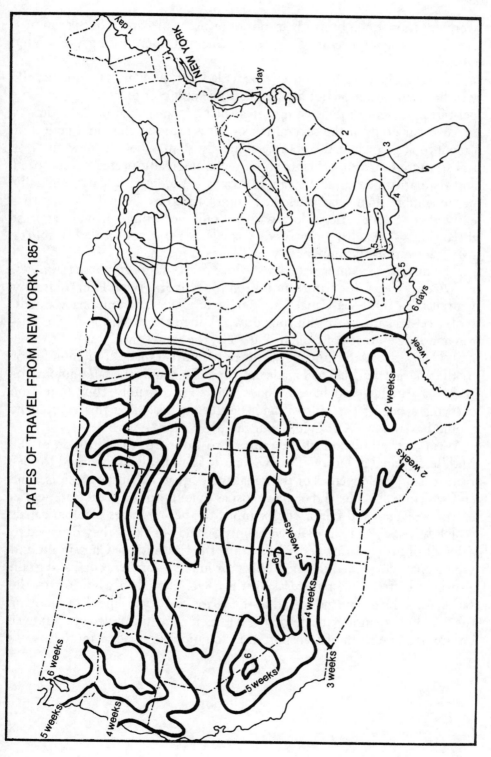

RATES OF TRAVEL FROM NEW YORK, 1857

were not shut down by freshets in the spring or dry spells in the summer and fall. Most important of all, they remained open during the winter months.

The steam locomotive not only provided fast, regular, dependable, all-weather transportation but also lowered the unit cost of moving goods by permitting a more intensive use of available transportation facilities. A railroad car could make several trips over a route in the same period of time it took a canal boat to complete one. By 1840, when the new mode of transportation had only begun to be technologically perfected, its speed and regularity permitted a steam railway the potential to carry annually per mile more than fifty times the freight carried by a canal. Even at that early date, Stanley Legerbott writes, "railroads could provide at least three times as much freight service as canals *for an equivalent resource cost*—and probably more nearly five times as much."

The history of competition on specific routes supports these estimates. For twenty years, the trip from Boston to Concord, New Hampshire, by way of the Middlesex Canal, the Merrimack River, and ancillary canals, took five days upstream and four down. When the extension of the Boston and Lowell reached Concord in 1842, the travel time was cut to four hours one way. A freight car on the new railroad made four round trips by the time a canal boat had made only one. To handle the same amount of traffic, a canal would have to have had approximately four times the carrying space of the railroad and, because of ice, even this equipment would have had to remain idle four months a year.

With the completion of the railroad to Concord, the historian of the Middlesex Canal points out "the waterway is immediately marked for defeat; in 1843 the expenses of the canal were greater than its receipts. The end has come." The end came almost as quickly to the great state works of Pennsylvania and Ohio. For example, the net revenues of Ohio canals which were $278,525 in 1849, were only $93,421 in 1855; they dropped to a deficit of $107,761 in 1860. For a time the Erie and the Chesapeake and Ohio canals continued to carry bulky products—lumber, coal, and grain—primarily from west to east. By the 1870s they had even lost to the railroad on the grain trade. And in the 1850s river boat lines lost much of the rapidly expanding trade of the Mississippi to the railroads. Never before had one form of transportation so quickly replaced another.

1979 AWARD

ABOUT THE SIGNIFICANCE
OF A SUPREME COURT DECISION

BY

DON E. FEHRENBACHER

Don Edward Fehrenbacher (born on August 21, 1920, in Sterling, Ill.) served with the United States Army Air Force during World War II and was decorated with the Distinguished Flying Cross and the Air medal with three oak leaf clusters. He earned his Bachelor degree at Cornell College in 1946, to which he added a Master of Arts degree at the University of Chicago in 1948. The following year he became assistant professor at Coe College in Cedar Rapids, Ia. After having received his doctorate of philosophy in 1951, he joined the staff of Stanford University as an assistant professor advancing to full professor during the next twenty years. In 1966 he became William R. Coe professor of American history. Meanwhile he had held guest lectures at several other Universities including Oxford, the College of William and Mary, Rutgers, Northwestern and Harvard. In 1978 he taught as Commonwealth Fund lecturer at the University of London. Fehrenbacher, a contributor of many articles for professional journals, is the editor of *History and American Society: Essays of David M. Potter*; *The Impending Crisis, 1848-1861*, and *Freedom and Its Limitations in American Life*. He is the author of *Chicago Giant: A Biography of Long John Wentworth*; *Prelude to Greatness: Lincoln in the 1850s* and *The Era of Expansion*. In 1979 Don E. Fehrenbacher became the recipient of the Pulitzer Prize for the best book on American history published during the preceding year. The winning work was entitled *The Dred Scott Case*.

THE DRED SCOTT CASE AS KEY JUDGMENT

[Source: Don E. Fehrenbacher: The Dred Scott Case. Its Significance in American Law and Politics, New York: Oxford University Press, 1978, pp. 1 - 4, 266; reprinted by permission of Oxford University Press, New York, N.Y.]

On Friday morning, March 6, 1857—a crisp, clear day for residents of Washington, D.C.—public attention centered on a dusky, ground-level courtroom deep within the Capitol. The Senate chamber directly above was quiet; Congress had adjourned on March 3. The inauguration ceremonies of March 4 were over, and James Buchanan had begun settling into his role as the fifteenth President. Now it was the judiciary's turn to be heard, as though the three branches of government were passing in review before the American people. Ordinarily, the Supreme Court carried on its business before a small audience and with only perfunctory notice from the press, but today the journalists were out in force and the courtroom was packed with spectators. A murmur of expectancy ran through the crowd and greeted the nine black-robed jurists as they filed into view at eleven o'clock, led by the aged Chief Justice. Acrimonious debate in the recent Congress had once again failed to settle the paramount constitutional and political issue of the decade. The Court, however, was ready to terminate the long struggle over slavery in the territories and, incidentally, decide the fate of a man named Dred Scott.

Neither of the two litigants was present in the courtroom. Scott remained at home in St. Louis, still a hired-out slave eleven years after he had taken the first legal step in his long battle for freedom. As for his alleged owner, John F. A. Sanford languished in an insane asylum and within two months would be dead. But then, both men had been dwarfed by the implications of their case and were now mere pawns in a much larger contest.

Roger B. Taney, who in eleven days would be eighty years old, began reading from a manuscript held in tremulous hands. For more than two hours the audience strained to hear his steadily weakening

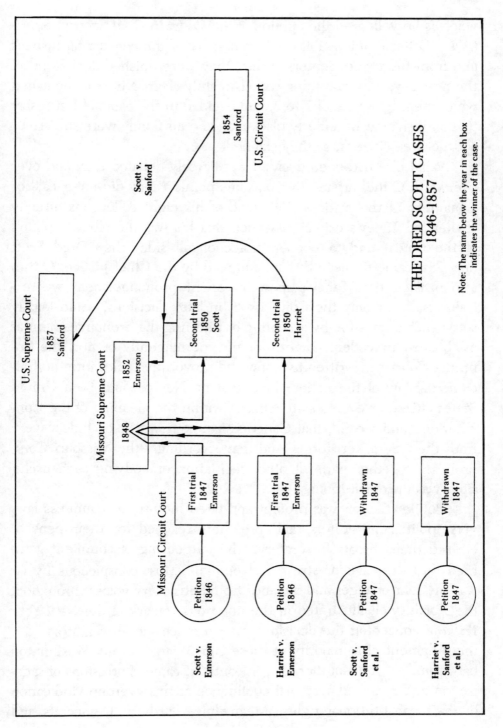

THE DRED SCOTT CASES
1846-1857

Note: The name below the year in each box
indicates the winner of the case.

voice as he delivered the opinion of the Court in *Dred Scott v. Sandford*. Other opinions followed from some of the concurring justices and from the two dissenters. When they were finished at the end of the next day, only one thing was absolutely clear. Nine distinguished white men, by a vote of 7 to 2, had decided in the court of last resort that an insignificant, elderly black man and his family were still slaves and not free citizens, as they claimed.

What else had been decided was fiercely debated then and ever afterward. Critics argued that on some points Taney did not speak for a majority of the justices. Yet none of his eight colleagues directly challenged Taney's explicit assertion that his was the official opinion of the Court, and in popular usage on all sides the "Dred Scott decision" came to mean the opinion read by the Chief Justice. Critics also insisted that Taney's most important pronouncement was extrajudicial, but only the Court itself, in later decisions, could legally settle such a question by accepting or rejecting the pronouncement as established precedent. Rightly or not, permanently or not, the Supreme Court had written two new and provocative rules into the fundamental law of the nation: first, that no Negro could be a United States citizen or even a state citizen "within the meaning of the Constitution"; and second, that Congress had no power to exclude slavery from the federal territories, and that accordingly the Missouri Compromise, together with all other legislation embodying such exclusion, was unconstitutional.

Public reaction was prompt and often intense, as countless lawyers, politicians, editors, and preachers reached for their pens or cleared their throats for oratory. The outpouring of comment gathered into three major streams of opinion. Most conspicuous by far was the roar of anger and defiance from antislavery voices throughout the North, well illustrated in the notorious remark of the New York *Tribune* conceding the decision "just so much moral weight as . . . the judgment of a majority of those congregated in any Washington bar-room." From southerners, in contrast, came expressions of satisfaction and renewed sectional confidence at this overdue vindication of their constitutional rights. Meanwhile, northern Democrats and certain other conservatives were confining themselves, for the most part, to exclamations of relief at the settlement of a dangerous issue and pious lectures on the duty of every citizen to accept the wise judgment of the Court.

In the years immediately following, the response to the decision proved to be much more important than its direct legal effect. As law, the decision legitimized and encouraged an expansion of slavery that never took place; it denied freedom to a slave who was then quickly manumitted. But as a public event, the decision aggravated an already bitter sectional conflict and to some degree determined the shape of the final crisis.

There is irony here, of course, if one views the Court's action as an effort at judicial statesmanship, intended to bring peace but instead pushing the nation closer to civil war. In this light, the Court majority appears incredibly unrealistic—indeed, so foolish as to pour oil rather than water on a fire. Yet Taney's opinion, carefully read, proves to be a work of unmitigated partisanship, polemical in spirit though judicial in its language, and more like an ultimatum than a formula for sectional accommodation. Peace on Taney's terms resembled the peace implicit in a demand for unconditional surrender. As one scholar has written, "The Dred Scott decision was nothing less than a summons to the Republicans to disband."

Thus perceived, the decision falls logically into place as one unusually bold venture in a desperate struggle for power, rather than being an evenhanded effort to resolve that struggle. And under close study it proves to be no less meaningful as a historical consequence than as a historical cause.

There are sharply defined historical events through which, like the neck of an hourglass, great causal forces appear to flow, emerging converted into significant consequences. Strictly speaking, this is illusion, and the translation is essentially a verbal one; for "cause" and "consequence" are subjective categories that serve to simplify and make intelligible the highly complex relationships among objective historical phenomena. Yet all explanation, being in some degree selective and synthetic, is to some degree a distortion of reality. The hourglass construct at least incorporates the flow of time and is chronologically sound. Like biography, moreover, the history of a single event provides a firm and convenient vantage point from which to observe the sweep of historical forces. The principal fallacy to be avoided is a tendency to view one's subject as the matrix of forces when it is usually instead a mere channel of their passage.

The Dred Scott decision, for example, was the Supreme Court's first invalidation of a major federal law. It is therefore a landmark in the history of judicial review. But the power to declare an act of Congress unconstitutional had frequently been asserted or implied in earlier decisions, and the existence of such power was widely assumed by the American people. That the power would have been exercised eventually, if not in 1857, seems about as certain as that someone else would have discovered America if Columbus had failed to do so. Thus the Dred Scott decision should probably be regarded as a prominent point of reference, but not as a major turning point, in the development of judicial review. And yet, since it was in 1857 that the Supreme Court first took this important step, it was in 1857 that Americans for the first time had to consider the operational scope and meaning of judicial review in national politics. What was the effect of such a decision beyond the specific judgment rendered? To what extent, for instance, would it inhibit the subsequent deliberations of Congress, and what recourse was left for the bitter critics of the decision? The heated argument of these constitutional questions had unmistakable political consequences.

1980 AWARD

ABOUT THE AFTERMATH
OF SLAVERY IN THE UNITED STATES

BY

LEON F. LITWACK

Leon Frank Litwack (born on December 2, 1929, in Santa Barbara, Cal.) received his Master of Arts degree at the University of California in 1952, after having earned his B.A. one year earlier at the same institute. From 1953 to 1955 he served with the United States Army. In 1958 the Doctor of philosophy degree was conferred on him and that same year he joined the staff of the University of Wisconsin as an assistant professor of history and, a few years later, was advanced to associate professor. He became member of the faculty of the University of California in 1965. Two years later he received there the Excellence in Teaching award. In 1971 Litwack became a full professor of history. Being the editor of *American Labor Movement* and the co-editor of *Reconstruction* he also wrote *North of Slavery: The Negro in the Free States, 1790-1860.* In 1979 *Been in the Storm So Long* was published. It was this work that made Leon F. Litwack the winner of the Pulitzer Prize for history the year after.

THE SUDDEN FEEL OF FREEDOM FOR BLACKS

[Source: Leon F. Litwack: Been in the Storm So Long. The Aftermath of Slavery, New York: Alfred A. Knopf, 1979, pp. 292 - 295; reprinted by permission of the autor and of Alfred A. Knopf, Inc., New York, N.Y.]

To THROW OFF A LIFETIME of restraint and dependency and to feel like free men or free women, newly liberated slaves adopted different priorities and chose various ways in which to express themselves, ranging from dramatic breaks with the past to subtle and barely perceptible changes in demeanor and behavior. But even as they secured family ties, sanctified marriage relations, proclaimed surnames, and encroached on the white man's racial etiquette, black men and women grappled with the most critical questions affecting their lives and status. To make certain of their freedom, would they first need to separate themselves physically from those who had only recently owned them? If so, where would they go, how would they protect themselves from hostile whites, for whom and under what conditions would they work? If they remained on the old place, what relations would they now enjoy with their former owners and how could they safely manifest their freedom?

Having lived in close, sometimes intimate contact with their "white folks," dependent on them for daily sustenance, conditioned by their demands and expectations, freedmen could not always quickly or easily resolve such questions. For many of them, however, that tension between the urge toward personal autonomy and the compulsions of the old dependency grew increasingly intolerable, and nearly every slaveholding family could affix a date to the moment when their former slaves resolved the tension. "On the 5th of August [1865] one of our young men left for Albany," the Reverend John Jones reported, "and on the 8th inst. (or night before) nine more took up the line of march, carrying our house boy Allen and a girl sixteen years old (Amelia, the spinner). This girl had been corrected for being out the most of Saturday night previously." Once that "dark, dissolving, disquieting wave of emancipation" (as he called it) broke over a particular region or plantation, many a planter family watched helplessly as the only world they had known collapsed around them. "I have been marking its approach for months," the Georgia clergyman wrote, "and watching its influence on our own people. It has been like the iceberg, withering and deadening the best sensibilities of master and servant, and fast sundering the domestic ties of years."

To experience the phenomenon was traumatic enough, but to seek to understand it could be a totally frustrating and impossible task. Ella Gertrude Thomas, the wife of a Georgia planter, tried her best, while viewing from day to day, and then confiding to her diary, the rupture of those affective ties which had provided her with such fond memories of a past now apparently beyond recovery. The experience of Jefferson and Gertrude Thomas reveals only the disruption of one household. But their ordeal, as they came to realize, was not unique. Like so many former slaveholders, the Thomases suffered the ingratitude of favorites, the impertinence of strangers, the exasperation of new "help," and the fears of race war. And like many others, Gertrude Thomas reached that point when nothing surprised her any longer and she could only utter the familiar cry of post-emancipation despair—"And has it come to this?" Most importantly, the legacy of distrust, bitterness, and recrimination emerging out of experiences like these helped to shape race relations in the South for the next several decades.

Except for those who had already experienced the anguish of wartime "betrayal," few knew what to expect from their black servants and laborers in the first months of emancipation. "Excitement rules the hour," Gertrude Thomas observed in May 1865. "No one appears to have a settled plan of action, the Negroes crowd the streets and loaf around the pumps and corners of the street. . . . I see no evidence of disrespect on the part of the Negroes who are here from the adjoining plantations." During the war, nearly all the Thomas slaves, both at the Augusta house and plantation (some six miles outside of town) and on the plantation in Burke County, had "proved most faithful." Only when Union troops entered Augusta, more than three weeks after the end of the war, did Gertrude Thomas resign herself to the inevitability of emancipation. While Yankee soldiers and blacks filled the streets, Jefferson Thomas performed the familiar rites of emancipation, advising the house staff that he would just "as soon pay them wages as any one else." The servants received the news with little show of emotion, though they evinced "a more cheerful spirit than ever" and Sarah "was really lively while she was sewing on Franks pants." Still, their apparent "faithfulness" pleased the Thomases, even as the future seemed dim. "Our Negroes will be put on lands confiscated and imagination cannot tell what is in store for us."

The news of freedom precipitated no spontaneous celebration or Jubilee among the Thomas blacks. None of them suddenly rushed out to test their new status. When they severed their ties with the Thomases, they did so quietly with a conspicuous absence of fanfare. There was no insubordination, there were no bursts of insolence, and the Thomas property remained undisturbed. Nor were there any tearful farewells. Like many freed slaves elsewhere, the Thomas servants did not betray their emotions, at least not in the presence of their former owners. Within less than a month after the Union occupation, nearly all of them left in much the same manner as they had received the news that they were free.

Among the most faithful and best liked of the slaves had been Daniel, the first servant Jefferson Thomas had ever owned. "When we were married," Gertrude Thomas recalled, "his Father gave him to us to go in the Buggy." Daniel was the first servant to depart, and he did so at night "without saying anything to anyone." He remained in town but the Thomases had no wish to see him again. "If he returns to the yard he shall not enter it." The day after Daniel's unexpected departure, Betsy went out to pick up the newspaper, "as she was in the habit of doing every day." This time, she never returned. "I suppose that she had been met by her Father in the street and taken away but then I learned that she had taken her clothes out of the Ironing room under the pretense of washing them." Shortly afterwards, Mrs. Thomas learned that the "disappearance" had been "a concerted plan" between Betsy and her mother, who had once been a servant in the house ("an excellent washer and ironer") but was found to be "dishonest" and had been transferred to the plantation in Burke County. "She left the Plantation, came up and took Betsy home with her." While disclaiming "any emotion of interest" in Betsy's departure, this loss obviously troubled Mrs. Thomas. Nor did the thought that familial ties had superseded those of mistress and slave console her in any way. "I felt interest in Betsy, she was a bright quick child and raised in our family would have become a good servant. As it is she will be under her Mothers influence and run wild in the street."

If the Thomases wondered who might leave them next, they did not have long to wait. But this time, at least, they had a premonition. Several days after Betsy's disappearance, Aunt Sarah seemed more diligent and cheerful than usual. "Sarah has something on her mind," Gertrude Thomas remarked to her husband. "She has either decided to go or the prospect of being paid if she remains has put her in a very good humor." That night, she left. By now, the Thomases were making a conscious effort to conceal their disappointment from the remaining servants, apparently in the belief that the others derived some pleasure from their discomfort. Meanwhile, Nancy had become a problem. After the departure of Sarah, she had been instructed to take over the cooking as well as perform her usual duties. Perhaps dismayed by her doubled work load, Nancy claimed that she was not well enough to work. When the "illness" persisted and the unwashed clothes accumulated in the ironing room, the much-annoyed mistress decided to take action. "Nancy," she asked, "do you expect I can afford to pay you wages in your situation, support your two children and then have you sick as much as you are?" Nancy stood there and made no reply. The next day, she left with her two children, claiming that she would return shortly. That was the last Mrs. Thomas saw of her..."

1981 AWARD

ABOUT THE DEVELOPMENTS IN AMERICAN EDUCATION POLICY

BY

LAWRENCE A. CREMIN

Lawrence Arthur Cremin (born on October 31, 1925, in New York, N.Y.) earned his Master of Arts degree at Columbia University in 1947 after having received a Bachelor's degree in Social Sciences one year earlier. He joined the staff of the Columbia Teachers College in 1948 and the following year the Ph.D. degree was conferred on him. Having been a Guggenheim fellow from 1957 to 1958, he advanced to Frederick A.P. Barnard professor of education in 1961. Twice, from 1964 to 1965 and from 1971 to 1972, Cremin held a fellowship of the Center for Advanced Study in Behavioral Sciences. In 1974 he became president of the Columbia Teachers College. A very prolific writer, Cremin is the author of the following book publications: *The American Common School*; *The Transformation of the School*, for which the Bancroft Prize of American history was awarded to him; *The Genius of American Education*; *The Wonderful World of Ellwood Patterson Cubberley*; *American Education: The Colonial Experience*; *Public Education* and *Traditions of American Education*. In 1981 Lawrence A. Cremin's *American Education: The National Experience, 1783-1876* was chosen by the Pulitzer Prize Board as best book on American history published during the preceding year.

NEW YORK CITY'S EARLY SCHOOL SYSTEM

[Source: Lawrence A. Cremin: American Education: The National Experience, 1783-1876, New York: Harper & Row, Publishers, 1980, pp. 444 - 447; reprinted by permission of Mrs. Charlotte R. Cremin, New York, N.Y.]

With respect to schooling, New York was subject to the same general influences that pressed for popularization across the country. By the 1790's there was a fairly large network of common pay schools in the city, which youngsters of either sex could attend at modest cost (the charge was between sixteen and twenty-four shillings per quarter), supplemented by a small number of charity schools conducted by various religious organizations and a variety of specialized entrepreneurial schools. In 1805, on the initiative of the Quaker philanthropist Thomas Eddy, the Free School Society was organized, "for the education of such poor children as do not belong to or are not provided for by any religious society." Committed to the Lancasterian system of monitorial instruction, the Society enlarged its activities quite rapidly, to a point where by 1820 it was reaching over two thousand children a year.

The legislature, cognizant of the fact that the city's poorest children were receiving their schooling primarily in institutions maintained by missionary organizations such as the Free School Society, the Orphan Asylum Society, and the Manumission Society (which ran the African Free Schools), apportioned most of the public money the city was due from the state common school fund to the support of these groups. Thereby were the grounds laid for the political conflict that began during the 1820's. As will be recalled, the various churches that conducted schools wanted a share of the funds at the same time as the Free School Society (renamed the Public School Society in 1826) wanted to monopolize them; and to complicate the political situation even further the leaders of the Roman Catholic church became increasingly assertive during the 1830's concerning their inability to use the schools of the Public School Society because of their decided Protestant bias. The controversy peaked in 1842, when the legislature enacted a law establishing a board of education for the city and placing the schools of the Society and all other eleemosynary institutions enjoying state support under the jurisdiction of the board. The Society went out of existence in 1853;

but the result of the legislation setting up the board was the development of two school systems in the city, the public system created in 1842 and the alternative system that the Roman Catholic authorities decided to create with their own money when they lost in the legislature. Politics aside, schooling was widely available in New York City by 1860, though varied in quality and differentially used. Of a total population of 813,669 that year, 153,000 were enrolled in the public schools; but the average daily attendance was only 58,000, reflecting an unusual degree of illness, truancy, and poor record keeping. In addition, 14,000 youngsters were enrolled in the Roman Catholic school system, and several thousand more were enrolled in independent schools and in schools managed by charitable organizations like the Children's Aid Society.

The higher learning also expanded in size, scope, and diversity during the nineteenth century. King's College, rechartered as Columbia College in 1784, increased its enrollment and enlarged its offering, but it remained in essence a small, elite institution until its transformation under Frederick A. P. Barnard, Seth Low, and Nicholas Murray Butler, beginning in the 1880's. Studies in law were conducted intermittently from 1794, when James Kent delivered his first lectures, until 1857, when the Faculty of Jurisprudence was formally organized. Studies in medicine were transferred to the College of Physicians and Surgeons in 1813, but then reestablished, de jure, when that college and Columbia formed an alliance in 1860. And studies in engineering were introduced with the founding of the School of Mines in 1863. In addition to Columbia, the city could boast the University of the City of New York (which became New York University), founded in 1831; St. John's College (which became Fordham), founded in 1841; St. Francis Xavier College (which awarded its degrees via St. John's until its own chartering in 1861), founded in 1847; the Free Academy (which became the College of the City of New York), also founded in 1847; and Rutgers Female College, founded in 1867. There were also numerous preparatory institutions, some of them connected with the colleges, all of them private or quasi-public (New York had no free public high school until 1897); and there were independent professional schools of law, medicine, theology, pharmacy, veterinary science, and dentistry. Most interesting of all these institutions, perhaps, was the Peter Cooper

Union for the Advancement of Science and Art, incorporated in 1857 as both an academy and a college; for, beyond the formal courses it offered in the arts and sciences, it featured an evening school for young ladies, mechanics, and apprentices (in effect, all those least able to find higher education elsewhere); lectures in languages, literature, oratory, telegraphy, design, and engraving; a reading room open to the public; an art gallery; and a museum of rare inventions.

The city also boasted a plethora of institutions for the advancement, preservation, diffusion, and sharing of culture. In addition to the New York Society Library, which dated from the provincial era and which by the 1830's had become the third largest in the nation, there was the Astor Library, founded in 1849 as a free noncirculating reference library, the Mercantile Library, the Apprentices' Library, the Printers' Free Library, the Women's Library, the New York Catholic Library, and the Maimonides Library. There was also the Athenaeum, modeled on the ones in Boston and Philadelphia, which included a reference library, a reading room containing periodicals, a museum, a laboratory for scientific experiments, and a lecture department; the Lyceum of Natural History; the Historical Society; the Literary and Philosophical Society; the Academy of Fine Arts; and, of course, Barnum's Museum. And beyond those there were the theatres, the opera houses, and the music halls that made the city a cultural as well as a commercial and manufacturing center, and there were the clubs (Union League, Century, Travellers, Welch, Young Cambrians, Société Lyrique Française, Vereine), the benevolent and fraternal associations (New England Society in the City of New York, St. Nicholas Society, Hibernian Universal Benevolent Society), and, more generally, the taverns and ale houses where diurnal social relations—and with them mutual education—proceeded apace.

Finally, New York City was a center of printing and publishing, with the result that books, pamphlets, tracts, and magazines of every sort and variety issued from its presses by the thousands. And it was the leader in the popularization of the newspaper.

1982 AWARD

ABOUT THE EYEWITNESS
REPORTS FROM THE CIVIL WAR

BY

C. VANN WOODWARD

Comer Vann Woodward (born on November 13, 1908, in Vanndale, Ark.) studied for two years at Henderson State College in Arkansas and entered then Emory University at Atlanta in 1928. He graduated in 1930 with a Bachelor of Philosophy degree, to which he added a Master's degree in political sciences from Columbia University in 1932. His dissertation *Tom Watson: Agrarian Rebel* earned Woodward a Ph.D. degree in 1937. During the late 1930s and early 1940s he shuttled from job to job in academia, teaching at Florida, Virginia, and Scripps, and serving a three-year stint as a Navy lieutenant in the Office of Naval Intelligence and the Naval Office of Public Information during World War II. In 1947 he joined the faculty of Johns Hopkins University, where he remained until he accepted a Sterling Professorship at Yale University in 1961. Meanwhile he served as Commonwealth Lecturer at the University of London in 1954, then taught for a term as the Harmsworth Professor of American History at the University of Oxford. In 1969 he was made president of both the Organization of American Historians and the American Historical Association. Woodward retired from Yale in 1977. Being the editor of the *Oxford History of the United States*, the scholar concentrated in his work as an author on the study of black history and the history of American race relations: *e.g. Origins of the New South, 1877-1913*; *Reunion and Reaction*; *The Strange Career of Jim Crow*; *The Burden of Southern History* and *American Counterpoint: Slavery and Racism in the North-South Dialogue*. In 1981 C. Vann Woodward completed another important project, which was his editing of Mary Chesnut's revision of her Civil War diary. *Mary Chesnut's Civil War* won the Pulitzer Prize in history of the following year.

THE GREAT DIARY BY MARY BOYKIN CHESNUT

[Source: C. Vann Woodward: Mary Chesnut's Civil War, New Haven - London: Yale University Press, 1981, pp. XV - XVII, 175; reprinted by permission of Yale University Press, London, GB.]

Literary critics who have written most thoughtfully about the work of Mary Boykin Chesnut have expressed some puzzlement and perplexity. They are generally as much disposed as historians have been to place high value on her book. "This diary," writes Edmund Wilson, "is an extraordinary document—in its informal department, a masterpiece." But he goes on to pronounce it "a work of art"—informal department or not. The puzzlement arises in assessing and understanding the character of the art involved. Mrs. Chesnut, in Wilson's opinion, evidently began the writing with "a decided sense of the literary possibilities of her subject." He goes further to say that he finds "the diarist's own instinct is uncanny" in anticipating such possibilities. "The very rhythm of her opening pages," he writes, "at once puts us under the spell of a writer who is not merely jotting down her days but establishing, as a novelist does, an atmosphere, an emotional tone. . . . Starting out with situations or relationships of which she cannot know the outcome, she takes advantage of the actual turn of events to develop them and round them out as if she were molding a novel." In general he finds "the brilliant journal of Mary Chesnut" to be "much more imaginative and revealing than most of the fiction inspired by the war."

Why the Civil War never inspired a literary treatment worthy of the subject is the question Daniel Aaron pursues in *The Unwritten War*. "The great War novel or epic everyone was calling for or predicting during the War and thereafter," in his opinion, "ought to have been written by a Southerner." Yet most of the Southern writing on the subject "was shot through with sentiment, moonshine, and special pleading." Of the three Southerners of the war generation whom he singles out as writing with detachment and insight, one was the poet Timrod, one the novelist Cable, and the third a diarist, Chesnut. Of these it was neither the novelist nor the poet but the diarist who was "the most likely candidate to write the unwritten Confederate novel." She it was who "had the eye and ear of a novelist as well as the temperament," even though she chose a form other than fiction. "Yet the *Diary*," he agrees with Edmund Wilson, "is more genuinely literary than most Civil War fiction."

What the critics had before them was, of course, clearly entitled a diary and was presented as such by its several editors. Moreover, it bore all the familiar characteristics of the genre. It proceeded from the start under dated entries beginning in February 1861 and continuing into July 1865. One break of nearly fifteen months occurs between August 1862 and October 1863, in which the diary form is abandoned and the author undertakes, she says, "to fill up the gap

36

Those sweet little Slidell girls -
So gentle and modest - clinging to
"Maman". Johnny said they spend their
months like mocking birds. Then
they all speak French. And Mrs Slidell
knows something of the world and its
ways - Beauregard is her brother in
law. She is a better general than I fancy —

My experience does not coincide
with the general idea of public
life - I mean the life of a politician
or statesman. Peace - comfort.
quiet. happiness, I have found away
from home. Only your own
family - those nearest and dearest
can hurt you. Wrangling.
Jows - heart burnings - bitterness
envy. hatred and malice - unbrotherly
love family snarls neighborhood
strife and ill blood - A lonely
word I have conjured up - But
they were all there - And for
these many years I have almost
forgotten them - I find them
always alive and rampant when
I go back to semi village life.

"Peace away from home." August 29, 1861

from memory." Apart from this section of about two hundred manuscript pages, the diary form is consistently maintained. Through forty-eight copybooks of more than twenty-five hundred pages, the diarist is narrator of her own experiences, and they are "real-life" experiences—flesh-and-blood people, real events and crises, private and public, domestic as well as historic. Recording them in her dated entries, Mary Chesnut adheres faithfully to the style, tone, and circumstantial limitations of the diarist and conveys fully the sense of chaotic daily life. To all appearances she respects the Latin meaning of *diarium* and its denial of knowledge of the future. Unforeseen events crowd in, unexpected guests arrive, messengers come and go. Each day brings its surprises. Illness, accident, violence, crime, death, and tragedy strike randomly and overwhelm. Ambitions, love affairs, conspiracies, and intrigues intimately traced in their day-to-day course, hang fire unfulfilled and await unforeseeable developments. Close friends pictured in the flush of triumph or the gaiety of the social whirl return next day from the front, as corpses. Over all hangs endless speculation, suspense, and anxiety about the fortunes of the war and the outcome of the struggle for Southern independence. The diarist agonizes over these uncertainties. She frets over interruption of her diary writing, weeps over the disappointments of her hopes and the tragedies of her friends, and rages over the beastliness of men, the unfairness of life, and the cruelties of fortune.

The Chesnut *Diary* in its published forms therefore appears to embody the cherished characteristics peculiar to the true diary—the freshness and shock of experience immediately recorded, the "real-life" actuality of subject matter, the spontaneity of perceptions denied knowledge of the future—all this in addition to its author's "uncanny" anticipation and exploitation of "the literary possibilities of her subject."

However that may be, we now know that the version of this work known to the public as "diary" was written between 1881 and 1884, twenty years after the events presumed to have been recorded as they happened. This information will be cause for concern among the many who feel indebted to Mary Boykin Chesnut for her vivid account of the Civil War and who have come to admire the author. The dating of the manuscript will inevitably raise questions among historians about the use of her writings and the way historians have used them extensively in the past. The bare fact of date of composition certainly changes the prevalent conception of the work and removes it from the conventional category of "diary." Much more than that, however, is to be learned from the surviving papers of Mary Chesnut about the sources of her work, the genuine diary she did keep, the subsequent drafts, abandoned experiments she tried, and the self-schooled apprenticeship she served before the writing of her book. The purpose here is certainly not to disparage her work, nor to extol it, but rather to understand and explain its true character and to remove some of the misapprehension and perplexity about it.

1983 AWARD

ABOUT THE TRANSFORMATION
OF EIGHTEEN-HUNDRED VIRGINIA

BY

RHYS L. ISAAC

Rhys Llywelyn Isaac (born on November 20, 1937, in South Africa) attended Rondebosch B. High School and then started studying at the University of Cape Town, South Africa, where he earned his B.A. and M.A. degrees. A Rhodes Scholarship enabled him to study at Oxford University, England, and to graduate there in 1962. The following year he moved to Australia in order to join the faculty of the University of Melbourne as a lecturer in history. Isaac became senior lecturer at La Trobe University in 1970 and in 1978 he became reader in history. Already in 1975 he held guest lectures as visiting professor at Johns Hopkins University. After a ten-year research effort Rhys L. Isaac published *The Transformation of Virginia, 1740-1790* in 1982, a work which earned him the Pulitzer Prize in history the year after.

THOMAS JEFFERSON AS A SYMBOL AND A LEGEND

[Source: Rhys L. Isaac: The Transformation of Virginia, 1740-1790, Chapel Hill, N.C.: University of North Carolina Press, 1982, pp. 273 - 276; reprinted by permission of the University of North Carolina Press, Chapel Hill, N.C.]

It is a Saturday in June 1826. At Monticello Thomas Jefferson sits in the study that commands a view away north along the outlines of the Blue Ridge and out across the low rolling hills of the Piedmont. The words he was writing are reproduced on the following page. They convey characteristically precise instructions concerning his tombstone.

Alas for the last wishes of a man who was becoming even in his lifetime a symbol and a legend! Far from destroying his monument "for the value of the materials," later generations first chipped it away for souvenirs and then, considering the prescribed proportions too modest for so great a man, ordered it replaced by the double-sized one that is now to be seen in the family burying ground on the southwestern brow of the little mountain.

Jefferson's modesty in reducing the list of his achievements to three has often been admired. Yet he did proudly focus attention on his successes as a philosopher-statesman. In 1776 the author of the Declaration of Independence had turned away from the affairs of the emergent union of states in order to assist in recasting the laws of the newborn Commonwealth of Virginia. In matters of franchise, governmental constitution, and education he was thwarted in his reformist aspirations. Only in religion did a great institutional transformation take place, and there the revolutionary statute was Jefferson's—although his formulation was not adopted until five years after he had retired from Virginia politics distressed and defeated. It is appropriate to inquire what made possible the passage of the "Act for Establishing Freedom of Religion" in 1786, after ten years of revolution, when so many of Jefferson's other radical proposals had been, or were about to be, rejected. What disputes was this statute expected to resolve at the time of its enactment by the General Assembly of Virginia?

Posterity has been inclined to endorse the pride that Jefferson took in the measure to establish religious freedom. Its form and content were designed to achieve a timeless expression of eternal truth that has deterred inquiry into the immediate contemporary meanings given to the act by the circumstances of its adoption. Since the 1780s, the principles proclaimed in the statute have become part of the idealized American way of life, and the passage of the bill through the legislature has been seen as a predestined triumph of progress. Yet the "Act for Establishing Freedom of Religion" was the outcome of a long and intense political struggle. It can only be understood historically in the context of the social and cultural reorientations that had been introduced by the

JEFFERSON'S INSTRUCTIONS ON HIS TOMBSTONE

popular evangelical and the patriotic republican revolutions at work in Virginia during the preceding decades. The situation that seven years of bitter warfare created must also be taken into account.

The decade that followed the declaration of independence was one of severe trial for Virginia. Already in the fall of 1775 there had been anxieties about the province's capacity to perform up to the high level of expectation expressed in the first patriotic enthusiasm. The young commonwealth that had been born amid demonstrations of self-sacrifice and martial valor—the stuff of republican virtue—soon entered a dark night of doubt, failure, and despair. Faced with the presence of invading forces in 1781, Virginia's leaders found themselves unable to organize effective resistance. For a war-weary populace the immediate response was too often an inglorious sauve qui peut.

The letters of leading patriots reveal a deep sense of disillusionment, but the feeling was not confined to those at the top—the mere disappointment of men too close to the initial expectations and the subsequent sobering realities of revolutionary politics. The low state of morale that sometimes prevailed among ordinary folk is revealed in a journal kept by a physician who lived and practiced in Hanover County, near the heart of Virginia's regions of settled population. Dr. Robert Honyman was an observer of rather than a participant in politics. As great events and the acts of the legislature impinged on his little part of Virginia, he filled his journal with a mixture of news and local opinion—reports of a distant war, comments on reactions at home. As early as 1778 he noted an unwillingness among neighboring farmers to fill draft quotas. Repeated rumors of peace were signs of a rather fainthearted longing for it. On March 16, 1780, Honyman commented sorrowfully: "The attention of the people of this state is very little taken up with the war at this time, or indeed for a year or two past. . . . The greatest part of the people are entirely taken up in schemes of interest of several kinds. Immense fortunes have been made by trade, or speculation . . . & almost all ranks are engaged in some sort of traffic or another." Soon he was to remark that although the "people interest themselves in Elections at this time more than ever," yet "they find fault with everything that has been done . . . [,] grumble exceedingly at the taxes . . . & choose those who make fair promises of altering things for the better." Honyman felt that in these circumstances "many of those chosen are men of mean abilities & no rank."

1984 AWARD

ABOUT THE WITHHOLD
OF THE HISTORY PRIZE

BY

PULITZER PRIZE BOARD

Since the members of the 1984 Pulitzer Prize History Jury in their report could not recommend any of the volumes received for the award, the Pulitzer Prize Board accepted the jury's proposal to give no award in this category.

NAMES OF THE BOARD MEMBERS VOTING FOR "NO AWARD"

Robert C. Christopher	Columbia University
Osborn Elliott	Columbia University
Michael Gartner	*Des Moines Register and Tribune*
Hanna H. Gray	The University of Chicago
Howard H. Hays	*Riverside* (Cal.) *Press-Enterprise*
James F. Hoge Jr.	*New York Daily News*
David A. Laventhol	*Newsday/Times Mirror Company*
Richard H. Leonard	*Milwaukee Journal*
C. K. McClatchy	*McClatchy Newspapers*
Eugene C. Patterson	*St. Petersburg Times*
Warren H. Phillips	*Dow Jones & Co.*
Joseph Pulitzer Jr.	*St. Louis Post-Dispatch*
William J. Raspberry	*The Washington Post*
Eugene L. Roberts Jr.	*The Philadelphia Inquirer*
Charlotte Saikowski	*The Christian Science Monitor*
Michael I. Sovern	Columbia University
Roger W. Wilkins	Joint Center for Political Studies
Thomas Winship	*The Boston Globe*

1985 Award

ABOUT THE PROTAGONISTS
OF THE U.S. REGULATION IDEAS

BY

THOMAS K. MCCRAW

Thomas Kincaid McCraw (born on September 11, 1940, in Corinth, Miss.) earned his B.A. degree at the University of Mississippi in 1962. During the following four years he served as an officer with the United States Navy. In 1966 he enrolled at the University of Wisconsin at Madison to earn there his Master of Arts degree two years later. That same year he joined the staff of the University of Wisconsin as a teaching assistant. After having received his Ph.D. degree in 1970, McCraw started teaching at the University of Texas as an assistant professor, being advanced to associate professor in 1974. As visiting associate professor he held lectures at the Harvard University Graduate School of Business Administration from 1976 to 1978. In 1978 he became full professor. McCraw, who has contributed numerous articles and chapters to various publications, is the author of *Morgan versus Lilienthal* and *TVA and the Power Fight, 1933-1939. Regulation in Perspective* is one of the works he has edited. In 1985 Thomas K. McCraw became the winner of the Pulitzer Prize in history for his *Prophets of Regulation*, which had been published one year earlier.

GOVERNMENT TRIALS TO REGULATE ECONOMY

[Source: Thomas K. McCraw: Prophets of Regulation. Charles Francis Adams, Louis D. Brandeis, James M. Landis, Alfred E. Kahn, Cambridge, Mass. - London: The Belknap Press of Harvard University Press, 1984, pp. 303 - 305; reprinted by permission of the author and Harvard University Press, Cambridge, Mass.]

Ideas about regulation, as Wilson implies, vary with time. During the 1930s, national policymakers generally held the powerful conviction that market mechanisms left to themselves would produce widespread injustice and even inefficiency. Hence they believed that an active federal government was essential for the protection of the public interest. So these political activists created a broad portfolio of new, independent agencies: the SEC, the FCC, the CAB, and so on. A few decades later, during the 1960s and 1970s, a new generation of policymakers embraced a very different idea. Rather than applauding the old activism, they became convinced that many of the independent commissions created during the 1930s had since been captured by the very interests that these agencies had been set up to regulate.

Partly as a result of the capture idea, there arose during the 1960s a curious two-pronged reform movement: pointing, on the one hand, toward deregulation and, on the other, toward a new wave of large-scale social and environmental regulation. These new rules were to be enforced not by independent commissions of the 1930s variety, which usually administered brief general statutes designed to give broad discretion to a group of commissioners acting collegially; but rather by an entirely different type of agency, with a single executive at its head (who could be held individually responsible for success or failure) and an agenda set in advance by the explicit provisions of extremely detailed legislation. New laws such as the Clean Air Act and the Occupational Safety and Health Act, often running to scores of pages in length, were calculated to minimize administrative discretion and to close all possible loopholes. Meanwhile, on the other prong, the deregulation movement—whose basic intellectual premise was that economic markets *do* work well—also advanced, simultaneously but contradictorily, gaining momentum alongside the companion movement toward growth of regulation in the areas of social and environmental policy.

The result, by the 1980s, presented a most peculiar spectacle. In an ironic historical example of the ways in which ideas can move policymakers in opposite directions, significant deregulation had been instituted for such industries as airlines, trucking, railroads, financial markets, and telecommunications. At the same time, additional social and environmental regulation had become firmly embedded in the structure of state and federal government in such a form as to make any capture by regulated interests very difficult, if not impossible.

The movement of ideas alone, of course, had not produced this ironic result. Despite the power of thought in the history of regulation, ideas in themselves could not determine concrete outcomes. Instead, ideas had to interact with particular economic and political circumstances to form a reciprocal relationship in which one or both might be altered. Nor, in any absolute sense, did the ideas themselves have to be demonstrably true in order to exert strong influence. We have seen, for instance, how Louis Brandeis' flawed idea of competition moved the hearts of his contemporaries. To cite a second example, the disparate sets of ideas underlying the initial imposition of regulation in airlines and trucking during the 1930s, and the later deregulation of these same industries in the 1970s and 1980s, could not both have been correct, in the absolute sense. Yet both sets of ideas became institutionalized. What had changed was the historical context in which opposing ideas about the legitimacy and actual performance of economic markets were defined.

During the 1930s, a period not only of depression but also of economic *de*flation, policymakers searched for some way to stabilize prices, as a means of preventing further economic decline. By the 1970s, however, deflation no longer provided the historical filter; indeed, it had become almost inconceivable as a problem for policy to solve. Instead, *in*flation was now the pressing issue, and thus the same protectionist regulations that had been applied in the 1930s to combat deflation now seemed inappropriate to the new economic context. Both ideas remained alive, but a different time meant a different choice for public policy. To state the same point in a more general sense, it is clear that in American history both the producer-oriented protectionist tradition, on the one hand, and the consumer-oriented anticartelist tradition on the other have remained hostage to immediate economic conditions. The strengths of each tradition have ebbed and flowed in response to several external forces: the business cycle, the different degrees of maturity reached by different product markets, and the conditions of international war and peace.

In speculating about the future, it is difficult to foresee with much additional precision what new historical contexts for regulation might develop. But if the past is any guide, a good deal of caution is in order. What I have called in this book the "economist's hour" of the 1970s and 1980s, for example, represents a phenomenon of unpredictable duration. Certainly the economist's hour in the history of regulation came relatively late, long after other notably different hours during which the muckraker and the lawyer alternately held center stage. This history makes it seem unlikely that any single approach to regulation will ever triumph. Therefore, although we may live in the golden years of regulatory economics and its practitioners, we should be in no hurry to crown the economist as permanent king of the regulatory hill.

1986 AWARD

ABOUT THE AMERICAN INVOLVEMENT IN SPACE AGE

BY

WALTER A. McDOUGALL

Walter Allan McDougall (born on December 3, 1946, in Washington, D.C.) enrolled at Amherst College and earned there his B.A. degree "cum laude" in 1968. During the following two years he served with the United States Army in Vietnam. For graduate study he attended the University of Chicago under a fellowship, and he received his Master of Arts degree in 1971. To his two academic degrees McDougall added a doctorate in philosophy in 1974. The next year he became assistant professor at the University of California, in Berkeley, advancing to associate professor in 1983. In 1981/82 he had been resident fellow of the Smithsonian Institution at the Woodrow Wilson International Center for Scholars and in 1982 at the National Air and Space Museum. In 1984 he was selected by *Esquire* as one of the "men and women under 40 who are changing America." The next year McDougall started working on a Harvard/Carnegie Study on the Prevention of Nuclear War. A contributor of a large number of articles to professional and scholarly journals, he is also the author of *France's Rhineland Diplomacy, 1914-1924: The Last Bid for a Balance of Power in Europe* and *The Grenada Papers*. In 1985 Walter A. McDougall published *... the Heavens and the Earth: A Political History of the Space Age*. This work earned him the Pulitzer Prize in history one year later.

STRATEGIES DURING THE EISENHOWER ERA

[Source: Walter A. McDougall: ... the Heavens and the Earth: A Political History of the Space Age, New York: Basic Books, Inc., Publishers, 1985, pp. 179 - 181; reprinted by permission of Harper Collins Publishers, New York, N.Y.]

Throughout the first half of 1958, while the space act was drafted and passed, the administration contemplated space law and policy. In the public domain, Eisenhower responded to American and world opinion, to his own hopes for control of technological competition, and to the needs of American propaganda, when he initiated exchanges with the USSR on outer space. In a letter of January 12, 1958, to Nikolai Bulganin, Eisenhower proposed "to solve what I consider to be the most important problem which faces the world today." He suggested that the United States and the USSR agree "at this decisive moment" to use outer space for peaceful purposes only. He recalled the failures of the previous decade regarding atomic power and urged a halt to the testing of missiles in outer space, as well as to their improvement and production. But "the capacity to verify the fulfillment of commitments is of the essence. . . ." Foster Dulles agreed that the time to control space development was now. In ten years it might be too late. Bulganin replied that the USSR was also prepared to discuss ICBMs and that the Soviets endorsed a multilateral petition to the UN including a ban on the military use of space, liquidation of foreign bases, and creation of "appropriate international control" and a UN agency to devise and supervise an international program for launching space rockets.

As usual, however, the two sides divided over procedure. UN Ambassador Lodge called first for a technical study of controls for all missile testing, leading later to a ban on the use of missiles that plied outer space for aggressive purposes. But controls on missiles, as opposed to just spaceflight, would rob the USSR of its mighty ICBMs and offer nothing in return. Besides, wrote Bulganin, it was not the missiles that threatened the world but the warheads they could carry in place of "peaceful sputniks." Of course, the first argument—that banning ICBMs would only hurt the USSR—was the same argument the Soviets rejected in 1946 when the United States enjoyed a weapons monopoly; and the second argument served no purpose unless the USSR permitted on-site inspection to determine the presence of warheads or sputniks. Throughout the summer of 1958, Khrushchev discussed a nuclear test ban treaty but never agreed to the technical study on means of controlling missiles and space.

In the meantime, Eisenhower ordered the NSC to do its own study and to draft an American strategy for space. Following the 1950 RAND report and the space act, this was the third, and most comprehensive entry, in the documentary history of the U.S. space program. It necessarily involved some compromise among the agencies: the BoB wanted to suppress alarmist language lest space command too many funds; State and the DoD conflicted on the extent of international cooperation to seek in space. But the draft paper was completed and approved by the President in mid-August 1958. It was NSC 5814/1, "Preliminary U.S. Policy on Outer Space."

"The USSR," the document began, "has . . . captured the imagination and admiration of the world." If it maintained superiority in space, it could undermine the prestige and security of the United States. The connection between long-range missiles and space boosters was intimate, but, the NSC declared, missile policy would be treated separately from space. This was a decision of great importance, for it meant that U.S. diplomacy, and thus UN controls, for space would be restricted to satellites. Even a UN agreement on "space for peace," therefore, would not mean a freeze on missile technology. NSC 5814/1 also explained that this policy statement was "preliminary" because the implications of space research were still largely unknown.

What was outer space? The NSC noted that no definition existed, although the question bore on the legality of overflight. It would, however, "appear desirable" to promote a common understanding of the term "outer space as related to particular objects and activities therein." In other words, the United States favored a functional definition of space (an object in orbit was ipso facto in space) rather than a schematic one (space starts fifty miles up). For while the United States did not want to forfeit its freedom to launch satellites of any sort, neither did it wish to give up the right to denounce hostile craft or develop aerospace craft that could fly in the atmosphere *and* orbit in space.

The NSC then underscored the scientific potential of spaceflight and its applicability to civilian and military missions alike. Imminent military systems included satellites for reconnaissance, communications, weather, electronic countermeasures, and navigation. Future missions included manned maintenance and resupply vehicles, manned antisatellite vehicles, bombardment satellites, and lunar stations. "Reconnaissance satellites are of critical importance to U.S. national security," the paper emphasized, and went on to describe the spy satellites then under development. They would serve missile targeting but also implement "Open Skies" policing of arms control. There were still potentially adverse implications, however, and "studies must be urgently undertaken in order to determine the most favorable framework in which such satellites would operate."

Policy on manned spaceflight was also crucial. Present space research could be carried on with unmanned vehicles, but "the time will undoubtedly come when man's judgment and resourcefulness will be required. . . ." Furthermore no unmanned experiments could substitute for manned flight in psychological effect.

International cooperation also appeared desirable from scientific, political, and psychological standpoints. The United States should cooperate in space so as to enhance its position as a leader in the peaceful uses of space, conserve American resources, speed up space progress by pooling talent, open up the Soviet bloc, and achieve international regulation. But genuine U.S./Soviet collaboration appeared unlikely. In March, at the time of Eisenhower's demarche to Bulganin, an NSC Ad Hoc Working Group on the Monitoring of Long Range Rocket Agreements found that much of the test data required for missile testing could be gleaned in the guise of "peaceful" space launches. It was American policy to try to prohibit the military use of space, but "contingent upon the establishment of effective inspection." Given continued Soviet secrecy, such a policy was probably barren. But since the UN would discuss space questions anyway, the United States ought to "take an imaginative position" in the General Assembly.

The legal problems of space were already manifold, the NSC continued, and more were not even identifiable as yet. "The only foundation for a sound rule of law is a body of ascertained fact." Thus many legal questions could not now be settled. The United States ought to reserve its position on whether celestial bodies were open to national appropriation and declare an insufficient basis for drawing the boundary between air and space. Instead, the United States ought to make an analogy to the proposed treaty on the Antarctic and seek agreement on which activities in space would be permissible or prohibited. *Generally speaking, rules will have to be evolved gradually* and pragmatically from experience. . . . The field is not suitable for abstract *a priori* codification."

1987 AWARD

ABOUT THE PRE-REVOLUTION PEOPLING IN THE UNITED STATES

BY

BERNARD BAILYN

Bernard Bailyn (born on September 10, 1922, in Hartford, Conn.) served from 1943 to 1946 with the United States Army. At the same time he enrolled at Williams College, where he received his Bachelor's degree in 1945. For graduate study he came to Harvard University and earned there his M.A. degree two years later. In 1953 he was granted his doctorate of philosophy and in the same year he joined the staff of Harvard as an instructor. He stayed at Harvard University and was advanced to full professor of history in 1961. The following year Bailyn became editor-in-chief of the John Harvard Library and in 1966 Winthrop professor of history. In 1981 Bailyn accepted the Adams University professorship at Harvard and served as president of the American Historical Association. In 1983 he became director of the Charles Warren Center for Studies in American History. The historian received honorary degrees from numerous Universities, e.g. Lawrence, Yale, Rutgers, Clark and Bard College. He is the author of several book publications, including *The New England Merchants in the 17th Century*; *Massachusetts Shipping, 1697-1714*; *Education in the Forming of American Society*; *Pamphlets of the American Revolution, 1750-1776*; *The Origins of American Politics*; *The Ordeal of Thomas Hutchinson* and *The Peopling of British North America: An Introduction*. 1967 was the publishing year of *The Ideological Origins of the American Revolution*, which earned Bernard Bailyn the Pulitzer Prize for the best book on history the following year. In 1987 the Pulitzer Prize Board selected for the second time a work by Bernard Bailyn. The award-winning book, published one year earlier, was entitled *Voyagers to the West: A Passage in the Peopling of America on the Eve of the Revolution*.

IMMIGRATION TO THE EAST COAST STATES

[Source: Bernard Bailyn/Barbara DeWolfe: Voyagers to the West: A Passage in the Peopling of America on the Eve of the Revolution, New York: Alfred A. Knopf, 1986, pp. 7 - 12; reprinted by permission of Professor Bernard Bailyn, Harvard University, Cambridge, Mass.]

IN THE years after the cessation of war in North America in 1760, the colonies experienced an extraordinary burst of expansion. By 1775 British North America, for all its remoteness, simplicity, and exotic strangeness, had become a place of interest for Britain, and to a lesser extent for Western Europe generally—talked about, written about, and visited with curiosity, and not merely because of the fame of the growing rebellion. The British North American colonies, still viewed as primitive outlands at the edge of civilization, were now immense in extent, and they were known to be potential gold mines in "futures": futures in land values, in consumer markets, and in supplies of colonial goods. Most important of all, they had acquired a powerfully intensified social role as a magnet and a refuge for the threatened, the discontented, the impoverished, and the ambitious of the western world.

The attractiveness of North America as a refuge and an opportunity was, of course, no new thing. From the beginning of British settlement, North America had been conceived of in those terms by people desperate enough and enterprising enough to consider overseas migration, and the attractiveness had increased in the eighteenth century as the colonies had grown and prospered. But after 1760 the increase in immigration became so great that it constituted a social force in itself, a force that added strain to the established relationship between the colonies and Britain. Even if there had been no political struggle between Britain and America, the relationship between them would have been altered by this growth of America as a powerful magnet and by the greatly increased flow of emigration. For the extraordinary territorial and demographic expansion of the mainland colonies after 1760 presented problems to the British rulers of North America that could not be solved within the limits of the ideas of the time and of the government's administrative capacity, and yet which, unsolved, led to increasingly troubling consequences.

While the world's attention was drawn to the question of the political and constitutional relations between Britain and America, these other problems were developing quickly and dangerously. First was the question of controlling settlement in the great new western land acquisitions. And closely interwoven with that question was the dilemma created by the enlarged emigration to the colonies—its consequences, if unregulated, in both Britain and America, and the apparent impossibility of regulating it.

The expansion of settlement that took place in North America after 1760 is a dramatic story that can be seen as a whole only from a very high vantage point. It began with the movement to the frontiers of isolated family and community groups moving here and there along a thousand-mile perimeter in search of new locations—a few hundred isolated clusters of people, at first, pulling loaded carts and sledges and driving wagons along Indian paths across the foothills and through the gaps in the first mountain barriers to the west, poling rafts loaded with farm equipment, animals, and household goods, and paddling canoes into the interior. Soon these movements of separate groups, which at first left no visible mark on the settlement maps of British North America, began to multiply, flowed together to form substantial human streams, and ended as a flood of migrants pouring west, north, and south outward from well-settled areas to form new centers of community life. The accelerating momentum of this postwar migration into the interior of America, its geographical range and ultimate numbers, astonished contemporaries, and they remain astonishing to anyone who sees this phase of frontier expansion in its proper historical context.

Hector St. John de Crèvecoeur, the Franco-American traveler, settler, and writer, gathering in the mid-1770s the experiences that would be distilled into his *Letters from an American Farmer,* personally joined the emigrants from Connecticut moving into the disputed Wyoming district of Pennsylvania. He was amazed at what he found: "the prodigious number of houses rearing up, fields cultivating, that great extent of industry open'd to a bold indefatigable enterprising people." It was the boldness of these migrants, the risks they were willing to take, their enterprise and gambling instinct, that most astonished him. He scarcely knew what to make of "the undiffidence with which these new settlers scatter themselves here and there in the bosom of such an extensive country without even a previous path to direct their steps and without being in any number sufficient either to protect or assist one another." So remarkable was this endless scattering of people that he despaired of properly describing even the one small part of it he personally experienced. All he could say was that he had seen, on his trips of 1774 and 1776, an extraordinary diaspora of various "sects and nations" on the western periphery. "Every spring," he recalled, "the roads were full of families travelling towards this new land of Canaan"; they came together as "a strange heterogeneous reunion of people . . . without law or government, without any kind of social bond to unite them all."

What Crèvecoeur witnessed was a small portion of an immense development. In a seemingly boundless proliferation, a new population, utterly different from the original native peoples whose territory this once had been, was spreading over a vast inland arc curving irregularly west and south from Nova Scotia to Florida, far removed from the coastal ports. (Map I.A.)

In the north the New England borderland was flung outward in an enormous expansion of settlement along three main routes of access. (Map I.B.) In Maine, the expansion was a bulging out westward from a long-established coastal fringe into the adjacent backcountry; in New Hampshire, in what would become Vermont, and in eastern New York land claims and population moved northward, in a V-shaped pattern reaching 150 miles north from the Massachusetts border, along the fertile upper reaches of the Connecticut and Hudson rivers. The number of towns founded annually in New England tripled, from an average of six per year before 1760 to eighteen per year after 1760—a total of 283 between 1760 and 1776, as some 20,000 migrants moved north across the border of Massachusetts, up through the broad corridor of the Connecticut River, and west from coastal New Hampshire. By 1776 all of New Hampshire save the northeast corner had been staked out and much of it at least thinly settled. The area of cultivation in Maine had doubled, and wide strips of land along both the east and west borders of Vermont—almost none of which had been settled in 1760—had been surveyed for towns and individual grants. New England's population as a whole rose 59% between 1760 and 1780.

In New York the heaviest concentrations of new settlements lay near the juncture of the Hudson and Mohawk rivers. (Map I.C.) North of the Mohawk, two clusters of wilderness clearings suddenly appeared: in the Saratoga district west of the Hudson, and around the stream known as Batten Kill east of the Hudson, scattering north to Lakes George and Champlain. But the more powerful magnet was south of the Mohawk—the great wedge of rich, well-watered land stretching more than 100 miles west from the Hudson to the Indian boundary line of 1768. Settlers swarmed into this fertile and accessible polygon of approximately 7,500 square miles (4.8

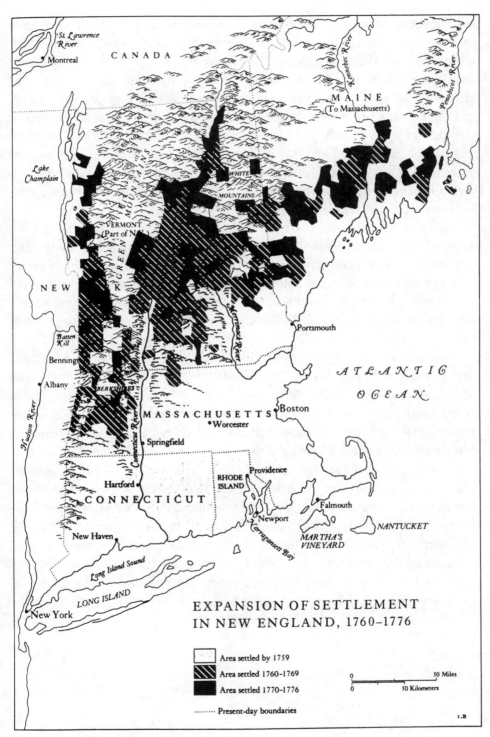

EXPANSION OF SETTLEMENT
IN NEW ENGLAND, 1760–1776

	Area settled by 1759
	Area settled 1760-1769
	Area settled 1770-1776
·········	Present-day boundaries

50 Miles

50 Kilometers

1.B

million acres) formed by the Mohawk, Schoharie, and upper Susquehanna river valleys, preceded by a legion of energetic land speculators, a few of whom, like Sir William Johnson, had lived in the area for years before the war, many of whom had been eyeing the region from afar. By 1776 the great Hudson-Mohawk wedge was a bewildering patchwork of patents, grants, and land claims of all sorts, many of which overlapped each other. And it was the scene of swiftly expanding settlements as thousands of migrants from New England, from lower New York, and from Britain located properties to rent or buy, cleared a few acres hurriedly, and threw up shelters for their first season on the land. New York's population rose 39% between 1760 and 1770 and 29% more in the decade that followed.

Some of this wave of expansion in the rich farming region of New York south of the Mohawk spilled over, through the Susquehanna River system, into northeastern Pennsylvania. But the great expansion of settlement in Pennsylvania lay not in the colony's north, which in 1776 remained largely uninhabited, but in the mountainous Appalachian plateau in the far south-western corner, which had been opened to settlement by the treaty line of 1768.

In few colonies did geology so completely dictate the pattern of expansion as it did in Pennsylvania. In 1760, after eighty years of settlement, the population was still almost completely confined to the gentle rolling plains in the southeastern corner of the colony, a fertile triangle blocked off by the diagonal barrier of the deep Appalachian ridges and valleys, formed as if by "some cosmic rake" dragged the length of the mountains. Behind that severe ridge system lay the 1,500-foot-high escarpment of the Allegheny Front. Only west of that natural wall could one find the tableland of the Appalachian Plateau, itself a formidable mountain land but intersected with twisting streams and capable of development into useful upland farms.

To this region of southwestern Pennsylvania migrants moved in large numbers in the 1760s and '70s, despite all the difficulties of traversing the ridges and clearing the hilly upland terrain. By 1770 most of the valleys in the ridge system had been explored and in part occupied...

1988 AWARD

ABOUT THE LAUNCHING
OF MODERN SCIENCE IN THE U.S.

BY

ROBERT V. BRUCE

Robert Vance Bruce (born on December 19, 1923, in Malden, Mass.) attended the Massachusetts Institute of Technology before he served with the United States Army in World War II. In 1945 he graduated from the University of New Hampshire with a degree in mechanical engineering and enrolled at Boston University for his M.A. degree. In 1947 he started working as an instructor at the University of Bridgeport, Conn. The following year he became master at Lawrence Academy, in Groton, Mass. After having received his Ph.D. degree in 1953, he became research assistant to Benjamin P. Thomas, in Washington. In 1955 he joined the staff of the University of Boston, where he was advanced to associate professor of history in 1960 and to full professor in 1966; in 1984 he became Professor Emeritus. Having been a Guggenheim fellow in 1957/58 and a Huntington fellow in 1966, Bruce is the author of several books, including *Lincoln and the Tools of War; 1877: Year of Violence* and *Bell: Alexander Graham Bell and the Conquest of Solitude.* For *The Launching of Modern American Science, 1846-1876.* Robert V. Bruce was awarded the 1988 Pulitzer Prize for the best book on American history published during the preceding year.

SOME TRENDSETTERS IN HIGHER EDUCATION

[Source: Robert V. Bruce: The Launching of Modern American Science, 1846-1876, New York: Alfred A. Knopf, 1987, pp. 326 - 329; reprinted by permission of Alfred A. Knopf, Inc., New York, N.Y.]

Postwar observers of higher education in America perceived what Ralph Waldo Emerson called in 1867 "a cleavage . . . in the hitherto firm granite of the past." They came to know it as "the new education." In cleaving the monolith of the old education, science was the wedge and technology the maul. Science-trained college presidents took the lead in the movement, while science widened and deepened its penetration of the curriculum. Technology, as the supposed offspring and actual partner of science, gave that movement the weight and force of economic incentive.

Many small colleges lacked the wherewithal for the new education, even when they had the will. Others resisted it on grounds of principle. The proud and long-established small colleges of New England in particular stood up for the traditional curriculum in the name of liberal culture and thereby heartened their daughter institutions further west, even to the Pacific. When the bright young chemistry professor Ira Remsen in 1872 asked Williams College for a small room to do research in, the president admonished him, "You will please keep in mind that this is a college and not a technical school. . . . The object aimed at is culture, not practical knowledge."

But the tide ran strong against them. Like Francis Wayland of Brown in 1850, Frederick Barnard of Columbia in 1870 blamed a decline in college enrollment per capita on college slowness to respond to science and technology. Wayland's diagnosis had proved to be premature. Postwar academic leaders sensed that Barnard's was not. Williams College gave Ira Remsen his little research lab before the year was out. At Princeton the conservative President James McCosh likewise came to terms with science, organizing a school of science in 1873, adding scientific equipment, and instituting graduate work. As a professor of philosophy McCosh had preached Scottish realism, and in academic policy he practiced it.

One of the ways in which science expanded its academic presence was through the system of elective courses. Harvard had tried it in the early 1840s and then drawn back for lack of resources. But by the late 1860s Harvard had money enough to revive it for half of the upperclassmen's courses. Cool toward it previously, the new president, Charles W. Eliot, embraced it in his inaugural address of 1869 and thereafter preached it so ardently that the public came to believe he had invented it. Electives freed the Harvard seniors first, then the juniors and sophomores, and by 1884 reached down to much of the freshman year. From Harvard the system spread throughout higher education. Conservatism limited it in the small New England colleges, poverty in the Southern state universities, but by the 1880s nearly all except the neediest colleges had adopted it to some extent.

The elective system decreased the proportion of students taking science courses, but those who did take them by choice (or at least by preference) were more apt to bring out the best in their teachers. They could also take more science and on a higher level. Specializing furthermore quickened the research spirit in professors. In the mid-1880s the historian Francis Parkman privately sounded out Harvard faculty opinion on the elective system. The scientists generally thought it had improved the quality of their students. Wolcott Gibbs, noted Parkman, "wants to abolish the old 'American college' and turn Harvard into a university [with] untrammeled election." As Gibbs implied, undergraduate electives paved the way for true universities. Frederick Barnard observed in 1879 that graduate courses were "a natural and necessary consequence" of the system.

Some who favored more science feared nevertheless that without some restraints students would choose foolishly, or dodge hard courses, or wall up their minds with overspecialization. For such doubters Yale's Sheffield School offered the "group system," under which students could choose a field such as chemistry or civil engineering, but had to take a "group" of courses tailored to it. Cornell and Johns Hopkins followed suit. Somewhat akin were "scientific departments," granting the B.S. degree for three years of study. More than twenty-five colleges created such departments during the sixties; and Rutgers, which had set up one in 1863 to edge out Princeton for New Jersey's land grant, lengthened its curriculum to four years in 1871.

Still more ambitious, at least in name, were the "scientific schools" affiliated with but not part of regular colleges. In 1873 the AAAS president commented sarcastically that "nowadays every college must have a scientific school attached, else it is not thought complete," though the supply of competent professors was far from adequate. According to the federal commissioner of education, the number of such schools increased from seventeen in 1870 to seventy in 1873 and the number of their instructors from 144 to 749. If he was right, the bottom of the barrel must indeed have been scraped hard for those instructors. Some leaders urged birth control for such schools, but the movement crested in 1873 of its own accord. Some of the weak schools expired during the ensuing depression, others in the relatively prosperous eighties.

As before the war, the scientific schools leaned heavily toward engineering and applied science, especially chemistry. Perhaps for that reason, perhaps also because of their detachment, inchoateness, shorter curriculum, and more transient students, they were still regarded by the colleges as inferior appendages and their students as of low caste.

At Yale, however, Sheffield students and faculty cheerfully acquiesced in the conservative President Noah Porter's salutary neglect. Indeed they would resist integration with the college until long after Porter had faded into the past he loved. Sheffield was thus free, for example, to organize a multidisciplinary course especially for two students in 1870. By 1871 Yale College proper had given up offering any classes for Sheffield students. That was the college's loss. Though Sheffield had its spells of short rations, its benefactor and namesake Joseph Sheffield enlarged its quarters in 1866 to make what George Brush called "an exceedingly well furnished building with convenient laboratories, lecture rooms, museums, etc." and provided a second building in 1873. Furthermore, segregation from the college did not stunt the scientific students' cultural growth. Their courses in the late 1860s included modern languages, literature, history, and political economy, all within Sheffield. In the early 1870s Professor Thomas Lounsbury of Sheffield revolutionized college teaching of English by turning it away from arid rhetoric and grammar to modern literature. Sheffield's enrollment rose from 120 in 1868 to 247 in 1873.

An alumnus of Harvard's Lawrence Scientific School, the chemist Frank Clarke, conceded in 1876 that Sheffield surpassed his alma mater in making scientists. A former Lawrence faculty member and acting dean, Charles W. Eliot, in two widely noticed *Atlantic Monthly* articles entitled "The New Education," charged in 1869 that Lawrence was a disjointed congeries of professorial fiefdoms. Unlike Sheffield, Eliot wrote, Lawrence required no meaningful entrance examinations, no courses common to all, and indeed no knowledge of any kind first and last other than that from "inconceivably narrow" study mostly under one professor. And it set a minimum residence requirement of only one year for the degree of Bachelor of Science.

1989 a AWARD

ABOUT THE CIVIL RIGHTS
MOVEMENT YEARS

BY

TAYLOR BRANCH

Taylor Branch (born on January 14, 1947, in Atlanta, Ga.) attended the
University of North Carolina at Chapel Hill and was granted his Bachelor of
Arts degree there in 1968. Afterwards he enrolled at Princeton University
for graduate study, which he pursued from 1968 to 1970. Having chosen a
career in journalism, he joined the staff of the *Washington Monthly* in
Washington, D.C. In 1973 he became member of the staff of *Harper's* in
New York and in 1975 he moved to *Esquire*. There he was a staff member
for about a year. Afterwards he has been a freelance writer. *Second Wind:
The Memoirs of an Opinionated Man*; *The Empire Blues* and *Labyrinth*
number among his book publications. Six years of research went into the
writing of the more than one thousand pages of *Parting the Waters:
America in the King Years, 1954-1963*. The book was published in 1988.
The following year Taylor Branch became the winner of the Pulitzer Prize
for history.

MARTIN LUTHER KING'S WASHINGTON SPEECH

[Source: Taylor Branch: Parting the Waters. America in the King Years, 1954-63, New York - London - Toronto - Sydney - Tokyo: Simon and Schuster, 1988, pp. 688 - 689, 881 - 883; reprinted by permission of Simon & Schuster, Inc., New York, N.Y.]

There were scattered cries for King, who was next and last. Although the program was running nearly a half-hour *ahead* of schedule, by a miracle from Bayard Rustin, people ached to stretch limbs and escape sunstroke. They were ready to go home. When Randolph introduced King as "the moral leader of our nation," small waves of applause lapped forward for nearly a minute in tribute to the best-known leader among them as well as to the end of a joyous day. Then the crowd fell silent.

It was a formal speech, as demanded by the occasion and the nature of the audience. By then, ABC and NBC had cut away from afternoon soap operas to join the continuous live coverage by CBS. King faced also a giant press corps and listeners as diverse as the most ardent supporters of the movement and the stubborn Congress at the other end of the Mall, where by quorum calls sullen legislators "spread upon the Journal" the names of the ninety-two absent members who might have let the march distract them from regular business. For all these King delivered his address in his clearest diction and stateliest baritone. Ovations interrupted him in the cracks of infrequent oratorical flourish, and in difficult passages small voices cried "Yes!" and "Right on!" as though grateful and proud to hear such talk. From the front, a woman could be heard to laugh and shout "Sho 'nuff!" when King told them about the freedom checks that had bounced. Five minutes later, when King declared that the movement would not stop "as long as our bodies, heavy with the fatigue of travel, cannot gain lodging in the motels of the highways and hotels of the cities," a shout went up from a pocket of the crowd so distant that the sound did not reach King for a second or two.

He recited his text verbatim until a short run near the end: "We will not be satisfied until justice runs down like waters and righteousness like a mighty stream." The crowd responded to the pulsating emotion transmitted from the prophet Amos, and King could not bring himself to deliver the next line of his prepared text, which by contrast opened its lamest and most pretentious section ("And so today, let us go back to our communities as members of the international association for the advancement of creative dissatisfaction"). Instead, extemporaneously, he urged them to return to their struggles ("Go back to Mississippi. Go back to Alabama . . ."), to believe that change would come "somehow" and that they could not "wallow in the valley of despair."

There was no alternative but to preach. Knowing that he had wandered completely off his text, some of those behind him on the platform urged him on, and Mahalia Jackson piped up as though in church, "Tell 'em about the dream, Martin." Whether her words reached him is not known. Later, King said only that he forgot the rest of the speech and took up the first run of oratory that "came to me." After the word "despair," he temporized for an instant: "I say to you today, my friends, and so even though we face the difficulties of today and tomorrow, I still have a dream. It is a dream deeply rooted in the American dream . . ."

Mindful of his audience, he held himself to a far more deliberate pace than in Detroit, or in Chicago the week before. Here he did not shout or smile, and there was no chance to build upon cascading rhythms of response, as in a mass meeting. The slow determination of his cadence exposed all the more clearly the passion that overshadowed the content of the dream. It went beyond the limitations of language and culture to express something that was neither pure rage nor pure joy, but a universal transport of the kind that makes the blues sweet. Seven times he threw the extremities of black and white against each other, and each time he came back with a riveting, ecstatic dignity.

The March on Washington will be remembered for King's "I Have a Dream" speech

The "Dream" sequence took him from Amos to Isaiah, ending, "I have a dream that one day, every valley shall be exalted . . ." Then he spoke a few sentences from the prepared conclusion, but within seconds he was off again, reciting the first stanza of "My Country 'Tis of Thee," ending, " 'from every mountainside, let freedom ring.' " After an interlude of merely one sentence—"And if America is to be a great nation, this must become true"—he took it up again: "So let freedom ring." By then, Mahalia Jackson was happy, chanting "My Lord! My Lord!" As King tolled the freedom bells from New Hampshire to California and back across Mississippi, his solid, square frame shook and his stateliness barely contained the push to an end that was old to King but new to the world: "And when *this* happens . . . we will be able to speed up that day when *all* God's children, black men and white men, Jews and Gentiles, Protestants and Catholics, will be able to join hands and sing in the words of the old Negro spiritual, 'Free at last! Free at last! Thank God Almighty, we are free at last!' " With that King stepped suddenly aside, and the March tumbled swiftly to benediction from Benjamin Mays.

Like most television viewers, President Kennedy was witnessing a complete King speech for the first time. "He's damn good," the President remarked to his aides at the White House. Kennedy was especially impressed with King's ad lib off the prepared text, and he was quick to pick out the most original refrain. As the principal leaders filed into the Cabinet Room from the march, he greeted King with a smiling "I have a dream," as a fellow speechmaker who valued a good line. The compliment made King feel slightly uncomfortable, as he alone had been showered with hosannas all the way over from the Lincoln Memorial. Deflectively, King asked President Kennedy if he had heard the excellent speech of Walter Reuther. The latter indeed had delivered a fiery oration containing the day's most pointed barbs at President Kennedy ("We cannot *defend* freedom in Berlin so long as we *deny* freedom in Birmingham!"), and the President in turn deflected mention of Reuther. "Oh, I've heard him plenty of times," he replied.

The President and King lacked the chemistry for small talk. Roy Wilkins was better. Once Kennedy had shaken hands all around, Wilkins embarked on a folksy monologue, craftily pointing out that the glowing success of the march could shift the heavy center of American opinion by diluting suspicions that the Negro and his cause were somehow inherently flawed.

1989 b AWARD

ABOUT THE ERA OF
THE AMERICAN CIVIL WAR

BY

JAMES M. MCPHERSON

James Munro McPherson (born on October 11, 1936, in Valley City, N.D.) earned his Bachelor's degree at Gustavus Adolphus College, magna cum laude, in 1958. Five years later he received his Ph.D. degree with highest distinction at Johns Hopkins University. Already one year earlier he had started to work as an instructor in history at Princeton University. During the following years he advanced from assistant professor of history (in 1965) to full professor (in 1972). Since 1982 he held the Edwards professorship of American History at Princeton. McPherson, who also contributed articles, reviews, chapters, and essays to various journals and books, is the author of numerous books, including *The Struggle for Equality: Abolitionists and the Negro in the Civil War and Reconstruction*; *Blacks in America: Bibliographical Essays* and *Ordeal by Fire: The Civil War and Reconstruction*. For *Battle Cry of Freedom: The Civil War Era*, James M. McPherson also became a full-winner of the Pulitzer Prize for history in 1989. His book had been published one year earlier.

ASPECTS AND BOOKS ON SPECIFIC QUESTIONS

[Source: James M. McPherson: Battle Cry of Freedom. The Civil War Era, New York - Oxford: Oxford University Press, 1988, pp. VI - VIII; reprinted by permission of Oxford University Press, New York, N.Y.]

Both sides in the American Civil War professed to be fighting for freedom. The South, said Jefferson Davis in 1863, was "forced to take up arms to vindicate the political rights, the freedom, equality, and State sovereignty which were the heritage purchased by the blood of our revolutionary sires." But if the Confederacy succeeded in this endeavor, insisted Abraham Lincoln, it would destroy the Union "conceived in Liberty" by those revolutionary sires as "the last, best hope" for the preservation of republican freedoms in the world. "We must settle this question now," said Lincoln in 1861, "whether in a free government the minority have the right to break up the government whenever they choose."

Northern publicists ridiculed the Confederacy's claim to fight for freedom. "Their motto," declared poet and editor William Cullen Bryant, "is not liberty, but slavery." But the North did not at first fight to free the slaves. "I have no purpose, directly or indirectly, to interfere with slavery in the States where it exists," said Lincoln early in the conflict. The Union Congress overwhelmingly endorsed this position in July 1861. Within a year, however, both Lincoln and Congress decided to make emancipation of slaves in Confederate states a Union war policy. By the time of the Gettysburg Address, in November 1863, the North was fighting for a "new birth of freedom" to transform the Constitution written by the founding fathers, under which the United States had become the world's largest slaveholding country, into a charter of emancipation for a republic where, as the northern version of "The Battle Cry of Freedom" put it, "Not a man shall be a slave."

The multiple meanings of slavery and freedom, and how they dissolved and re-formed into new patterns in the crucible of war, constitute a central theme of this book. That same crucible fused the several states bound loosely in a federal *Union* under a weak central government into a new *Nation* forged by the fires of a war in which more Americans lost their lives than in all of the country's other wars combined.

BATTLE CRY OF FREEDOM

The original words and music of this sprightly song were written in the summer of 1862 by George F. Root, one of the North's leading Civil War composers. So catchy was the tune that southern composer H. L. Schreiner and lyricist W. H. Barnes adapted it for the Confederacy. The different versions became popular on both sides of the Mason-Dixon line. Reproduced here are Verse 3 and the Chorus of each version.

VERSE 3

Union: We will wel-come to our num-bers the loy-al, true and brave,
Confederate: They have laid down their__ lives on the blood-y bat-tle field,

Shout - ing the bat-tle cry of Free-dom, And al - though he may be poor Not a
Shout, shout the bat-tle cry of Free-dom; Their__ mot-to is re-sis-tance, To

man shall be a slave, Shout - ing the bat - tle cry of Free - dom.
ty - rants we'll not yield! Shout, shout the bat - tle cry of Free - dom.

CHORUS

The Un - ion for - ev - er, Hur - rah, boys, Hur - rah!
Our Dix - ie for - ev - er, she's never at a loss

Down with the trai-tor, up with the star; While we ral - ly 'round the flag, boys,
Down with the ea - gle, up with the cross. We'll__ ral - ly 'round the bonnie flag,

ral - ly once a-gain, Shout - ing the bat - tle cry of Free - dom.
we'll rally once a - gain. Shout, shout the bat - tle cry of Free - dom.

Americans of the Civil War generation lived through an experience in which time and consciousness took on new dimensions. "These are fearfully critical, anxious days, in which the destinies of the continent for centuries will be decided," wrote one contemporary in a sentence typical of countless others that occur in Civil War diaries and letters. "The excitement of the war, & interest in its incidents, have absorbed everything else. We think and talk of nothing else," wrote Virginia's fire-eater Edmund Ruffin in August 1861, a remark echoed three days later by the Yankee sage Ralph Waldo Emerson: "The war . . . has assumed such huge proportions that it threatens to engulf us all—no preoccupation can exclude it, & no hermitage hide us." The conflict "crowded into a few years the emotions of a lifetime," wrote a northern civilian in 1865. After Gettysburg, General George Meade told his wife that during the past ten days "I have lived as much as in the last thirty years." From faraway London, where he served his father as a private secretary at the American legation, young Henry Adams wondered "whether any of us will ever be able to live contented in times of peace and laziness. Our generation has been stirred up from its lowest layers and there is that in its history which will stamp every member of it until we are all in our graves. We cannot be commonplace. . . . One does every day and without a second thought, what at another time would be the event of a year, perhaps of a life." In 1882 Samuel Clemens found that the Civil War remained at the center of southern consciousness: it was "what A.D. is elsewhere; they date from it." This was scarcely surprising, wrote Twain, for the war had "uprooted institutions that were centuries old . . . transformed the social life of half the country, and wrought so profoundly upon the entire national character that the influence cannot be measured short of two or three generations."

Five generations have passed, and that war is still with us.

1990 AWARD

ABOUT THE UNITED STATES INFLUENCE IN SOUTHEAST ASIA

BY

STANLEY KARNOW

Stanley Karnow (born on February 4, 1925, in New York, N.Y.) served with the United States Army Air Forces during World War II. He graduated from Harvard with a Bachelor's degree in 1947 and attended the Sorbonne, University of Paris, during 1947/48 and from 1948 to 1949 the Ecole des Sciences Politiques. After his studies, he began his journalistic career in Paris in 1950 as a *Time* correspondent. After covering Europe, the Middle East and Africa - he was bureau chief in North Africa from 1958 to 1959 - he went to Asia for *Time* and *Life*, and subsequently reported from there for the London *Observer*, *The Saturday Evening Post*, *The Washington Post* and *NBC News*. He was an editor of *The New Republic* from 1973 to 1975 and a columnist for *King Features*. Then he became affiliated with the German Marshall Fund. Karnow is the author of *Southeast Asia* and *Mao and China: From Revolution to Revolution*. As chief correspondent he worked on the PBS series *Vietnam: A Television History*, for which he won six Emmys as well as DuPont, Peabody and Polk awards. In 1990 Stanley Karnow's *In Our Image - America's Empire in the Philippines* was selected by the Pulitzer Prize Board as best book on American history published during the preceding year.

AMERICA EXPORTS ITSELF TO THE PHILIPPINES

[Source: Stanley Karnow: In Our Image - America's Empire in the Philippines, New York: Random House, 1989, pp. 196 - 198; reprinted by permission of the author, Potomac, Md.]

Under a slate sky on a sultry August morning in 1901, a converted cattle ship, the *Thomas,* steamed into Manila Bay. Crowding its decks were five hundred young Americans, most of them recent college graduates, the men wearing straw boaters and blazers, the women in long skirts and large flowery hats. Like vacationers, they carried baseball bats, tennis rackets, musical instruments, cameras and binoculars. Few had ever been abroad, and they scanned the exotic landscape with a mixture of fascination and anticipation. Precursors of the Peace Corps volunteers of a later generation, they were arriving as teachers. They quickly fanned out across the archipelago to set up schools and soon became known as "Thomasites," after the vessel that had brought them. The label, pinned on all American teachers of the time, had the ring of a religious movement. But their vocation, though secular, did have an evangelical design. Education would Americanize the Filipinos and cement their loyalty to the United States. "We are not merely teachers," Philinda Rand later wrote to her family in Massachusetts from the island of Negros. "We are social assets and emissaries of good will."

Not all Americans who landed in the Philippines during those early years were so dedicated. There were swindlers, hucksters and dubious adventurers among them. Many who began with noble motives became lonely and discouraged and vented their bitterness in racial slurs against the Filipinos. But many—doctors, engineers, agronomists, surveyors, sanitation specialists and teachers like Philinda Rand—were driven by an unflagging faith in the virtue of their commitment.

The U.S. conquest of the Philippines had been as cruel as any conflict in the annals of imperialism, but hardly had it ended before Americans began to atone for its brutality. Inspired by a sense of moral obligation, they believed it to be their responsibility to bestow the spiritual and material blessings of their exceptional society on the new possession—as though providence had anointed them to be its savior. So, during its half-century in the archipelago, the United States refused to be labeled a colonial power and even expunged the word *colonial* from its official vocabulary. Instead of establishing a colonial office, as the British did to govern their overseas territories, President McKinley consigned the Philippines to the Bureau of Insular Affairs, an agency of the War Department. Nor did Americans sent out to supervise the islands call themselves colonial civil servants, a term that evoked an image of white despots in topees, brandishing swagger sticks at cringing brown natives. In their own eyes, they were missionaries, not masters.

The venture had originally been infused with apostolic fervor when McKinley divulged his divine directive to "uplift and civilize" the Filipinos—a goal he had earlier advertised as "benevolent assimilation." Elihu Root, his secretary of war, codified the doctrine in his instructions to William Howard Taft to promote the "happiness, peace and prosperity" of the natives in conformity with "their customs, their habits and even their prejudices." Seconding that sentiment soon after becoming governor, Taft intoned: "We hold the Philippines for the benefit of the Filipinos, and we are not entitled to pass a single act or to approve a single measure that has not that as its chief purpose."

Compared to European colonialism, the United States was indeed a model of enlightenment. Americans were banned by law from acquiring large tracts of land in the Philippines—a sharp contrast to Britain's mobilization of coolies on Malayan rubber plantations or France's forced recruitment of native labor to cultivate huge rice fields in Vietnam. The Americans avoided such egregious schemes as the opium monopolies, maintained by the British, French and Dutch in their Asian dominions to raise revenues. Nothing they did to preserve order even remotely matched the repression of the French in Vietnam, who in 1930 executed nearly seven hundred native dissidents without trial. Even the supposedly benign British summarily imprisoned a hundred thousand Indians for civil disobedience during the same period. On the other hand, the Filipinos renounced violent opposition to U.S. supremacy after Aguinaldo's defeat— precisely because they finally concluded that American rule would not be harsh.

Aware from the start that the Filipinos would judge them by actual deeds, the Americans launched practical programs to demonstrate their benevolence. They bought and redistributed the rural estates held by the Catholic friars, whose excesses had provoked Filipinos to rebel against Spain. To improve the economy, they constructed dams and irrigation facilities, expanded markets, developed mines and timber concessions, built roads, railways and ports. Their legal reforms gave the archipelago, for the first time in its history, an honest judiciary under native magistrates. They introduced a tax system to make the country self-sustaining, and renovated the financial structure, which had been a chaos of currencies. Unlike the Europeans elsewhere in Asia, who plundered their colonies for their own profit, they displayed deep concern for the welfare of the natives. Their expenditures on health helped to double the population from 1900 to 1920, and schools spurred a climb in the literacy rate from twenty percent to fifty percent within a generation. Fearful of mutinies, the Europeans forbade native troops from outnumbering their own soldiers and maintained their forces at the expense of the colonies. By the 1920s, more Filipinos than Americans were serving as army regulars and police in the Philippines.

The United States also accorded the Filipinos unusual latitude to govern themselves, even though its motives were less than idealistic. Taft encouraged the ambitions of the upper classes to subvert diehard native nationalists, and the Republicans back home endorsed liberal moves to deflect their Democratic critics. But whatever the reasons, Filipinos were running for local office even before the Americans had fully conquered the archipelago. They conducted elections for a national legislature as early as 1907.

But the U.S. performance in the Philippines was flawed. The Americans coddled the elite while disregarding the appalling plight of the peasants, thus perpetuating a feudal oligarchy that widened the gap between rich and poor. They imposed trade patterns that retarded the economic growth of the islands, condemning them to reliance on the United States long after independence. The American monopoly on imports into the Philippines also dampened the development of a native industry. At the same time, the unlimited entry of Philippine exports to the United States bound the archipelago inextricably to the American market. Economically at least, the Filipinos were doomed to remain "little brown brothers" for years—though many, despite their nationalist rhetoric, found security in the role.

Above all, the U.S. effort to inculcate Filipinos with American ethics proved to be elusive. Filipinos readily accepted American styles and institutions. They learned to behave, dress and eat like Americans, sing American songs and speak Americanized English. Their lawyers familiarized themselves with American jurisprudence, and their politicians absorbed American democratic procedures, displaying unique skills in American parliamentary practices. But they never became the Americans that Americans sought to make them. To this day, they are trying to define their national identity.

Taft oversaw U.S. rule of the Philippines for thirteen years, first as governor in Manila and later from Washington as secretary of war and president. He undertook the gigantic task of implanting in the archipelago the foundations of a modern state. Rather than steer them toward independence, he sought to convince the Filipinos that their own interests would best be served by a close and permanent bond with the beneficent United States. But he underestimated the dynamics of nationalism, which drove Filipinos to push for sovereignty despite their recognition of America's generosity. Nor did he anticipate the shifting pressures that came from changing attitudes in Congress and the White House. Thus, while he left an indelible imprint on the islands, U.S. policies in the archipelago lacked consistency.

1991 AWARD

ABOUT THE LIFE IN
EIGHTEEN-HUNDRED MAINE

BY

LAUREL T. ULRICH

Laurel Thatcher Ulrich (born on July 11, 1938, in Sugar City, Id.) attended the University of Utah and received there her Bachelor of Arts degree in 1960. She enrolled for graduate study at Simmons College, where she earned her Master's degree in 1971. At the University of New Hampshire she started to teach English and from 1976 to 1980 she worked as an instructor in history. She was granted her doctorate of philosophy from the University of New Hampshire in 1980. That same year Mrs. Ulrich was advanced to associate professor of history. She has joined the Organization of American Historians and the National Women Studies Association. Being the contributor of scholarly articles and personal essays to various journals, she is also the author of *Vertuous women found: New England ministerial literature, 1668-1735*; *A friendly neighbor: Social dimensions of daily work in Northern Colonial New England*; *Good Wives: Image and Reality in the Lives of Women in Northern New England, 1650-1750* and *Psalm-tunes, periwigs and bastards: Ministerial authority in early eighteenth century Durham*. In 1990 Laurel T. Ulrich published *A Midwife's Tale. The Life of Martha Ballard, Based on Her Diary, 1785-1812*. This work made her the recipient of the Pulitzer Prize for history one year later.

A WOMAN FROM THE KENNEBEC RIVER REGION

[Source: Laurel Thatcher Ulrich: A Midwife's Tale. The Life of Martha Ballard, Based on Her Diary, 1785-1812, New York: Alfred A. Knopf, 1990, pp. 3 - 5; reprinted by permission of the author and of Alfred A. Knopf, Inc., New York, N.Y.]

Eight months of the year Hallowell, Maine, was a seaport. From early April to late November, ocean-going vessels sailed up the Kennebec, forty-six miles from the open Atlantic, bringing Pennsylvania flour, West Indian sugar, and English cloth and hardware, returning with shingles clapboards, hogshead and barrel staves, white ash capstan bars, and pine boards destined for Boston or Bristol or Jamaica. In late autumn, ice blockaded the river, sometimes so suddenly that though a man had been expecting it for weeks, he was caught unprepared. One year, on November 25, after the last ships had sailed from the town, Jonathan Ballard pushed off from his father's sawmill with a raft of boards destined for Long Reach on the coast. He got no farther than Bumberhook Point, three miles below, before the Kennebec closed around him. It didn't open again until April 1.

Hallowell folks remembered openings and closings of the river the way people in other towns remembered earthquakes or drought. In 1785, the year of the long winter, the ice was still firm enough on April 22 to hold a sleigh bearing the body of Samuel Howard, one of the original settlers of the town, to his burying place at Fort Western. Not until May 3 did the first vessels arrive from "the westward," bringing corn and pork to the straitened town. People both welcomed and feared the opening of the river. In bad years ice jams made ponds of fields and rafts of fences, backing up water in the mill creeks that cut through the steep banks on both sides. In good years, the opening water sent mill hands flying through April nights, ripping logs and securing lumber unlocked by the spring thaw. Sometimes the greatest danger was not from the river itself, though high water might pitch a man from a raft to his death before his fellows could reach him, but from the raging creeks on the shore.

In 1789, the river opened on April 7 in a heavy rain that took away the bridge over Ballard's brook, made a breach in the mill dam, and washed out the underpinning of the north side of the house. "But we are yet alive & well for which we ought to be thankful," Martha Ballard told her diary. She was fifty-four years old, a midwife. She and her family had lived at the mills since 1778, seven years after the incorporation of the town. Though she

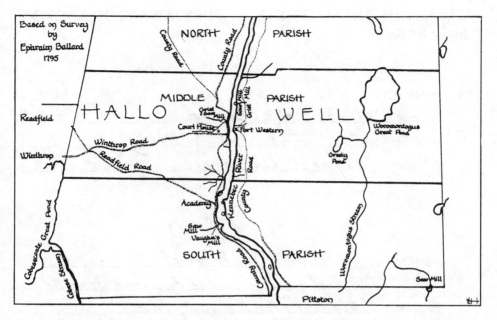

knew little of the sea, she had traveled much of the Kennebec, by water, by ice, and, during those treacherous seasons when the river was neither one nor the other, by faith.

The year Old Lady Cony had her stroke, Martha Ballard crossed the river in a canoe on December 2, pushing through ice in several places. On December 30 of another year, summoned by a woman in labor, she walked across, almost reaching shore before breaking through to her waist at Sewall's Eddy. She dragged herself out, mounted a neighbor's horse, and rode dripping to the delivery. Necessity and a fickle river cultivated a kind of bravado among Hallowell folks. "People Crost the river on a Cake of ice which swong round from the Eddy East side & stopt at the point below Mr Westons," Martha wrote on December 15 of one year. On April 1 of another she reported walking across on the ice after breakfast, adding drily in the margin of the day's entry, "the river opened at 4 hour pm."

Martha Moore was born in 1735 in the small town of Oxford, near the Connecticut border in Worcester County, Massachusetts, but the real story of her life begins in Maine with the diary she kept along the Kennebec. Without the diary her biography would be little more than a succession of dates. Her birth in 1735. Her marriage to Ephraim Ballard in 1754. The births of their nine children in 1756, 1758, 1761, 1763, 1765, 1767, 1769, 1772, and 1779, and the deaths of three of them in 1769. Her own death in 1812.

WINNERS OF THE AMERICAN HISTORY AWARD, 1992 – 2002 *
- Space for Notes -

1992 Winner(s):

Name(s) *Mark E. Neely, Jr.*

Book Title *The Fate of Liberty*

Publisher *Oxford University Press*

1993 Winner(s):

Name(s) *Gordon S. Wood*

Book Title *The Radicalism of the American Revolution*

Publisher *Alfred A. Knopf, Inc.*

1994 Winner(s):

Name(s) _____

Book Title _____

Publisher _____

1995 Winner(s)

Name(s) _____

Book Title _____

Publisher _____

* The listings of the annual Pulitzer Prize-winners as well as further background information about the awards will be available in the *New York Times*, New York, N.Y.

1996 Winner(s):

    Name(s) _____

    Book Title _____

    Publisher _____

1997 Winner(s):

    Name(s) _____

    Book Title _____

    Publisher _____

1998 Winner(s):

    Name(s) _____

    Book Title _____

    Publisher _____

1999 Winner(s):

    Name(s) _____

    Book Title _____

    Publisher _____

2000 Winner(s):

    Name(s) _____

    Book Title _____

    Publisher _____

354

2001 Winner(s):

Name(s) _____

Book Title _____

Publisher _____

2002 Winner(s):

Name(s) _____

Book Title _____

Publisher _____

INDEX

362

The Pulitzer Prize Archive
A History and Anthology of Award-winning Materials in Journalism, Letters, and Arts

Series Editor: Heinz-Dietrich Fischer
1987 onwards. 16 volumes. Bound

Part A: **Reportage Journalism**

Vol. 1   INTERNATIONAL REPORTING 1928 - 1985
From the Activities of the League of Nations
to present-day Global Problems
1987, LXXXVI, 352 pages

Vol. 2   NATIONAL REPORTING 1941 - 1986
From Labor Conflicts to the Challenger
Disaster
1988, LXII, 388 pages

Vol. 3   LOCAL REPORTING 1947 - 1987
From a County Vote Fraud to a
Corrupt City Council
1989, LII, 388 pages

Part B: **Opinion Journalism**

Vol. 4   POLITICAL EDITORIAL 1916 - 1988
From War-related Conflicts to
Metropolitan Disputes
1990, LXXIV, 376 pages

Vol. 5   SOCIAL COMMENTARY 1969 - 1989
From University Troubles to a
California Earthquake
1991, XLVI, 400 pages

Vol. 6   CULTURAL CRITICISM 1969 - 1990
From Architectural Damages to
Press Imperfections
1992, LII, 420 pages

Part C: **Nonfiction Literature**

Vol. 7   AMERICAN HISTORY AWARDS 1917 - 1991
From Colonial Settlements to
the Civil Rights Movement
1993, LXVIII, 366 pages

Future Volume

Vol. 8   BIOGRAPHY/AUTOBIOGRAPHY AWARDS 1917 - 1992
will be published in 1994

Columbia University
in the City of New York

THE PULITZER PRIZES IN LETTERS,
DRAMA AND MUSIC

Excerpt from the Plan of Award

The following provisions govern the award of the Pulitzer Prizes and Fellowships established in Columbia University by the will of the first Joseph Pulitzer:

1. The prizes and fellowships are awarded by Columbia University on the recommendation of The Pulitzer Prize Board. The prizes are announced during the Spring.

2. Entries must be submitted in writing and addressed to the Secretary of The Pulitzer Prize Board. (See reverse side for address.) Entries for letters awards must be submitted on or before July 1 of the year of publication in the case of books published between January 1 and June 30 and on or before November 1 in the case of the books published between July 1 and December 31. Competition for prizes is limited to work done during the calendar year ending December 31, except in drama and music. For the drama prize, works produced during the twelve months from March 2 through March 1 are considered. For the music award, works performed between March 15 in one year and March 14 of the subsequent year are considered, and entries should be received by March 1 if possible.

3. For the prizes in letters, four copies of each book published before June 30 shall be sent to the Secretary of the Pulitzer Prize Board by July 1. Books published between July 1 and December 31 shall be submitted by November 1. (Books scheduled for publication in November and December must be submitted no later than November 1 in galley proof.) For the prize in drama, entries shall be made while the work is being performed together with up to six published or manuscript copies of each work, where requested, and an agreement from the producer to permit the purchase of tickets by the Secretary of The Pulitzer Board for those concerned in the judging, not to exceed two each. For the prize in music, entries similarly shall be accompanied by an agreement from performing organizations to submit scores and recordings or, when necessary, to make arrangements for the judging in the same manner as the drama prize. All entries should include biographies and pictures of entrants and each entry in letters and music must be accompanied by a handling fee of $20 made payable to Columbia University / Pulitzer Prizes.

The Pulitzer Prize Board

November, 1991